Thomas Jefferson on Wine

JOHN HAILMAN

UNIVERSITY PRESS OF MISSISSIPPI / JACKSON

www.upress.state.ms.us

The University Press of Mississippi is a member of the
Association of American University Presses.

First published in paperback 2009
∞
Library of Congress Cataloging-in-Publication Data

Hailman, John R., 1942–
  Thomas Jefferson on wine / John Hailman.
    p. cm.
  Includes bibliographical references and index.
  ISBN 978-1-60473-370-9 (pbk. : alk. paper) 1. Jefferson, Thomas,
1743–1826—Knowledge—Wine and wine making. 2. Wine and wine
making—Virginia—Albemarle County—History. 3. Monticello (Va.)—
Social life and customs. 4. Jefferson, Thomas, 1743–1826 Travel—France.
5. Jefferson, Thomas, 1743–1826—Travel—Germany. 6. Wine and wine
making—France—History. 7. Wine and wine making—Germany—
History. I. Title.
  TP547.J44H36 2009
    641.2′2—dc22   2009015522

British Library Cataloging-in-Publication Data available

This book is dedicated to the

women in my life: my wife, Regan,

and my daughters, Allison and Lydia,

and to James A. Bear, Jr., scholar and friend,

and Daniel P. Jordan, with eternal gratitude

Contents

Contents

PREFACE

This book is intended for the general reader. Although its scholarly under-pinnings are solid, it is not meant to be a learned treatise, but a book to be read for pleasure, a private exploration of a largely obscure facet in the life of one of the most intriguing figures in American history. The book is meant not only for those attached to Thomas Jefferson or just those who love wine. It is offered especially to those who know only a little about either wine or Jefferson, but would like to learn more about both in a relatively painless way. If portions become too technical or detailed, the patient and amiable reader can simply skim over them. Endnotes and bibliography appear at the back of the book for those who wish to know sources or delve more deeply into the subject.[1]

The book treats Jefferson's wines chronologically, as he discovered them, tracing the evolution of his tastes. The first chapter, "Early Wines," begins with a brief background of the man and the character of his times, including his first recorded wine-drinking experiences. These occurred mainly at Williamsburg, after his college days at William and Mary, while he was studying law under George Wythe, one of the great legal scholars of the revolutionary period. The Wythes, like most Virginia gentry of the late 1700s, drank primarily Madeira and claret, and Jefferson's first refer-ences are to those wines. Soon he established his first cellar, noting with meticulous accuracy just what wines he possessed, in what quantities he bought them, and how much they cost.

Chapters two, three, and four deal with his five formative years as American minister in Paris. What Jefferson did not learn at the salons and dinner tables of Paris, he sought out in the vineyards themselves during two lengthy, incognito wine tours. Extensively excerpted are his eminently readable journals of those trips: the first to Burgundy, Bordeaux, southern France, and northern Italy, and the second to the Rhine, the Mosel, and Champagne. Also included are scores of little-known letters to and from his wine suppliers and producers, some of whose descendants still produce the same wines on the same properties.

Chapter five recounts his difficult return to life in America, beginning with his four years in New York and Philadelphia as secretary of state, when he ordered and wrote extensively about wine, trying to obtain in America the same quality and variety he had known in Paris. Then came three years of "retirement" at Monticello when he tried unsuccessfully to reestablish vineyards there. During the succeeding four years, while he was vice president, again in Philadelphia, there are fewer discourses on wine, but still many references in his letters, account books, and tavern bills.

Chapter six recounts the golden age of wines for Jefferson in America: the eight years he spent as president. Primary sources are again his letters, contemporary accounts of dinners at the White House, and a fascinating list, in his own handwriting, entitled "Wine Provided at Washington," which he compiled later from memos made while he was president.

Chapter seven examines the seventeen years of his active retirement, when he conducted extensive correspondence on wines with European suppliers, employing a wine vocabulary familiar to any modern amateur of wines. It also has brief sections on his Monticello brewery and his annual crops of hard cider, which he called "more like wine" than any other beverage.

Chapter eight reviews Jefferson's lifelong efforts to establish vineyards at Monticello and their current reconstruction by the Thomas Jefferson Memorial Foundation. Jefferson had an avid interest in grape growing, maintaining an active correspondence with several Europeans who sought to establish vineyards in America. He made periodic plantings of vines at Monticello, but his continual absences while in public office prevented him from properly overseeing them. His plans and failures along this line are documented by Jefferson himself in two primary sources: his *Garden Book*, a sort of botanical journal which he kept in his own hand from 1766 until his death in 1826, and his *Farm Book*, a journal of his land holdings and plantings.

The epilogue delves briefly into the latest Jefferson controversy: the appearance in 1985 of a case of old bottles of Bordeaux alleged to have belonged to Jefferson and which have sold at auction for hundreds of thousands of dollars.

Despite Jefferson's own intense interest in wine, it occurred to me during the years it took to research and write this book that it might be a somewhat frivolous exercise to devote an entire book just to the drinking habits of a great man, even one who wrote with what some called such a "curious felicity of expression." In the end it was Jefferson himself who answered the question: *he* must have considered wine worthy of such serious interest. Otherwise, why would he have taken the time and trouble to preserve copies of literally hundreds of letters, just about wine, to such persons as Washington, Adams, Franklin, and Monroe, not to mention all the scientists, ambassadors, winemakers, and others with whom he seriously corresponded on the subject. As Jefferson himself once wrote: "The letters of a person, especially of one whose business has chiefly been transacted by letters, form the only full and genuine journal of his life." If Jefferson considered his letters on wine worth preserving, then he would no doubt be pleased to see them included in a single volume for study as a whole.

Thomas Jefferson had numerous wine cellars in his long life, including at least two at Monticello (one under the dining room, one under the South Pavilion), one at his father's house at Shadwell (which burned), one at the Governor's Mansion in Williamsburg (destroyed by the British), at least two at the White House, two in Paris, two in Philadelphia, one in New York, one at his recently restored octagonal second home at Poplar Forest near Lynchburg, and possibly one at Elk Hill, his wife's house where they first lived, another at Chancellor George Wythe's house in Williamsburg where Jefferson studied law, and still another at Annapolis where he lived with James Monroe. Jefferson also visited scores of wine cellars throughout Europe and Virginia.

On July 4, 2006, a statue honoring Jefferson is being dedicated in Paris. It is located, fittingly, near the Seine between Musée d'Orsay and the former Hotel de Salm, Jefferson's favorite building in Paris, which now houses the Académie Française

PBS is airing this year a one-hour special on Jefferson's influence on American wine called "A Cultivated Life." Filmed in the vineyards of France, Virginia, and California in the format popularized by Ken Burns, it is narrated by Hal Holbrook. Produced by Alessandro (Sam) Santarelli and John Harrington of Madisonfilm in Alexandria, Virginia, it features eighteen excellent commentators, including Jefferson experts Daniel Jordan, Peter Hatch, Lucia Cinder Stanton, and Susan Stein of Monticello; Jefferson and wine historian James Gabler, who has just written a book on Jefferson and Franklin; White House historian William Seale; Tuscan winemakers Filippo and Francesco Mazzei, direct descendants of Jefferson's neighbor Philip Mazzei; French winemakers Alexandre de Lur-Saluces of Yquem and Jean-Bernard Delmas of Haut-Brion of Bordeaux; Francois Parent of Burgundy; Michel Chapoutier of the Rhône Valley; and American winemakers Robert Mondavi, Jay Corley, and Bob Long of California. The many able winemakers of Virginia are represented by one of the ablest, Gabriele Rausse, who makes the wines at Monticello, including a very fine 1999 Sangiovese.

ACKNOWLEDGMENTS

A project of such scope could never be accomplished without much help and encouragement. It began with a phone call in 1973 from James A. Bear, Jr., then director of the Jefferson Foundation at Monticello. Jim had read a column I wrote on old Madeiras for the *Washington Post* and suggested a little "pamphlet" on Jefferson and wine. After a lifetime of stops and starts, it is at last completed. After Jim Bear, my biggest helper at Monticello was Lucia Cinder Stanton, another terrific person. When Jim retired, my fellow Mississippi native Dan Jordan took over and has graciously opened every door for me like a genie from the Arabian nights. Curator Susan Stein has been warmly supportive, as have winemen Peter Hatch and Gabriele Rausse, library director Jack Robertson, photographer Charles Kelly, *Papers* editor Jeff Looney and, not least, the modest and generous Kim Curtis, who exceeded all expectations in finding and obtaining high-quality illustrations. Then there is Felicia Warburg Rogan, doyenne of the Albemarle wine scene, who opened for me the new universe of fine Virginia wines. Thanks also to Robert de Treville Lawrence, the pioneer of *vinifera* wines in Virginia.

At Princeton, the late Dr. Julian Boyd was surprisingly available, as was his able assistant Ruth Lester, who personally made for me hundreds of photocopies of original, unedited letters about wine in Jefferson's own handwriting. While I was legal counsel to the late Senator John Stennis, a Virginia graduate and Jefferson admirer, the eminent scholar Daniel Boorstin and his staff guided me through their maze of microfilm at the Library of Congress. The Colonial Williamsburg Society also assisted greatly with documents for chapter one. Historian William Seale got me into the White House for three full days of quiet, private explorations of the cellars and dining rooms, where I sat for hours imagining what they must have been like for Jefferson.

In France my friends Alfred Tesseron and Franck Pouey of Bordeaux taught me the secrets of classified growths. Robin Kelley O'Connor of the Bordeaux Wine Bureau in New York was also a great teacher and great company, as was Dixie Gill of Premium Ports and Madeiras. In Italy, Count Buonacasi of Capezzana helped me with the wines of Florence. In Provence my old friend Claude Blanc introduced me to the Bergasse family history. In Saumur brothers Roger and Paul Fillia-treau showed me how Cabernet Franc could be shipped from the Loire as "claret," just as Jefferson said. Mireille Guiliano of Veuve Clicquot Champagne kindly made me a judge of her wine book competition for several years and annually enriched my library with scores of review copies. The Parent family helped me in Burgundy, as did Pam Hunter in Champagne and Beaujolais. My two years as a student in Paris were unforgettable, as others have discovered.

At the University of Mississippi, with my adjunct law professor's ID, I was allowed to check out many scores of books from the John D. Williams Library, and the books were stamped due *one year* from the date I received them. To the late John Grisanti of Memphis and to my first editor at the *Washington Post*, William Rice, who had faith in an unknown writer trained by Eudora Welty, I owe a huge debt of gratitude, as I do to Dr. William H. Baskin of North Carolina and Dr. William S. Woods of Tulane, my mentors in things French. Miss Eudora Welty tried her best to teach me to write while at Millsaps College. Then there were the selfless secretaries, especially Brenda Gill and Joan Case, who gave evenings and weekends to type perfectly my countless drafts.

Charles Overby, now CEO of the Freedom Forum, but formerly my editor, along with John Johnson and Angela Terrell, at Gannett while I was a syndicated wine columnist, gave me a generous expense account to help me pursue my Jefferson wine interests in conjunction with my weekly columns. Dr. William Ferris, former director of the National Endowment for the Humanities, along with computer master Samuel James Baker, were perhaps my biggest enablers. Special honor is due to Larry and Dean Faulkner Wells of Oxford and the late Willie Morris, aided and abetted by Shields Hood, the South's best palate, who refused to let me quit this project. Thank you also to my friends at Square Books of Oxford, the "Best Little Bookstore in the South," who always found for me everything I needed without using the Internet.

Jefferson scholar and fellow law professor Annette Gordon-Reed kindly recommended my manuscript for publication, as did the eminent Dr. Richard P. Vine, who not only directs top international wine competitions, but selects the wines for American Airlines. Perhaps most important of all were my soulmates and fellow wine judges at the top yearly international wine competitions over the past twenty years in Los Angeles, San Diego, San Bernardino, Riverside, Dallas, Atlanta, Oregon, Washington, and Torgiano, Italy. Dr. Bob Small, David Lake, Nathan Chroman, Peter M. F. Sichel, Don Galleano, Robin Daniel Lail, Dan Berger, Darrell Corti, Fred Dame, the antipodean twins Daryl Groom and Nick Goldschmidt, Richard Peterson and his daughters Heidi and Holly, Parks Redwine, and others too numerous to name here have made my life in wine judging pleasingly unforgettable.

Then there was Fred Weck, who hired me at two dollars an hour to unload wine by the truckload at the Original Wine & Cheese Shop in Georgetown, now sadly closed, then made me a "wine consultant" when he learned I could speak French, and patiently taught me the glories of Burgundy and the Rheingau. I will always treasure my three wonderful years with our compatriots at the shop: Con Buckley, snooker champion of Ireland, and Larry, Alan, Carlos, and Harvey, wine experts all, who taught me everything from decanting '47 Cheval Blanc to the mysterious charms of the wines of the Saar.

Most recent are my friends at the University Press of Mississippi. I went there to discuss writing a memoir of my thirty years as a prosecutor in Faulkner country, but editor Craig Gill artfully persuaded me to delay that idea and finish first my languishing project on Jefferson's wines. I shall be eternally grateful to him for his influence and wise counsel, as I will to editor Shane Gong for keeping me straight, and to Todd Lape for his outstanding design work. To those which space has required me to omit, you are not forgotten. I only wish my parents were here to enjoy this moment with me.

Thomas Jefferson on Wine

Introduction

In his approach to wine, Jefferson seems remarkably modern in the breadth of his tastes. He liked the red and the white, the dry and the sweet. He epitomized his own searching and mentally adventurous age in his incessant experiments with every available variety, his constant seeking of new sensations and knowledge. He expressed a preference for French wines, especially certain Burgundies, Bordeaux, Champagnes, and Rhônes, and often insisted on particular vintages. He also cellared, drank, and praised some wine of just about every other winemaking country at one time or another, especially Italy, Spain, and Portugal.

Jefferson's letters about wine, in the scope and variety of their curiosity, read remarkably like a Hugh Johnson wine book or a Gerald Asher column. In his everyday table wine selections, Jefferson was very much a precursor of present-day American wine drinkers. When his favorite Burgundies and Bordeaux became too expensive, he turned to the thriftier wines of southern France, Italy, and Portugal. What have been called "country wines," from such regions as Languedoc and Roussillon, were regulars on Jefferson's table. Of Italian wines Jefferson drank quite a variety, including Chianti, Orvieto, Gattinara, and Marsala, as well as the ancestor of Soave and various Moscatos and Vin Santo dessert wines. His favorite was Montepulciano, a wine once seldom seen in America, whose cousins the Chiantis dominated Italian imports. In the past decades that has changed, and Montepulciano and Jefferson's other Tuscan wines, such as Carmignano, Pomino, and Castello di Ama, are once again among the highest-rated and most sought-after wines of Italy, and again imported into America under their own names.

Among Spanish wines Jefferson preferred "pale" Sherry and St. Lucar, today called Manzanilla. He also served to guests, while president, quantities of Mountain, a dessert wine obtainable today as Malaga. He prescribed for his daughter Maria, in her final illness, old Spanish Paxarete and Pedro Ximénez. He once served Monticello visitor Daniel Webster a "Grecian Islands" wine which Webster called "Samian," apparently the famous Muscat of Samos.

In addition to Madeiras, many of Jefferson's everyday wines were also Portuguese. Some came from the vineyards of the Marquis de Pombal, ruler of Portugal from 1750 to 1777, for whom a well-known rosé is now named. Most of Jefferson's everyday Portuguese whites like "Lisbon" no longer appear in America under those names, but the crisp whites and full-bodied reds of Portugal are still available as wine values in America.

In bringing such a wide variety of wines into what was largely a wilderness, Jefferson faced obstacles unknown to us. There were, of course, no wine shops or wholesalers, although there were wine merchants in the major ports. Shipping was a big problem. If the wines were sent at the wrong season, the slow and rough ocean voyages alternately froze or boiled them as they lay in the holds of the old sailing ships. Other hazards were the eighteenth-century pirates, whom Jefferson called "the lawless rovers of the ocean." More than once pirates raided the ships bearing his wines from Europe. Even more deadly to the safe arrival of Jefferson's wines were what he called "the rascally boatmen" of the Potomac and James rivers, who tapped his wine barrels, drank much of the wine, then refilled them with water.

In 1815 things got so bad that Jefferson lamented to a wine merchant that "[d]isappointments in procuring supplies have at length left me without a drop of wine." On another occasion, being notified that a priceless shipment of wines was lost to a storm in the West Indies, he wrote to a friend that he received the news with "much mortification of the palate." To order wine, Jefferson had to specify in each letter the ship, the captain, the ports of exit and entry, how the wine should be packaged, and how he would get payment across the ocean and determine and pay the customs duties. That he took such pains shows just how much he desired fine wine.

Another major problem for Jefferson was bottling. Unstable wines like Champagne and Italian Nebbiolos often burst their bottles en route or spoiled. There were few bottle factories back then, so his many Portuguese and Spanish wines were shipped in barrels to be bottled at Monticello, where bottles often cost more than the wines they contained.

Corks were so hard to obtain that Jefferson tried, without success, to produce his own corks from the bark of cork oak trees planted at Monticello. The Jefferson Foundation revived the experiment, in conjunction with the replanted Monticello vineyards, and created a nursery of cork oak trees at the Virginia estate, but they too found the climate there too cold.

As his ample cellar lists attest, Jefferson was equal to every challenge in obtaining wines he wanted. He preferred to order his wines directly from the proprietors who made them, and advised Madison and Monroe never to deal with brokers or middlemen. He never hesitated to use his official positions, whether as secretary of state or president, to receive his wines via diplomatic channels. He usually ordered and paid through the U.S. consul of the port nearest the vineyards whose wines he wanted. So expert at importing wines did he become that the tax collectors at American ports sometimes asked Jefferson how much duty they should charge him on his wines, conceding that no one knew as much about the subject as he did.

WHAT WAS WINE LIKE IN JEFFERSON'S TIME?

Fortunately, we still know quite a bit about eighteenth- and early nineteenth-century wines, thanks to excellent contemporaneous books on the subject, including *Ancient and Modern Wines* by Cyrus Redding (1814) and *The History of Ancient and Modern Wines* by Alex Henderson (1824). Then there are great wine histories such as *Vintage: The Story of Wine* by Hugh Johnson (1989) and *Bottlescrew Days* (1926) by Andre Simon, among the finest wine writers of the last century. When one compares the wines preferred by Jefferson to those listed by Redding and Henderson, it is apparent that the American president was well versed in the subject. The wines mentioned among Jefferson's purchases are almost invariably those which have survived to this day, while those wines listed by Redding that Jefferson did *not* buy have largely passed from the scene. It is not unreasonable to ask whether we might use Jefferson as a standard of judgment, and ask how the specialists of his age measured up to him, rather than the other way around. At the very least it is safe to rank Thomas Jefferson as one of the most knowledgeable wine amateurs of his age.

As Simon's title indicates, it was not long before Jefferson's time that the use of corks as bottle stoppers was rediscovered and used on a commercial scale for the first time since the Romans. Before the eighteenth century, wines were served directly from the wooden barrels in which they were shipped, passing at most through a pitcher to be carried to the table. What few bottles did exist were used mainly as serving vessels, and not for aging wine. As such, they were flat-bottomed, bulbous affairs like ships' decanters, made so that not even the tipsy could knock them over.

The rediscovery of the cork seems to have happened in Portugal and several other places around the same time, but it was most important in Champagne. In the 1690s Spanish monks apparently brought to a monastery in Champagne wine bottles stoppered with the bark of cork oak trees native to Spain. When Dom Perignon, the famous blind monk and cellar master of the monastery, tried bark as a stopper in his still white wines, he found that it trapped the small, natural bubbles that formed during fermentation and made the wine sparkling. He thereby created Champagne as we know it. Today one of the finest and most expensive modern Champagnes is aptly named Dom Perignon in his honor.

Ironically, Jefferson denounced sparkling Champagne, which he insisted was a fad that would never catch on. Today a little nonsparkling Champagne is still made, my favorites by Moet's Chateau de Saran and the old house of Ruinart, which already existed in Jefferson's time. Called Coteaux Champenois, the still variety of Champagne is steely dry and subtle and can be a uniquely fine wine.

Rediscovery of the cork also had a profound impact on other wines. Previously, most wines were drunk young, straight from the cask, usually in the year after they were made. In barrels, air leaked in and often turned the wine to vinegar before it could age, so that, prior to the renewed use of the cork, aged wine was virtually unknown. It is said that as late as Henry VIII, English kings still used rags as bottle stoppers.

Jamming pieces of cork in bottlenecks did create one problem: how to get the cork back out? One answer was port tongs, a device still used today, which basically consists of breaking the neck off the bottle, taking the cork with it. Or you could slice it off with a saber, which is easier than it sounds, and is often done for show at Champagne tastings. But wine bottles were expensive and hard to get, and Jefferson had to reuse his. To his gadget-oriented mind, there was a more ingenious and appealing invention: the bottlescrew, or "corkscrew," as we call it. Numerous *Memorandum Book* entries from 1783 onward show that he purchased many corkscrews both before and after going to France. Also preserved at the Smithsonian is a corkscrew on Jefferson's elaborate pocket knife, which bears an uncanny resemblance to a modern "Swiss Army" knife.

One criticism which might fairly be made of Jefferson's wine evaluations is that they are too uniformly positive. He was cautious to criticize but quick to praise—an excellent quality in a politician, but less desirable when one is seeking useful comments on wines. However, since many of his comments were intended for those who either produced the wines or procured them for him, often against great obstacles, Jefferson's tendency to be positive is understandable. His biographer Dumas Malone noted that overuse of superlatives was a weakness of Jefferson's in all areas, whether due to his positive, optimistic nature, or just from innate courtesy.

Malone once called it "a blurring of the dim line between courtesy and deception." John Adams's grandson Charles Francis expressed it in a subtle way:

> More ardent in his imagination than in his affections, he did not always speak
> exactly as he felt towards either friends or enemies. As a consequence, he has left
> hanging over a part of his public life a vapor of duplicity or, to say the least, of indi-
> rection, the presence of which is generally felt more than it is seen.[1]

John Adams himself, who knew both the public and private Jefferson (and preferred the private one), thought it was Jefferson's method of expressing himself which caused him to be accused of "double-dealing," even on such a relatively nonpolitical subject as wine, and one senses so much of the diplomat in Jefferson that it can leave questions as to what he *really* thought.

A second criticism which might be made of Jefferson's expertise in wine is his spelling, where he seemed to enjoy variety, often spelling the same wine four or five different ways. Perusal of wine books of the period, however, shows that this was neither ignorance nor idiosyncrasy. As N. M. Penzer stated in his interestingly esoteric *Book of the Wine Label* (1947), the eighteenth century was a period with "an almost medieval richness of orthography." There were, as Penzer shows with copies of old silver neck labels, often four or five different but equally acceptable spellings for the name of a single wine.

Jefferson was thus not confused when he spelled the great wine city of Beaune in Burgundy both "Vaune" and "Vioune," even though it was easily confused with the nearby "Vone," now called Vosne-Romanee. In his time that was how they spelled it. Nor were his renderings of the Italian wine grape Nebbiolo as "navioule" or the great Riesling grape of Germany as "rhysslin" erroneous. It was simply the practice then to permit phonetic and sometimes arbitrary spelling.

JEFFERSON HIMSELF: HIS WINES AS A WINDOW TO HIS TRUE NATURE

In studying Jefferson's comments on wine, one is constantly led back to Jefferson himself. What was he like? How did he find time for this enormous interest in wines, which would have been a full-time hobby for someone with nothing else to do? Was he a wine snob? Didn't he sometimes carry the subject to extremes, like some Americans of our own time? After spending more than three decades with Jefferson's letters on wines as a more or less constant project, I've come to think that he simply had more energy and curiosity than ordinary mortals. He went at wine as he did every subject, from the weather to the New Testament (which he rewrote the way he thought Jesus would have wanted it). Jefferson became the foremost wine expert of his time, while holding the most demanding public offices, because he was unique in his energy, talent, and ability to concentrate.

For us, an important by-product of Jefferson's interest in wine is the light it tends to throw on his personality. In a sense he is more approachable from this avenue because it is a more personal side of him, which he was less likely to color or rearrange for political consumption. His love of wine is also of special interest to us because wines have changed less than most other objects in the past two hundred years, thus giving a more common frame of reference for us and for Jefferson than almost any other. As F. Scott Fitzgerald once said: "Perhaps life really is better seen through a single window after all."

If someone had wanted to create the ideal observer of wine in early nineteenth-century America, he would have created Jefferson: a Virginia planter, well-travelled, a cultivated and urbane writer with an excellent palate, plenty of money to buy and try any wine from any part of the world he wanted, and enough fluency in French to speak and write to winemakers and connoisseurs in their own language. Jefferson lived at the heart of American and European social life. He could taste and discuss wine with the most famous and knowledgeable men and women of his day.

For me it is difficult to picture Jefferson's wines without picturing Jefferson himself. Fortunately, several excellent portraits and descriptions of his appearance and personal habits remain. Easily the most colorful descriptions were left by Isaac Jefferson, a servant who was with Jefferson for nearly forty years. Isaac knew Jefferson well, not only at Monticello, but at Williamsburg and Richmond when he was governor, and in Philadelphia when he was secretary of state. There Jefferson apprenticed Isaac for four years in ironworking and tinning, a trusted position. Later, at Monticello, he was in charge of Jefferson's nail-making factory, the only business venture in which Jefferson was ever successful.

Isaac knew Jefferson in his public offices and throughout his retirement at Monticello.

In 1847, Isaac Jefferson was discovered and interviewed by Charles Campbell, whose handwritten accounts of their interview have been edited and republished three times, most thoroughly by James Bear, whose edition is followed here.[2] To our ears some of the former slave's phrases sound at first as if they were put in his mouth by a condescending Confederate, but when you read the narrative as a whole, they sound remarkably consistent and historically authentic. His native intelligence and gift for vivid detail make him one of the most valuable observers of Jefferson. Isaac also left several eyewitness comments on Jefferson's wines that confirm the written evidence left by Jefferson and others.

Isaac always referred to Jefferson with as much affection as respect, and for a former slave was on rather familiar terms with Jefferson. He still called him "Old Master" twenty years after Jefferson's death, but his comments show the easy familiarity of one who knew Jefferson on an everyday basis rather than the overawed reverence for "Mr. Jefferson" that some modern admirers show. Isaac spoke of Jefferson candidly, without artificially glorifying or vilifying him as a historical character as more remote observers have done.

One reason Isaac knew some of the better Jefferson anecdotes was, as he explained it, because "Old Master used to talk to me mighty free." He described Jefferson as a "tall, thin-visaged man" with a "light-red head" and

> as tall, straight-bodied a man as ever you see, right square-shouldered. Nary man in this town walked so straight as my Old Master. Neat a built man as ever was seen in Vaginny, I reckon, or any place—a straight-up man, long face, high nose.

Although respectful, Isaac was not obsequious. Commenting on the rather too-flattering portrait of Jefferson in Linn's contemporary biography, which Campbell apparently had shown him, Isaac scoffed: "Old Master never was dat handsome in dis world."

Edmund Bacon, Jefferson's overseer at Monticello from 1806 to 1822, when he emigrated to Kentucky and became a successful horse farmer, gave a similar description of Jefferson:

> Six feet two and a half inches high, well proportioned, and straight as a gun barrel. He was like a fine horse; he had no surplus flesh. He had an iron constitution and was very strong. He had a machine for measuring strength. He always enjoyed the best of health. I don't think he was ever really sick until his last sickness . . . He had blue eyes.

Isaac, always a colorful observer, recalled that Jefferson had brought back a "great many clothes from France," including

> a coat of blue cloth trimmed with gold lace; cloak trimmed so too. Dar say it weighed fifty pounds. Large buttons on the coat as big as half a dollar; shine like gold. In summer he war silk coat, pearl buttons.

Isaac also described Jefferson's mannerisms, giving us another way of visualizing him: "Mr. Jefferson bowed to everybody he meet; talked with his arms folded."

When it came to describing Jefferson's drinking habits, again it was Isaac who left the most vivid picture, saying Jefferson always had "[p]lenty of wine, best old Antigua rum and cider; very fond of wine and water. Isaac never heard of his being disguised in drink."

FACES OF JEFFERSON: LIFE PORTRAITS OF AN EVOLVING WINE DRINKER

Even with the reliable verbal portraits from Isaac and Bacon, it is still hard to picture a man without, so to speak, a picture. For that reason included here are reproductions of some of the most authentic and evocative portraits of Jefferson, from John Trumbull's red-headed likeness of the young Virginia planter in his thirties to his Paris portrait of a much more sophisticated Jefferson in his forties, while American minister to France in 1788, complete with powdered wig and wearing the French silk coat with large pearl buttons later described by Isaac.

There is one portrait of Jefferson which may tell more about his private side than any other, particularly the wine-loving Jefferson. It is an unusual amateur aquatint done in Philadelphia in 1798 by, of all people, the Revolutionary War hero and Polish patriot, General Thaddeus Kosciusko. Really more of a friendly caricature, the Kosciusko portrait shows a convivial, almost madcap Jefferson, wearing a laurel wreath, his head tipped back and chin jutting out in a fun-loving and most unpresidential pose. The expression is that of a happy wine drinker. It is easy to understand why this portrait was little publicized or circulated when Jefferson was in politics. And when he graduated to being a revered ex-president and Founding Father, it was out of keeping with the sober-sided image thought to be necessary in schoolbooks, on nickels, or on two-dollar bills, especially during Prohibition.

The Kosciusko picture seems an usually accurate portrait of Jefferson the good companion, who loved the pleasures of the table and good conversation. It is reminiscent of the bachelor Jefferson who wrote youthful letters to friends in pig Latin and formed a group called the Flat Hat Club. That merry Jefferson necessarily disappeared during the rigors of the Revolution. No sooner did that ordeal end than his wife died, a misfortune from which in a sense he never really recovered. His later positions as secretary of state, vice president, and president left him with little time for frivolity, so the Kosciusko portrait is probably unique in capturing visually that playful side of his nature.

There also exists another striking portrayal of the spirit of Jefferson the wine man. It is the anonymous, undated "silhouette," or shadow portrait of him in tall boots and long coat, which vividly shows the "loose, shackling air" he was described as having. Although not absolutely authenticated by undisputable evidence as being Jefferson, it is a persuasive likeness.

In stark contrast to both Trumbull's rustic revolutionary of 1776 and the Parisian dandy of the 1780s is the mature politician portrayed by

Rembrandt Peale in his 1800 Philadelphia portrait, painted just before Jefferson was elected president. The Peale portrait shows a solid, ambitious mesomorph with a hard set to the eyes, the sort of man you could imagine serving the most expensive wines, perhaps as much for their social effect as for the wines themselves.

If one *really* wanted to speculate, he could find in the preceding Jeffersons three rather different wine drinkers. The first was a hard-riding frontier planter who drank Madeira laced with brandy and whatever local taverns made available. The second was a pleasantly bewildered American in Paris, slightly lost, as Jefferson said, "on the vaunted scene of Europe," from the boudoirs of the women to the political intrigues of the men, and drinking the great Burgundies, Bordeaux, and Champagnes that such a life entailed. The third Jefferson would be a rich and ambitious label flaunter, freshly returned from Paris and rubbing his countrymen's noses in his European tastes and sophistication. Patrick Henry accused Jefferson of as much when he said he had "abjured his native victuals" for fancy French cuisine. Some even said he was "Frenchified."

The most moving portrait, in its candid revelation of the ravages of age on a once-powerful man, is the 1821 study by Thomas Sully, made from life at Monticello when Jefferson was seventy-eight. It shows a decidedly old man with a sort of resigned expression. This was the Jefferson of the late-life correspondence with John and Abigail Adams, where he described them all as too tired and infirm to "decant over our palates another vintage." Ironically, it was during that period when he had most time to write and reflect on wines, and some of his best comments on wine are from his old age. Considering the enthusiasm and vigor of his writing in those days, perhaps the Sully portrait simply shows an old man tired of posing for the painter.

In a striking way, Jefferson's life portraits correspond with his evolution as a wine drinker as shown by his cellar lists and letters. He began as a hunter and outdoorsman drinking strong Madeira, evolved into a mature and well-travelled public official enjoying Champagne and Bordeaux, and ended as a genteel, impoverished retiree with a cellar full of well-chosen but inexpensive wines.

Was Jefferson a Wine Snob?

It is curious how differently biographers have viewed Jefferson. Most saw him as an eloquent, liberal statesman, but others as a rather slippery politician not unlike the species we are familiar with today. One biographer thought him a "cold, forbidding person with strong but repressed passions." Some wondered how he could be both connoisseur of wines and a populist, at the same time the best fiddler and the finest violinist in Virginia.

A still pertinent treatment of this diversity of views is *The Jefferson Image in the American Mind* by Dr. Merrill Peterson (1960). Opinion today is just as divided, and this book attempts to deal with the contradictions in Jefferson's personality as reflected in his contrasting tastes in wine and his varied comments on a wide spectrum of wines throughout his long life as a wine drinker.

In the 1970s came *Thomas Jefferson: An Intimate History* by the late Fawn Brodie, who closely examined his love life, and was attacked therefor by traditionalist supporters of "Mr. Jefferson" and his image as an American icon. Since then, DNA tests and a reasoned and perceptive analysis of the evidence by a New York University law professor have shown Brodie was probably right. (See *Thomas Jefferson and Sally Hemings: An American Controversy* by Annette Gordon-Reed [1997].)

One of those periodic reexaminations of Jefferson's character is now under way. With computer technology making research easier and quicker, armies of scholars are redissecting the man and his contradictions. He has recently been called by reputable scholars both a "sphinx" and a "grieving optimist," and blamed for conducting a "vendetta" against Aaron Burr and even for helping to cause the Civil War by his utopian support for small farmers and failure to oppose slavery more effectively.[3] Much of the new scholarship has tended to bring Jefferson down, stressing the tension between his powerful rhetoric on freedom while he held and sold fellow humans in slavery, which one historian likened to a "tin can tied to his reputation."[4]

His current reputation is such that he can be declared "greatest man of the millennium" by filmmaker Ken Burns one moment and then finish behind Ronald Reagan in a national poll on the Discovery Channel the next. As Jefferson's role as an icon is questioned, the reputations of overlooked heroes like the feisty Adams, the serious Washington, the witty Franklin, and the steely Hamilton are undergoing positive reevaluations. In our contentious age, a settled view of Jefferson the man is difficult to find.[5] Perhaps examining this practical idealist, who built brick by brick his own ivory tower at Monticello, might be better done through the prism of his wines, in a sort of biography written in wine.

When Patrick Henry charged that Jefferson had "abjured his native victuals," he implied a related wine snobbery. Was there any basis for that charge? Available records allow us at least to speculate on an answer. It is clear that long before he ever went to France, Jefferson was interested in wine. His Williamsburg law tutor, George Wythe, and Francis Fauquier, the Huguenot governor of Virginia, saw to that. With his Tuscan-born neighbor Philip Mazzei, he planned to grow grapes and make a Chianti-like wine. Through Hessian officers who were prisoners of war near Charlottesville, Jefferson learned about German wines. From his letters throughout his long life, it is clear that he had a sincere and abiding interest in the subject, both in his youth and in his old age, and was far more than a mere name dropper.

Jefferson did take wine rather seriously at times, but would certainly have deplored wine snobbery, which to him would have smacked of Tory colonialism and been contrary to the democratic spirit of equality he favored. To him wine was a natural, enjoyable beverage and not an object of art, and certainly not a profitable "investment," a subject he was notoriously bad at anyway. He drank wine for pleasure and liked to share his pleasure with others, constantly sending friends in other cities and on other continents new wines he had discovered.

Henry's charge that Jefferson "abjured his native victuals" might have been partly right as to *food*, but Jefferson's everyday *wines* were usually inexpensive and unpretentious. Like Henry himself, Jefferson sometimes used beer and hard cider as his "table drinks." Jefferson and his wife brewed their own beer at Monticello, from corn and wheat. He boasted that his homebrew was far superior to the "meagre" and "vapid" products then sold commercially. He even left a design for a Monticello "brew-house," drawn on lined architect's paper in his own careful hand. Typically, his one-room brewery was of a handsome, arched, Palladian design. For guests and servants, he also made his own fruit brandies, which he referred to in the idiom of the day as "perry" and "peach mobby."

One has to admit that at his most enthusiastic, Jefferson probably qualified as a *wine bore*, a fanatic somewhat like those one sees in America today. He took his wine *very* seriously, too seriously for those around him who were not persuaded that wine was such an important subject. John Quincy Adams once said as much in grumbling about Jefferson's White House dinners and their endless conversations about wines, which he found "not very edifying." Jefferson tended to be compulsive, pursuing in depth whatever subject came to his attention. Wine and its trappings were made to order for him, and held a fascination for him similar to his interests in music and architecture.

One theoretical blot on Jefferson's reputation as a connoisseur of wines is the intriguing comment by Isaac about Jefferson's liking "wine and water." Did he mean that Jefferson watered his wine? What kind of connoisseur waters his wine?

Jefferson's cellar lists of wines in barrel, especially those of southern France or Portugal, suggest that he often used cheap wines slightly watered as mealtime beverages. He apparently saved his finer wines to highlight and appreciate with guests after dinner, somewhat like a modern wine tasting. And we know that he did so on his trips from Monticello to his other home at Poplar Forest near Lynchburg. During his retirement, he took his grandchildren and had regular picnics along the way, as one granddaughter recalled:

> My grandfather travelled in his own carriage. It took us nearly three days to make the hundred miles. His cheerful conversation, so agreeable and instructive, his singing as we journeyed along, made the time pass pleasantly. Our cold dinner was always put up by his own hands; a pleasant spot by the roadside chosen to eat it, and he was the carver and helped us to our cold fowl and ham, *and mixed the wine and water to drink with it* [emphasis added].[6]

Were these family picnics the only time Jefferson watered his wines? His letter to American consul Joseph Fenwick of Bordeaux in September 1790 suggests not. After ordering thirty dozen bottles of Château d'Yquem for George Washington and ten dozen for himself, and twenty dozen Château Latour for Washington and ten dozen Château Rausan and others for himself, Jefferson concluded:

> To these I must beg you to add 10. dozen for me of a good white *vin ordinaire*, or indeed something better, that is to say of such a quality as will do to mix with water, and also be drinkable alone.[7]

Thus it appears certain that Thomas Jefferson mixed water with his ordinary wines on some occasions. That should in no way detract from his reputation as a connoisseur, but merely shows that he was practical, and also tends to rebut the charge that he was a wine snob. After all, Napoleon watered his Chambertin, and Homer said that the great warrior Achilles, when greeting guests, ordered his servants to "put less water in the wine."

JEFFERSON AND FOOD: WAS THE GREAT CONNOISSEUR A VEGETARIAN?

Jefferson's love of fine food was once better known than his love of fine wines. Bacon and Isaac agreed on his love of food. In the White House chapter are excerpts from his maitre d's shopping lists which show what fine fare Jefferson served, although he never seemed interested in the current hot topic of wine/food matching.

Jefferson wrote certain letters in his old age, especially to *doctors*, stressing a preference for vegetables over the rich, elaborate dishes he favored earlier. Even Bacon had to admit Jefferson was a fanatic for fine food:

> He was never a great eater, but what he did eat he wanted to be very choice. He never eat much hog meat. He often told me, as I was giving out meat for the servants, that what I gave one of them for a week would be more than he would use in six months.

Although not fond of "hog meat," apparently, Jefferson had his preferences:

> He was especially fond of Guinea fowls; and for meat he preferred good beef, mutton, and lambs. Meriwether Lewis' mother made very nice hams, and every year I used to get a few from her for his special use. He was very fond of vegetables and fruit and raised every variety of them.

Bacon recalled that whenever Jefferson returned to Monticello, the first thing he would ask, after inquiring of everyone's health, was: "What have you got that is good [to eat]?" Bacon's comments are corroborated by those of White House maitre d' Etienne Lemaire, whose handwritten Day Book of food purchases from 1805 to 1809 corroborates and expands on what Bacon said.[8]

Isaac told of a similar Jefferson at Monticello, but with more stress on the opulence of his hospitality, and without overlooking the wines: "He never would have less than eight covers at dinner if nobody at table but himself. Had from eight to thirty-two covers for dinner. Plenty of wine." The serving of thirty-two different dishes is itself on the opulent side, but the idea that Jefferson would have served for himself at least eight dishes when dining alone suggests a *serious* interest in food. And his later wine lists show that he had appropriate wines for every one.

In this context, President Kennedy's famous remark to a group of Nobel laureates—that they were the greatest collection of talent at a White House dinner since Thomas Jefferson dined alone—takes on renewed significance. Jefferson's interest in food, even when he dined alone, shows a talent for the pleasures of the table as well as those of the mind. And his love of fine wines was at least equal to his love of fine foods.

Wine and the Other Founding Fathers

Jefferson appears to have been the most knowledgeable of the Founding Fathers about wine, but several others were avid wine drinkers, and many left records of wines served to them, even during the Continental Congress and Revolutionary War. John Hancock, a wealthy shipowner and wine importer, became involved in revolutionary activities partly due to his objections to British taxes on his Madeiras. When the British prosecuted him in 1769 for smuggling, John Adams defended Hancock and had the charges dismissed on a technicality after several weeks of trial.[9] So protracted were the proceedings that Adams said in his diary how he hated the bell which "bongled me out of bed each morning" to go to court.

Adams was another of the great wine lovers among the Founding Fathers, personally touring Bordeaux and later sharing with Jefferson the world's finest wines in Paris, New York, Philadelphia, and elsewhere.

George Washington, while not the connoisseur Jefferson was, never went without his glass of Madeira or claret, and received many cases of the finest French wines via Jefferson after the latter was minister to Paris. French generals who served with Washington recalled vividly his love of fine claret and the lively suppers for his officers where Alexander Hamilton led the toasting. Washington's letters show that in 1759, just a few months after his marriage to Martha, he was already ordering Madeira by the barrel straight from the best "houses" on the island, with the typically stern Washingtonian admonition: "let it be secured from pilferers."[10] He ordered his "Rhenish" or Rhine wine in thrifty one-pint tasting bottles.[11]

In 1768 Washington ordered vine cuttings from Madeira, hoping to establish a successful vineyard at Mount Vernon to stock the vaulted brick wine cellar he was building there.[12] His Madeira orders were always from the best suppliers: the Newtons, the Searles, and Scot, Pringle & Cheap, as well as the American consul on Madeira, John Pintard,[13] who supplied Madeiras to Alexander Hamilton, who said of one shipment, "I anticipate from its excellent quality a regale in due time to my friends and myself."[14]

Washington's tastes in wines, as in most matters, generally remained more restrained than those of the peripatetic Jefferson. He once ordered "4 Neat and fashionable Cut glass Decanters with broad Bottoms, that they may stand firm on the Table," and "2 1/2 Dozen Wine Glasses, to be rather low and strong as well as Neat."[15] Typical of Washington's stolid attitude toward food and drink was his own summary of his hospitality: "A glass of wine and a bit of mutton are always ready." Mutton is not quite so popular as it was in Washington's time, when it sometimes competed with such delicacies as cow's udder. As one Englishman noted in his diary during that era: "[A]t the chaplain's table dined upon a roasted tongue and udder. . . . I shall not dine on a roasted tongue and udder again very soon."[16]

Perhaps the greatest wine lover of the Founding Fathers next to Jefferson was Franklin, who has a well-deserved reputation as a ladies' man and bon vivant who loved to drink Champagne. Franklin, the least stuffy of the Founding Fathers, was a tremendous favorite with the French when he was American minister in Paris preceding Jefferson. And Franklin, whom Jefferson referred to as the "venerable and beloved Franklin," already had a fair cellar in his Paris residence as early as 1778, as will be discussed in chapter two.

But no Founding Father except Jefferson left the kind of extensive written comments about wines that would interest a modern wine drinker. Nor did they try as many kinds of wines as Jefferson did. In fact, many of their references to wine were in replying to letters from Jefferson, who was clearly the prime mover in discussing wine, especially in taking seriously the "appreciation" of wine, as people would say nowadays.

Was Thomas Jefferson Addicted to Alcohol?

To some it might seem surprising that Jefferson drank so *much* wine in his lifetime. Despite solid health and enormous intellectual achievements, Jefferson did ingest a lot of alcohol in his eighty-three years, however moderate each separate dose. And there are in history numerous examples of people who drank heavily yet remained at the peak of achievement for many years: Winston Churchill comes immediately to mind. Was Jefferson one of those? Could he have been addicted to alcohol?

Several comments by Jefferson, all made late in life, show that either he was thinking of the subject or others were asking him about it. In a letter of 1819, when he was seventy-six, Jefferson admitted that he doubled, and even tripled, with a friend, Dr. Benjamin Rush's recommended daily measure of wine: 1 1/2 glasses. Jefferson stressed that he drank only on a full stomach, and drank no wines with brandy added.[17] Such a "measure" is still a substantial one. Depending always on the size of the glasses, 4 1/2 glasses could be most of a normal-sized bottle. Yet Jefferson must not have been concerned about his consumption or he would not have admitted it.

During the War of 1812 he made another candid comment in a letter to a supplier: "Wine from long habit has become an indispensable for my health, which is now suffering by its disuse."[18] It is possible he referred to his digestion, but it is also arguable that he could not stand withdrawal from wine. In another letter four years later to Stephen Cathalan in Marseilles, who supplied many of his wines in his old age, he said: "You are not to conclude that I am become a *buveur* [drinker]. My measure is a sober one of 3 or 4 glasses at dinner, & not a drop at any other time."[19] This rather defensive comment was volunteered by Jefferson without a question on that line from Cathalan to provoke it.

While president in 1803, when he learned he could not get his favorite pale Sherry, Jefferson wrote to his supplier that it was "a privation which I shall feel sensibly once a day."[20] Of course, taking these isolated comments from a lifetime of letters written about wine is perhaps not fair, especially since they are all there is to suggest Jefferson might have been unable to stop drinking wine. And it was never suggested during his life that he became intoxicated. He was constantly inveighing against excessive drinking, which was rampant among some of his servants, and even his own family, including his son-in-law Randolph and Thomas Bankhead, who married one of his favorite granddaughters, Anne Cary.

Isaac decisively exonerated Jefferson on this score in his graphic way, saying, "Isaac never heard of his being disguised in drink."[21] Such a comment means not only that Isaac never saw it, but that there was no gossip about it either. That point should be conclusive: after a lifetime in the public eye, subject to rumors of everything from being an atheist to ignoring his alleged children by an enslaved quadroon concubine, never did any political opponent accuse Jefferson of abusing alcohol. All were aware of his interest in expensive French wines, so if there had been any pretext for a charge of drinking problems, it would certainly have been made. Readers will, of course, judge for themselves, but there seems no evidence that Thomas Jefferson ever had a problem with alcohol abuse.

Thomas Jefferson in fact strongly believed that wine promoted sobriety. He was more adventuresome than Washington, but when compared to the free-wheeling Franklin, Jefferson was a regular Puritan in his interest in wines, and has long been quoted as an apostle of good health through wine. Jefferson thought wine a healthier beverage than whiskey or brandy. It would be no exaggeration to say that he thought of wine as akin to medicine. He was quite modern in his belief that diet and exercise were the keys to good health, and he recommended wine as an aid to digestion and a mild sedative or analgesic for the ill.

Jefferson took concrete actions to encourage wine drinking. Both as president and as secretary of state, he urged the lowering of import duties on table wines, believing that wine drinking would decrease alcohol abuse. On one occasion, after hearing that import taxes on wines might be reduced, he wrote with enthusiasm to M. de Neuville, a French friend:

> I rejoice, as a moralist, at the prospect of a reduction of the duties on wine by our national legislature. It is an error to view a tax on that liquor as merely a tax on the rich. It is a *prohibition* of its use to the middling class of our citizens, and a condemnation of them to the poison of whiskey, which is desolating their houses.
>
> No nation is drunken where wine is cheap; and none sober, where the dearness of wine substitutes ardent spirits as the common beverage. It is, in truth, the only antidote to the bane of whiskey.[22]

Yet Jefferson was cautious in his optimism about wine supplanting whiskey and other hard liquors in American life:

> This reformation, however, will require time. Our merchants know nothing of the infinite variety of cheap and good wines to be had in Europe; and particularly in France, in Italy, and the Graecian islands.

Cautious as he was about progress in bringing Americans to the moderate drinking of dinner wines, little did he imagine how prophetic was his use of the word "prohibition," and that wine would actually one day be outlawed in America.

Jefferson Controversies: Wine and Women

Of the famous trilogy wine, women, and song, only song has never caused a Jefferson controversy. His propensity to hum and sing to himself as he walked and rode around Monticello, as noted by Isaac, and his skill in playing the violin in duets with his wife have brought him only praise and admiration. One can even buy at the Monticello Museum Shop reproductions of CDs of the music he played, recorded from preserved copies of his and his wife's sheet music. His relations with women, however, are another matter.

His dalliance in Paris, while he was a widower, with the beautiful, blonde, married, Anglo-Italian painter Maria Cosway, has caused much chatter and several books. As discussed in chapters two and three, he never hid the liaison. Jefferson even kept among his papers copies of the love letters he wrote to and received from Mrs. Cosway.

Then there was the beautiful Sally Hemings. Half-sister of his late wife, Sally Hemings was long a house servant at Monticello and personally attended to Jefferson's private quarters. A slave with fair skin and long, straight, black hair, she spent some eighteen months with him in Paris and many years at Monticello as a lady's maid to his daughter Maria.

Jefferson's political enemies referred to Sally Hemings as "dusky Sally," and employed the most vicious racist epithets in painting her as Jefferson's enslaved concubine. In a recent film she was portrayed as a sort of conniving servant. At Monticello, however, she was known as "dashing Sally" for her good looks and polished demeanor. A more accurate image for the modern mind would be an eighteenth-century version of the actress Halle Berry or singer Whitney Houston: a beautiful, well-dressed, articulate, and otherwise believable (if illegal) intimate companion for the vigorous widower Jefferson, who swore to his wife on her deathbed in the presence of Sally Hemings that he would never remarry or put a stepmother over their daughters. But that controversy, however interesting and important it is for Jefferson's status as an American icon, is beyond our subject, especially since no one ever mentioned her in connection with Jefferson's wines.[23]

The latest Jefferson controversy, more pertinent here, concerns the sudden appearance twenty years ago on the auction market of a case of mysterious bottles of Bordeaux from the 1780s. Claimed to have been found in a bricked-up cellar in Paris, some of these bottles of the famed Châteaux Yquem, Lafite, Mouton, and Margaux have sold for over one hundred thousand dollars each and created quite a stir. That controversy will be briefly touched on chronologically in connection with Jefferson's wine orders, and then more comprehensively in the epilogue. At least it is one controversy for which Jefferson was apparently not personally responsible.

If Thomas Jefferson Returned

In the past forty or so years, Jefferson's vision of wine in America has at last begun to come true. After a century and a half of whiskey and Prohibition, the wine "explosion" of the 1960s and 1970s made America one of the leading wine-producing, wine-consuming and even wine-exporting countries of the world. Beginning with returning soldiers from World War II, who had seen European wines firsthand, and continuing with waves of American tourists, the United States rediscovered wine. And with that rediscovery, a tremendous amount of typically American ingenuity and enthusiasm have poured into improving the methods of producing wine, as well as the scientific study of the qualities and characters of wines. This enthusiasm and spirit of inquiry seem, in retrospect, remarkably Jeffersonian.

It is interesting to speculate what Jefferson might think of the current wine scene in America. All fifty states now have commercial wineries, so our current wine scene seems a fair replica of Jefferson's dream of a winemaking, wine-drinking America. Recent reports show wine has become America's most popular alcoholic beverage. There is now a successful Monticello Winery in California's Napa Valley that is modeled on Jefferson's ideas and plans, and which makes highly successful versions of the Cabernets, Chardonnays, Pinot Noirs, and late-harvest wines that Jefferson wanted to produce.

But it is in Virginia that Jefferson would find the true realization of his dream. That state now has over eighty successful commercial wineries. From Chrysalis vineyards in Middleburg in the north to former governor Mark Warner's Rappahannock vineyards in the east to the sixty-five-thousand case Château Morrissette along the Blue Ridge Parkway in the south and the impressive Kluge Winery near Monticello, which employs famed consultant Michel Rolland, Virginia is bristling with beautiful new wineries.

More established wineries are also doing quite well, including Barboursville Winery, owned by the Zonin Wine Corporation of Italy, Oakencroft Winery, owned by the doyenne of Virginia wine, Felicia Warburg Rogan, and Montdomaine Cellars, now known as Horton Winery under the dynamic entrepreneur Dennis Horton. They have pioneered not only the traditional Chardonnays and Cabernets, but red Rhône varieties such as Syrah, Mourvedre, and Grenache, and white Rhône varieties such as Viognier and Marsanne, which Jefferson would have readily recognized. Horton has made good wines from the Virginia-based red varietal Norton and from the famous white wine of the Republic of Georgia, Rkatsiteli. Among my personal favorite Virginia whites is his Petit Manseng, made from the grape from Béarn responsible for the great Jurançon wines of southwest France.

In Jefferson's beloved Albemarle County the Bureau of Alcohol, Tobacco, and Firearms has now approved a special appellation, or AVA, for Monticello, and it is there that Virginia wine has reached its summit. The Viogniers of Oakencroft are among the best I have tasted in the United States. The spectacular King Family Winery, which has its own picnic grounds and polo field beside the tasting room, produces an entire line of wines from Cabernet Franc, similar to a Loire Valley red, to Pinot

Noirs in the style of Burgundy, where winemaker Michael Shaps earned his degree in winemaking from the University at Beaune. Shaps now also makes a rare late-harvest style Viognier which Jefferson would have admired as similar to white Hermitage. Shaps also has a lovely house and is a partner in a winemaking venture in Meursault, the little town that was home to Jefferson's favorite white Burgundy, his original Chardonnay.

As discussed at length in chapter eight, the two vineyards at Monticello have now been restored with the same grape varietals Jefferson planted there. An excellent Italian winemaker, Gabriele Rausse, has been nurturing them for several years. His 1999 Sangiovese Monticello is an excellent wine. Visitors to Monticello can follow a clearly marked Monticello Wine Trail around Charlottesville, stopping for a lengthy tasting at the beautiful Jefferson Vineyards just south of Monticello. The latter winery is particularly noteworthy because its vineyards occupy Colle, the former estate of the Florentine Philip Mazzei, which Jefferson gave Mazzei to use in founding a Virginia wine industry. This book also treats at length Jefferson's relations with Mazzei, who brought laborers and vine cuttings from Tuscany and established at Colle a large vineyard which flourished for a while in the 1770s and even made some wine. It may well have been Mazzei who was most responsible for Jefferson's early interest in wines, especially Italian wines.

Direct descendants of Philip Mazzei, including current CEO Filippo Mazzei and his brother Francesco, still manage his estate near Castellina, and make fine Chianti called Fonterutoli. Lapo Mazzei, now eighty, a Florentine banker and father of Filippo, was president of the Chianti Growers' Consortium for twenty years. The contemporary Mazzeis have visited Monticello and several of the thriving new Virginia wineries. In New York City a restaurant on Second Avenue is named for Mazzei.[24] Jefferson would no doubt have been pleased to know how well Colle turned out.[25]

Current Colle (Jefferson Vineyards) winemaker Frantz Ventre, a native of Bordeaux and graduate of its winemaking school, and who trained with Michael Shaps, makes excellent Bordeaux-style blends known as Meritages, as well as fine pure Cabernet Francs, Merlots, and Pinot Gris. His current assistant, Benjamin Abric, is from the southern

French wine region of Costières de Nîmes, one of Jefferson's favorite places in France. Jefferson Vineyards sits on a 650-acre estate with good southern exposure and well-drained soils, and the four 50-acre parcels planted to European varietals promise to make some of the better wines in the country as the vines mature.

In October of each year a Monticello wine festival is now held at the Boar's Head Inn at Charlottesville where visitors can taste the wines of the region. Hot air balloon rides over the vineyards are also available, which would have pleased Jefferson, who was an eyewitness to the earliest balloon flights in Paris by the famous Mongolfier brothers. A combination wine bar/wine store/restaurant called Tastings now exists in Charlottesville where he could taste and buy, hassle free, all his favorites from a real wine expert and raconteur, Bill Curtis. Nearby is Vavino, a wine bar and shop devoted mainly to Virginia wines, where he could taste and discuss nightly the realization of his dreams with Virginia winemakers, who serve behind the bar.

Indeed, if Thomas Jefferson returned to America today, he would be pleasantly surprised at how many of his wine dreams have come true. Not only are wineries thriving, but if he entered a local wine shop, or searched any of the multitude of Internet sites on wine, he would immediately recognize most wines. His favorites are all still around. In fact, Jefferson might find that, of all the many objects of his insatiable curiosity, wines have changed least of all in the two centuries since he was president. And of all the places he could visit in modern America, he might well find himself more at home in a wine shop than in any other place.

CHAPTER ONE

Early Wines

To understand the complex and enigmatic Thomas Jefferson, especially in his role as a connoisseur of wines, it is helpful to picture him in his own setting.[1] He was born in 1743 at Shadwell, his father's plantation at the foot of the Blue Ridge Mountains near Charlottesville. The area was then a wild, "silent country of far-flung patriarchal seats." When Jefferson was only two, his family moved to Tuckahoe, the home of his mother, farther east near Richmond.

Jefferson's mother was a Randolph, one of the most powerful and socially prominent families of Virginia's coastal, or Tidewater, aristocracy. His early childhood at Tuckahoe was a privileged one; his first memory was of being carried on a pillow by a servant from one house to another.

When he was nine the family moved back to the more rugged world of Shadwell. There Jefferson learned to ride and hunt with his father, Peter Jefferson, a physically powerful frontiersman whose own rustic background was probably the basis for Jefferson's later democratic attitudes. His father had no formal education, but had great respect for education and loved books.

Peter Jefferson's family was said to have come from Wales, and it was perhaps from this Celtic side that Thomas got his gift for writing, the famous "running pen," which caused Franklin and Adams to choose him to write the Declaration of Independence. Despite his great strength,

Peter Jefferson died before he was fifty, when his oldest son, Thomas, was only fourteen years old.

During his years at Shadwell, Jefferson led an isolated but interesting life. The local Indian tribes were frequent visitors there, and made a lifelong impression on him. The woods which surrounded Shadwell were filled not only with abundant game but with wolves. The entire setting was nearly primeval. Nearby, within sight, was the small, round-topped mountain where he later built the famous Monticello.

In 1760, when he was seventeen, Jefferson began college at William and Mary in Williamsburg, then the colonial capital. Obviously precocious, he was soon playing string quartets with the royal governor, a descendant of French Huguenots named Francis Fauquier. He also attended Fauquier's best dinner parties. An interesting character, Fauquier liked fine wines, leaving to his successor a cellar full of them at the Governor's Palace, a partial inventory of which still remains.

It is likely that Jefferson's first contacts with good wine came through Fauquier, although no written record of it survives. If not from Fauquier, then Jefferson certainly learned of wine from his law tutor, the great scholar George Wythe, whose house is one of the finest still preserved at Williamsburg. Wythe definitely liked fine wines and even had a vaulted brick wine cellar built under his beautiful Georgian house, where Jefferson lived while studying law. Some of Jefferson's later references indicate the drinking of fine wines, especially Malmsey Madeiras, at Wythe's house.[2]

During holidays from school, Jefferson continued to reside at Shadwell, where he had a small cellar of his own. Shadwell burned to the ground in 1770, destroying nearly every paper and book Jefferson owned except for a few of his pocket account books, which are the sole source of his brief comments on wine prior to 1770, when he was already twenty-seven.

His earliest comments on wine are thus lost to us, but the fire did perhaps have a positive side: it was one cause for Jefferson's lifelong habit of keeping an extra copy of everything he wrote, which has made his life one of the best documented of all the Founding Fathers.

Other reliable records of the period still remain to give us a fairly accurate idea of what wines his contemporaries drank. Documents preserved by the Colonial Williamsburg Society show that the best wines in the colony seem to have been in the large cellars under the Governor's Palace.[3] Governor Fauquier's successor, Lord Botetourt, left a cellar list for 1770 showing that the large "Binn Cellar," where brick bins were used for laying down and aging fine wines, contained over twenty-three hundred bottles. Included were not only many dozens of Madeira, Port, and claret, but also eleven dozen hard-to-ship Burgundies and a remarkable twenty-five dozen bottles of Hock, the British term for wines of the Rhine.

In a smaller, vaulted cellar Lord Botetourt listed Malmsey Madeira, three bottles of "Champaine," and several bottles of two different kinds of arrack, one of the most popular drinks of the day. Generally speaking, arrack was an inexpensive spirit distilled locally from whatever was handy. Arrack is the Arab word for "juice," which gives a pretty good idea of the local product. Almost unknown in America today, it is still popular in the Orient and parts of the Arab world, where it is made from everything from dates and figs to rice and palm-tree sap. Some of it in the Governor's Palace 1770 cellar, described as "fine," was a kind of rum imported from the East Indies. Its main use was for mixing with water, sugar, or fruit juices in making punch.

Arrack was certainly well known to Jefferson. The land rolls show, in the jocular style of the day, that the price his father paid for the land where Shadwell stood was "Henry Weatherbourne's biggest bowl of arrack punch." Jefferson's early account books show several purchases of arrack.

The Williamsburg Society has published lively accounts of dining and wine-drinking customs of the period, based on contemporary diaries, in a book entitled *Colonial Virginians at Play*.[4] It gives a vivid image of drinking habits during Jefferson's youth and young adulthood. One major wine-drinking occasion prior to the Revolution was a royal birthday, always celebrated by large parties featuring much honorary cannon fire and the drinking of "loyal healthes" in Madeira, claret, and arrack. Surprisingly modern sounding were the "barbecues" and "fish fries," which also featured the same drinks, to the extent that some observers called them mere "drinking parties."

While attending sessions of court or meetings of the House of Burgesses, colonial Virginians like Jefferson and George Washington did not maintain town houses but stayed in local inns and taverns called ordinaries. Both of them noted fees for tavern clubs, dinners, arrack, and wines. Jefferson customarily stayed at the small inn of Mrs. Anne Ayscough, who had been the cook for Governor Fauquier, which no doubt reflects that Jefferson liked her cuisine and even followed it.[5] While I have not found a record of it, one would probably be safe in assuming that her wine list was one of the better ones, given her past experience.

There are also excellent records of the lists of wines offered by early Virginia taverns both before and after the Revolution. Food and beverage prices at the time were fixed by law in each county by the local court, which issued decrees as to how much innkeepers could charge for each item of food, drink, or lodging. The Williamsburg Society has kindly furnished copies of several of those decrees for various Virginia counties for the years 1760–1780.

Those tavern prices reveal much about the society of the day and the role of wine therein. They also tend to show comparative values of products. Wine, for example, was apparently something of a luxury item then, as it remains to some extent today. In nearly every county, even the worst bottle of wine cost more than a full meal or two nights' lodging. Of course, it is also true that in some ordinaries "lodging" meant sleeping four or five to a bed, crossways, so it is hard to put an accurate value on such accommodations.

The first ordinary list available, that for coastal Lancaster County in 1760, shows only three wines: Madeira, Port, and Claret. Prices are quoted not only in English pounds, shillings, and pence, but also in pounds of tobacco, indicating this agricultural region still relied in part on a barter economy. The list shows that hard liquors, especially rum and rum punch with "loaf sugar," were more popular than wine. It reveals likewise that brandy, and expensive brandy at that, was already being made in Virginia.

A slightly more varied list from Richmond County in 1763 offered "French" claret. While there was no promise that it came from Bordeaux, there was at least hope that it was made somewhere in France.

On the Richmond list appeared "good" French brandy and "French white wine." The origin of the latter was decidedly vague, but it cost more than Madeira, so it must have had some pretensions to quality.

Perhaps most surprising of all was the price of the arrack, which was nearly three times as expensive as the wines, equalling both West Indian rum and even French brandy in price. The Richmond list, like the others, showed on the whole a populace in the taverns with little taste for lighter, drier wines, but a great thirst for something high in alcohol which would intoxicate quickly and effectively. The colonists also had a pronounced sweet tooth, or else their wines were not that good and the sweetness was needed to mask the flavors.

One exception was the 1767 list for coastal Middlesex County, reproduced here in full because of its inclusiveness. Of all lists of the period, it comes closest to representing the variety seen in the great private houses of Virginia, even if not quite up to the cellars of the Governor's Palace. Only on the Middlesex list were the wines given pride of place at the head of the list. Also specified were such luxuries as "clean sheets" with the lodging, and the specific varieties of apples used in the ciders were listed. All in all, a Middlesex County tavern sounds like not such a bad place to be in 1767.

ORDINARY RATES FOR MIDDLESEX COUNTY IN 1767

	SHILLINGS	PENCE
Canary Wine or Malaga the Quart	4	
Sherry the Quart	3	
Madeira Wine the Quart	4	
Claret the Quart	5	
White Wine the Quart	3	
Rhenish the Quart	4	
Fyall Wine the Quart	1	6
Nants or French Brandy the Gallon	16	
Rum the Gallon	10	
English or Virginia Brandy the Gallon	6	

	SHILLINGS	PENCE	
A Quart of Arrack made in Punch	10		
A Pint of Rum made into Punch with White Sugar	1	6	
A Quart of Madeira Wine made into Sangaree or Lemonade with White Sugar	4	6	
A Pint of English or Virginia Brandy made into Punch with White Sugar			1
English strong Beer or Ale the Bottle	1	6	
The same per Quart	1	3	
Virginia Ale the Quart		7 1/2	
Virginia Small Beer the Quart		4	
Good Cyder the Gallon	1	3	
Good Boiled Cyder the Gallon	1	6	
Good Hughe's Crab Apple Cyder the bottle		8	
A Dinner with good Small Beer	1	3	
A Diet with good Small Beer	1		
A Night's lodging with clean Sheets		6	
Pasturage for a Horse per Day		6	
Stablage for a Horse per Day		6	
Corn or Oats per Gallon		6	

The Middlesex list shows the importance of water transport in the eighteenth century. All of the wines came from areas on navigable rivers easily accessible to an ocean port. Many came from islands in the Atlantic even nearer America. A prime example is Fyall, now spelled Fayal, named for the island in the Azores where it was made. Several Azores wines appear on Jefferson's lists, and he bought Fayal even when he was in Paris and had access to French wines. Today, although the U.S. maintains an air base on those strategic mid-Atlantic islands, few of their inexpensive wines are exported here, most being drunk locally or shipped to Portugal.

Malaga, also known as Mountain and so called by Jefferson while president, was and is a sweet dessert wine from the town of that name in deep southern Spain. Although relatively high in alcohol, 15–16 percent, it customarily did not have brandy added, which was Jefferson's taste. The best-known wine of Spain, Sherry, was later to become a real Jefferson favorite while he was president. Rhenish, the old term for German Rhine wine, was praised by him during a visit there in 1788, but he later described it as too acidic, especially the quality of it available in America.

Canary, or the wines of the Canary Islands off the west coast of Africa near Madeira, were of two types in Jefferson's time. The "modern" type was a dessert wine with brandy added. The earlier Canary was a light, quaffable beverage wine like the "Canary Sack" immortalized by Shakespeare's Falstaff two centuries earlier. As Mistress Quickly described that kind of Canary wine in *Henry IV, Part Two*:

> But in faith, you have drunk too much Canaries, and that's a marvellous searching wine, and it perfumes the blood ere one can say: What's this?[6]

Canary Island wines were proclaimed "better than any in Spain" as early as 1564 by Sir John Hawkins on a visit there. They were very popular in the American colonies, and both Jefferson and George Washington noted purchasing them, although Jefferson never had much comment on what he thought of them. In 1785, while Jefferson was living in Paris as American minister, only sixteen thousand gallons of Canary were exported to England. By 1815, however, when Jefferson was retired at Monticello and ordering Canary wines again for his cellar, the islands exported over seven hundred thousand gallons to England. Whether the wines had improved that much in thirty years, or had been modified by brandy to please Anglo-Saxon tastes, or made more available by wars and politics, they were certainly exceedingly popular. Alex Henderson said in his *History of Ancient and Modern Wines*, published the year after Jefferson died, that his contemporaries thought Canary wine to be

> the richest, the most firm, the best bodied and lastingest wine, and the most defecated from all earthly grossness of any other whatsoever. It nutrifieth also, being a glutinous, substantial liquor.

If good wine carrieth a man to heaven, surely more English go to heaven
this way than any other, for I think there is more Canary brought into England
than to all the world besides.[7]

Today the Canary Islands produce over nine hundred thousand gallons
of wine each year, but hardly a drop reaches the United States, much of it
being drunk in the islands themselves, and tourists there are just about the
only living Americans to have tasted real Canary wine.

Another intriguing entry on the Middlesex list is the "Madeira wine
made into Sangaree or Lemonade." In no record does Jefferson mention
Sangaree, or Sangria as we know it today, but it was widely popular in
his day, so he no doubt tasted it, and it deserves a mention in light of its
popularity in our own time.

Sangria, or Sangaree, comes from the Spanish word *sangre*, meaning
blood. Not a very appetizing name at first, it means simply that the drink
originally was made from red wine. Today it is still normally made from
red wine with either orange or lemon juice and sugar added, as well as
spices and all manner of other ingredients. Since its purpose was to make
a not-very-good base wine more palatable, it was a natural for the eighteenth century when, according to the *Oxford English Dictionary*, it began
its evolution:

1726.   Mr. Gordon, a Punch-seller in the Strand, has devised a new
         Punch made of strong Madeira wine and called Sangre.

1796.   Sangaree = water, Madeira wine, nutmeg and sugar.

1843.   Which enabled the fortunate owner to take his last tumbler of
         port-wine Sangaree.

1865.   The Anglo-Indian is generally believed to be a luxurious idler,
         whose life is spent in hookah-smoking and sangaree-drinking.[8]

Despite its lapses into small beer, Sangaree, and boiled cider, the Middlesex
list appears to have offered as much variety as Jefferson could have hoped
to find in the taverns he frequented while studying and practicing law prior
to the Revolution. It should also be noted that, as any modern restaurant

patron knows, just because certain wines were on the list does not mean that they were actually available in stock at any particular tavern.

The other lists showed only slight variations on the same theme: lots of liquors and few wines. The Louisa County list for 1768 showed Western Island (Azores) wines, Spanish brandy, London beer, "continent" rum, English cider, and "whiskey." Richmond County for 1769 added Teneriffe, another Canary wine named for the capital city and chief port of the islands, a wine which Jefferson was still cellaring nearly twenty years later in Paris. The York County list for 1772 had Welsh ale and Virginia "middling" beer.

By 1777, just after the Declaration of Independence, wine prices had climbed by 50 percent, but variety had decreased only a little. But by 1780, with a full-scale revolutionary war raging, and shipping interrupted, prices had jumped on all wines and spirits by over 1,000 percent. A quart of any good wine, which had cost only four shillings in 1767, cost eighteen pounds by 1780. More ominously, the 1780 tavern lists did not mention a single wine by name, giving only the reference "wine per quart."

When one considers the ordinary lists of the period, it is obvious that the elaborate connoisseur's vocabulary and enjoyment of comparative tastings which Jefferson exhibited later had no place in the revolutionary Virginia of his young adulthood. It is no wonder that he left few specific comments about wine before departing for France in 1784.

The first wine mentioned by Jefferson of which we have a record is "claret." His pocket account book for August 18, 1768, noted: "Pd. w. Crow for claret 4/." "Claret" is a term which apparently described in Jefferson's America any light red wine. Today "claret" is less used in America as a wine term, being encountered almost exclusively as the common British word for the red wines of Bordeaux. It comes from the earlier French term "clairet," meaning "clear" in the sense of "light-colored." It was first used to describe the light red wines sold from the port of Bordeaux as opposed to the darker "black wines" from farther inland, upstream in Bergerac and Cahors along the river Dordogne, home country of Cyrano and the French essayist Montaigne.

Claret was also made in the Bordeaux region in the early days by blending lighter wines with darker. Sometimes whites were mixed with reds to make a kind of early rosé, but that term for pink wine was not widely used until the twentieth century.

Many "clarets" in Jefferson's time did not even originate in Bordeaux, although most were shipped, or were said to be shipped, from there. As Jefferson later noted in his travel journals, few Cabernet Franc red wines from the château country of the Loire Valley in western France were ever heard of by their own names outside France, since they were sold instead under the more popular and saleable name of "claret."

Adulteration of wines was common in Jefferson's time, one popular recipe for "claret" being: "mix a quart of cider with a quart of port, shake well, then let stand for a month [and] the best judge will not be able to distinguish it from good Bordeaux."[9] The judges must not have been that great either.

Whatever the term "claret" meant to American colonists in Jefferson's youth, the French had long since ceased to use it, as Jefferson learned when he lived there. While president, he advocated that the very name itself be deleted from the official list of imported wines compiled for tax purposes: "The term claret should be abolished, because unknown in the country where it is made, and because indefinite here."[10] From his first mention of buying claret in 1768 to that comment about the word in 1807, Jefferson obviously evolved greatly in his knowledge of wines.

Thomas Jefferson's second written reference to wine came in his account book for March 9, 1769: "Pd. John Coleman for wine at election." Although Jefferson does not mention *what* wine it was he bought for the election, we know that the purchase was made before the election was held, and that it was not purchased for use in celebrating a victory. It was a basic part of electioneering in the era when Jefferson sought his first political office.

A particularly apt description of election-day drinking habits in colonial Virginia is provided by Professor Malone in his description of Jefferson's election in May of 1769 to the House of Burgesses:

> The campaigning of that era, which they called "burgessing," was wholly per-
> sonal and consisted of providing drinks and other refreshments at or before

elections: "swilling the planters with bumbo," as one observer put it. Jefferson and Carter may have provided rum jointly, and the former recorded other expenditures for drinks and cakes.[11]

Quite a contrast to present-day elections when by law all liquor and wine stores are often closed on election day as long as the polls are open.

THOMAS JEFFERSON'S FIRST WINE CELLAR AT MONTICELLO

In the fall of 1769, after his election to the House of Burgesses, Jefferson began having a cellar dug out under the new house he was planning atop the mountain he finally decided to call Monticello. At first he had referred to it in his *Garden Book* as the "Hermitage," but later struck through that word and inserted "Monticello." He noted in his account book for 1769 that: "four good fellows, a lad and two girls of abt. 16 each in 8 1/2 hours dug in my cellar of mountain clay a place 3 f. deep, 8 f. wide and 16 1/2 f. long." That cellar was apparently not yet a wine cellar. It was under the South Pavilion at Monticello, the first portion constructed, and the portion into which he later moved as a sort of honeymoon cottage with his new bride, Martha Wayles Skelton, in 1772.

In 1769 Jefferson was still living, when not travelling the legal circuit, at Shadwell. It must have been there that he located his first embryonic wine cellar, noted in his account book entry of September 1, 1769: "bottles now in possn. doz. bottles . . . 4. with Lisbon wine for common use . . . 3. with Madeira." This entry, despite its brevity, is revealing. Lisbon wine, in the parlance of the day, referred to white table wine of Portugal shipped from the port of Lisbon. Since there were few glass works then, wine was generally shipped in barrels. Portuguese whites, having a higher alcohol content than most French wines, withstood better the rough sea voyages in the holds of sailing ships, and were thus popular in the American colonies. Since nearly all "Lisbon wines" were produced in the region surrounding Lisbon itself, or could be easily shipped there by boat, they were also less expensive than French whites like Burgundies or Champagnes, which had far to go by wagon and river before even reaching the sea, and often arrived spoiled or adulterated.

"Lisbon" in Jefferson's time could be either a light table wine to be drunk with meals or a sweet dessert wine laced with brandy for drinking after the table was cleared. In colonial Virginia, and even well into the nineteenth century, the fashion in America was to drink wine not with meals but after meals. Since Lisbon could be either type, it is possible that Jefferson was already either ahead of, or out of step with, his own time in this respect. But it is risky to infer much from the presence of 50 percent Lisbon wine in Jefferson's first cellar, since we just do not know what his "common use" was. The name "Lisbon" also appeared on some early tavern lists, so obviously others were drinking Lisbon, whatever type it was.

Madeira, the other wine appearing prominently in Jefferson's first cellar, was and still is a true dessert wine, and the favorite wine of the American colonies. Madeira was not Jefferson's own favorite all his life because it was "fortified" with brandy. Later in life he even denounced it for this reason, demanding that all his wines be "pure" and unbrandied. He urged his countrymen to drink lighter, less alcoholic wines than Madeira. Nevertheless, he still bought and cellared more Madeira in his lifetime than any other wine, and even imported it into France when he first lived in Paris. Whether this was because his guests preferred it, or because he liked it himself more than he admitted, we can only speculate.

Since Madeira was *the* American wine of Jefferson's time, and the wine of choice of most of the Founding Fathers, it deserves further description at this point.

THE HISTORY OF MADEIRA WINE: ZARCO THE BLUE-EYED[12]

Zarco the Blue-eyed, a sea captain for Prince Henry the Navigator, discovered the island of Madeira in 1419 some four hundred miles due west of Casablanca, Morocco, in the South Atlantic. Calling it "steep as an iceberg, green as a glade," Zarco named the uninhabited volcanic island "madeira,"

Portuguese for "wooded," because of its incredibly dense foliage, which was so heavy that sailors were unable to hack out a clearing for settlers.

In one of the great anti-ecology acts of all time, Zarco put the entire island to the torch to clear it. After burning for seven years, the fertile soil of Madeira was so impregnated with smoke and ash that natives still say the great fire imparted some of the characteristic smoky taste which all Madeira wines retain to this day. It is an unlikely story.

Madeira became the best-known and most popular wine in colonial America by quirks of geography and politics. First, the Gulf Stream and trade winds which pass Madeira carried sailing ships naturally toward our ports. In 1664 Charles II put heavy taxes on all French wines going to British colonies in America. Later it was required that European goods travel only on British ships. Since Madeira was technically in Africa, its wines were exempt from such requirements, and soon swept the colonies. By the late eighteenth century it was considered patriotic to drink Madeira and thereby avoid taxes to the Crown, and Madeira thus became the veritable mother's milk of the American Revolution. Madeira also suited the colonials' taste for sweet wines.

John Adams once declared that a few glasses of Madeira made anyone feel capable of being president. Madeira was especially popular in the South, and cellars from Savannah to Natchez to Charleston were filled with it. Madeira finally caught on in England only when returning redcoats carried back a taste for it acquired in America.

Today relatively little Madeira is drunk in the U.S. Most is exported to Scandinavia, Germany, and France. Americans now seem to want light, quick-drinking wines, and Madeira, which is heavy and must be sipped and savored at leisure, is like daytime baseball: a wonderful institution, made for the spirit of another age. Really fine Madeiras are today the Edsels of the wine world: a handful of fanatics hoard them and talk about them, but most people have never tasted one, let alone bought one.

Madeira is now a "fortified" wine, an alcoholic spirit being added to stop fermentation. In Madeira the spirit is often made from sugar cane, and raises the alcohol content to roughly 20 percent, compared to roughly 12 percent for normal wines. After fermentation, Madeira is heated for months in *estufas*, stove-like rooms which darken this basically white wine and give it a smoky, caramel quality unlike any other.

Because of its high alcohol and stoving treatment, Madeira is very stable and travels better and lives longer than any other wine. Hundred-year-old Madeiras are commonplace, and a few still exist from the eighteenth century, when the vinification process was little different from today's.

In Jefferson's time, the era of sailing ships, casks of Madeira were deliberately sent on long, rough sea voyages around the capes to the East Indies and South America because the heat of the ships' holds and the jostling of the sea were found to age and improve them. Old bottles often had parchment labels listing the bottles' various ships and voyages like pedigrees.

Just weeks after noting the contents of his first cellar of Lisbon and Madeira, Jefferson, a newly elected member of the House of Burgesses and an eligible bachelor planter who was probably doing considerable entertaining, left another inventory in his account book:

LIQUORS AND BOTTLES ON HAND ABOUT 3. GALLS. RUM A HHD. MADEIRA R.C. - 2 BT. 3 GALLS.

DOZ.

0–11	Lutherns of Madeira
3–1	L. 69.
2–11	M. 70
2–1	M
0–10	Port
2–5	small beer
9–2	empty
0–1	do. Luthern
2–7	with mescellanes in closet.
Doz 24–2	present stock

This second Jeffersonian cellar, with its slightly expanded variety in wine selections and evidences of rebottling, offers our first real glimpse into the making of the greatest American wine connoisseur of his age. That this aspect of Jefferson's life remained so little known for two centuries is surprising since Jefferson's notes on the subject are not difficult to decipher. Even his wine jargon and abbreviations are fairly simple compared to some present-day wine terminology.

The abbreviation "hhd" stands for a hogshead, a large wooden cask holding anywhere from approximately fifty-five to eighty U.S. gallons of Madeira, which shows that Jefferson had begun buying his wine in bulk and bottling it himself. The reference "do." sometimes means dozen and sometimes means "ditto." L. 69 apparently refers to Lisbon wine received in 1769, and the M. refers to Madeira. Less clear is the reference to "70," which could not have referred to wines received that year, since it was then only 1769.

Another mystery is the "Luthern," apparently a type or size of bottle or cask. From the context it might mean a large bottle of Germanic provenance akin to the jeroboams and Methuselahs that still exist today. It could also refer to a clay bottle, or luther, which were common in the days when glass was expensive and hard to obtain. There was also a colonial bottle maker named Henry Luther.

Port, the classic eighteenth-century Englishman's wine, made its first appearance in this September 15, 1769, cellar. Although Jefferson later insisted several times that Port was not one of his favorite wines because it so often had brandy added to it, he obtained it pure when he could; it appeared on cellar lists throughout his life, and he mentioned it in his letters early and late.

The inclusion of "small beer," i.e., beer low in alcohol, in Jefferson's 1769 cellar is not surprising. Jefferson proclaimed beer a healthful and pleasant drink and at one point hired his own brewer to live at Monticello and even drew plans for building his own brewery. During his retirement years, after the close of his second term as president, Jefferson wrote long letters to Madison on the art of brewing and had his own men teach Madison the secrets of this popular American art. Included in the chapter on his retirement are several Jefferson letters and comments extolling the excellence of his own beer and cider, and how they were made during his life at Monticello.

It is noteworthy that Jefferson always kept track of his empty bottles almost as closely as his full ones. In eighteenth-century America, especially during the Revolution, glass was hard to obtain, and bottles often cost as much or more than their contents. Consequently no bottle was ever thrown away. Lack of proper bottles apparently cost Jefferson several barrels of wine, which spoiled because no bottles, and sometimes no corks, were available to preserve the wine, which turned to vinegar from getting too much air in wooden barrels.

Jefferson and his contemporaries knew many of the "hows" of keeping and ageing wine, but knew little of the "whys." Pasteur did not discover until later why wine fermented or why it turned to vinegar if exposed too long to the presence of air. Unless promptly bottled, wine evaporated, or "ullaged," as Jefferson correctly stated, in its wooden casks, and quickly spoiled, but even the inquisitive Jefferson did not at that time know why.

The 1769 list includes the inevitable colonial rum, which Jefferson used as a young man to make punch before his tastes for unfortified wines became set. Later he always kept a good rum cellar for his guests and servants. And, as in everything else, if he was going to do it, he went first class, importing his rum from the West Indies, as Isaac stated: "The wine cellar was full. Old Master had plenty of wine and rum, the best. Used to have Antigua rum, twelve years old."[13]

Skipping ahead twenty-five years, we can see from his account book that as late as May 24, 1794, Jefferson was still as concerned with the empty bottles in his Monticello cellar as with the full:

STACKED THE FOLLOWING EMPTY BOTTLES.

short English.	261
long do.	160
French	670
=	1091

There are besides about 500 full bottles in ye house.

On October 2, 1769, Jefferson made yet another inventory of his young cellar:

LEFT OUT 51/2 BOTTLES OF BEER. LIQUORS LEFT IN EODEM TEMPORE IN CELLAR

L.	69.	146/102 bottles
M.	15	bottles
R.	64.	65. R. 67. 3 R 69. 16
O.	21	

The above shorthand notations may be largely, if not entirely, deciphered. Aside from the lapse into Latin by the use of *eodem tempore*, meaning "at the same time," Jefferson apparently used the initials L. for Lisbon, M. for Madeira, R. for rum, and C. for cider, to which he later devoted an entire room of his cellar. He still referred to wine as a subcategory of "liquors."

Hard cider was always a favorite Jeffersonian drink. Several barrels of it were made at Monticello each year for everyday drinking, and Jefferson considered it in every way superior to rum and whiskey. He was quite firm about how it should be made, specifying the blend of varieties of apples to be used. In a March 19, 1826, letter to his granddaughter Ellen Randolph Coolidge, he was lavish in his praise of the best cider: "They [the taliaferro apples] yield unquestionably the finest cyder we have ever known, and more like wine than any liquor I have ever tasted which was not wine."[14]

The cryptic notations on his October 2, 1769, cellar do not themselves indicate the size or type of bottles referred to, or specify that he had any wine at all other than the Lisbon and Madeira, but they do show the very close watch which the young Jefferson was already keeping on his incipient wine cellar, since it was his third inventory in a month.

His next review of his cellar, entered on January 7, 1770, as a notation in the 1767 volume of his account books, casts further light on the meaning of his earlier system of abbreviations:

ON MY RETURN HOME FOUND MY LIQUOR IN THE CELLAR AS FOLLOWS.

L.	69	221	bottles	27. loss bottles
M.		5	10	
R.	64	13	71	
C.		14	7	

Of these 26 of the bottles were left empty. The other 89 were carried off or broke.

This entry shows, among apparent thefts and acts of vandalism to the Jeffersonian hoard, that someone was drinking a lot of Madeira while others were carrying away the rum.

No further references to this first cellar appear in the account books, probably because when Shadwell burned later in 1770, the cellar burned with it. Since Monticello was not then habitable, he no doubt returned to the tavern wines of Williamsburg for a while, not to mention the fine Madeiras at Mr. Wythe's. In 1773 he noted, for some reason in his *Garden Book*, that "Mrs. Wythe puts 1/10 very rich superfine Malmsey to a dry Madeira and makes a fine wine."[15]

His granddaughters much later recounted the family story that on his wedding night, arriving at the then one-room South Pavilion of Monticello on a snowy night in January of 1772, after midnight and freezing with cold, Jefferson and his new bride found the place deserted, but had a decanter of Madeira to keep them warm. Otherwise, Jefferson's records for the next years have few references to wines.

Wine at the Continental Congress

On occasion Jefferson no doubt did have the opportunity to taste a better and more varied selection of wines. Yet prior to 1774, he had only once travelled outside Virginia. On that trip he visited New York, Philadelphia, and Annapolis, but never mentioned wine in his letters about the trip. His first extended exposure to the world outside Virginia was at the age of thirty-two when he attended the Continental Congress in Philadelphia in the fall and winter of 1774. As accounts of the period reveal, the meetings of the Congress in Philadelphia were accompanied by considerable imbibing of the better wines of the day. Samuel Eliot Morrison describes the ambience:

> The First Continental Congress met at Philadelphia in September 1774. The Philadelphians outdid themselves in hospitality. John Adams, in addition to generous, noble Sentiments and manly Eloquence in Congress, enjoyed at Dr. Rush's "the very best of Claret, Madeira and Burgundy, and at Chief Justice Chew's four o'clock dinner, I drank Madeira at a great Rate and found no inconvenience in it."[16]

These festive revolutionaries later

> showed a Puritan streak common to most revolutions, in a vote of Congress to "discourage every species of extravagance and dissipation, especially all horse-racing, gaming, cock-fighting, shews, plays and other expensive diversions" including elaborate funerals. Congress also voted to give up drinking imported tea, madeira, and port wine. But the local product, rum, was still permissible.[17]

Faced with the deprivation of imported wines, Jefferson hatched a scheme to grow grapes and make wine in Virginia, enlisting George Washington to help him. The catalyst and key actor in what was later to be called the Virginia Wine Company was Jefferson's neighbor, the Italian Philip Mazzei.

THE ITALIAN INFLUENCE: PHILIP MAZZEI

If it was George Wythe and Governor Fauquier who first interested Jefferson in wine *drinking*, it was his unusual neighbor Philip Mazzei who first interested him in vineyards and grape growing. Mazzei was born near Florence in 1730 on an estate where his family had made Chianti for over three hundred years and where it is still made by his direct descendants today. He intended to emigrate to South America, but first practiced medicine briefly in Smyrna, now known as Izmir and part of Turkey.

Mazzei later relocated to London, where he was a successful wine merchant and met Benjamin Franklin, then commercial agent there for Pennsylvania. Mazzei came to Virginia in 1773 with the idea of establishing a wine industry. Had the Revolution not occurred, he might well have succeeded. As it was, Mazzei became an ardent revolutionary patriot, and was later the agent of the new Commonwealth of Virginia in Paris, and in that capacity was captured and imprisoned for a time by the English.

Later still, following financial problems with which Jefferson tried to help him, Mazzei entered on an even more improbable career: secret agent in Paris for the king of Poland. Finally he returned to Italy where he lived a less exotic but equally energetic life, dying in 1816 at eighty-five, an age which no one who knew him in his youth ever thought he would reach.

In November of 1773 Mazzei arrived in Virginia, where he was greeted, according to Mazzei, by none other than George Washington himself. After staying for a brief period with Francis Eppes, Mazzei came by Monticello for a visit on his way to set up vineyards on lands given to him by Thomas Adams and the Virginia legislators. But when he learned that the four thousand acres they planned to give him were made up of numerous small, scattered parcels, he declined and settled instead on two thousand acres given to him by Jefferson, lands located just over two miles east of Monticello. There Mazzei established himself on a small estate which he called Colle (now locally pronounced "collie"). Whether this title, which means "hill" in Italian, was chosen to distinguish it from Jefferson's more imposing estate at Monticello (Italian for "little mountain"), or whether Mazzei simply named it for the town of Colle in Italy is unknown, although it is the subject of speculation by Jefferson scholars.[18]

While his house was being constructed, Mazzei lived at Monticello with the Jeffersons. With Mazzei and the gardeners, or *vignerons*, Mazzei brought from Tuscany, Jefferson began the famous vineyards at Monticello, which are chronicled in chapter eight.

SEDIMENT IN THE SYRACUSE:
JEFFERSON DISCOVERS MUSCAT WINES

Not long after Philip Mazzei became his neighbor, Italian wines began to appear in Jefferson's records. In 1775 an unusual entry compares, with Jeffersonian precision, the cost of Madeira with the cost of flasks of wine from Syracuse, on the island of Sicily:

> If a pipe of Madeira yields 30. doz. bottles, we drink it at 7. years old for 3/ a bottle, which includes the 7. years interest. Such a bottle holds 15. common wine glasses. A flask of Syracuse holds about 7 3/4 common wine glasses, call them 7 1/2 because of the extraordinary sediment. To drink it then as cheap as the best Madeira it should be but about 1.d. the flask, or 6—0 the gross.
>
> A pipe of new Madeira will yield 40. doz., which brings the price (there being no interest) to 20/ a doz. or 20. d. when drank new.

Later, when president, Jefferson made similar calculations on the cost of Champagne, then continued to spend lavishly on it anyway, ignoring his own analysis of the costs.

In 1775 Jefferson was not yet so extravagant, or at least carefully calculated the extent of his extravagance. Especially Jeffersonian is his allowing for the *interest* which his money would have gained if he had invested it rather than tying it up for seven years in holding wine until it was ready to drink. Few present-day wine "investors" who buy Bordeaux or Burgundy calculate the returns on their purchases with such precision.

Financial considerations aside, the 1775 comment on sediment in the Syracuse also shows that Jefferson had already become interested in, and knowledgeable about, the wines he was able to purchase in colonial Virginia.

On April 7, 1775, Jefferson again noted Syracuse wine in his account book: "In three months and one week (excluding the time we have been

absent) we have used at Elk Hill . . . 8 do. pint Flasks of Syracuse." Elk
Hill was a small plantation in Goochland County inherited by Jefferson's
wife from her father. It was later ravaged and largely destroyed by General
Cornwallis in 1781, and there is now no record of there being an Elk Hill
wine cellar.

From his description of the heavy sediment in his Syracuse wine, it
is relatively certain *which* Syracuse wine Jefferson was referring to. The
ancient city of Syracuse, on the southeast corner of the island of Sicily, an
independent kingdom in Jefferson's time, produced mainly Muscat wines.
The best and best known one exported to America was its red Muscat,
which would also have been the one to throw the most sediment. It was
described by Cyrus Redding, the most authoritative wine expert of his
time in the English-speaking world, as "equal to any other in the world,
if not superior."[19]

This evaluation by the foremost wine author of Jefferson's time tends
to give one pause at first. Could a "Muscatel" ever be one of the world's best
wines? Did Jefferson just follow fashion? The problem is one of history.

Muscat wines, brought to Europe from the Middle East by returning Crusaders, were thought for centuries to be among the greatest of
wines. The word *Muscat* itself is old Persian, meaning "strong-scented."
One of the most beautiful cities in the world is Muscat, the capital of
the Sultanate of Oman, which is named for that grape. Muscats should
not be confused with native American Muscadines like the Scuppernong,
a totally different species of grape. Like Rieslings, Chardonnays, and all
other great wine grapes, Muscats are of the species *Vitis vinifera*. Muscadines are *Vitis rotundifolia*.

Muscat wines are as popular in Mediterranean Europe today as ever,
and many of them are excellent. Only in the United States had the Muscat
until recently fallen upon evil days. The problems began when Prohibition
ended. Demand for wine was immediate and overwhelming. American
winemakers were desperate for any grape that could be made quickly into
wine. They pressed into service, so to speak, some very poor strains of
Muscat bred for use only as table grapes and raisins, not wine grapes.
Heavily dosed with sugar and cheap brandy, they were rushed to market

to satisfy the deadened palates of a generation of Americans trained on bathtub gin. The result was the infamous Muscatel, pariah of the wine world, wino wine par excellence.

THE NEW AMERICAN MUSCAT WINES

Bad Muscatel damaged the reputation of good Muscat wines in America for generations, and only very recently are good Muscat wines again being made in California. Now the grape name is carefully defined on the label to separate them from Muscatel, and such excellent wines as Moscato d'Oro of Robert Mondavi and various Muscats are widely available. The word Muscatel is seldom used here.

Europe, having suffered neither Prohibition nor the sort of vinous Reconstruction which followed it, has always produced and enjoyed local Muscats. The famous Asti Spumante is a Muscat, and some Muscadelle, a French strain, goes into French Sauternes. Some red or "black" Muscats, as they are often called, are now being produced in California, and a few are entered in comparative wine-tasting competitions. The orange Muscat of Quady winery, called Essensia, is very fine, as is the inexpensive, light Moscato of Sutter Home, an excellent aperitif. The finest is a red Muscat now made by the Don Galleano Winery, from the red Aleatico grape, which won a gold medal in the Los Angeles County Fair Wines of the World Competition in 2005.

Thus Jefferson's early reliance on a Muscat from Sicily as his main alternative to Madeira shows a broadening of his tastes and an open mind to learning about new ones. Jefferson's account book for the following month even shows him switching roles from student to teacher. On May 5, 1775, he wrote to his former teacher from Shadwell days, William Small, who had returned to England, that he was sending him six dozen bottles of Madeira which "has been kept in my own cellar eight years."[20] This letter is a premonition of the mature Jefferson, who was constantly bombarding Washington, Monroe, and others with bottles of good vintages and advice about how and when to drink them.

The letter to Small does present an interesting question: if the cellar at Shadwell was destroyed, where had Jefferson kept all this Madeira in "my own cellar" for eight years, or since 1767, a year before his first recorded purchase of wine and two years before his first recorded purchase of Madeira? Perhaps a few casks were saved from Shadwell and moved to Monticello, although there is no record of it.

In any event, Jefferson clearly had not abandoned Madeira. On October 31, 1775, he noted: "Pd. for common stock of Madeira 6-13-3." Sounding ever more like some knowledgeable English lord with a cellar full of wine, he noted on January 28, 1776: "Broached a pipe of Madeira, 1770 Vintage."

Since a pipe of Madeira held about 110 American gallons or 44 twelve-bottle cases of wine, this was likely the wine Jefferson drank just before he went off to write the Declaration of Independence. He was away from home when he did the actual writing, however, so tavern wine was probably his companion on that occasion. In fact there is only one more reference to wine by him that year, on June 19, 1776, when he wrote: "pd. Greentree for wines 6/." His references to wine for the next several years were similar and few, and serve mainly to show how expensive it was and the tremendous inflation brought on by the war.

In 1775, Jefferson was named commander in chief of the militia for his county, Albemarle, by the Virginia Committee of Safety, the executive arm of the revolutionary convention. Although never trained as a soldier, Jefferson was in command of the military, such as it was, for his area, and entitled to be called "colonel." Despite that fact, and despite his being one of the main instigators of the Revolution, its early years were peaceful ones for him.

One surprisingly pleasant duty was supervising the Hessian officers captured at Saratoga, New York, and sent to Virginia to be interned. Jefferson presented a bill in Congress offering free land and American citizenship to all foreign mercenaries who would desert the British and join the Americans. The plan was not very successful, but Jefferson pursued it with his usual vigor, often inviting the Hessian officers to Monticello for meals and musical evenings with his family. Since these officers came from the Rhineland, one of the prime German wine-growing areas, it is almost certain they discussed wines; Jefferson later visited one of them in Germany in the late 1780s, and they even went on a wine-tasting trip down the Rhine.

In 1776 both Jefferson's mother and his only son died, but through that year and 1777 and 1778, while Washington was at Valley Forge, Jefferson lived an otherwise peaceful life at Monticello. His own ordeals began in 1779 when he was elected governor of Virginia to succeed Patrick Henry.

Jefferson convinced his wife to join him at Williamsburg, where the old Governor's Palace with its wine cellar was still a relatively pleasant place to live. Because of the danger of British attack, however, and with virtually no troops to defend it, the capital was soon moved further inland to Richmond. There the "palace" was a ramshackle frame dwelling, and had no vaulted brick wine cellars like those at the old colonial palace at Williamsburg.

THE REVOLUTIONARY WAR:
GROSS INFLATION IN THE WINE MARKET

Inflation became rampant. With the seas unsafe, supplies of wine were hard to come by. There were, nevertheless, 191 taverns in the state, so things were far from dry. A few wines were still available, at exorbitant prices, but Jefferson's account books reflect no wine purchases at all for either 1777 or 1778.

The next account book entry, in 1779, in the midst of the economic holocaust which laid waste Jefferson's finances, he noted without comment the cost of a single bottle of wine: 48 shillings, or nearly 2 1/2 colonial pounds sterling. He did not mention the size of the bottle or its type or country of origin.

On September 27, 1779, Jefferson noted another large expenditure for wine: "Pd. Sam Berll for wine from Cart. Braxton 151^L." Then: "8 Apr. 1780 pd Majr. Mercer for wine ^{L}463/10." So great were the economic uncertainties that in May of 1780 Jefferson's salary as governor was changed from pounds sterling to pounds of tobacco. At that time he was paid sixty thousand pounds of tobacco. A chicken cost three pounds. On August 15, 1780, he made this entry in his account book: "pd. Jas Buchanan for wine 258^L." The rampant inflation shown by the Williamsburg Society Ordinary Lists for the 1780s was affecting even rich planters like Jefferson, and his letters and accounts show virtually nothing on wine purchases for some four years thereafter.

A lone entry for October 31, 1780, shows how things were going. Simon Nathan, purchasing agent for the Virginia troops, billed Jefferson for two quarter casks of wine. The price was three thousand pounds of tobacco at Philadelphia prices.

Tavern lists of the period show similar gross inflation. A single quart of wine, which had cost from four to six shillings in 1776, by 1780 had risen to eighteen pounds of sterling silver, so the prices Jefferson was paying for wine in bulk were in line with going rates. They also show that, whatever the cost, he was a wine drinker.

The year 1781 was a critical one for Jefferson, in which he suffered the greatest humiliation of his life, both personally and as a public official. A British naval force, under the personal leadership of the traitor Benedict Arnold, sailed up the James River to Richmond, catching Jefferson's ill-equipped Virginia militia unprepared, and overran Richmond, forcing Jefferson and the other officials to flee.

As luck would have it, the servant Isaac, then a boy of six, was present at Richmond when the British arrived. He vividly described the scene:

> The British sarcht the house but didn't disturb none of the furniture; but they plundered the wine cellar, rolled the pipes out and stove 'em in, knockin' the heads out. The bottles they broke the necks off with their swords, drank some, threw the balance away. The wine cellar was full.[21]

Although Jefferson escaped, the legislature later ordered an official inquiry into his conduct during the incident, which cleared Jefferson of blame, but remained an embarrassment for him the rest of his days. The British soon left, however, and Jefferson was able to return.

In April of 1781 he first met General Lafayette, thereafter a close friend for life. Oddly, perhaps because Lafayette was from the Auvergne region of France, which is not known for its wines, not a word about wine was ever recorded as having been discussed between Jefferson and his best-known French friend. Perhaps Lafayette was not interested in the subject, or they had more pressing better things to talk about, or just did not bother to write down their wine talks.

For security reasons, the capital was moved to Charlottesville, still farther from the British lines, and Jefferson could again stay at Monticello. This was essential for his family because on April 15, 1781, his two-year old daughter, Lucy, died, leaving his wife, Martha, again devastated. She had borne six children in ten years, and half of them died. Within eighteen months, she too would die, leaving Jefferson with three small daughters to raise alone, plus the six children of his widowed sister, Martha, whose husband, Jefferson's best friend, Dabney Carr, had also died.

On June 2, 1781, just as it seemed he might have a chance to pull his family affairs together—he had resigned as governor effective June 4—a force of British soldiers from Tarleton's command was overheard at the Cuckoo Tavern, forty miles from Monticello, heading for Charlottesville in a sneak attack to take prisoner Governor Jefferson and the leading revolutionaries.

Legend has it that a Captain Jack Jowett overheard the plot and made a ride exceeding that of Paul Revere to warn Jefferson. He is said to have arrived at Monticello at sunrise, his face scarred for life by the whipping he received from the branches as he rode through the dark, dense woods. Legend further has it that Jefferson revived him at breakfast with fine old Madeira before fleeing over nearby Carter's Mountain just ahead of the advancing British troops. Apparently the great Monticello cellar was still not empty.

As his granddaughter Sarah Randolph described it in her book *The Domestic Life of Thomas Jefferson*:

> Jefferson was made Governor of Virginia in 1779: and when Tarleton, in
> 1781, reached Charlottesville, after his famous pursuit of "the boy" Lafayette,

who slipped through his fingers, it was expected that Monticello, as the residence of the Governor, would be pillaged. The conduct of the British was far different.

Captain McLeod commanded the party of British soldiers who were sent to Monticello to seize the Governor, and he went with "strict orders from Tarleton to allow nothing in the house to be injured". When he found that the bird had flown, he called for a servant of the house, asked which were Mr. Jefferson's private apartments, and being shown the door which led to them, he turned the key in the lock and ordered that every thing in the house should be untouched.[22]

Monticello and its wine cellar were saved, and Jefferson and his family returned there to live again in July 1781.

In October of that year, Cornwallis was trapped at Yorktown and surrendered, a portent to both sides that the British were finished and that the war might soon be over. Washington and Madison wrote constantly to Jefferson to join them in some office at this critical juncture of the Revolution, when the new country was to be formed. Preoccupied with personal matters and criticisms of his conduct as governor, Jefferson stayed in seclusion at Monticello. His wife was gravely ill, and it is no wonder that he made no mention of the nonserious subject of wine after the destruction of his expensive cellar at Richmond.

Chastellux Drinks Wine with Washington, but Only Punch with Jefferson

The first person to visit him after that event who left an account of his visit was the Marquis de Chastellux, another of those fascinating characters brought together by the American Revolution. Also called the Chevalier de Chastellux, this major general of the French army was a native of upper Burgundy with a castle near Chablis which dated back to the Middle Ages. His family had always been soldiers, and he had considerable combat experience in the Seven Years War, had fought a successful duel, and was a veteran of the Yorktown campaign with Washington and Lafayette, who had travelled through more of the American colonies than had Jefferson himself when the two met.

More unusual was Chastellux's experience as a professional writer, *philosophe*, and member of the exclusive French Academy. He arrived in America with a glowing personal recommendation from Benjamin Franklin, and was the perfect chronicler of the French view of the American Revolution and its leaders. Chastellux immediately took to Jefferson as his favorite, and they remained close friends when Jefferson later came to Paris as an American commissioner.

Most important of Chastellux's roles in the Revolution was as personal interpreter between Washington and the French commander, General Rochambeau, since neither man spoke a word of the other's language. Chastellux had an Irish wife, and apparently spoke English perfectly. As part of his duties, Chastellux attended all the dinners of Washington and Rochambeau, and served as a sort of unofficial spokesman for one when the other was absent. So Americanized did he become that some French officers referred to him as *l'Américain*.

Chastellux spent three years with the American Revolutionary Army, during which he travelled the length and breadth of the thirteen colonies. He published a two-volume journal of his experiences which was translated and published in two volumes as *Travels in North America in the Years 1780, 1781 and 1782*. Jefferson himself reviewed and approved the initial drafts on Virginia. The journal was edited and superbly translated by Jefferson scholar Howard Rice, Jr. (1963).

Like any true Frenchman, Chastellux devoted much of his journal to foods and wines he sampled along the way. As much as any contemporary I have found, Chastellux gives a context to Jefferson and his knowledge of wines before he went to live in France in 1784. His only slipup was being a bit too specific in his descriptions of the habits and appearances of some of the American ladies, which caused the first edition of his journal to be greeted with storms of protest in the colonies. Typical of his indiscretions was referring to a leading society belle as "a bit contraband." Jefferson, as a known friend, had to defend Chastellux and redact his more offending passages.

Whatever his errors as to the ladies, no one better described early American wine-drinking customs than Chastellux. Particularly interesting were his accounts of the wine-drinking habits of Washington and his officers. From Chastellux we learn that it was Jefferson who toned down the excessive drinking of toasts at early American dinner parties.

George Washington on the "Hilarity" Produced by a Good Glass of Claret

No other contemporary comes close to Chastellux as a chronicler of Washington's love of good wines and good company. Particularly revealing is an exchange of letters between the two men in July 1781, not long before the decisive action at Yorktown. Chastellux, having heard that Washington was low on his favorite claret, and knowing Washington's rule against accepting gifts, nevertheless endeavored to offer him some. The personalities of the two men and the relationship between them is revealed in the following exchange of letters:

Dear General,

Your excellency knows very well that it is an old precept to offer tithes of all earthly goods to the ministers of God. I think in my opinion that the true ministers of God are those who at the risk of their life employ their virtues and abilities to promote the happiness of mankind, which consists for the greatest part of freedom and liberty. Accordingly, I believe I am bound in duty to present your excellency with one of *ten* barrils of claret that have just been received.

If you was, dear general, unkind enough not to accept of it, I should be apt to think that you want to prevent the blessings of heaven to fall upon me, or, as I was saying yesterday, that you are an enemy to French produce and have a little of the tory in your composition.

Whatsoever be the high opinion that I entertain of your excellency, I wish to judge by that criterion and to guess by it your dispositions for the French troops and for myself.[23]

Washington replied in kind, showing a side of himself not often revealed in grammar-school texts:

> You have taken a most effectual method of obliging me to accept your Cask of Claret, as I find by your ingenious manner of stating the case that I shall, by a refusal, bring my patriotism into question, and incur a suspicion of want of attachment to the French Nation, and of regard to you.
>
> In short, my dear sir, my only scruple arises from a fear of depriving you of an Article that you cannot conveniently replace in this Country. You can only relieve me by promising to partake very often of that hilarity which a Glass of good Claret seldom fails to produce.
>
> G. Washington[24]

As can be seen from this exchange, either we were sorely misled in grade school about what sort of goody-goody the father of our country really was, or else Chastellux was unusually good at provoking his less sober and haughty side. Whichever, Chastellux certainly gives us an intriguing picture of Washington.

Like the Frenchman he was, regardless of his extreme liking for Americans, Chastellux could not resist analyzing the wine, women, and food of the New World as he observed them. His observations of a typical meal with Washington and his officers on November 24, 1780, during the heart of the Revolution, are particularly evocative of the spirit of the period:

> The meal was in the English fashion, consisting of eight or ten large dishes of meat and poultry, with vegetables of several sorts, followed by a second course of pastry, comprised under the two denominations of "pies" and "puddings." After this the clothe was taken off, and apples and a great quantity of nuts were served, which General Washington usually continued eating for two hours, "toasting" and conversing all the time.
>
> About half past seven we rose from the table, and immediately the servants came to take it down and shorten it into a smaller one a quarter the size; for at dinner it was placed diagonally to give more room. I was surprised at

this maneuver, and asked the reason for it; I was told they were going to lay the cloth for supper. At the end of another half hour, I was informed that his Excellency expected me at supper.

The supper was composed of three or four light dishes, some fruits, and above all a great abundance of nuts, which were as well received in the evening as at dinner. The cloth being soon removed, a few bottles of good Bordeaux and Madeira were placed on the table.

Having spent half the day eating, Washington and his officers apparently planned to drink away the evening. As Chastellux described it:

Less accustomed to drink than another, I accommodate myself very well to the English "toast": you have very small glasses, you pour yourself out the quantity of wine you choose, without being pressed to take more, and the "toast" is only a sort of refrain punctuating the conversation, as a reminder that each individual is part of the company and that the whole forms but one society.

Chastellux elaborated on the toasts:

I observed that there was more solemnity in the toasts at dinner: there were several ceremonious ones; the others were suggested by the General and given out by his aides-de-camp, who performed the honors of the table at dinner, for one of them is seated each day at the head of the table, near the General, to serve all the dishes and distribute the bottles. The toasts in the evening, however, were proposed by Colonel [Alexander] Hamilton, as they occurred to him, without order or formality. This supper, or conversation, commonly lasted from nine to eleven, always free and always agreeable.[25]

Not all "toasting" suppers in America were so agreeable, as Chastellux remarked about other American dinners he attended while travelling through the colonies:

These healths, or "toasts," as I have already observed, have no inconvenience, and only serve to prolong the conversation, which is always more lively at the end of the repast; they oblige you to commit no excess, wherein they greatly differ from the German healthes, and from those we still drink in our garrisons and in our provinces.

But absurd and truly barbarous is the custom, the first time you drink, and at the beginning of dinner, of calling out successively to each individual, to let him know you are drinking his health. The actor in this ridiculous comedy is sometimes ready to die of thirst, while he is obliged to inquire the names, or catch the eyes of, twenty-five or thirty persons, and the unhappy persons to whom he addresses himself are dying of impatience, for it is certainly not possible for them to bestow much attention on what they are eating and on what is said to them, being incessantly appealed to from right and left.

Another custom completes the despair of poor foreigners, if they be ever so little absent-minded or have good appetites: these general and partial attacks terminate in downright duels. They call to you from one end of the table to the other: "Sir, will you permit me to drink a glass of wine with you?" The bottle is then passed to you, and you must look your enemy in the face, for I can give no other name to the man who exercises such an empire over my will; you wait till he likewise has poured out his wine, and taken his glass; you then drink mournfully with him, as a recruit imitates his corporal in his drill.

But to do Justice to the Americans, they themselves feel the ridiculousness of these customs borrowed from Old England, and since laid aside by her. They have proposed to the [French ambassador] the Chevalier de La Luzerne to dispense with them, knowing that his example would have great weight; but he has thought proper to conform, and very rightly so.[26]

It was not until twenty years later, when Jefferson was president, that the old custom of excessive toasting was finally abolished by his rule that in the president's house "[y]ou drink as you please and converse at your ease." Today one of the few countries in the world where the venerable custom of toasting and "drinking healthes" still persists is the beautiful Republic of Georgia, where the role of *tamada*, or toastmaster, once filled by Hamilton, still thrives among those drinking fine Georgian wines such as Rkatsiteli, now grown in a few U.S. vineyards.

Another old dispute which Chastellux seems to put to rest is whether our forefathers drank wine with meals or only after meals. According to the marquis, they seem to have drunk before, during, and after, toasting and eating simultaneously.

George Grieve, who translated Chastellux's journals, left another story on Washington and wine from October 1782:

> The General observing it [the ague], told me he was sure I had not met with a good glass of wine for some time, an article then very rare. He made me drink three or four of his silver camp cups of excellent Madeira at noon, and recommended to me to take a generous glass of claret after dinner. I mounted my horse next morning, and continued my journey to Massachusetts, without ever experiencing the slightest return of my disorder.

To know that George Washington liked to drink wine, and plenty of it, is somehow reassuring, and makes him more accessible. But to some contemporaries, Chastellux seemed like just another French upstart criticizing American foods and wines. In a later edition of his *Travels*, where he tried to remedy his comments on colonial ladies, he explained that he wrote so much about food and drink in America because that is what his French readers were interested in, and because that is what he found most striking. Sounding like a sort of culinary Tocqueville, Chastellux described American wine-drinking habits prophetically: "Wine is an article of luxury in America, so that finding it in an inn there is as unusual as for a traveler in France to find lodging in rooms hung with damask and ornamented with mirrors."[27] Wall mirrors *are* standard in France now, and everywhere in America you can find excellent wines, but it has not been that way for so very long. Just a few years ago you were lucky to find any good wines in the standard motel restaurant dining room, and even now if you stray far from the beaten path your choices will likely be few. Yet we have come a long way in the past forty years. Wine is still an article of luxury in too many people's minds, but things have improved, especially with the coming of age of American wines. Chastellux would hardly recognize the place.

In the spring of 1782, when he opened the door of an ordinary near Jefferson's home, Chastellux saw a harbinger of the current epidemic of obesity in America. He also saw the stark contrast between the habits of Jefferson and those of some of his neighbors:

> This man, called Mr. Johnson, has become so monstrously fat that he can no longer move out of his armchair. He is a good humored fellow, whose manners are not very strict, who has loved good cheer and all sorts of pleasures to such an extent that at the age of fifty he has so augmented his bulk and diminished his fortune that by two opposite principles he is near seeing the termination of both; but this does not in the least affect his gaiety.
>
> I found him stretched out in his armchair, which served him for a bed; for it would be difficult for him to lie down, and impossible for him to rise. A stool supported his enormous legs, in which were enormous fissures on each side, a prelude to what must soon happen to his belly.
>
> A large ham and a "bowl of grog" served him for company, like a man resolved to die surrounded by his friends. He reminded me in short of that country mentioned by Rabelais, where men had their bellies hooped [like barrels] to prolong their lives, and especially of the Abbe, who having exhausted every possible resource, resolved at last to finish his days by a great feast, and invited all the neighborhood to his *bursting*.[28]

The inn nearest Monticello, where Chastellux finally decided to stay, did not sound much better. In an understatement Chastellux called the supper "frugal," and the "whiskey, or corn spirits, that we had mixed with water, was very bad." He liked the breakfast, noting like any veteran Frenchman visiting the U.S. today that "we were perfectly accustomed to the American habit of drinking coffee as a *beverage* with meat, vegetable, or other food." Jefferson himself apparently followed the French custom of drinking his coffee only at breakfast and after meals, not as a beverage to accompany food.

On April 13, 1782, Chastellux arrived at Monticello, remarking the unusual location for a private house in early America: on top of a small mountain. He also noted the "antique" and "Italian" style of Monticello, which "resembles none of the other [houses] seen in this country," convincing the Frenchman that "Mr. Jefferson is the first American who has consulted the Fine Arts to know how he should shelter himself from the weather."

Finding Jefferson at first "grave and even cold," Chastellux was soon sitting up with him till all hours, walking, talking, and "toasting." In Jefferson he had found a kindred spirit with whom he enjoyed that "satisfaction experienced by two persons who in communicating their feelings and opinions invariably find themselves in agreement and who understand each other at the first hint—all these made my four days spent at Monticello seem like four minutes."[29]

Despite his many jolly evenings with Washington and his fellow soldiers, Chastellux seemed most impressed by Jefferson of all the Americans he met. In his published diary he gave this much-quoted portrait of Jefferson in 1782:

> Let me then describe to you a man, not yet forty, tall, and with a mild and pleasing countenance, but whose mind and attainments could serve in lieu of all outward graces; an American who, without ever having quitted his own country, is Musician, Draftsman, Surveyor, Astronomer, Natural Philosopher, Jurist, and Statesman; a Senator of America, who sat for two years in that famous Congress which brought about the Revolution and which is never spoken of here without respect.
>
> [He has] a gentle and amiable wife, charming children whose education is his special care, a house to embellish, extensive estates to improve, the arts and sciences to cultivate—these are what remain to Mr. Jefferson, after having played a distinguished role on the stage of the New World, and what he has preferred to the honorable commission of Minister Plenipotentiary in Europe.[30]

Little did Chastellux imagine that by September Jefferson's amiable wife would die from complications of childbirth.

The most surprising thing about Chastellux's visit is his failure to mention wine. The only drink he says was served during the four days was punch. A great wine lover himself, as his letters to Washington show, and a native of Burgundy, it seems unusual for him to omit that he and Jefferson discussed wines. But Chastellux had noted during his trip from North Carolina to Jefferson's home that Virginia, with its "patriarchal agriculture," offered little wine: "As to drink, they are obliged to content themselves with milk and water until their apple-trees are large enough to bear fruit, or until they have been able to procure themselves stills to distil their grain."[31]

It seems that a man so impressed by Jefferson, and so full of praise for his every taste and idea, would certainly have said *something* about wines Jefferson served, if he had served any. One can only surmise that the war had made wines, or at least wines fit to serve to a French marquis, unobtainable for Jefferson.

Following the death of his wife in September of 1782, Jefferson went into a period of mourning and depression. He refused the post of minister to France offered by Washington and left few records of his activities, being engaged primarily in bringing up alone his three small daughters and adjusting to his loss.

In November 1783 Jefferson attended the boisterous party honoring Washington in his retirement as commander of the American revolutionary army. By all accounts, it was one of the great festive occasions of early American history. Thirteen straight toasts were drunk to the departing commander in chief. Jefferson apparently did nothing to damage his reputation as a strictly moderate drinker, or at least there was no one else there sober enough to record any excesses on his part.

Just about his only preserved writing relating to wine during the period 1782–84 is an irate letter from Jefferson to Simon Nathan, purchasing agent for Virginia troops in the war. On May 18, 1783, Jefferson wrote to Nathan concerning two quarter casks of unnamed wine he'd bought and paid for in full in October of 1780 at the prevailing rate of exchange for tobacco. When Nathan tried to profit from the new exchange rate, Jefferson refused to be cheated, particularly since the wine was lost in the 1781 British raid.[32]

While a member of Congress for Virginia in 1783 and 1784, he travelled considerably from Philadelphia to Trenton, Princeton, Baltimore, Annapolis, and New York. During this fractious and dispiriting period he had more on his mind than what vintages he was or was not drinking. While rooming with Monroe in Annapolis, however, they did hire a French cook, showing he had not lost his taste for fine foods. Monroe, speaking no French, had to rely on Jefferson to instruct the French-speaking cook how to prepare his eggs in the morning.[33]

Jefferson Departs for France, Drinking German Wines and Reading *Don Quixote* in Spanish

On May 7, 1784, Congress appointed Jefferson to join Franklin and Adams as commissioners in Paris to establish commercial treaties with the nations of Europe for the newly freed colonies.[34] It was a position Jefferson had coveted since 1776, when he had been named to a similar post but could not serve due to the Revolution he helped launch.[35]

In 1784 Jefferson's activities picked up dramatically. He spent the spring writing his Notes on Coinage, where he proposed use of the dollar as the unit of currency and the decimal system as its basis.[36] He wrote to ask Colonel David Humphreys to live with him in Paris. Humphreys was both a soldier and a Connecticut poet close to Washington. He also asked lawyer William Short, a bright young Phi Beta Kappa from William and Mary, to be his personal secretary. Short later became like a son to Jefferson and shared his interest in wines.[37]

The peripatetic Mazzei had begun to get on Jefferson's nerves, for he wrote James Madison:

> I am induced to the quick reply to [your letter] by an alarming paragraph in it, which is that Mazzei is coming to Annapolis. I tremble at the idea. I know that he will be worse to me than a return of my double quotidian headache.[38]

Little did Jefferson know that not only was Mazzei coming to Annapolis before he left, but that he would be in Paris to greet him when he arrived. The Italian had become a bitter antagonist of Franklin's, and despite their great common interest in wines, Jefferson for a while tried to avoid him.

In June 1784 Jefferson wrote to Franklin in Paris, saying he would leave in July and see him in France.[39]

As American treaty commissioner, Jefferson was empowered to deal officially with all the major leaders of the world as it then existed, from the "Most Serene Elector of Saxony" to the Turkish "Sublime Porte." In the process Jefferson was going to be in a position to learn about the wines of all those countries as well, and from among their most knowledgeable and distinguished men and women. On his list of countries for negotiation of treaties of commerce were France, where he would be based, as well as Spain, Portugal, and the various German and Italian kingdoms, which pretty well covered the important wine countries of his day.[40] His stay in Europe was to make him the foremost American wine expert of his time.

On July 1, 1784, he noted in his account book his first recorded purchase of wine in nearly four years: "pd. for 4 doz. Hock 7/54."

He was obviously getting in the mood for the trip.

CHAPTER TWO

Thomas Jefferson Goes to Paris

(1784–1787)

On July 5, 1784, Jefferson set sail from Cape Cod with his daughter Martha, then almost twelve. The voyage to England took only nineteen days over a sea "calm as a river" as Martha later described it. There were only six passengers aboard, and Jefferson brought along four dozen bottles of "Hock," or Rhine wine, he had just bought. En route he amused himself by reading *Don Quixote* with a Spanish dictionary.[1] He never mentioned why he was not practicing French or drinking French wines on his way to France, but Jefferson was never conventional. He had long wanted to learn Spanish in order to read in the original the early histories of America, many of which had not been well translated from Spanish to English. And he apparently knew German wines from his time spent with the Hessian officers quartered near Monticello.

On the twenty-fifth they arrived in England, and on the thirtieth crossed the channel to France, putting in at Le Havre seasick. Upon arrival it became apparent that Jefferson's knowledge of written French was little help with the spoken language, and he had to rely on an Irishman to interpret for them and guide them to a lodging. On the third of August they proceeded to Rouen on the Seine, which was to be the port of entry for most of Jefferson's wines while he was in Paris, rivers then being the main channels of commerce for heavy and fragile shipments like wine.

Arriving in Paris on August 6, Martha noted about the French: "It is amazing to see how they cheat the strangers."[2] Jefferson set out to follow the sartorial advice of John Adams:

> The first thing to be done in Paris is always to send for a tailor, a perukemaker and a shoemaker, for this nation has established such a domination over fashion that neither clothes, wigs nor shoes made in any other place will do in Paris. [3]

There has been some dispute as to how far Jefferson went in adopting a Parisian dress code, but it is certain that he followed it to some extent, as the dandified Mather Brown portrait shows. As his successor, Gouverneur Morris, said, however, the longer he stayed there the more he decided to remain conspicuously American in appearance. That was Franklin's "fur cap" approach, and it worked to perfection with the French, who have always enjoyed exotics and originals.

JEFFERSON'S FRENCH

One of the first things Jefferson tried to do in Paris was learn French. In his time as in ours, an ability to speak French opened doors which would otherwise have been closed to him. The French have always been intensely attached to their language, and generally it is only to someone familiar with it that they will unlock the secrets of their wines. There is no way of knowing just how well Jefferson *spoke* French except for scattered comments about it in his letters, and those seem more humorous modesty than serious assessment. We know that he sent his secretary, Short, to live in a French family for a while because neither of them was learning any French at Jefferson's house while they spoke English together. Jefferson recommended the same thing to his future son-in-law Thomas Mann Randolph.[4]

On August 30, 1785, after he had been in France for over a year, he wrote to his brother-in-law Francis Eppes that "Patsy is well. She speaks French as easily as English; while Humphries, Short and myself are scarcely better at it than when we landed."[5]

Franklin had said the same upon arriving in France: "I understand the French so imperfectly as to be uncertain whether those with whom I speak and myself mean the same thing."[6]

By 1788, after his second daughter, Maria, joined him, Jefferson said that she spoke French easily, and no longer added that he could not. From his letters quoted later, it is apparent that he wrote it quite well, and from his solo travels through France in 1787 and 1788 it appears that by then he must have spoken it better. During his retirement, he called the French language "an indispensable part of education."[7]

In his first month, while living in a hotel on the rue des Petits Augustins, Jefferson began buying wineglasses, plates, cutlery, and other furnishings for a fairly elaborate household. He also made his first wine purchase, which was partly of "American-taste" dessert wines, noting in his account book for August 20, 1784: "rec'd from Mr. Barclay [American consul at Paris] 2 doz. Madeira, 1 1/2 doz. Frontignac (red) & 1 1/2 doz. Muscat. Pd. duty of do. & portage 27 f." In the same entry, he recorded the first of many purchases of the finest dry dinner wines: "Pd. for 18 doz. Bourdeaux @ 2 f. 5 & the portage 498 f. 12. (note: reds and whites of great distinction)." Thus the "savage from the mountains of Virginia," as he called himself in a letter home, had already begun to take up the habit, and the vocabulary, of drinking wines "of distinction."

On October 8, 1784, he bought more Bordeaux, without designating any origin, vintage, or even whether they were red or white. They were slightly more expensive than the first batch, so they too were probably "wines of distinction": "Pd. for 59 bottles Bourdeaux 208 f."

With the help of his old friend Chastellux, Jefferson enrolled his daughter Martha in the fashionable boarding school–convent of Panthemont, and saw her only on Sundays. For most of 1784 his household consisted mainly of servants until his secretary, William Short, arrived. Jefferson sounded homesick in this bachelor establishment, calling himself "a being withdrawn from his connections of blood, of marriage, of friendship [and] of acquaintance in all their gradations."[8]

He said little of wines. His first letter to show any interest in the subject was to his brother-in-law Francis Eppes, whose family had been keeping Jefferson's other two daughters. In December of 1784 Jefferson sent Eppes some English porter and Stilton cheese, and wrote that he was sending him a gross of Château Haut-Brion, the great red wine of Graves. He ordered the wine, along with another gross for himself, through John Bondfield, the French-speaking American consul at Bordeaux, who was originally from Quebec. Bondfield had been Franklin's Bordeaux supplier, and it was apparently at Franklin's table that Jefferson first encountered and approved the Haut-Brion.

Bondfield acknowledged the order, but did not ship the wines until the next spring, Jefferson receiving his on May 8, 1785, and paying for it in July 1785, as noted in his account books. Bondfield sent Eppes's wine by an American ship at Jefferson's insistence, but against Bondfield's better judgment.[9] With the exception of those few letters, the primary source of information on Jefferson's wine purchases during his first two years in Paris are his voluminous account books, also called memorandum books.

Fascinating reading in themselves, the account books are by no means dry financial records. They contain a constant stream of pithy, Pepys-like observations on the multitude of new objects and customs that Jefferson observed in Europe. For his entire five and a half years there, he dutifully recorded in his account books every monetary transaction, from how much he tipped his barber to how much he paid for seeing a "learnèd pig."

Given the active social life he led and the large sums he spent setting up his household, Jefferson's spending on wines during his first two years in Paris was modest, especially when compared to the tremendous amounts he spent on wines while president fifteen years later.

Of course wines were cheaper in Paris, and it is possible that some of his everyday *vins ordinaires* were included in his category of "cuisine." For the first year or so, wines were included in the monthly bills to his *traiteur*, or caterer, who provided the household's meals.

American Commissioner:
"Lowest and Most Obscure of the
Whole Diplomatic Tribe"

On October 16, 1784, Jefferson rented a private house in the Cul-de-Sac Taitbout (now Rue Helder) near the opera and the present Chaussée d'Antin. He immediately began to notice the extravagant cost of Parisian life in the days of Louis XVI. Writing to John Jay, who resigned and returned to America as secretary of foreign affairs partly because he could not afford the lifestyle of an American minister in Europe, Jefferson complained: "I desire no service of plate, having no ambition for splendor. My furniture, carriage, and apparel are all plain; yet they have cost me more than a year's salary."[10] Since Jay was responsible for approving Jefferson's expenses, the latter was addressing the right man. For more sympathetic help, he also wrote to Monroe, asking that he solicit either a raise in his salary or an expense account from Congress:

> I must say a word on my own affairs because they are likely to be distressed. Congress in the moment of my appointment struck off 500 guineas of the salary, and made no other provision for the outfit but allowing me to call for two quarters' salary in advance. The outfit has cost me near a thousand guineas, for which I am in debt, and which, were I to stay here *seven years*, I would never make good by savings out of my salary, for be assured *we are the lowest and most obscure of the whole diplomatic tribe* [emphasis added].
>
> I ask nothing for my time, but I think my expenses should be paid in a style equal to that of those with whom I am classed.[11]

Back in America, Monroe had problems of his own with the French-speaking servant Jefferson had left him:

> Partout and myself agree very well, only now and then we require the aid of an interpreter. I have had one or two comfortable solitary dinners upon little more than vegetables and coffee cream. He says: [in translation: "Since you dine alone, Sir, you must reduce your rations."][12]

Jefferson may have been a Francophile, but there is no record that he ever let his French servants put him on reduced rations.

In October 1784, Jefferson noted his next wine-related purchases: "Pd. for 6 1/2 doz. china plates, a sallad dish & 3 doz. caraffes 1266 f. 18." Assuming the French have not changed habits dramatically in the interim, these carafes were certainly meant to hold wine, not water, and three dozen shows a gearing up for service of wines to large companies of guests. Nor did he neglect his Madeiras, noting on November 5: "pd. Mr. Williams for 21 bottles Madeira 63 f."

A "SEASONING" OF ILLNESS

On November 11, 1784, the three American commissioners in Paris— Franklin, Adams, and Jefferson—made their first official report to Congress. They were meeting frequently that month, and it is likely that at least some of the foregoing wines were drunk together. Jefferson travelled often to Auteuil, then a village outside Paris where the Adamses lived, and both Jefferson and Adams dined at Passy, the village where the invalid Franklin lived.

On the date of their report, Jefferson wrote to Nicholas Lewis that his health had been good "till lately." By November 20, he reported to another friend that he had "relapsed into that state of ill health in which you saw me in Annapolis, but more severe. I have had few hours where I could do anything."[13] His illness continued more or less unabated all during the winter of 1784–85, and was no doubt made worse when Lafayette arrived in January of 1785 with the news that his youngest daughter, Lucy Elizabeth, had died of whooping cough.

Abigail Adams reported that Jefferson was confined entirely to his bed for six weeks, and John Adams griped that with both of his fellow commissioners confined to their beds, he was nothing but a "go-between" from Auteuil to Passy to Paris all winter. Finally, as April in Paris approached, Jefferson began to recover, noting in a letter to Monroe on March 18, 1785, that

I have had a very bad winter, having been confined the greatest part of it. A "season-ing" as they call it, is the lot of most strangers: and none I believe have experienced a more severe one than myself. The air is extremely damp, and the waters very unwholesome. We had for three weeks past a warm visit from the sun (my almighty physician) and I find myself almost reestablished. I begin now to be able to walk 4. or 5. miles a day and find myself much the better for it.[14]

By May of 1786 his health was "at length firmly reestablished."[15] Being ill, Jefferson had less energy to entertain, but purchased wines for his household and noted them in his account books. An entry for March 17, 1785, reads, "Pd. Jonathan Williams for . . . bottles of Madeira & . . . of rum 180 f," and there is one for April 28, 1785: "Pd. for 12 bottles Frontignan 32 f. 10." Frontignan is a white Muscat which still thrives today without being much known in America. A little is made in California, notably by Beau-lieu Vineyards. Jefferson later visited the real town of Frontignan, and its wines became favorites.

His household's consumption of Madeira appeared to remain steady; he noted on May 27, 1785, "Inclosed W. Short to pay for 88 bottles Madeira @ . . . 300 f."

Jefferson Is Named American Minister

On May 17, 1785, he presented his credentials as American minister pleni-potentiary to the king of France, succeeding the ailing Franklin. Being min-ister required a much more expensive lifestyle and proved to be "a school of humility" because the other nations had not granted full recognition to the upstart new government in America.[16] But Jefferson enjoyed his new post, and it certainly put him in the way of Paris's best wines. He made use of his introductions to Parisian society from Lafayette, Chastellux, Franklin, Adams, and Mazzei. He frequented the Condorcets, Rochefoucaulds, and other remnants of the eighteenth-century *philosophes* of Paris. The stimu-lating literary salons of the seventeenth and early eighteenth centuries had given way to more political groupings, but licentiousness still prevailed.

To celebrate his elevation from commissioner to minister, he gave an elaborate dinner, attended by Lafayette, the Adamses, John Paul Jones, and other French and American notables. Young Abigail Adams noted that Jefferson had already adopted, to her mind too quickly, French dining customs. He continued to dress more or less like an American, but had started to eat and drink like a Frenchman. The evolution of Jefferson's tastes in food did not come overnight. As far back as Governor Fauquier he had fancied a French approach. Then there was the French servant that he and Monroe had shared in Annapolis, and, upon arriving in Paris, Jefferson apprenticed James Hemings, one of his servants brought from Monticello, to a *traiteur* to learn French cooking methods.

For once in his life Jefferson took a direct interest in the preparation of food. As discussed in Marie Kimball's *Thomas Jefferson's Cook Book*, during his first year in Paris Jefferson made in his own hand a list of his preferred French dishes. Written in French with some English words added, the list occupies eight printed pages, and includes basic recipes and descriptions for puff pastry, galantines, veal cutlets, stuffed pullet, eels, rabbit filets in sorrel sauce, pike in red wine, soups devised by the great chef Careme, and several ways of preparing game and squab. Jefferson was deadly serious about his food, approaching the subject with his customary thoroughness. He could do no less for wines.

After being named American minister in May of 1785, he began to dine each Tuesday with the diplomatic corps, and, while claiming not to be impressed with them except for the Baron Grimm, he no doubt learned much about food and wine from such well-travelled company. In later years it was the wines and the company that he recalled most from those diplomatic dinners, rather than the business, citing them as authority for his opinions on what wines were best regarded by those with reason to know.

Jefferson's most enjoyable and knowledgeable dinner companions at first were the Adamses, including their precocious son, seventeen-year-old John Quincy, and he dined often with them. Through them and through Franklin he also met several jolly clergymen called abbés, or abbots. These free-spirited intellectuals were among Franklin's favorites, and Jefferson later called them perhaps the best company in all France.[17] He exchanged visits and letters with several of them for years thereafter.

A particular favorite was the Abbé Morellet, like Chastellux a member of the French Academy. It was he who translated Jefferson's only book, *Notes on Virginia*, into French. Its appearance in Paris greatly enhanced Jefferson's reputation in Paris society as a "man of letters." Typical of Abbé Morellet was a drinking song he once wrote accusing Franklin of instigating the American Revolution mainly to replace English tea with the French wines he liked so well.

Franklin was a favorite with the French not only because of his wise demeanor and witty sayings, but for his style as a bon vivant and lover of good food and wine. He had an excellent wine cellar long before Jefferson ever came to Paris. As early as 1778 it contained over a thousand bottles:[18]

WINE	NO. OF BOTTLES
Red & White Bordeaux	258
Old Bordeaux	15
Champagne	21
White Mousseux ("bubbly")	326
Red Burgundy	113
Xeres [Sherry]	148

Unlike the serious Jefferson, Franklin had a jocular attitude toward wine—as he did toward many subjects. He wrote to the Abbé Morellet, in response to his jibe about the cause of the American Revolution, a letter which tells much about what both men must have been like:

> You have frequently cheered me, my very dear friend, with your excellent drinking songs. In return I am going to edify you with a few Christian, moral and philosophical reflections on the same subject.
>
> "In vino veritas," says the Sage. The truth is in wine. Before Noah, therefore, men having only water to drink, became abominably wicked, and were justly exterminated by the water it pleased them to drink. It is customary to speak of the conversion of water into wine at the Marriage of Cana as a miracle, but by the goodness of God this conversion takes place every day before our

eyes. Water falls from the skies onto our vineyards. There it penetrates the grapes of the vine and is changed into wine, a continual proof that God loves us and that he likes to see us happy. The particular miracle at Cana was done merely to perform this operation in a sudden case of need.

My good brother, be as kindly and well disposed as He, and do not spoil the good work He has done, wine for our rejoicing. When you see your neighbor at table pour wine into his glass, do not hasten to pour water after it. Why should you wish to drown the truth?

Franklin concluded, after several other wine anecdotes:

P.S. To confirm you in your piety, and recognition of Divine providence, reflect on the position Providence has given the elbow. Man, who was destined to drink wine, has to be able to carry the glass to his mouth. If the elbow had been placed closer to the hand, the forearm would have been too short to bring the glass to the mouth; if it had been closer to the shoulder, the forearm would have been so long that it would have carried the glass beyond the mouth.

Let us then adore, glass in hand, this beneficent Wisdom. Let us adore and drink.

This was the same Benjamin Franklin whose Poor Richard professed that the first article of virtue was: "Temperance—Eat not to dullness, drink not to elevation." One suspects that if he placed it at the top of the virtues, Franklin must have considered temperance a difficult accomplishment. He said similar things about chastity, but they are beyond the scope of our subject.

Another Franklin story further illustrates his character. One evening at a fashionable salon, the subject of flatulation came up. Franklin was asked why he had not yet invented a cure for this embarrassing social phenomenon. Noting that "sophistication" consisted of saying the naughtiest things in the nicest way, Franklin got sophisticated and announced his cure for flatulation, which consisted of drinking a potion of dried rhubarb and attar of roses, dissolved in wine. The object was not, he assured them, to *prevent* flatulation, but to give it the aroma of rose petals, so that its occurrence would no longer be considered a grave social error, but a rare treat.

These stories show why Franklin so appealed to Parisians, and why Jefferson feared he would be thought dull in the salons of Paris beside the philosopher from Philadelphia. They also help explain that the Parisian society Jefferson knew was not of that earnest type which would sit around reading vintage charts. They took their wine for pleasure and amusement, and that is probably why there are not more analytical comments by Jefferson about what people were saying about particular wines at Paris tables.

Due in part to his excessive indulgence in the pleasures of the table, Franklin was so gout-ridden by July of 1785, when he returned to America, that he had to be carried from Paris on a litter provided personally by King Louis XVI. Before he left, Franklin introduced the bachelor Jefferson to the ladies of Paris, including his favorites, the zany Madame Helvétius and the beautiful Comtesse d'Houdetot, model for the Julie of Rousseau's *Confessions*. With the famed Madame de Staël, Lafayette's aunt Madame de Tessé, the Greek Madame de Tott, and several others, Jefferson had quite a circle of aristocratic lady friends. It was at about this time that he began to powder his hair, as shown in the Mather Brown portrait.

In May of 1785, the same month Jefferson was named American minister, John Adams left for London to be minister there. That departure deprived Jefferson of his best friends and dinner companions. But it also led to an extensive correspondence, which began shortly after the Adamses arrived in London, and was provoked by a wine problem. When Adams learned he might have to pay high import duties on the everyday table wines from his Paris cellar, he wrote Jefferson to head them off:

London May 27, 1785

Upon Enquiry I find that I cannot be exempted from paying duties upon my Wines, because no foreign Minister is, except for a less quantity than I have of the best qualities in my Cellar at the Hague, so that I must stop all that I have in France if I can. To pay six or Eight Shillings Sterling a Bottle upon the Small Wines I packed at Auteuil would be folly. I must beg you then if possible to stop it all except one Case of Madeira and Frontenac together. Let me beg you too to write to Mr. Garvey and stop the order for five hundred Bottles of Bourdeaux.

I am sorry to give you this Trouble but I beg you to take the Wine, at any
Price you please. Let your own Maitre D'Hotel judge, or accept it as a present.

My Esteem & Regards as due. Yours affectionately

JOHN ADAMS[19]

Jefferson did his best to oblige, but was too late:

Paris June 2, 1785

The day before the receipt of the letters of the 27th, we had had your cases
brought to the barrier of Paris. From there they were put on board the boat
for Rouen and their portage paid. In the instant of receiving your letter I sent
Petit off to try to stop them if not gone. The boat was just departing and they
declared it impossible to reland them: and that could it be done, a new passport
from the [Count] de Vergennes would be necessary for the part not landed.

I was very sorry we could not stop the wine. It would have suited me perfectly to have taken it either at the prices it cost you, if known to Petit, or if not
known, then at such prices as he and Marc should have estimated it at: and this
would have saved you trouble.

TH: JEFFERSON[20]

Not having received Jefferson's letter of June 2, Adams tried to remain
calm, sending Jefferson a bantering letter on how tough life must be for
a king:

Bath Hotel Westminster June 7, 1785

To be obliged to enter into Conversation with four or five Thousand People of both
Sexes in one day and to find Small Talk enough for the Purpose, adapted to the
Taste and Character of every one, is a Task which would be out of all Proportion to
my Forces of Mind or Body.

Adams concluded, however, by panicking:

For Mercy Sake stop all my Wine but the Bourdeaux and Madeira, and Frontenac.
And stop my order to Rouen for 500 Additional Bottles. I shall be ruined, for each

Minister is not permitted to import more than 5 or 600 Bottles which will not more than cover what I have at the Hague.

Adieu.

John Adams[21]

As was often his wont, Jefferson answered John Adams's letter by writing to Abigail. To make it more confusing, both Mrs. Adams and her nineteen-year-old daughter were named Abigail, and the daughter served for a time as secretary for her father, so it is difficult without seeing the handwriting on the originals to know who is writing or for whom. After informing Mrs. Adams on June 21 that he had done his best to stop wines, Jefferson wrote again two weeks later to report the arrival of a sixty-gallon mystery cask:

Paris July 7, 1785

Dear Madam

I had the honour of writing you on the 21st of June, but the letter being full of treason has waited a private conveiance. Since that date there has been received for you at Auteuil a cask of about 60. gallons of wine. I would have examined it's quality and ventured to decide on it's disposal, but it is a cask within a cask, and therefore cannot be got at but by operations which would muddy it and disguise it's quality. As you probably know what it is, what it cost, & /c. be so good as to give me your orders on the subject and they shall be complied with.

Th: Jefferson[22]

In the meantime, Adams learned that he could avoid the import duties on most of his wines anyway. He had not yet received Jefferson's letter on the mystery cask, however:

Grosvenor Square Westminister

July 16th, 1785

I have been so perplexed with Ceremonials, Visits, Removals and eternal applications from Beggars of one Species and another, besides the real Business of my Department, that I find I have not answered your favour of the second of June, which I received in Season. I have received from Mr. Garvey all but my wine and have written him today to forward that and will run the risque of it, as I believe I shall easily obtain an order to receive it without paying duties.[23]

Adams followed up on the mystery cask:

Aug. 7, 1785

As to the Cask of Wine at Auteuil, it is not paid for. If you will pay for it and take it, you will oblige me. By a sample of it, which I tasted, it is good Wine and very, extremely cheap.

JOHN ADAMS[24]

Jefferson agreed to take it:

TO ABIGAIL ADAMS

Paris Sep. 25, 1785

Dear Madam

The cask of wine at Auteuil I take chearfully. I suppose the seller will apply to me for the price. Otherwise, as I do not know who he is, I shall not be able to find him out.

TH: JEFFERSON[25]

In December 1785, Jefferson received a letter from one Gazaigner de Boyer of Gaillac in southwestern France which finally settled the matter. In his account book for December 21, 1785, Jefferson noted:

Paid Mr. Andrier for le sieur Gazaigner 74-8-9 for a barrique of wine de *Gaillac dit du Cocq* which contains 215 bottles. It took 600 bottles of Bordeaux to fill it up. Note this is the wine which Mr. Adams had bought, and which he desired me to take.

Boyer had sent the case unsolicited, hoping to develop a market for his wines in America. Jefferson never said what he thought of the Gaillac, but saw fit to top up the cask with Bordeaux, which indicates he at least thought it worth saving. His accounts also show that he bought five hundred empty bottles and six hundred corks about that time, so he may have bottled the blend as well.[26]

Most of his other wine expenditures that year were predictable. On July 5 he paid 590 f. 8 for the 24 dozen bottles of Château Haut-Brion he had ordered from Bondfield the previous December. In November he paid 180 francs for 240 bottles of simple "white wine," and the same for 240 bottles of red "ordinaire." More unusual was his first Paris purchase of a Greek wine, from Cyprus, which he lumped together with a small lot of Muscat of Frontignan, the total costing 42 francs.[27]

JEFFERSON'S VILLA ON THE CHAMPS-ELYSÉES: PLEASURES OF THE TABLE

Late in 1785 Jefferson remodeled and moved into a striking three-story town house more in keeping with his new status as the American minister. Modern for its time, it had inside bathrooms, or "lieux anglaises," as the French called them (English "loos"). Known as the Hotel de Langeac, the house was an elegant one with a courtyard, a large wine cellar, and a fine garden behind, where Jefferson planted "Indian" corn and other American vegetables. In 1788, after his trip to the Rhine and Moselle, he planted grapevines there from Germany's finest vineyards.

Designed by the architect who later designed the nearby Arc de Triomphe, the house was intended for the mistress of one the king's ministers. The windows looked out on the Champs-Elysées, which were then more true to their name, having fields and gardens and more of a country setting. Not far from the Bois de Boulogne, where he rode each day, the house was within walking distance of the Grille de Chaillot, the city gate where wines and other goods entered Paris from the countryside and local customs duties were paid.

By the time he moved into the Hotel de Langeac, Jefferson had begun forming opinions of France and French society. To Carlo Bellini, professor of modern languages at William and Mary, he wrote:

Behold me at length on the vaunted scene of Europe: you are perhaps curious to know how this new scene has struck a savage of the mountains of America. Not advantageously I assure you. I find the general fate of humanity here most deplorable. The truth of Voltaire's observation offers itself perpetually, that every man here must be either the hammer or the anvill.

I have endeavored to examine more closely the condition of the great, to appreciate the true value of the circumstances in their situation which dazzle the bulk of the spectators, and especially to compare it with that degree of happiness which is enjoyed in America by every class of people.

Intrigues of love occupy the younger, and those of ambition the more elderly part of the great. Conjugal love having no existence among them, domestic happiness, of which that is the basis, is utterly unknown.[28]

Jefferson did allow as how Paris was not *all* bad:

In the pleasures of the table they are far before us, because with good taste they unite temperance. They do not terminate the most sociable meals by transforming themselves into brutes. I have never yet seen a man drunk in France, even among the lowest of the people.[29]

Jefferson began housekeeping at the Hotel de Langeac by stocking his wine cellar. On January 24, 1786, he wrote to Bondfield requesting twelve more cases of red Bordeaux and twelve more cases of white, both of the finest to be had. He also asked him to send three cases of pint bottles of Frontignac (Frontignan) to Francis Eppes in Virginia.

In a letter to Eppes of the same date, he informed his brother-in-law that he *still* had never heard "what was the fate" of the gross of Haut-Brion he had ordered for Eppes in 1784.[30] On June 24, 1786, Bondfield noted Jefferson's January 1786 order: "I have forwarded by the publick Roullier who will arrive in Paris 13 or 14 July, Twelve Doz. Claret and twelve Doz. Vin de grave in eight Cases of three Doz. bottles each which I hope will get safe to your hand."[31]

This shipment, one of the few sent not by sea but by wagon, arrived quickly, Jefferson noting on August 10: "The wine is come to hand, and the cost of it shall be paid when you please. We find the red wine excellent. The Grave is a little hard."[32] Since the red was apparently the great first growth of Haut-Brion, it is no wonder Jefferson found it good. The other Graves, from an unspecified source, was never identified.

OF ALL FRENCH WINES, SAUTERNES HIT THE PALATE OF AMERICANS BEST

While visiting Bordeaux, Jefferson noted that people there seemed to prefer the drier white wines of the Graves region, while in Paris the sweeter white wines of Sauternes were favored. Jefferson voted with the Parisians. He found the same to be true of most Americans, both in Paris and later in Washington when he was president. Sauternes "hit their palate," as he put it.

During January and February of 1786, Jefferson let his servant Marc purchase his everyday wines, noting in his account books reimbursements to Marc for "wine" in both months. It was probably the last time Jefferson ever let anyone else buy his wines for him. In 1785 his old neighbor Mazzei arrived in Paris and

> went immediately to look for Jefferson. He was living in that charming little villa with a pretty garden at the end of the Champs-Elysees, within gunshot of the stockade through which one must pass on the way to Versailles. I had informed him of my arrival so that he was expecting me daily. Nevertheless our meeting was very touching to both of us.[33]

Next to Lafayette and Chastellux, it was Mazzei who had given Jefferson introductions to more French friends than anyone else. In particular the Duc de la Rochefoucauld, Marmontel, Reyneval, and the Count de Vergennes were among those whom Jefferson came to know chiefly through the energetic Mazzei.[34]

At no time in 1784 or 1785 did Jefferson give any indication that he had thought about the vineyards he had planted at Monticello. Finally, on February 5, 1786, he wrote in English to Antonio Giannini, one of Mazzei's Tuscan vineyard workers, or *vignerons*, as they were called, to ask about them. This much-publicized letter has often been quoted as evidence of what an avid vineyardist Jefferson was. Reading the entire letter, however, one wonders. It occupies two full printed pages, but the entire reference to wine is in three brief sentences:

> How does my vineyard come on? Have there been grapes enough to make a trial of wine? If there should be, I should be glad to receive here a few bottles of the wine.[35]

The rest of the letter deals with requests for more than three dozen kinds of seeds Jefferson wanted Giannini to send him from Monticello, including persimmons, pokeweed for salad, sassafras, and sweet potatoes. Jefferson's only letter in three years about his vineyards actually devoted more space to discussing his apple orchard than his vineyard.

In June Giannini replied, in Italian, that the vines were improving "marvelously," but no wine had been made because each year the grapes were all picked illicitly before they were ripe. He promised to resolve the matter and make some wine in the fall of 1786 and send it to Jefferson in Paris.[36] So far as is known, none was ever made.

A VISIT TO ENGLAND

In March of 1786 John Adams invited Jefferson to England on short notice. Adams sent his new son-in-law, Colonel William Stephens Smith, to Paris to hand-deliver his invitation, which he considered both serious and confidential. Adams simultaneously notified Jay by diplomatic note of his plan, stressing the importance of concealing the purpose of Jefferson's trip from the British. Smith and Jefferson arrived in London on March 11. In a letter to Jay, Jefferson stated that *his* primary motive in making the trip was the possibility of concluding treaties with Tripoli and Portugal.[37] The pirates of Tripoli were constantly capturing and holding American seamen for ransom, and helping them was one of Jefferson's most challenging duties while minister. This experience later convinced him while president to expand the U.S. Navy and subdue the Barbary pirates, which he did.

A treaty with Portugal had several trading advantages, not the least of which was to make available more readily in the United States Portugal's multitude of good and cheap wines. A treaty was signed with the Portuguese during Jefferson's visit, although its effect on the import of Portuguese wines does not appear to have been significant.

Like many another visitor to England, Jefferson noted with special displeasure English food, even blaming it for flaws in the English character:

> I fancy it must be the quantity of animal food eaten by the English which renders their character unsusceptible of civilization. I suspect it is in their kitchens, and not in their churches that their reformation must be worked, and that missionaries from hence would avail more than those who should endeavor to tame them by precepts of religion or philosophy.[38]

Yet the England of that day was not an unmerry place. It was the era of James Boswell and Dr. Samuel Johnson, not to mention Addison's sprightly *Spectator*. Jefferson managed to enjoy himself pretty well there. The wines he encountered at what he called a "Sunday evening rout" at the French ambassador's he pronounced among the finest he had yet tasted in Europe.

In a letter to Jay, his portrait of the Prince of Wales gives us an idea of how and when wine was drunk in London at that time:

> The information I most rely on is from a person here with whom I am intimate, who divides his time between Paris and London, an Englishman by birth, of truth, sagacity and science. He happened, when last in London, to be invited to a dinner of three persons. The Prince came by chance, and made the fourth.
>
> He ate half a leg of mutton; did not taste of small dishes, because small; drank Champagne and Burgundy as small beer during dinner, and Bourdeaux after dinner, as the rest of the company. Upon the whole, he ate as much as the other three, and drank about two bottles of wine without seeming to feel it.[39]

One enjoyable English escapade involved a very un-Jeffersonian evening known as "The Interlude at Dolly's Chop House." It featured

Colonel Smith, Adams's son-in-law, Jefferson, and Richard Peters, former secretary of war in the Revolution. Peters had already been prominently mentioned by Chastellux in his journal as an excellent singer of drinking songs at parties. As the story goes, Adams had invited them to dinner, as he usually did during Jefferson's visit to England, but none of their names appear on the guest list. Instead there appears in the records a piece of not-bad doggerel, signed with a circle composed of their signatures, called the "Round robin":

> *An Interlude at Dolly's Chop House*
> *1/2 past 1—Dolly's*
> *One among our many follies*
> *Was calling in for steaks at Dolly's*
> *Whereby we've lost—and feel like Sinners*
> *That we have miss'd much better dinners*
> *Nor do we think that us 'tis hard on*
> *Most humbly thus to beg your pardon*
> *And promise that another time*
> *We'll give our* reason *not our* rhime
> *So we've agreed—our Nem: Con: Vote is*
> *That we* thus jointly *give you notice*
> *For as our rule is to be clever*
> *We hold it better late than never*[40]

The England trip renewed Jefferson's interest in travelling in France and caused him to appreciate better the virtues of France and the French. Returning to Paris was more like going "home" than before:

> I am much pleased with the people of this country. The roughnesses of the human mind are so thoroughly rubbed off with them, that it seems as if one might glide through a whole life among them without a jostle.[41]

From his own comments, which are contradictory and seem to depend a lot on who he was writing to at the time, it is hard to tell which French social customs Jefferson adopted, and how far he took them. It is certain that he began to entertain a great deal, and was well known for the excellence of both his wines and his foods. As American minister, he made his house a gathering place for the American community, and every traveller from America passing through Paris seemed to try to have dinner at Jefferson's.

Abigail Adams on a Jefferson Dinner

One regular was John Paul Jones. Equally intriguing was John Ledyard, an adventurer from Massachusetts who had sailed to Tahiti with Captain Cook and wrote to Jefferson from such spots as Cairo and Siberia. Since he had mainly American dinner guests, it is difficult to imagine Jefferson going wholly French. Yet there exists a letter from Abigail Adams to her niece which suggests he went pretty far, at least when the majority of his guests were French:

> To Miss Lucy Cranch
>
> Auteuil, 7 May 1785
>
> Well, my dear niece, I have returned from Mr. Jefferson's. When I got there, I found a pretty large company. It consisted of the Marquis and Madame de la Fayette; a French Count, who had been a general in America, but whose name I forget; Commodore Jones; a Mr. Bowdoin, an American also; the Chevalier de la Luzerne and Mr. Short; though one of Mr. Jefferson's family, as he has been absent some time, I name him. He took a resolution that he would go into a French family at St. Germain, and acquire the language; and this is the only way for a foreigner to obtain it.
>
> They have some customs very curious here. When company are invited to dine, if twenty gentlemen meet, they seldom or never sit down, but are standing or walking from one part of the room to the other, with their swords on, and their *chapeau de bras*, which is a very small silk hat, always worn under the arm. These they lay aside whilst they dine, but reassume them immediately after.
>
> At dinner, the ladies and gentlemen are mixed, and you converse with him who sits next you, rarely speaking to persons across the table, unless to ask if they will be served with any thing from your side. Conversation is never general,

as with us; for, when the company quit the table, they fall in *tête-a-tête* of two
and two, when the conversation is in a low voice, and a stranger, unacquainted
with the customs of the country, would think that everybody had private
business to transact.[42]

Mrs. Adams's letter is the most intriguing written about Jefferson's
dinner parties in Paris. Although it does not mention the wines served,
it gives a tantalizing glimpse of the dinners themselves. Did Jefferson go
around carrying an arm hat? Doubtful. Yet she is saying Jefferson went
pretty far in adopting French customs as to how dinner was served and
how the guests conducted themselves. If that is so, he had probably also
abandoned the American practice of serving no wines until after the cloth
was removed, which was totally alien to the French.

Upon his return from London, Jefferson ordered his first Champagne,
fifty bottles for 175 francs, about the price of his best Bordeaux. They were
obtained for him by the Chevalier de la Luzerne, brother of the French
minister to the U.S.[43] As always, he used his best contacts to insure getting
the best wines. On June 21, 1786, Jefferson paid six francs "to see Tetu go
off in his balon." Hot-air ballooning was yet another subject Jefferson was
keen on, writing long letters on it, with handwritten diagrams of how the
balloons operated.[44] How he would have enjoyed the multicolored balloons
that now float over the vineyards of California and, recently, Virginia.

Having had an unfortunate experience with French water during his
first winter, Jefferson opted in 1786 for the best: Perrier from the original
Perrier brothers themselves. On July 10 he noted in his account book: "pd.
Perrier for a year's supply of a muid [240 liters] of water a day from the
1st inst. 50 f. pd. do. for fixing pipes &c. 50 f." Nowadays not even in Bev-
erly Hills could you get a real Perrier to fix your pipes, but for Minister
Jefferson, it was nothing but the best.

Later that month Jefferson received from Lisbon an invoice for 140
bottles of assorted wines to try, recommended to him by the Portuguese
minister whom he had met in London.[45] His cellar list for 1787 shows the
wines were Port, Malvoisie, Calcavallo (now Carcavelos), Pico (Azores),
and Setubal, the great Portuguese Muscat.[46]

Malmsey Madeira from Estate Sales

Malvoisie is the French word for what we call "Malmsey" in English. In August of 1786 Jefferson confirmed receipt of the 140 bottles and, writing in English, ordered more Malmsey, his favorite Madeira ever since he was a law student living with the Wythes in Williamsburg:

> When Mr. Pecquet was here I asked him if he would send me some very good Malvoisie de Madeire. He told me that by attending the sales of wine after decease, he could purchase what was old and fine, and at a reasonable price.
>
> I therefore desire him [to do so]. Perceiving that there are only 30. bottles of Malvoisie de Madeire in the parcel sent, I will beg [the favor of you] to send me six dozen bottles more of that kind of wine of what is old and good.[47]

On October 15 the wines had already arrived at Rouen, and included not just 72 but 212 bottles of Malvoisie de Madeire, plus 72 bottles of Frontignac Muscat from Marseilles and 36 bottles of Cyprus wine from Greece via Leghorn, Italy.[48]

The extra 140 bottles of Malmsey came from New York. Half were for the Marquis de Lafayette, as confirmed by Jefferson's July 17, 1786, account book and a later memo from Jefferson to Lafayette's secretary showing payment for a pipe of Madeira "de l'Amérique" on August 2, 1786. Jefferson's April 1787 cellar list further confirms "183 Madeira of which 154. is from N. York."[49]

Thus we have the odd circumstance of the Frenchman, Lafayette, importing Portuguese wine into France from America. But considering Lafayette's attachment to America and all things American, it is not surprising. At his house in Paris, Lafayette's children spoke mainly English, and he had an American Indian servant, in full native costume, to handle his errands and give the place an exotic air of the New World.[50]

Lafayette's bringing of coals to Newcastle, so to speak, is less surprising when one considers that long sea voyages were thought to improve Madeiras, and this pipe, having been to America and back, should have been doubly improved. Nor was Lafayette eccentric in developing a taste for Madeira in America. Even the British did not drink much Madeira until after returning Redcoats started demanding it, having developed a taste for it during their unsuccessful campaign against the former American colonies.

In all, 1786 turned out to be one of Jefferson's better wine years. Having recovered his health and settled in a fine house with a good wine cellar, he began to enjoy Paris. In a letter to Humphreys on August 14, Jefferson at age forty-three sounded younger than he had in a long time, and less moralistic than usual:

> Your friends here are well. La Comtesse d'Houdetot asks kindly after you. The public papers continue to say favourable and just things of your poem.
>
> The Marquis [Lafayette] is gone into Auvergne for the summer. The rest of the beau monde are also vanished for the season. We give and receive them in exchange for the swallows.[51]

Yet to other friends back in America, the ever-elusive Jefferson showed a totally different face that same year:

> I am here burning the candle of life without present pleasure or future object. A dozen or twenty years ago, this scene would have amused me, but I am past the age for changing habits.[52]

And not *all* of what he called the "beau monde" (beautiful people) had gone from Paris. In addition to friends met through Lafayette, Mazzei, and his diplomatic contacts, Jefferson began in the summer of 1786 to frequent a group of artists. One, the painter John Trumbull, son of the governor of Connecticut, moved in with Jefferson at the Hotel de Langeac while painting the portraits of famous Americans. Trumbull not only did some of the best-remembered paintings of Jefferson and the other Founding Fathers, but introduced Jefferson to the great love of his Paris years.

Maria Cosway, a twenty-seven-year-old Anglo-Italian painter with golden curls and a coquettish manner, changed Jefferson's mind about the emptiness of transitory love affairs in Paris. Her husband, Richard, an effete painter of miniatures and snuff boxes, was little competition for the lonely Jefferson. During the summer of 1786 he *really* entered Parisian life, spending nearly every day with her somewhere, often in the Bois de Boulogne. He also wrote her what were, for him, passionate love letters.

During an afternoon with her in September of 1786, Jefferson fell, under circumstances he later described in veiled terms, saying he had fallen while doing something "from which no good could come, but harm may."[53]

Some say that in a moment of elation over his affair with Maria, the champion of domestic virtue tried to jump over a kettle in his garden and missed the attempt. However it really happened, it is clear that he severely injured his right wrist. He first thought it was just dislocated and badly set, but it was probably broken.

By October the pain in his wrist still kept him awake all night and he could not use it at all. In November he said the hope of recovering its use "walks before me like my shadow" out of reach. In December he wrote Madison that the swelling remained constant and was a "real martyrdom." He began writing letters with his left hand, doubting the stiffness would ever leave the right. He never played the violin again. On December 31, he paid his surgeon for *twenty* visits to his home. Finally, on January 30, 1787, he wrote to Madison that he was going to visit the mineral waters at Aix-en-Provence to see if they would restore his aching and still-swollen wrist.[54]

The Great 1787 Wine Tour

His trip to the south of France had another purpose: to allow him to visit the vineyards and cellars of Burgundy on the way down and those of Bordeaux on the way back. Jefferson had been planning such a trip ever since he came to France as an exercise in what he described to Lafayette as "combining public service with private gratification."[55]

There were, of course, official purposes for such a trip. He wanted to view and obtain plans of classical architecture as models for American public buildings, which he did with great success. *Someone* needed to visit the great southern French ports of Marseilles and Bordeaux to check on the potential for American exports of tobacco and whale oil. The Canal of Languedoc, a great engineering project carried out under Louis XIV, was to be a model for similar canal projects all over the United States. It too needed visiting. Jefferson was interested in numerous species of plants from southern France for cultivation in the southern United States, and wanted to obtain a type of rice which allegedly could be grown with less water than what was then planted in America.

Last, and far from least, was Jefferson's desire to build a great American wine industry based on the French model. To study French viticulture would alone have been worth the trip, a project in which public service and private gratification meshed with little conflict. To his paymaster Jay, Jefferson also wrote of a certain shadowy Brazilian who wanted to meet secretly and talk about driving the Portuguese out of Brazil. His daughter Martha, not taken in by any of the reasons except the mineral waters, wrote to him from her convent that the whole thing sounded like a pleasure trip to her.[56] Whatever its motives, the tour changed Jefferson's habits as a wine drinker forever, and was the greatest single factor in his becoming the foremost American wine expert of his age.

Jefferson left Paris on February 28, 1787, and did not return until June 10. Although he was known as a traveller, most of his trips were short ones, undertaken for business. His three-month jaunt through southern France and northern Italy was the longest of his life. Jefferson travelled southeast from Paris toward Fontainebleau, touching the corner of the province of Champagne, but not visiting any vineyards. He returned to Champagne the next year, however, and visited its vineyards in depth. He also passed through part of the Yonne, commenting unfavorably on the wines there, not realizing how close he was to wines which would later be considered among France's finest under the name Chablis. It is one of the few wines he never mentioned.

Travelling in the worst possible season, under rain, sleet, and snow, he headed straight for Burgundy, stopping first at Dijon. There, still incognito and referring to himself only as a "foreign gentleman," he hired a servant named Petitjean, who remained with him for the rest of the trip, not knowing Jefferson was the American minister. Jefferson had planned to change servants, as he did horses, at every major town. But Petitjean proved so satisfactory that Jefferson hated to lose him and never changed. After passing several days in Burgundy, Jefferson wrote to Short from Lyons that he had "rambled thro' their most celebrated vineyards, going through the houses of the laborers, cellars of the vignerons, & mixing and conversing with them."[57]

Jefferson's main guide through the vineyards and cellars of Burgundy was Etienne Parent, who had been recommended by the Abbé Morellet. Parent was a master cooper and barrelmaker, and also what we would now call a *négociant*, or wine blender and shipper. It was from him that Jefferson thereafter ordered all his Burgundies, trusting Parent's ability and honesty in choosing the best vats and obtaining decent prices. In his account book for March 7, Jefferson noted a payment of six francs for "guide to Pommard, Voulenay, Meursault."

On March 8 Jefferson noted that at Aussy (now spelled Auxey) he "Pd. Parent guide to this place which is depot of wines of Monrachet 6 F." So much did Jefferson like the white Montrachet that, despite its high price, he wrote back to Parent from Lyons on March 13 and asked him to buy and bottle a whole *feuillette* of it (a cask of some 130 gallons) from the 1782 vintage that Jefferson had tasted with him on March 8. Jefferson also requested Parent to ship him cuttings from the finest vines of Montrachet, the Clos de Vougeot, and Chambertin.[58]

Lest he forget any of Parent's tips on Burgundies, Jefferson also asked for detailed, written information from Parent on the prices and relative qualities of the wines of Chambertin, Vougeot, Romanee, Vosne, Nuits, Beaune, Pommard, Volnay, Meursault, and Montrachet. He particularly asked about a vineyard near Montrachet which made wines of quality similar to Montrachet, but which were much cheaper because they were less well known. He spoke of Meursault. His signature remains to this day in the guest book of the Château de Meursault.

The list Jefferson requested was never found; his later writings on the wines of Burgundy indicate that Parent probably sent it, but it was lost after

Jefferson had translated the contents. Some passages in his next letter to Parent, written in June, just three days after he got back to Paris, seem to indicate that he did receive the information, since he asked not only for a *feuillette* of Meursault, but for wine of the particular vineyard called the Goutte d'Or (drop of gold). Thereafter he generally ordered that wine as his preferred white Burgundy, a fine but less expensive substitute for the great Montrachet.

On occasion Jefferson modestly claimed to French correspondents that he could not write letters in French. This was obviously incorrect, since his papers are filled with them, and I have personally translated scores of them written in Jefferson's unmistakable handwriting. To show what Jefferson's French was like, reproduced in a footnote is the letter he wrote to Parent requesting the Meursault and Volnay. Parent's French was natural and colloquial, even homey beside the correct prose of Jefferson. The letters also show, as do his later exchanges with the aristocratic wine proprietors of Bordeaux, that Jefferson's French spelling was as good as, and usually better than, most of his native correspondents'.[59]

Jefferson's request in a P.S. is especially interesting. It asks Parent to mark on the cases of his fine Volnays and Meursaults "Ordinary Wines." Whether this was to avoid the high import duties into Paris or to discourage theft of the wines is not clear. Either way, it was an interesting request from the always-thinking Jefferson.

OUR "PRINCIPAL CONSUMMATION" IS OF WHITE WINES

Parent's reply, written just six days later from Beaune, shows that mail service in eighteenth-century France was not that bad. Parent had acquired the Meursault Goutte d' Or white of the 1784 vintage, but had substituted another red for the Volnay, which Parent rendered as Comarenné of the 1785 vintage.[60] In his reply of July 21, Jefferson acknowledged receipt of all the wines in six hampers, and said that he had tasted both wines and found them good. He told Parent that his household's "principal consummation" was of white wines and that in future he would require mainly whites.[61]

Much later, when he was president, and even in his retirement some thirty-five years later, Jefferson still recalled fondly Parent's Comarenné, the red which he spelled "Caumartin" in his 1787 cellar book. This spelling caused me for some time, before I rediscovered Parent's June 20 letter, to suspect Jefferson of misspelling "Chambertin." When one reads phonetically, however, as one must do with eighteenth-century words, it is perfectly clear that Parent sent Jefferson what we now call Commaraine, or, more precisely, Clos de la Commaraine. It is one of the four best Premiers Crus (first growths) of the commune of Pommard. It is adjacent to Volnay, as Parent suggested, and its wines have similar characteristics. Its vineyards now cover ten acres and are owned entirely by the Jaboulet-Vercherre family.

Even more intriguing is the Domaine Parent, one of the leading grower-winemaker families of Pommard, whose great bottles have been the centerpieces of many fine evenings for my wife and me. Today's Parent domaine descends directly from Jefferson's old supplier, and whenever we drink their wines, we always think of Jefferson and his faithful supplier. I met one of Parent's descendants at the International Pinot Noir Celebration in Oregon, tasted Parent wines with him, and kept the corks in remembrance. Anne Parent, the current director, has even visited the somewhat remote Oxford, Mississippi.

After Burgundy, Jefferson travelled through Mâcon and into the Beaujolais, which he proclaimed "the richest country I ever beheld." At the Château de Laye Épinaye, he stayed to dine with a good friend of his Paris chums, the Abbés Arnoud and Chalut, but he said little of the wines of Beaujolais.

There may be a reason. It was not until relatively recently that the Gamay reds of Beaujolais gained worldwide fame. Only once, many years later while he was president, do his records show a purchase of Beaujolais, which was spelled "Barjolais," apparently by his maitre d', and that wine was a *white* Beaujolais. Until recently, that wine was rarely seen in America, since often sold under the name of its neighbor, Mâcon.

After four days in Lyons, culinary capital of France then and now, Jefferson passed on to Vienne and the Rhône Valley, where his account book shows he paid for "guides to Côte Rotie 1 F 4." He later spoke highly of Rhône wines, discussed them at length in the journal, and asked about a reliable supplier. Still later, while president, he received some of the finest and rarest of them, called Hermitage *paille*, or "straw wine," which now is only made once every several years, when the grapes are exceptionally ripe.

His account book for March 17 shows he paid nine francs for wine at Tains, the principal town for the great red Syrahs of Hermitage and the white Viogniers of Château Grillet. He tasted them on the spot, calling them "justly celebrated." Later he ordered mainly white Hermitage made from the Roussanne and Marsanne grapes, whose California versions are now winning gold medals in the best international competitions. Good examples are those of Rideau, Marilyn Remark, Eberle, and Orfila wineries.

From Tains Jefferson proceeded through Orange, near where the Châteauneuf-du-Pape wine is now made, and on west across the Rhône to Nîmes, heartland of the Roman ruins he had long wanted to visit. While not overlooking the remains of Roman grandeur, he also noted that Nîmes had the best and least expensive red *vin ordinaire* he had found anywhere.

At Nîmes Jefferson made one of his most curious acquisitions. Known as the *askos*, and of ancient Greek origin, it is an elegantly shaped brass object looking somewhat like a glorified gravy boat with a lid. Jefferson had his copy specially made in wood and later reproduced in sterling silver and brought back to Monticello, where it still remains. When Jefferson died, the *askos* passed on to his daughter Martha, who called it "the duck" because of its shape, and used it as a serving dish for her children's jams, jellies, and chocolates.

Askos is the old Greek word for wine skin, and it was originally used for that purpose: decanting wine. The long flat design and large open mouth, which looked like a duck's bill to Jefferson's grandchildren, make it easy to decant from, and serve to provide maximum aeration of the wine's surface so the wine can "breathe" to the fullest. The lid he added can also be closed if that is desired. Several wine accessory companies have now reproduced them, most in crystal with silver trim so you may see the wine better. Many are reasonably priced.

From Nîmes, Jefferson finally went to Aix-en-Provence, his original destination, arriving there March 25. With typical Jeffersonian intensity he took forty douches for his wrist in just four days. Feeling no improvement, he prepared to leave. Although the mineral waters at Aix did Jefferson no good, he was well impressed with the city otherwise, writing to Short that

> [t]he man who shoots himself in the climate of Aix must be a bloody-minded fellow indeed. I am now in the land of corn, wine, oil, and sunshine. What more can man ask of heaven? If I should happen to die at Paris, I will beg of you to send me here and have me exposed to the sun. I am sure it will bring me to life again.[62]

The following day Jefferson left for the great port of Marseilles, arriving March 29 and staying a week. During his visit he wrote Chastellux, in English, to thank him for his introduction to M. de Bergasse, who "united for me all objects: a good dinner, good company, and information." Jefferson visited Bergasse's enormous wine cellar, which he described in the journal, and may have adopted at Monticello his method of keeping his wines cool by covering them with wet sand on the floor of the cellar.

When Jefferson was back in America, Bergasse became one of his favorite suppliers of everyday reds, and one of his preferred correspondents during his retirement. An old French friend of mine, Claude Blanc, whose father lived in Marseille, says that a direct descendant of Henri Bergasse was mayor of the city not long ago.

On April 4 Jefferson wrote to Mazzei, offering to lend him money to tide him over a rough patch. Mazzei accepted, but spent most of his letter telling Jefferson how the cook for the powerful Prince de Condé had taken on Jefferson's cook, James Hemings from Monticello, as an apprentice while the prince was out of town, and charged him an exorbitant twelve francs a day for ten days.[63] As usual, Jefferson did not seem overly concerned about the money. After all, such tutoring put Jefferson's cook near the pinnacle of Parisian cuisine, and he cheerfully wrote the matter off:

> The plan of my journey, as well as of my life, being to take things by the smooth handle. A travellor, sais I, finds how few are our real wants, how cheap a thing is happiness, how expensive a one pride.[64]

Proclaiming Marseilles on the whole a "charming place," Jefferson left it and headed east to Nice via the port of Toulon. At that time the city of Nice was not in France, but part of the independent Kingdom of Savoy. Jefferson had wisely obtained a passport to enter it before leaving Paris.

From Nice he wrote to Lafayette a much-quoted description of himself as a traveller, advising Lafayette that he needed to make the same trip to know his own country better:

> In the great cities, I go to see what travellers think alone worthy of being seen; but I make a job of it, and generally gulp it all down in a day. On the other hand, I am never satiated with rambling through the fields and farms, examining the culture and cultivators with a degree of curiosity which makes some take me to be a fool, and others to be much wiser than I am.
>
> And to do it most effectually, you must be absolutely incognito, you must ferret the people out of their hovels, as I have done, look into their kettles, eat their bread, loll on their beds under pretense of resting yourself, but in fact to find if they are soft.[65]

True to his word, Jefferson travelled incognito, without trappings, in order to observe better the people he met. He also travelled alone because, as he later wrote to John Bannister: "I think one travels more usefully when alone, because he reflects more."[66]

Some politically oriented observers have suggested Jefferson's main purpose in making the trip was to calculate for Lafayette and his friends the chances of a revolution in the countryside. Reading his writings in context, however, that seems as doubtful as the idea that his entire purpose in making the tour was to visit vineyards and taste wines. As always with Jefferson, his motives were numerous, subtle, and mixed.

In his journal at Nice, Jefferson praised the wine as "good, tho' not of the first quality." Later, back in America, he would refer to its leading red, Bellet, as the "best everyday wine in the world."

A Little Voyage Across the Alps

Leaving his carriage at Nice, Jefferson mounted a mule and crossed the Alps, noting later that his dream of tracing Hannibal's route was impossible due to a lack of sufficient landmarks remaining from his time.[67] Arriving at Turin on April 16, he noted their unusual way of training the wine-grape vines. He also tasted his first Nebbiolo, the grape from which the great Piedmont wines Barolo, Barbaresco, Gattinara, and Carema are made. Those wines, rich and slow to age, can also have a slight sparkle or fizz, which used to make them hard to ship without breakage, as Jefferson discovered to his dismay after his return to the U.S. Upon his first taste of Nebbiolo, he gave a candid description of it which has never really been bettered: "Very singular. It is about as sweet as the silky Madeira, as astringent on the palate as Bordeaux, and as brisk as champagne. It is a pleasing wine."[68]

By "silky" Jefferson usually meant what we call *demi-sec*, or "half-dry," and by "brisk" he meant *pétillant*, or just perceptibly bubbly. In quick succession he tasted Monferrato, which he described as "thick and strong," and the now-famous Gattinara, of which he tasted both a red and a white. The latter he compared to the full-bodied white Carcavellos (or Calcavallo as he spelled it) of Portugal. Moving on to Milan, he noticed the Italians' old method of letting the grapevines grow up trees and across poles from tree to tree which, although picturesque, for centuries injured the quality of their wines; far better wines are now produced from well-pruned vines.

At Rozzano Jefferson stayed up all night to watch them make genuine Parmesan cheese and described the process in detail. Passing through Genoa and along the Italian Riviera, he made his way back to Nice, arriving on the first of May, again travelling by mule. Apparently because of the difficulties of the trip, he neglected or did not carry his account book, there being no entries in it for purchases of wine while he was in Italy. Or perhaps he felt the journal itself sufficed and took its place.

Retracing his steps across southeastern France, he went from Nice to Aix to Marseilles by May 4, once again in his own carriage, renting post horses. While in Marseilles, Jefferson dined with Stephen Cathalan and his family; he later helped Cathalan obtain the lucrative post of American consul there. Cathalan became another of his most reliable wine suppliers and a favorite wine correspondent. Writing from Marseilles to his friend Madame de Tott, Jefferson revealed that not every moment there was occupied in fine dinner parties and good wines, saying his inn presented at first glance

[n]othing but noise, dirt and disorder and four thousand three hundred and fifty market-women (I have counted them one by one) brawling, squabbling, and jabbering patois (dialect), three hundred asses braying and bewailing to each other and to the world their cruel oppressions and all this in the street under my window, and the weather too hot to shut it.[69]

From Marseilles, Jefferson proceeded back through Aix to Avignon, where he noted in his account book on May 9 "wine de Rochegude 2 F. 8." In his journal he stated that the white wine of M. de Rochegude resembled dry Lisbon. Since the white wine of Avignon is similar to what we would call today white Châteauneuf-du-Pape, a little-seen wine of good quality and interesting taste, it gives us some idea of what his Lisbon may have been like. Today Rochegude is on the southern tip of the Coteaux de Tricastin, and known mainly for its good red wines.

After passing Nîmes again, Jefferson stopped at Lunel, where he studied the making of its fine Muscat wines, still popular in France, although little known in America. At Frontignan on May 12 Jefferson met Dr. Lambert, a winemaking doctor and a professor on the medical faculty at the nearby University of Montpellier. Posing as just a foreign tourist, Jefferson was entertained and instructed on wines without ceremony by Lambert, who was greatly chagrined and apologetic when he later learned that his guest was the American minister.[70] Jefferson, however, was not at all displeased either by Lambert or his wines. He continued to order them in quantity for most of the rest of his life, not only for himself, but as gifts for friends such as the Count de Moustier, French ambassador to the U.S., whom he sought to please and impress.

From Frontignan Jefferson proceeded to the seaport of Cette (Sète), later infamous as the source of adulterated wines in the eighteenth and nineteenth centuries. Known as "Quack Vintners" or "midnight chemists," these eighteenth-century con men specialized in fabricating famous wines by fraud. A most colorful description of them was left by Joseph Addison in his *Tatler* #31:

> There is a certain fraternity of chemical operators, who work underground in holes, caverns, and dark retirements, to conceal their mysteries from the eyes and observations of mankind. These subterraneous philosophers are daily employed in the transmutation of liquors, and by the power of magical drugs and incantations, raising, under the streets of London, the choicest products of the hills and valleys of France. They can squeeze Bordeaux out of the sloe, and draw Champagne from an apple.[71]

William Younger, in his colorful work *Gods, Men and Wine*, says that the eighteenth century was a terrible time for wine frauds, and that Cette was the most notorious place for it in all France. So bad did it get that some said there was hardly any pure claret in all of England in 1775, and far more "sherry" and "port" were sold in England than were produced in Spain or Portugal.[72]

Jefferson was aware of the practice, and usually ordered his fine wines direct from the producers. Yet he also relied for many years for his everyday wines on the blenders of southern France, especially his friends Bergasse and Cathalan of Marseilles. He often received wines shipped from Cette, and either never had a problem with adulteration, or it was so well done he never noticed it.

At Cette, Jefferson took the wheels off his carriage and placed it on a small barge on the Canal du Languedoc, whose operations he had said were one of the main things he wished to learn and take back to America to assist in the construction of similar canals. Travelling at a rate of one to three miles per hour, Jefferson travelled over two hundred miles on the canal. As he described it to Short:

> Of all the methods of traveling I have ever tried this is the pleasantest. I walk the greater part of the way along the banks of the canal, level & lined with a double row of trees which furnish shade. When fatigued I take seat in my carriage, where, as much at ease as if in my study, I read, write, or observe. My carriage being of glass all around, admits a full view of the varying scenes thro' which I am shifted.[73]

THE CANAL DU LANGUEDOC

The canal was built about a century before Jefferson visited. Its purpose was to allow French produce to travel smoothly from the Mediterranean to the Atlantic without ever leaving France. In his day it was the main wine route from the large-volume vineyards of the deep south to the port of Bordeaux on the Atlantic.

An amazing feat of engineering for its time, it combined Roman-style aqueducts over the rivers with water tunnels through mountains. Today it is less important commercially, but the seventeenth-century lockkeepers' houses still stand and often serve as vacation houses. A major use for the canal today is tourism, as Jefferson used it. Its primary commercial cargoes are still casks of wine, which float on barges little different from those Jefferson knew except that they are now diesel powered instead of being pulled by oxen. The canal is especially attractive because it is not cut out in a straight line like a commercial ditch, but follows the natural contours of the land, thereby both saving money and being more natural to the eye.

Recently the canal has fallen upon hard financial times, partly from high fuel costs and partly because its locks are too narrow to accommodate wide modern barges. It is now used for floating restaurants and vacation homes. In the nineteenth century the canal was joined to several others to form one long Canal du Midi, on which one can now travel inland by water all the way from the Rhine-Rhône network to Bordeaux and the Atlantic Ocean. A beautiful book on the canal was published in English in 1983 by Thames and Hudson. Called simply *The Canal du Midi*, it has magnificent photographs of life on the canal as it looked both in Jefferson's time and today.

Jefferson's descriptions of the canal were later used on several projects in the U.S., so his trip did have practical uses, although he did not convince his elder daughter. A letter he wrote to her, dated May 21, 1787, convinced her that he was not on a business trip:

> I write you, my dear Patsy, from the canal of Languedoc, on which I am at present sailing, as I have been for a week past, cloudless skies above, limpid waters below, and on each hand a row of nightingales in full chorus.[74]

Closing the letter with an admonition to Martha to "be industrious" was perhaps not too diplomatic either, considering that while he floated along the canal listening to nightingales, she was locked up studying in a convent.

At Toulouse, Jefferson reluctantly left the canal and pushed on to Bordeaux. In just four days, from May 24 to May 28, he learned about and committed himself to writing a thorough evaluation of the wines of Bordeaux which is still quoted today as an authoritative work on the Bordeaux wine trade as it stood in 1787. His discussion is rather complete in itself, so I will not elaborate on it here, saving it for discussion later in the context of his correspondence with leading proprietors, merchants, and friends.

In 1788, after his two wine tours were completed, Jefferson was asked for advice on travelling in Europe by two young Americans, Thomas Lee Shippen, son of a Philadelphia surgeon, and John Rutledge, son of the governor of South Carolina. Rutledge's father asked Jefferson for advice. His reply is a fitting introduction to the journals of his own travels. Although written after his trips, they are useful reading beforehand, because they often tell more than either the journals or the letters written during the trips just *how* Jefferson observed what he did, and how he obtained his information on so many subjects in so short a time.

Jefferson's Advice to Americans Travelling in Europe[75]

General Observations

Buy Dutens [travel guides]. Buy beforehand the map of the country you are going into. On arriving at a town, the first thing is to buy the plan of the town, and the book noting it's curiosities. Walk round the ramparts when there are any. Go to the top of a steeple to have a view of the town and it's environs.

When you are doubting whether a thing is worth the trouble of going to see, recollect that you will never again be so near it, that you may repent the not having seen it, but can never repent having seen it. But there is an opposite extreme too. That is, the seeing too much. A judicious selection is to be aimed at.

Take care particularly not to let the porters of churches, cabinets &c. lead you thro' all the little details in their possession, which will load the memory with trifles, fatigue the attention and waste that and your time. It is difficult to confine these people to the few objects worth seeing and remembering. They wish for your money, and suppose you give it more willingly the more they detail to you.

When one calls in the taverns for the vin du pays (local wine) they give you what is natural and unadulterated and cheap; when vin etrangere (imported wine) is called for, it only gives a pretext for charging an extravagant price for an unwholsome stuff, very often of their own brewing.

The people you will naturally see the most of will be tavern keepers, Valets de place, and postillions. These are the hackneyed rascals of every country. Of course they must never be considered when we calculate the national character.

With that introduction, here is Jefferson's greatest journal, carefully excerpted from his forty-four-page handwritten manuscript. Where needed, one-word translations have been inserted in brackets.

Memorandums Taken on a Journey from Paris into the Southern Parts of France and Northern Parts of Italy in the Year 1787.[76]

CHAMPAGNE, March 3. SENS TO VERMANTON. . . . The plains of Yonne are of the same [mulatto] colour. The plains are in corn, the hills in vineyard, but the wine not good.

Few chateaux. No farm houses, all the people being gathered in villages.
Are they thus collected by that dogma of their religion which made them
believe that, to keep the Creator in good humor with his own works, they must
mumble a mass every day? The people are illy clothed. Perhaps they have put
on their worst clothes at this moment as it is raining. But I observe women and
children carrying heavy burthens, and labouring with the hough. I see few beggars. Probably this is the effect of a police.

BURGUNDY. Mar. 4. The people are well clothed, but it is Sunday. They
have the appearance of being well fed.

DIJON. The tavern price of a bottle of the best wine (e.g. of Vaune) is 4.
pound (hereafter #). They have very light waggons here for the transportation of
their wine. They are long and narrow, the fore wheels as high as the hind. Two
pieces of wine are drawn by one horse in one of these waggons.

March 7. 8. From LA BARAQUE TO CHAGNY. On the left are plains which
extend to the Saône, on the right the ridge of mountains called the Côte. The
plains are in corn, the Côte in vines. The former has no inclosures, the latter is
in small ones of dry stone wall.

They are now planting, pruning, and sticking their vines. They begin to
yield good profit at 5.# or 6. years old and last 100. or 150. years.

A vigneron at Voulenay carried me into his vineyard which was of about
10. arpents. He told me that some years it produced him 60. pieces of wine,
and some not more than 3. pieces. The latter is the most advantageous produce,
because the wine is better in quality and higher in price in proportion as less
is made; and the expences at the same time diminish in the same proportion.
Whereas when much is made, the expences are increased, while the quality and
price become less. In very plentiful years they often give one half the wine for
casks to contain the other half. The cask for 250. bottles costs 6# in scarce years
and 10^e in plentiful.

The FEUILLETTE is of 125. bottles, the piece of 250., and the QUEUE, or
BOTTE of 500. An arpent [1 1/2 acres] rents for from 20.# to 60#. A farmer of 10.
arpents has about three labourers engaged by the year. He pais 4. Louis [a Louis
= 20 gold francs] to a man, and half as much to a woman, and feeds them. He
kills one hog, and salts it, which is all the meat used in the family during the
year. Their ordinary food is bread and vegetables.

At Pommard and Voulenay I observed them eating good wheat bread; at Meursault, rye. I asked the reason of the difference. They told me that the white wines fail in quality much oftener than the red, and remain on hand. The farmer therefore cannot afford to feed his labourers so well. At Meursault, only white wines are made, because there is too much stone for the red. On such slight circumstances depends the condition of man!—

The wines which have given such celebrity to Burgundy grow only on the Côte, an extent of about 5 leagues long, and half a league wide [a league = 3 miles]. They begin at Chambertin, and go on through Vougeau, Romanie, Veaune [Vosne], Nuys, Beaune, Pommard, Voulenay, Meursault, and end at Monrachet. The two last are white; the others red. Chambertin, Voujeau, and Veaune are strongest, and will bear transportation and keeping. They sell therefore on the spot for 1200.# the Queue, which is 48. sous the bottle.

Voulenaye is the best of the other reds, equal in flavor to Chambertin &c. but being lighter, will not keep, and therefore sells for not more than 300# the Queue, which is 12. sous the bottle. It ripens sooner than they do and consequently is better for those who wish to broach at a year old. In like manner of the White wines, and for the same reason, Monrachet sells at 1200# the Queue (48s. the bottle) and Meursault of the best quality, viz. the Goutte d'or, at only 150# (6s. the bottle) [a queue = 456 litres].

It is remarkeable that the best of each kind, that is, of the Red and White, is made at the extremities of the line, to wit, at Chambertin and Monrachet. It is pretended that the adjoining vineyards produce the same qualities, but that, belonging to obscure individuals, they have not obtained a name, and therefore sell as other wines.

In the margin of his journal, Jefferson made a small diagram of the layout of the villages and their vineyards in relation to the road through Burgundy south of Dijon. The modern highway follows basically the same route. The vineyards where the red and white wines are produced are marked respectively "r" and "w." It is remarkable how little the vineyard area has changed in comparison with how the vineyard owners have changed. The biggest change was, of course, the subdivision of ownership of church-owned lands during the Revolution. Burgundy is now a region of small proprietors. Bordeaux, having fewer church properties at the time of the Revolution, is still primarily a land of great estates.

Jefferson's List of the Villages of Burgundy

la baraque

Chambertin r.

Vougeau r.

Romanie r.

Veaune r.

Nuys r.

Beaune r.

Pommard r.

Voulenaye r.

Meursault w.

Montrachet w.

Chagny[77]

Vougeau [Vougeot] is the property of the monks of Citeaux, and produces about 200 pieces. Monrachet contains about 50 arpents, and produces one year with another about 120 pieces. The best wines are carried to Paris by land. The transportation costs 36# the piece. The more indifferent go by water. Bottles cost 4 1/2 sous each.

March 9. CHALONS. On the left are the fine plains of the Saone; on the right, high lands, rather waving than hilly, sometimes sloping gently to the plains, sometimes dropping down in precipices, and occasionally broken into beautiful vallies by the streams which run into the Saône, their sides in vines, and their summits in corn. The vineyards are inclosed with dry stone walls.

I passed three times the canal called le Charollis, which they are opening from Chalons on the Saone to Digoin on the Loire. It will reanimate the languishing commerce of Champagne and Burgundy, by furnishing a water transportation for their wines to Nantes, which also will receive new consequence by becoming the emporium of that commerce.

BEAUJOLOIS. This is the richest country I ever beheld. It is about 10. or 12. leagues in length, and 3. 4. or 5. in breadth. The whole is thick sown with farm houses, chateaux, and the Bastides [villas] of the inhabitants of Lyons. The people live separately, and not in villages. The hillsides are in wine and corn: the plains in corn and pasture.

They have a method of mixing beautifully the culture of vines, trees and corn. Rows of fruit trees are planted about 20. feet apart. Between the trees, in the row, they plant vines 4. feet apart and espalier them. 100. toises [2,000 yards] of vines in length yield generally about 4. pieces of wine. In Dauphiné, I am told, they plant vines only at the roots of the trees and let them cover the whole trees. But this spoils both the wine and the fruit. Their wine, when distilled, yields but one third it's quantity in brandy. The wages of a labouring man here are 5. Louis, of a woman one half. The women do not work with the hough: they only weed the vines, the corn, &c. and spin. They speak a Patois [dialect] very difficult to understand.

LYONS. DAUPHINÉ. March 15. 16. 17. 18. In the neighborhood of Lyons there is more corn than wine, towards Tains more wine than corn.

Nature never formed a country of more savage aspect than that on both sides of the Rhone. A huge torrent, rushing like an arrow between high precipices often of massive rock, at other times of loose stone with but little earth. Yet has the hand of man subdued this savage scene, by planting corn where there is a little fertility, trees where there is still less, and vines where there is none. On the whole, it assumes a romantic, picturesque and pleasing air. The hills on the opposite side of the river, being high, steep, and laid up in terrasses, are of a singular appearance.

A league below Vienne, on the opposite side of the river is COTE ROTIE. It is a string of broken hills, extending a league on the river from the village of Ampuys to the town of Condrieux. The soil is white, tinged a little, sometimes with yellow, sometimes with red, stony, poor and laid up in terrasses. Those parts of the hills only which look to the sun at Midday or the earlier hours of the afternoon produce wines of the first quality. 700 vines 3 feet apart, yield a feuillette, which is about 2 1/2 pieces to the arpent.

The best red wine is produced at the upper end in the neighborhood of Ampuys, the best white next to Condrieux. They sell of the first quality and last vintage at 150# the Piece, equal to 12.s the bottle. Transportation to Paris is 60 and the bottle 4.s so it may be delivered at Paris in bottles at 20s. When old it costs 10. or 11 Louis the Piece. There is a quality which keeps well, bears transportation, and cannot be drunk under 4. years. Another must be drunk at a year old. They are equal in flavor and price. The best of white are at Chateau grillé by Madame la veuve Peyrouse.

The wine called HERMITAGE is made on the hills impending over the village of Tains; on one of which is the hermitage which gives name to the hills for about two miles, and to the wine made on them. There are but three of those hills which produce wine of the 1st quality, and of these the middle regions only. They are about 300 feet perpendicular height, 3/4 of a mile in length and have a Southern aspect. It is in sloping terrasses. They use a little dung. 700 plants 3. feet apart, yield generally about 3/4 of a piece. When new the Piece is sold at about 225$^{\#}$, old at 300$^{\#}$. It cannot be drunk under 4. years, and improves fastest in a hot situation.

There is so little White made in proportion to the red, that it is difficult to buy it separate. They make the White sell the Red. If bought separately it is from 15. to 18. Louis the piece, new, and 3 the bottle old. To give quality to the Red, they mix 1/8 of white grapes.

Portage to Paris is 72$^{\#}$ the piece, weighing 600 lb. There are but about 1000. pieces of both red and white of the 1st. quality made annually. Vineyards are never rented here, nor are labourers in the vineyard hired by the year. They leave buds proportioned to the strength of the vine: sometimes as much as 15. inches.

The last Hermit died in 1751.

In 1788 Jefferson elaborated on Hermitage in his Travelling Notes:

Tains. Do not go to the tavern at the Post House, the master of which is a most unconscionable rascal. There is another before you get to that which has a better mien.

On the hill impending over this village is made the wine called Hermitage, so justly celebrated. Go up to the hermitage on the top of the hill, for the sake of the sublime prospect from thence.

Be so good as, for me, to ask the names of the persons whose vineyards produce the Hermitage of the very first quality, how much each makes, at what price it is sold new, and also at what price when fit for use.

Be particular as to the white wine, and so obliging as to write me the result.[78]

Apparently Jefferson had mislaid his notes on the growers of the best Hermitage, or perhaps his notes referred mainly to the reds and he wanted more particulars on the whites, which he favored all his life.

Mar. 18. Principality of ORANGE . . . Here begins the country of olives, there being very few till we enter this principality. They are the only tree which I see planted among vines.

March 19. to 23. LANGUEDOC. Pont St. Esprit. Bagnols. Connault. Valignieres. Remoulins. St. Gervasy. Nismes. Pont d'Arles.

An excellent road, judiciously conducted, thro very romantic scenes. The summit has sometimes a crown of rock, as observed in Champagne. At Nismes the earth is full of limestone.

Numbers of people in rags, and abundance of beggars. The Mine of wheat, weighing 30. lb., costs 4# 10.s, wheat bread 3.s the pound. Vin ordinaire, good and of a strong body 2.s or 3.s the bottle. Oranges 1.s apiece.

[From Travelling Notes]

Nismes. The name of the hotel I lodged at the first time I was there was, I think, le petit Louvre, a very good inn. The 2d. time I lodged at the Luxembourg, not so good.

The vin ordinaire here is excellent and costs but 2. or 3. sous a bottle. This is the cheapest place in France to buy silk stockings.[79]

March 24. From Nismes to Arles.

An olive tree must be 20 years old before it has paid it's own expences. It lasts for ever. In 1765, it was so cold that the Rhone was frozen over at Arles for 2. months. In 1767, there was a cold spell of a week which killed all the olive trees. From being fine weather in one hour there was ice hard enough to bear a horse. It killed people on the road. The old roots of the olive trees put out again.

March 25. 26. 27. 28. AIX. The country is waving, in vines, pasture of green sward and clover, much inclosed with stone, and abounding with sheep.

On approaching Aix the valley which opens from thence towards the mouth of the Rhone and the sea is rich and beautiful: a perfect grove of olive trees, mixt among which is corn, lucerne [alfalfa] and vines.

In the morning they eat bread with an anchovy, or an onion. Their dinner in the middle of the day is bread, soupe, and vegetables. Their supper the same. With their vegetables they have always oil and vinegar.

They drink what is called *Piquette*. This is made after the grapes are pressed, by pouring hot water on the pumice. On Sunday they have meat and wine.

Mar. 29. MARSEILLES. Monsieur de BERGASSE has a wine cellar 240 pieds [feet] long, in which are 120 tons of from 50. to 100 pieces each. These tons are 12 pieds diameter; the staves 4.I. thick, the heading 2 1/2 pouces [inches] thick. The temperature of his cellar is of 9 1/2 degrees of Réaumur [approx. 55% fahrenheit]. The best method of packing wine, when bottled, is to lay the bottles on their side, and cover them with sand.

[From Travelling Notes]

Visit M. Bergasse's wine cellar. Buy here a plan of the Canal of Languedoc.[80]

April 9. ANTIBES. NICE. The wine made in this neighborhood is good, tho' not of the first quality. There are 1000 mules, loaded with merchandize, which pass every week between Nice and Turin, counting those coming as well as going.

Nice. I lodged at the Hotel de York. It is a fine English tavern, very agreeably situated, and the mistress a friendly agreeable woman.

The wine of Nice is remarkably good. You may pass many days here very agreeably. It is in fact an English colony.

Call here on Monsr. de Sasserno, a merchant of this place and very good man. Be so kind as to present him my compliments and assure him that I retain a due sense of his friendly attentions. I was recommended to him by the Abbé Arnoud.[81]

Before entering Italy buy Addison's Travels. He visited that country as a classical amateur, and it gives infinite pleasure to apply one's classical reading on the spot. Besides, it aids our future recollection of the place.

Cross the Alps at the Col de Tende, hire mules and a carriage at Nice to take you to Limone, which is three days journey. Descending the Alps on the other side, you will have that view of the plains of the Po and of Lombardy in general which encouraged the army of Hannibal to surmount the difficulties of their passage. Speckled trout on all the road from Nice to Turin.[82]

April 14. TENDE. A very inconsiderable village, in which they have not yet the luxury of glass windows.

April 15. 16. LIMONE. CONI . . . TURIN.

We cross the Po in swinging batteaux. Two are placed side by side, and kept together by a plank floor, common to both, and lying on their gunwales. The carriage drives on this, without taking out any of the horses.

April 17. 18. *Turin*. There is a red wine of Nebiule made in this neighborhood which is very singular. It is about as sweet as the silky Madeira, as astringent on the palate as Bordeaux, and as brisk as Champagne. It is a pleasing wine. At Moncaglieri, about 6 miles from Turin, on the right side of Po . . . The soil is mostly red and in vines, affording a wine called Montferrat, which is thick and strong.

April 19. VERCELLI

There is a wine called Gatina made in the neighborhood of Vercelli, both red and white. The latter resembles Calcavallo. There is also a red wine of Salusola which is esteemed. It is very light.

In the neighborhood of Vercelli begin the RICE fields. Poggio, a muletier, who passes every week between Vercelli and Genoa will smuggle a sack of rice for me to Genoa; it being death to export it in that form.

April 20. NOVARA. BUFFALORA. SEDRIANO. MILAN. From Vercelli to Novara the fields are all in rice. From Novara to the Ticino it is mostly stony and waste. From the Ticino to Milan it is all in corn. There is snow on the Appenines near Genoa. They have still another method here of planting the vine. Along rows of trees they lash poles from tree to tree. Between the trees are set vines which passing over the pole, are carried on to the pole of the next row, whose vines are in like manner brought to this, and twined together; thus forming the intervals between the rows of trees alternately into arbors, and open space.

April 21. 22. MILAN. Figs and pomegranates grow here unsheltered. They had formerly olives; but a great cold in 1709 killed them, and they have not been replanted. The nights of the 20. and 21st. inst. the rice ponds freezed half an inch thick. About 5. years ago there was such a hail as to kill cats. The trade of this country is principally rice, raw silk, and cheese.

Milan. Excursion to Rozzano to see the Parmesan cheese made, and the management of their dairies. See their ice houses. Learn the method of storing snow instead of ice.[83]

April 23: PARMESAN CHEESE. It is supposed this was formerly made at Parma, and took it's name thence, but none is made there now. It is made thro' all the country extending from Milan 150. miles.

Apr. 26. GENOA. Strawberries.

April 28. NOLI, into which I was obliged to put by a change of wind, is 40. miles from Genoa. There are 1200 inhabitants in the village, and many separate houses round about. The wine they make is white and indifferent.

April 29. ALBENGA. If any person wished to retire from their acquaintance, to live absolutely unknown, and yet in the midst of physical enjoiements, it should be in some of the little villages of this coast, where air, earth and water concur to offer what each has most precious. Here are nightingales, beccaficas, ortolans, pheasants, partridges, quails, a superb climate, and the power of changing it from summer to winter at any moment, by ascending the mountains. The earth furnishes wine, oil, figs, oranges, and every production of the garden in every season. The sea yields lobsters, crabs, oysters, thunny, sardines, anchovies &c.

May 1. VENTIMIGLIA. MENTON. MONACO. NICE. A superb road might be made along the margin of the sea from Laspeze where the champaign country of Italy opens, to Nice where the Alps go off Northwardly and the post roads of France begin, and it might even follow the margin of the sea quite to Cette. By this road travellers would enter Italy without crossing the Alps, and all the little insulated villages of the Genoese would communicate together, and in time form one continued village along that road.

May 8. VAUCLUSE. AVIGNON. The vin blanc de M. de Rochegude of Avignon resembles dry Lisbon. He sells it at 6. years old for 22s. the bottle, the price of the bottle &c included.

May 10. NISMES. LUNEL. *Lunel* is famous for it's vin de muscat blanc, thence called Lunel or vin Muscat de Lunel. It is made from the raisin muscat, without fermenting the grape in the hopper. When fermented, it makes a red Muscat, taking that tinge from the dissolution of the skin of the grape, which injures the quality. When a red Muscat is required, they prefer colouring it with a little Alicant wine. But the white is best. The price of 240. bottles, after being properly drawn off from its lees, and ready for bottling, costs from 120. to 200. of the 1st quality and last vintage. It cannot be bought old, the demand being sufficient to take it all the first year.

May 11. MONTPELIER. With respect to the Muscat grape, of which the wine is made, there are two kinds, the red and the white. The first has a red skin, but white juice. If it be fermented in the cuve, the colouring matter which resides in the skin, is imparted to the wine. If fermented in the cuve [vat], the wine is white. Of the white grape, only a white wine can be made.

May 12. FRONTIGNAN. The territory in which the vin muscat de FRONTIGNAN is made is about a league of 3000 toises long, and 1/4 of the league broad. There are made about 1000 pieces (of 250 bottles each) annually, of which 600 are of the first quality made on the coteaux [hillsides].

The 1st. quality is sold, brut, for 120.[#] the piece. But it is then thick, must have a winter and the fouet [whisk] to render it potable and brilliant. The fouet is like a chocolate mill, the handle of iron, the brush of stiff hair. In bottles this wine costs 24.s the bottle &c. included. It is potable the April after it is made, is best that year, and after 10. years begins to have a pitchy taste resembling it to Malaga. It is not permitted to ferment more than half a day, because it would not be so liquorish. The best colour, and it's natural one, is the amber. By force of whipping it is made white but loses flavor.

There are but 2. or 3. pieces a year of red Muscat made, there being but one vineyard of the red grape. This sells in bottles at 30.s the bottle included. The coteaux yield about half a piece to the Setterie, the plains a whole piece. The inferior quality is not at all esteemed. It is bought by the merchants of Cette, as is also the wine of Bézières, and sold by them for Frontignan of 1st. quality. They sell 30,000 pieces a year under that name. The town of Frontignan marks it's casks emptied . . . was offered 40.[#] for the empty cask by a merchant of Cette.

The town of Frontignan contains about 2000 inhabitants. It is almost on the level of the ocean. [In the notes he added]:

M. Lambert, médecin, will give you any information you desire on your calling on him *de ma part* (on my behalf). He is a very sensible man.[84]

CETTE. There are in this town about 10,000 inhabitants. It's principal commerce is wine. It furnishes great quantities of grape pomice for making verdigriese.

[From Travelling Notes]

May 13. *Agde*. Here you may either go in the post boats [on the canal] which pass from hence to Thoulouse in 4. days, or you may hire a small boat and horse and go at your leisure, examining every thing as you go. I paid 12 livres a day for a boat, a horse and driver. I was 9 days going, because I chose to go leisurely.[85]

May 14. BEZIERES. A wine country. It is here in fact that they make most of the wine exported under the name of Frontignan.

May 15. ARGILIES. LE SAUMAL. Considerable plantations of vines. Those on the red hills to the right are said to produce good wine.

The bark in which I go is about 35. f. long, drawn by one horse, and goes from 2. to 3. geographical miles an hour. The canal yields abundance of carp and eel. I see also small fish resembling our perch and chub.

May 18-21. CARCASSONNE. CASTELNAUDARI. VILLEFRANCHE. At Toulouse, the canal ends. It has four communications with the Mediterranean. Of these 4. communications, that of Cette only leads to a deep sea-port, because the exit is there by a canal and not a river.

May 24. BORDEAUX. When we cross the Garonne at Langon we find the plains entirely of sand and gravel, and they continue so to Bordeaux. Where they are capable of any thing they are in vines.

Near Langon is Sauterne where the best white wines of Bordeaux are made. The elm tree shows itself at Bordeaux peculiarly proper for being spread flat for arbours. Many are done in this way on the quay des Charterons.

May 24. 25. 26. 27. 28. BORDEAUX. The cantons in which the most celebrated wines of Bordeaux are made are MEDOC down the river, GRAVE adjoining the city and the parishes next above; all on the same side of the river. In the first is made red wine principally, in the two last, white.

The grafting of the vine, tho' a critical operation, is practised with success. When the graft has taken, they bend it into the earth and let it take root above the scar. They begin to yield an indifferent wine at 3. years old, but not a good one till 25. years, nor after 80, when they begin to yield less, and worse, and must be renewed.

They dung a little in Medoc and Grave, because of the poverty of the soil; but very little; as more would affect the wine. The journal yields, communibus annis [in a typical year], about 3. pieces of 240. or 250 bottles each. The vineyards of first quality are all worked by their proprietors. Those of the 2d. rent for 300. the journal: those of the 3d. at 200. They employ a kind of overseer at four or five hundred livres [pounds] a year, finding him lodging and drink; but he feeds himself. He superintends and directs, but is expected to work but little. If the proprietor has a garden the overseer tends that. They never hire labourers by the year. The day wages for a man are 30. sous, a woman's 15. sous, feeding themselves. The women make the bundles of sarment [vine shoots], weed, pull off the snails, tie the vines, gather the grapes. During the vintage they are paid high and fed well.

Of RED WINES, there are 4. vineyards of first quality, viz.

1. Chateau Margau, belong to the Marquis d'Argicourt, who makes about 150 . tonneaux of 1000 bottles each. He has engaged to Jernon a merchant.
2. [Chateau] La Tour de Ségur, en Saint Lambert, belonging to Monsieur Mirosmenil, who makes 125. tonneaux.
3. Hautbrion, belonging 2/3 TO M. le comte de Fumelle, who has engaged to Barton a merchant, the other third to the Comte de Toulouse. The whole is 75. tonneaux.
4. Chateau de la Fite, belonging to the Président Pichard at Bordeaux, who makes 175 tonneaux. The wines of the three first are not in perfection till 4 years old. Those (of) de la Fite being somewhat lighter, are good at 3 years, that is the crop of 1786 is good in the spring of 1789. These growths of the year 1783 sell now at 2000.# the tonneau, those of 1784, on account of the superior quality of that vintage sell at 2400.# those of 1785 at 1800.#, those of 1786 at 1800.#, tho' they sold at first for only 1500.#.

RED WINES of the 2d quality are ROZAN belonging to Madame de Rozan, Dabbadie, ou Lionville, La Rose Quirouen [Kirwan], Durfort; in all 800 tonneaux, which sell at 1000.# new.

The 3d. class are Calons, Mouton, Gassie, Arboete, Pontette, de Terme, Candale. In all, 2000 tonneaux at 8 or 900.#. After these they are reckoned common wines and sell from 500.# down to 120.# the ton. All red wines decline after a certain age, losing colour, flavour, and body. Those of Bordeaux begin to decline at about 7. years old.

Of white wines those made in the canton of Grave are most esteemed at Bordeaux. The best crops are 1. pontac which formerly belonged to M. de Pontac, but now to M. de Lamont. He makes 40. tonneaux which sell at 400.# new. 2. st brise belonging to M. de Pontac, 30 tonneaux at 350.#. 3. de carbonius [Carbonnieux], belonging to the Benedictine monks, who make 50 tonneaux, and never selling till 3. or 4. years old, get 800.# the tonneau.

Those made in the three parishes next above Grave, and more esteemed at Paris are 1. sauterne, the best crop belongs to M. Diquem at Bordeaux, or to M. de Salus his son in law. 150 tonneaux at 300.# new and 600.# old. The next best crop is M. de Fillotte's [Filhot] 100 tonneaux sold at the same price. 2. prignac. The best is the President de Roy's [now Chateau Suduiraut] at Bordeaux. He makes 175 tonneaux, which sell at 300.# new, and 600.# old. Those of 1784, for their extraordinary quality sell at 800.#. 3. Barsac. The best belongs to the Président Pichard, who makes 150. tonneaux at 280.# new and 600.# old.

Sauterne is the pleasantest; next Prignac, and lastly Barsac; but Barsac is the strongest; next Prignac, and lastly Sauterne; and all stronger than Grave. There are other good crops made on the same paroisses of Sauterne, Prignac, and Barsac; but none as good as these.

There is a Virgin wine, which tho' made of a red grape is of a light rose colour, because, being made without pressure the colouring matter of the skin does not mix with the juice.

There are other white wines from the preceding prices down to 75.#. In general the white wines keep longest. They will be in perfection till 15. or 20. years of age. The best vintage now to be bought is of 1784, both of red and white. There has been no other good year since 1779.

The celebrated vineyards before mentioned are plains, as is generally the canton of Medoc, and that of Grave. The soil of Hautbrion particularly, which

I examined, is a sand, in which is near as much round gravel or small stone, and a very little loam; and this is the general soil of Medoc. That on Pontac, which I examined also, is a little different. It is clayey, with a fourth or fifth of fine rotten stone; and of 2. feet depth it becomes all a rotten stone.

The principal English wine merchants at Bordeaux are Jernon, Barton, Johnston, Foster, Skinner, Copinger and McCarthy. The chief French wine merchants are Feger, Nerac, Brunneau, Jauge, and du Verget. Desgrands, a wine broker, tells me they never mix the wines of first quality: but that they mix the inferior ones to improve them.

June 1. 2. The country from Nantes to LORIENT is very hilly and poor. The cultivated parts are in corn, some maize, a good many apple trees, no vines.

June 6. 7. 8. NANTES. ANCENIS. ANGERS. TOURS. About the limits of Bretagne and Anjou the lands change for the better. There are some considerable vineyards in the river plains, and after that, where the hills on the left come into view, they are mostly in vines. There is very good wine made on these hills; not equal, indeed to the Bordeaux of best quality, but to that of good quality, and like it. It is a great article of exportation from Anjou and Touraine, and probably is sold abroad under the name of Bordeaux.

All along both hills of the Loire is a mass of white stone, not durable, growing black with time, and so soft that the people cut their houses out of the solid stone with all the partitions, chimnies, doors &c. The hill sides resemble coney burrows, full of inhabitants. The borders of the Loire are almost a continued village.

After stopping at Tours and Orleans, Jefferson finally arrived in Paris on June 10, 1787. He noted he had travelled "something upwards of a thousand leagues," or more than three thousand miles in three months, mainly by carriage and horseback over eighteenth-century roads. As he wrote to his daughter Martha:

To Martha Jefferson
From Genoa to Aix was very fatiguing—the first two days having been at sea, and mortally sick—two more clambering the cliffs of the Appenines,

sometimes on foot, sometimes on a mule, according as the path was more or less difficult—and two others travelling through the night as well as day without sleep.[86]

Oddly, he never said once, that I have seen, that his wrist hurt him on the voyage, despite its rigors. Perhaps the waters of Aix worked for him after all.

CHAPTER THREE

Jefferson Stocks His Paris Wine Cellar

(1787–1788)

Once back in Paris, Jefferson reflected on his journey, writing to acquaintances of all ages and conditions, trying to digest what he had seen. The most important and pleasurable trip he ever took, it also gave him mixed emotions about travel. As he wrote his nephew Peter Carr:

> Travelling makes men wiser, but less happy. When men of sober age travel, they gather knowledge, which they may apply usefully for their country; but they are subject ever after to recollections mixed with regret; their affections are weakened by being extended over more objects; and they learn new habits which cannot be gratified when they return home.[1]

Whatever the hardships of his trip, and whatever lessons he learned from it, Jefferson the wine drinker would never be the same. His horizons on the subject had been infinitely expanded. Back in Paris he began writing about the new wines he'd learned, ordering Bordeaux, Burgundies, Muscats, and Champagnes. He also began recommending wines to others, as he was to do for the remainder of his life.

His travels in the provincial parts of France, away from Paris and the hothouse atmosphere of the court, gave him a different view of France and the French as a people.[2] Having seen the poverty and ignorance of the countryside, he took a different view of the extravagances of the court—and its drinking. While trying to be positive toward Louis XVI, who had helped the American Revolution at a critical time, even if purely for his own interest in weakening England, Jefferson found it difficult to support him. Writing to Madison on June 20, 1787, he gave forebodings of the collapse from decadence which was only two years away:

> The King loves business, economy, order and justice, and wishes sincerely the good of his people; but he is irascible, rude, very limited in his understanding, and religious bordering on bigotry. He has no mistress, loves his queen, and is too much governed by her. She is capricious like her brother, and governed by him; devoted to pleasure and expense, and not remarkable for any other vices or virtues.
>
> Unhappily, the King shows a propensity for the pleasures of the table. That for drink has increased lately, or at least it has become more known.[3]

Jefferson was hardly one to tut-tut credibly against the pleasures of the table, but his comment on the king's excessive drinking proved accurate. As he wrote melodramatically to Adams:

> Paris August 30, 1787
>
> The King, long in the habit of drowning his cares in wine, plunges deeper and deeper. The Queen cries, but sins on.[4]

By fall he was writing to Jay that the government was out of the hands of Louis XVI:

> Paris October 8, 1787
>
> The King goes for nothing. He hunts one-half the day, is drunk the other, and signs whatever he is bid.[5]

Continuing his critique of Parisian society, Jefferson wrote that year a satirical portrait of a lady of fashion:

> To Mrs. William Bingham
>
> To what does the empty bustle of Paris tend? At eleven o'clock it is day, *chez madame*. Propped on bolsters and pillows, and her head scratched into a little order, the bulletins of the sick are read, and the billets of the well. She writes to some of her acquaintance, and receives the visits of others.
>
> She flutters half an hour through the streets, by way of paying visits, and then to the spectacles. These finished, another half hour is devoted to dodging in and out of the doors of her very sincere friends, and away to supper.
>
> After supper, cards; and after cards, bed; to rise at noon the next day, and to tread, like a mill horse, the same trodden circle over again. Thus the days of life are consumed, one by one, without an object beyond the present moment.
>
> If death or bankruptcy happen to trip us out of the circle, it is matter for the buzz of the evening, and is completely forgotten by the next morning.[6]

To escape this life, Jefferson began that summer one of his most unusual associations, frequenting a retreat of Catholic lay brothers where a vow of silence was observed during the day. Called the Mont Calvaire or Mont Valérien, it was located beyond the Bois de Boulogne on a hill overlooking the village of Suresnes. It is now the American military cemetery in Paris. One of its unique features was a large and thriving vineyard, which was unusual for Paris even in that day. Jefferson kept his horse at Mont Valérien and rode there, and often shared with the brothers their evening meals and their Paris-made wines.[7]

Back in America, not everyone perceived Jefferson as dining quietly with monks. John Jay, secretary of foreign affairs, to whom Jefferson officially reported, seemed somewhat cool in reviewing the purposes of Jefferson's three-month jaunt through the south of France. Perhaps, like Martha, he wondered if it was strictly business. Perhaps he had heard rumors of the liaison with Maria Cosway. With thinly veiled sarcasm, Jay wrote that Congress "regret[s] the circumstance which calls you to the

South of France, but are perfectly satisfied that you should make that or any other journey which your health may require."[8]

Jay was no doubt recalling the relatively miserable time he had spent in Europe earlier, dragging his wife from place to place, meeting mainly discomfort and rejection, and no doubt wondered what the bachelor Jefferson did for his health by crossing the Alps on a mule.[9] Later, when Jefferson offered to send Jay any wines he desired from the vineyards he had visited, the latter declined coolly, saying Congress was too busy moving around for him to have a place to keep them. The implication was that he did not have as much time on his hands to worry about trifles like wine as certain other public servants seemed to have.[10] Perhaps I read too much into his letter, but it certainly sounds that way. If so, he got his revenge later when he negotiated with England what became known as Jay's Treaty, whose provisions caused Jefferson to repay a second time his prewar debts to English creditors, and was a factor in his eventual bankruptcy.

Jefferson's reception from Adams was quite different:

Grosvenor Square July 10, 1787

Dear Sir

I received with great pleasure your favour of the first. Your excursion, I dare answer for it, will be advantageous in many respects to our country. The object of mine to Holland was to procure Money.

Tell Mazzei he cannot conceive what an Italian I am become. I read nothing else, and if he writes to me it must be in that language: but he must remember to make his Letters so plain that I can see them.

You too write Italian, and if you like it, you will oblige me. But I am not yet presumptuous enough to write a Line in any Thing but rugged American."[11]

In this same letter Adams informed Jefferson of the safe arrival of his second daughter, Maria, by boat from America. Maria stayed with the Adamses while waiting for Jefferson to return. Adams added kindly, "In my life I never saw a more charming Child." Maria was accompanied by James Hemings's younger sister, Sally Hemings, then fourteen.

Jefferson was especially relieved when his second daughter arrived. Just about the only matter which did not work out for him in 1787 was his relationship with the other Maria, the beautiful Maria Cosway. After his return to Paris, they exchanged many letters, even after he was back in America, but their love affair was basically over.

Most notable of Jefferson's letters to Maria was the one usually titled "A Dialogue Between My Head And My Heart," a debate between his passion for Maria and his reason, which tells him she is married. More relevant to our subject is Franklin's amusing earlier letter entitled "Dialogue Between Franklin and the Gout," in which the old philosopher debates whether to give up wine or pain. As for Maria Cosway, after she and Jefferson parted, she eventually ended her days in an Italian convent as Baroness Cosway of Lodi. Her letters to and from Jefferson did not surface until the 1940s.[12]

One major conclusion Jefferson reached from seeing French vineyards firsthand was that they would not be profitable in the United States. To his old mentor Wythe, Jefferson put the matter starkly:

> I do not speak of the vine, because it is the parent of misery. Those who cultivate it are always poor, and he who would employ himself with us in the culture of corn, cotton &c. can procure in exchange for that much more wine, and better than he could raise by its direct culture.[13]

Jefferson wrote a similar letter to William Drayton of South Carolina, for whom he had risked his freedom smuggling rice out of Italy, and who had also taken an interest in grape growing and winemaking.[14] After his return to America, Jefferson softened these views, and by the time he retired from the presidency, he was once again a proponent of an American wine industry.

THOMAS JEFFERSON'S PARIS CELLAR LIST

His Paris cellar list, begun in 1787 by Petit while Jefferson was on his tour and added to by accretions as he bought new wines, appears at the end of his 1790 account book. It is reproduced here for readers' reference, since it contains the bulk of his best Paris wines, and enables one to survey them all together.

STOCK OF WINE ON HAND APR. 7, 1787

1787.	BOTT[LES].	
Apr. 7.	88.	Bourdeaux. from Bondfield in 1785 & 1786.
	95.	Grave. from Bondfield in 1786.
		Cayusac.
	29.	Champagne. Chevr. Luzerne.
	100.	Gayac. [Gaillac]
	183.	Madeira. of which 154. is from N. York.
	18.	Setubal
	20.	Port
	19.	Pico
	15.	Calcavallo
		Malvoisie
	10.	Chipre [Cyprus]
	8.	Eleatico

1787.		
May	124.	Monrachet. from Parent. de la Tour's. 274^L + 65^L + 34-10
July 4	250.	Frontignan. white. Lambert 300^L + 25^L + 213^L
	33.	Frontignan. red. Lambert 49-10
7	72.	Pacaret. Mr. Grand.
13.	124.	Meursault de M. Bachey de 1784. goutte d'Or 78^L + 48. at Beaune.
	126.	Caumartin. (Commaraine of Pommard) 125 bottles. 84^L en futaille (cask) = 13s - 4d & 48^L bottles &c = 21s the bottle
Aug.	180.	Chateau-Margot. from Messrs. Feger, Grammont & Co. Note I sent 124 bottles of this to A. Donald

1788		
Feb. 12.	248.	Meursault de M. Bachey de 1784. goutte d'Or. 200^L + 100^L + 66^L.
	123.	Voulenaye. 90.^{L} + 50^L + 33^L +
Apr. 23.	250.	Sauterne. de Comte de Lur-Saluce. 312^L = 10 + 28 at Bord. bott. includd.

1789		
Mar. 1.	248.	Meursault de 1784. 170^L + 102^L = 272^L is 13 3/4s. + 8 1/4s. = 22s. pr. bottle delivd. at Beaune. Add 66.^{L} transportn. = 338^L is 27 3/4s. the bottle.

Jefferson's cellar was surprisingly diverse, and not limited to French wines. Even among his French wines, not all were famous names, notably the two wines from Gaillac in the southwest, Gayac and Cayusac, phonetic spellings for Gaillac and Cahusac, respectively.

Gaillac, located in the modern French *département* known as the Tarn, after the beautiful river which flows through it, has produced good wines for centuries, and was a special favorite of the Plantagenet kings. One old writer waxed so eloquent as to say that its aftertaste left the scent of roses in the mouth.[15] Until recently its wines had lost some of their reputation, but with replantings going on all over southern France, it is an appellation which, for both reds and whites, seems to be improving. Jefferson ordered more Gaillac after he was back in America, but left few meaningful comments on what the 1787 version was like. He received it via Bondfield and Bordeaux, noted that it was red and that the Frenchman Gazaigner de Boyer had first sent it to John Adams hoping he would like it and thus establish an American market for his wines.[16]

The Cahusac or Cayusac is another Gaillac, apparently mainly white, from a property belonging to the Rochefoucauld family. This wine also arrived in cask via Bordeaux. Jefferson noted in his January 26, 1787, account book that it held 250 bottles, for which he paid only 98 F.

Cahusac is an obscure wine in the United States today, but I once tasted a dry one at a small wine shop in Georgetown whose name I've now forgotten. The wine was ordinary and sold under what the French call a "simple" appellation, meaning no appellation at all so far as the law is concerned. The name of the proprietor was given, however, as Mr. Guérard, which is always a good sign, and for about two dollars a bottle in 1973 it was not bad value, probably just the sort of wine Jefferson was looking for as his finances crumbled.

Cahusac, now called Cahuzac-sur-Vère, is a pretty town in the beautiful Gaillac region. It is entitled, along with forty-eight other hillside villages, to call its wines "Gaillac," which is much more saleable. Only the white wines are allowed this label. Their alcoholic strength must be at least 10.5 percent.[17] Sweet, unbrandied dessert wines are also produced, called *vin doux nouveau*, some fine examples of which I tasted there in fall

2005. It is likely Jefferson tried these, since he distinguishes between the dry Cahusacs and the others in his orders. Present-day Cahuzacs have relatively full bodies for white wines, and are also made sparkling, or "brisk," as Jefferson once described a white Gaillac.

Jefferson's only Greek wine in Paris, the "Chipre," or wine of Cyprus, as mentioned earlier, was apparently a sample. The only other time anyone said Jefferson had any Greek wines was when Daniel Webster noted drinking Muscat of the Isle of Samos at Monticello during Jefferson's retirement (see chapter seven).

Despite his friendship with Philip Mazzei, his old neighbor and a merchant of Italian wines, the only wine of that country on his Paris list was Eleatico, today spelled Aleatico. It is a red Muscat dessert wine of fine aroma and flavor which is still grown in several areas of Italy. A few vintners of Italian origin have also made it in California, notably Don Galleano. It is likely that Philip Mazzei put Jefferson onto this wine. He must have liked it, for he imported it again, served it in the White House while president, and planted Aleatico vines at Monticello in 1807. This particular lot is undoubtedly the one referred to in the account book entries of January 24 and February 9, 1787, as coming from Count Carbouri, 28 bottles for 168 francs the first time and an unspecified number of bottles for 170 francs the second time.

There was likewise only one Spanish wine on Jefferson's 1787 Paris cellar list, Pacaret, or Paxarete, as it is now spelled. A wine of the deep south like Sherry, it appeared in different styles, both dry and sweet. I have never found any comment on who drank it or preferred it among Jefferson's household or Paris guests, but it was generally considered what they called in the eighteenth or nineteenth centuries a "ladies' wine," eminently suited for what was then the American custom of drinking wines mainly after dinner.

The Paris Pacaret first appears in the account book not long after Jefferson returned from his southern France tour. A July 5, 1787, entry states: "pd. portage 72 bottles Pacaret from Grand 5 f 2." Grand was Ferdinand Grand, Jefferson's Paris banker, who handled the rent on his house and other financial transactions including, on occasion, paying for wines.

That fact unfortunately obscures rather than clarifies the source of this Spanish wine, since Grand was apparently not connected with any particular broker or region.

The 1787 cellar list corroborates the account book, but is no more revealing as to how, why, or from whom Jefferson got six cases of the only Spanish wine he recorded having during his five and a half years next door to Spain. The most likely source for his Spanish wine was, as with his Portuguese wines in Paris, the diplomats from those countries that he dealt with. While in Paris, Jefferson tried hard to negotiate a treaty with Spain, but had little success.

That Jefferson had no regular supplier of Spanish wines in Paris is also shown by a letter from one Pierre de Labat, from Cadiz, a great port for the fine dessert wines of southern Spain, written October 7, 1788. In the letter, which is three pages long and in French, Labat says he is under the patronage of the Commandeur de Bausset of France, and asks Jefferson if he would like to order any wines from southern Spain, noting he supplies "Lords, Ambassadors and Persons of Distinction from the different Courts of Europe." He enclosed a price list for all his different vintages, qualities, and types of wines. Sadly, it has been lost.[18]

After he became president and moved to Washington, Jefferson began ordering large quantities of Spanish wines, including Pacaret. Whether that was because he found them more to the taste of Americans, or whether it was there that he found a reliable supplier is open to question. Whatever the reason, it is remarkable that the second most popular wines in Jefferson's White House cellars, ranking behind only Madeira and ahead of even his favorite French wines, were the dessert wines of Spain, the very wines he mostly ignored when he was next door to them in Paris.

The same might be said of his Paris "Calcavallo," now spelled Carcavelhos, which he first tried in Paris, then ordered often while president fifteen years later. Named for the village of that name near Lisbon, Carcavelos has traditionally been mainly a dessert wine. In the first half of the nineteenth century, over three hundred thousand gallons a year were produced, and it was highly popular in England.

Today less Carcavelos is made, much of its land having been swallowed up by suburban development in the nearby seaside resort of Estoril. Most of the wine that remains is brandied, sweet, and 19 percent alcohol like Port or Madeira, but still retains its characteristic almond taste. Like the Graves region in the suburbs of Bordeaux, Carcavelos survived the terrible vine diseases of the nineteenth century only to be more devastated by the land-development mania of the twentieth. One can still occasionally find a dry Carcavelos, and it can be a good, somewhat unusual-tasting aperitif.

The quality of Jefferson's Carcavelos is uncertain. In his era many of the common wines from Lisbon were shipped to England and America under the names Carcavelos, even though they did not deserve it. On the other hand, some true Carcavelos wines of that era were relatively dry, natural white wines without any brandy added. As wine historian William Younger has stated:

> It is of course impossible to say that today we can drink Portuguese wines of exactly the same type and texture as those drunk by the Georgians for we cannot be certain of the proportions of different grapes in the vintages of 18th-century Portugal. Nor can we be certain of the degree to which the gathered grapes were dried in the sun before pressing. But there is a remarkable correspondence between a description of Carcavellos, written in 1793, and the description of it which I have given today. It was then 'a white wine of an agreeable sweetness, with a pungent taste' and so it is in our own time.[19]

Given Jefferson's strong preference for natural, unbrandied wines and his evident care in ordering from specific vineyards, it is possible that *his* Carcavelos were dry table wines and not sweet dessert wines.

A unique white dessert wine from Portugal which may still be found in good wine stores is the golden Setubal, noted both on Jefferson's 1787 cellar list and his White House list. Still made in the same beautiful area not far from Lisbon, Setubal is one of the oldest and finest dessert wines of the world. Allegedly named for Tubal, grandson of Noah, it is pronounced "shtew-bahl" in Portuguese, almost like the mythical racehorse. The deep-gold color and unforgettable wild-honey taste of Setubal appear to have changed little since Jefferson's day.

Port, the other Portuguese wine on Jefferson's Paris list, was apparently only a sample, and rarely mentioned by him otherwise. Port was traditionally *the* Englishman's wine, and given the unpleasantness between him and the English, it is not surprising that he did not rave about it. He did, however, order it several times while president, and of the best, which says quite a bit.

Despite his obvious enjoyment of variety, Jefferson still leaned overwhelmingly to the classic Bordeaux and Burgundies when it came to stocking his Paris cellar. Of the nearly twenty-four hundred bottles on the list, over sixteen hundred, or two-thirds, were Bordeaux or Burgundies. More surprisingly, nearly two-thirds of *that* total were Burgundies, a heavy preference that one would not have suspected given recent stress on Jefferson's love of Bordeaux.

Jefferson's Favorite Burgundies

It has been assumed by many that Jefferson liked Bordeaux better than Burgundies. It is certainly true that he *wrote* more about them. He also ordered more Bordeaux than any other nondessert wine after his return to America. Yet he was also very attached to Champagne, and during his early years in Washington it predominated over all other wines except the ever-present Madeira.

But what of Burgundy? Are its Pinot Noirs and Chardonnays not fully as good as Bordeaux, both in its red Cabernets and Merlots and its white Sauvignons and Semillons? And was it not the same in Jefferson's time, if we can believe what others said of it then? If all that is so, why did Jefferson stop ordering it? Is that evidence that, having tasted the best wines of both regions, Jefferson finally opted for Bordeaux as his unquestioned favorite?

Reading his accounts and letters as a whole, one suspects not. It appears he probably liked the two wine regions about equally, but ordered more Bordeaux while in America for at least three reasons: (1) Burgundies were *said* not to travel well; (2) Burgundies lay far inland and were harder to obtain than Bordeaux; and (3) there were no large proprietors and no American consul in Burgundy for Jefferson to rely on. He had only his faithful cooper, Parent, who was no match for the counts and presidents at Bordeaux, not to mention Bordeaux's advantage of having the son of George Mason in Bordeaux working for Jefferson's main supplier. When you put all those factors in the balance, it is easy to speculate why Jefferson ordered more Bordeaux from America than he did Burgundy.

In May of 1787, while Jefferson was still on his long tour, Petit noted on the cellar list that he had 124 bottles of 1782 Montrachet, procured by Parent direct from the producer, M. de la Tour. It had cost a rather stout three pounds per bottle.

On July 13, after the return, 124 bottles of Meursault "Goutte d'Or" vintage 1784, "came to hand," at one pound per bottle. There arrived still in cask some 126 bottles of what Jefferson called "Caumartin" red (actually Pommard, Clos de la Commaraine), vintage 1785, costing one pound, one shilling each.[20]

It is interesting that Jefferson's red Burgundies were younger than his whites. In his tour notes he said that the whites of Bordeaux were also thought to age longer and better than the reds, a striking contrast with current experience and opinions (except for certain Sauternes). It no doubt says a lot about winemaking practices of his era, and that the reds may have received less contact with the skins than reds do today, reducing their aging potential but making them drinkable younger.

The same summer, Jefferson had 88 red Haut-Brions and 95 dry white Graves from Bordeaux, which he supplemented with 180 bottles of Château-Margot (Margaux), but sent on 124 bottles of the latter to Alexander Donald in Virginia. In all, Jefferson thus had in his Paris cellar from May through August of 1787 some 374 bottles of Burgundy and only 239 bottles of Bordeaux, not that this is some contest of numbers.

On December 17, 1787, Jefferson sought to secure more Burgundy, writing to Parent at Beaune:

> Your letter, Sir, of June 20, informed me that Mr. Bachey still had at that time four
> feuillettes [casks of 114 American gallons] of Meursault "Goutte d'Or" wine, of the

same growth and quality as that which you had sent me. I found it so good that I
will take three feuillettes, if so much still remains.

If there is no more, please be so kind as to procure for me one feuillette of
the same quality as the "Goutte d'Or," or whichever you find of the best kind,
and send it to me in bottles as soon as possible.

I ask also that you send me one feuillette of red wine of Volnay, in
bottles also.

TH: JEFFERSON[21]

Parent replied with an alacrity unusual for eighteenth-century France,
writing Jefferson on Christmas Eve:

at Beaune this 24 December 1787

In reply to your honored letter of the 17th instant, in which you wrote me
to buy for you three casks of white Goutte d'Or, I have been to Mr. Bachey's,
who still has three casks, but only wishes to sell two at this time, and he wants a
hundred pounds per cask, and not less.

I also went to Mr. Latour's. He has no more 1784 Montrachet, but has
some 1785 and wants 300 pounds a cask for it, and not less.

There is a farmer in Chagny, Dents de Clermont, who has 6 casks of 1784
for which he wants 300 pounds each, but I believe it is better than that of
Mr. Latour.

I did not wish to buy you any without advising you, so please let me know
whether or not you will take it at that price or not by the first mail because
he told me yesterday that he had sold one cask two weeks ago and awaits a
response on three others.

I helped him sell 22 barrels (pièces) of Volnay for 340 pounds a week ago
and he promised me that he would hold these two casks for me awaiting your
response.

Or, if you wish, I will send you a cask of white Meursault, which will cost
you 84 or 86 pounds per cask for the first quality, and which will not be as
good because in the past two months prices on old wines have risen greatly in
our area.

As for the vine cuttings of the Clos de Vougeot, Romanée, Chambertin and Montrachet, I will send them to you if you still want them. If I had not been sick from October till the end of November, I would have sent them to you as promised.

Parent[22]

The mails growing ever swifter, Jefferson got Parent's December 24 letter on December 28 and answered it the same day, telling him to buy the two casks of '84 from Bachey for a hundred pounds "if his price will not come down." He also requested one cask of first quality Volnay 1784, bottled. As for the high-priced Montrachet, Jefferson decided to pass on it for the moment, but might order some later, and asked that Parent please go ahead and ship the Meursault and Volnay right away, and forward the vine cuttings as soon as convenient.[23]

On January 16, 1788, Parent confirmed the transactions were complete and the wines packed, but that it was too cold to send them; they would freeze and the bottles might break. He promised to send them and the vine cuttings as soon as the weather was better.[24] By February 3 the freeze had lifted and Parent notified Jefferson of the name of the carter who would be delivering six hampers of wine, around February 12, including two of Volnay and four of Meursault Goutte d'Or.[25] As indicated by his grammar and the way he signed his name, Parent was not a man of erudition, but his manner was honest, and his instructions to Jefferson had a Burgundian earthiness. On this occasion, he instructed Jefferson to pay sixteen pounds ten sous for each hamper and *no more*, implying the carter would certainly try to beat Jefferson on the transaction. He concluded with a downright Jeffersonian listing of precisely what he had charged him for bottling, corks, wax, straw for packing, and even how much the string cost to tie up the hampers.[26]

Petit later noted on the bottom of Parent's letter the totals of all the charges and that 372 bottles had arrived with only one broken, which would not be a bad record even today.[27]

A letter from Short, mailed from Beaujolais, recounted how he was retracing Jefferson's steps, staying at the same hotel in Dijon and ordering the Irish potatoes Jefferson had so much approved:

September 24, 1788

The next morning we went to Beaune. I wished to spend that day there. The first thing I did was to go to Parent's. Unfortunately he was gone some distance from home. A heavy rain was falling, but still his wife insisted on sending for him.

After the posthorses were put to and we in the carriage, Parent arrived. He assured us he should have been able to have shewn us several cellars where the wine was still making. It was now too late and we were obliged to go on. I saw with a great deal of pleasure Volnais, Meursaut and Montraché.

They made us pay at the tavern at Beaune three livres for a bottle of Volnais. I do not however think it equal to a wine we had at Auxerre for the same price and which I think was made in the neighborhood. It was of the year 84.[28]

Short's reaction to the wine of Auxerre, which is hard by Chablis and once was better known and better regarded than Chablis, is interesting. Obviously Short was not just slavishly following whatever Jefferson dictated to him, as some of his detractors later accused him of doing. He placed the wine of Auxerre above that of Volnay, one of Jefferson's favorites. What we do not know is whether the Auxerre was a white, as it mostly was, or a red, which would make the comparison more equitable, since otherwise Short may just have preferred whites to reds.

Short checked out something else Jefferson had missed: what the Burgundy grapes themselves were like. Jefferson, travelling in March, had missed that experience. Short filled him in:

I ate of the grape of which the Volnais is made. I was struck with its resemblance to some of our wild grapes in Virginia and particularly some that grow in Surry [county] on my father's estate. The shape of the bunch, the size and color, and still more the taste of the grape so absolutely the same that I think it would be impossible to distinguish one from the other.

The vine at my father's grew on an oak tree which stood in an old field quite separate from any other, so that the sun acted on it with its full force. I could wish much to see a fair experiment made on the grapes of that tree.[29]

So much for Short the connoisseur. If he liked the wines made from wild Virginia grapes, some of them growing up trees, his palate was possibly not to be trusted. No wonder he liked the Auxerre better than the Volnay.

In January of 1789 Jefferson contacted Parent for more Burgundy. As Jefferson wrote to Madame de Bréhan, sister-in-law of the former French minister to the U.S., the weather was the reason:

We have had such a winter, Madame, as makes me shiver yet whenever I think of it. All communications almost were cut off. Dinners and suppers were suppressed, and the money laid out in feeding and warming the poor, whose labors were suspended by the rigors of the season.

Loaded carriages passed the Seine on the ice, and it was covered with thousands of people from morning to night, skating and sliding. Such nights were never seen before and they continued two months.[30]

Despite the cold, Jefferson was still thinking of white Burgundy, as he informed Parent:

January 22, 1789

For several weeks now, Sir, I have wanted to order from you a shipment of Meursault. But the season has been so rude that I thought it would be better to await milder weather. The delay has lasted to the point that I now find myself with a pressing need. I ask you therefore to send me immediately two hundred fifty bottles of wine, Meursault "Goutte d'Or." I have become so attached to that of Mr. Bachey of the 1784 vintage that if he still has any I would prefer it.

If he has none, would you please be so good as to obtain for me whatever there is that is best of this type of wine. I rely on you always for the quality, and let the price be what it has to be, always however considering quality more than price.[31]

That concluding statement sums up Jefferson's attitude toward wine: quality always came first, worries about price later.

Parent was alert and obliging, sending Jefferson pears as well as wines:

I shipped 4 hampers wrapped and tied and packed in straw and marked P.S. 1, 2, 3, and 4, one of which contains twenty-five Bonchretien pears, which I send to you because I believe they must be rather rare in Paris because of the ice we have had this winter.

There are 248 or 249 bottles in the four baskets, which left the 14th and should be received late in the month or by the first of March at the latest.

The wine all went off in good condition; I sent all the better wine of 1784. Wine prices have risen extremely in the past few days. The growers say that the vines are almost entirely lost due to cold weather.

I bought two casks as soon as I received your letter, yet it cost 170 pounds, plus 60 pounds for the bottles, 28 pounds for the basket and packing, and 14 for straw and corks, in all 272 pounds.

I have been to Mr. Bachey's, but he has no more of his old Goutte d'Or, he has only '87s, which are not at all of good quality, neither whites nor reds, and yet was very expensive and of very bad quality; But he still has seven (60-gallon) barrels of his Goutte d'Or which are excellent, but wants five hundred pounds for each 120-gallon barrel. At present he has already sold half at this season's price.

If you should wish any, please let me know. It is of good quality this year, and will be ready for bottling at the end of autumn. I hope to see you in Paris in May on my way to Rouen.[32]

Despite the weather and prices, Parent found Jefferson some Meursault, whose receipt Jefferson noted on March 11, 1789:

I have received in good condition the four hampers of Meursault wine which you were so good as to send me, and I will be ready to pay the bill on your order whenever you wish to present it. Indeed I ask that you send it immediately because I count on departing next month for America, from whence I shall not return until Autumn.

At that time I shall need to request from you some Monrachet, Meursault and Voulenaye. The Meursault of Mr. Bachey that you have heretofore sent me has rendered me a bit difficult. The shipment which you have just sent me is not so perfect. I would have said it was from another year than 1784 if you had not assured me that it was from that year.

I hear that last year [1788] was excellent for the quality of its wines. Thus it is of that year that I will ask you to send me this autumn.

I send you a thousand thanks for the pears which you were so kind as to send me. They were truly superb and indeed rare.

TH: JEFFERSON.[33]

Little did Jefferson suspect that when he arrived in the U.S. he would find himself appointed secretary of state, and that he would never see Parent or Burgundy again.

Learning that his wealthy American customer was going to the United States, Parent let it be known just how bad his personal situation really was:

at Beaune this 18 March 1789

SIR

I ask you to do me the favor of placing my 14 year-old son. You indicate that you are leaving soon for America, so I see that you are in a position to help him. If you can do it soon, I would be greatly obligated to you. In our present state we can hardly make ends meet, all merchandise being at present too expensive.

I ask you to consider what I have asked about my son, and ask your pardon for taking the liberty of asking it of you.

I hope to go to Paris toward the month of May.

PARENT[34]

The desperate straits of honest working men like Parent were building toward the violence of the French Revolution. When men like Parent felt compelled to send their fourteen-year-old sons to America to seek a better life, things were in desperate shape indeed.

Jefferson did not reply to Parent's March 18 letter until May, but when he did it was with a kindness of tone and a succinctness of expression in French that would be hard to equal. As a writer of business and official letters that manage to sound natural and human, Jefferson was unsurpassed:

> SIR
>
> Paris this 7th of May 1789.
>
> Not having received reply to my letters to America requesting permission to go there for a few months, it is very possible that you will find me in Paris if your plan to come here during the first few days of this month comes to pass.
>
> I would be indeed happy to see you and to speak with you about your son. In explaining to me your ideas on the matter, I would know whether I could be of some use to you, and I would be so with pleasure.
>
> TH: JEFFERSON[35]

On May 27, 1789, Parent sent the last letter exchanged between the two men, informing Jefferson that he had hurt his leg in decanting some wine and could not leave Beaune before the fifteenth or twentieth of June.[36] Had Parent known that Jefferson too would be delayed, and not leave for America until October, he would probably have succeeded in sending his son to America. But in that case his descendants might not have been around to tend the wine business at Beaune where they have, ironically, prospered better in France than some of those of Jefferson in America.

THE MYSTERIES OF JEFFERSON'S BORDEAUX

The best-known Jefferson quotes about ordering wine have been about Bordeaux. It is clear that Jefferson did *write* more about Bordeaux, but he did more writing than he did purchasing. Before his trip there in 1787, he had already written and received over a dozen letters about Bordeaux, but had only received two shipments, one of Haut-Brion and one of Margaux.

After his trip, Jefferson wrote and received at Paris at least twenty-eight letters *about* ordering it, but really only placed three orders: one for Haut-Brion, one for Yquem, and one for Lafite. Only in the case of Yquem did he receive what he ordered. When he ordered Haut-Brion, he was sent 180 bottles of Château Margaux, 124 bottles of which he then gave to Alexander Donald of Virginia. When he ordered Lafite, its proprietor Pichard wrote the American consul that he had no more available. The consul, Bondfield, tried to replace the Lafite with Haut-Brion, but his cooper accidentally shipped Jefferson's wine to someone else, and by the time the mistake was discovered, Jefferson was ready to return to America and called off the order.

A much-quoted Jefferson dictum is that you should never order Bordeaux from anyone but the proprietor who makes it. This is a precept he seldom followed, however, since nearly all his ordering was done through consuls, bankers, or brokers. While in France, the only proprietor he ever successfully ordered wine from was the Count de Lur-Saluces of Château d'Yquem. Otherwise, he dealt successfully only through Bondfield and Feger, Grammont.

Jefferson had reason to warn his friends against intermediaries because doctored and fraudulent Bordeaux was prevalent in the eighteenth century. Hermitage, Gaillac, and other rich wines were freely blended into the Médocs of Bordeaux for body and color, even though the additions changed the character of the wine. Wine writers of the period said that many Englishmen became so used to blended Bordeaux that they did not like the genuine article when they tasted it. Perhaps there was some justification for the practice in thin years because, after all, the Syrah of Hermitage is a great wine. And many consumers actually sought, and brokers advertised, claret that was "hermitagé," or had Hermitage openly added to give it body and depth. Today Syrah is often blended with cabernet, both in the U.S. and Australia, but it is so noted on labels. It is thus an ongoing experiment.

To appreciate Jefferson's problems in obtaining Bordeaux as he wanted it, one must examine his letters in context, in detail, and chronologically. That approach shows more clearly just how and why he failed to receive many of the Bordeaux he discussed. His own words, in context, also show better which ones he liked most and least. A more specific question has lately arisen, as mentioned in the introduction: did Jefferson really possess, or at least order, the famous dozen or so bottles, bearing his initials, of Lafite, Yquem, Margaux, and Mouton of the years 1784 and 1787 recently sold at auction? For students of claret, and those who love a historical detective story, the matter is dealt with in the epilogue.

As shown by the list of his baggage for America, which is meticulous and perfectly preserved, it is clear that he took a little over 30 cases of wine, 363 bottles to be exact, and not a single one of them was a red wine. His only Bordeaux was Château d'Yquem, of which he shipped 72 bottles, 2 dozen for Monticello, 2 dozen for New York, where the government was, a dozen for his brother-in-law at Eppington, and one case for consumption en route as "Seastores."

Once he was back in America and realized he had to accept Washington's offer to be secretary of state and could not return to France for some time, if ever, he immediately began ordering claret. Still later, after he was elected president more than a decade later, he again began ordering first-growth claret for himself. But his first orders seem to have been primarily for the great claret lover George Washington, and only secondarily for Jefferson himself. And his White House claret orders were minor compared to a dozen or so other wines. Could it be that red Bordeaux was not his personal favorite?

It was possibly a matter of price and availability. During and after the French Revolution, the Bordeaux wine world was in chaos. Supplies could not be counted on. Many of the aristocrats who had controlled the great wine estates were either guillotined or in exile, and the market was turbulent. His suppliers changed with the political winds, as America changed consuls at Bordeaux from Franklin's old friend Bondfield to Joseph Fenwick, a protégé of George Mason of Virginia, whose son John was sent to Bordeaux as a partner of Fenwick to handle sales of Virginia tobacco to the French.

Taking his clarets in detail, it is fairly clear that prior to his 1787 visit to Bordeaux, the wines that Jefferson actually possessed from Bordeaux were the 144 bottles of red Château Haut-Brion sent by Bondfield according to his April 19, 1785, letter. Jefferson acknowledged those as received and approved them as "good" in his letter of May 20, 1785.[37]

The second shipment was of 144 red Chateau Margaux and 144 white Graves, sent by Bondfield June 24, 1786, and acknowledged as received by Jefferson's letter of August 8, 1786,[38] as also verified by his account book. Jefferson said the red was "excellent" but the Graves too "hard." When he returned to America, he left the Graves, Haut-Brion, and Margaux in his Paris cellar.

In the midst of his 1787 stop at Bordeaux, Jefferson wrote to his claret-loving brother-in-law Francis Eppes:

May 26, 1787

Making a tour round the sea-ports of this country on matters of business, and meeting at this place with Capt. Gregory, just sailing for Portsmouth, I cannot deny myself the pleasure of asking you to participate of a parcel of wine I have been chusing for myself.

I do it the rather as it will furnish you a specimen of what is the very best Bourdeaux wine. It is of the vineyard of Obrion, one of the four established as the very best, and it is of the vintage of 1784, the only very fine one since the year 1779.

Six dozen bottles of it will be packed separately addressed to you.[39]

On June 2, 1787, the firm of Féger, Grammont of Bordeaux, wrote that additional wine ordered for him and Eppes had been shipped. This wine was not the Haut-Brion which he described to Eppes, but part of a whole cask of Château Margaux he had personally selected:

We have loaded, as per your orders, six dozen bottles of the wine of Chateaux Margaux, in three cases, on the ship Comte d'Artois, addressing them to Mr. Francis Eppes at Eppington.

And we are sending today the rest of a hogshead of wine, in four cases of 45 bottles, to Mr. Garvey at Rouen, with a request to forward them to you, and we are sending him also the bill of lading.[40]

His cellar list corroborates receipt in August 1787: "180 Bottles Chateau Margot from Messrs. Féger, Grammont & Cie." He did not mention the vintage, but there is no cellar list or account book entry for Haut-Brion in 1787. Jefferson made continuing notes on the 1787 list. Beside this Margaux entry, in his own handwriting, is written: "Note I sent 124 bottles to A. Donald."[41]

"GENUINE WINES CAN NEVER BE HAD BUT OF THE VIGNERON"

During the summer following his tour of southern France, Jefferson renewed his correspondence with his former law partner Edmund Randolph, then attorney general of Virginia, offering to procure for him and his wife "books, fruits, modes, or anything else," including good Bordeaux wines:

> Paris, August 3, 1787
>
> As to wines, I have the best Vignerons of Bordeaux, Burgundy and Frontinan. Genuine wines can never be had but of the Vigneron.
>
> The best of Bordeaux cost three livres the bottle, but good may be bought for two. Command me freely, assured that I shall serve you cheerfully.[42]

Apparently neither Jefferson nor Randolph followed up on the offer.

Later that summer he responded to good friend Wilson Miles Cary, who had asked him about the tobacco market at Bordeaux. Jefferson answered him about Bordeaux wines instead:

> Paris Aug. 12. 1787
>
> You ask if we know a merchant in Bordeaux who may be recommended for a consignment of tobacco. My acquaintance there is not extensive. There is a Mr. John Bondfield of whom I have a good opinion. He is an American and is Agent there for the United States.

If wine is your object, he is a good judge of that. He supplies me, as he had before done Doctr. Franklin, with very good. They cost now 30 sous a bottle, and 2 livres when 3 years old, which is the age before which they should not be drank.

If you like white wines, ask for Sauterne, which is the best in that country, and indeed is excellent.[43]

He also kept in touch with Alexander Donald, former vice-consul at Bordeaux, who Jefferson hoped would be a source of wines when he returned to the United States. Jefferson promised to obtain wines for Donald from France, assuring him of his good connections:

Paris 17 Sept. 1787

I can undertake to procure for you in the cellars of the persons who make it, any wines of [this country] which you may desire. I have visited all the most celebrated wine cantons, have informed myself of the best vignobles [vineyards] and can assure you that it is from them alone that genuine wine is to be got, and not from any winemerchant.[44]

On December 18 of 1787 Jefferson wrote to Bondfield at Bordeaux, enclosing a letter in French for M. Diquem, who Jefferson assumed was still owner of the great château, telling Bondfield he had already been in contact with the other owners of first growths to obtain their wines direct:

Having in the course of my journey the last spring examined into the details relative to the most celebrated wines of France, and decided within my own mind which of them I would wish to have always for my own use, I have established correspondences directly with the owners of the best vineyards.

It remains for me to do this at Sauterne. I have therefore written the inclosed letter to M. Diquem, who makes the best of that name, to begin a correspondence on this object, and to ask of him for the present 250 bottles of Sauterne of the vintage of 1784.

I have taken the liberty to tell him you would receive the package and forward them to me by a waggon: and I have assured him that his draught on me shall be paid at sight. But he does not know either my name or character, public or private, and may have doubt. Will you be so good as to remove them both for the present and future, and even for the supply now asked for to offer to pay him, assured that your draught on me for reimbursement shall be honoured at sight. I must ask you also to add on the letter the address of M. Diquem, with which I am unacquainted, and to inform me of it for my future government.

Perhaps I should have addressed myself to Monsr. Salus, his son in law, as I am not certain whether he is not either jointly or solely interested at present in the vineyards.[45]

The enclosed letter to the proprietor of the Château d'Yquem read, in translation, as follows:

Paris, 18 December 1787

I shall have need for some small supplies of white wine of Sauternes for my annual consumption during my stay in France, and even after my return to America when that takes place.

I know that yours is one of the best growths of Sauternes, and it is directly from your hand that I prefer to receive it, because that way I will be sure to receive it natural, good and sound.

Permit me therefore Sir to ask whether you still have any of your wine of Sauternes, first quality, of the year 1784, and if you would be so kind as to let me have 250 bottles?

In the event that you can do me this favor, I would ask that you have the packing done under the supervision of your own manager. Your draught on me at Paris for the amount will be paid at sight, and Mr. John Bondfield, American Consul at Bordeaux, will receive the cases or hampers and forward them to me.

Permit me further, if you will, to contact you directly each time I need a supply of white wine of Sauternes for my own use, and accept assurances of my etc.

TH: JEFFERSON[46]

Jefferson's study where he wrote hundreds of letters about wine, making copies on his "polygraph" machine, courtesy of Robert C. Lautman/Thomas Jefferson Foundation, Inc.

The dining room at Monticello with dumbwaiters at each end of the fireplace to carry up wine bottles from the cellars below, courtesy of Robert C. Lautman/Thomas Jefferson Foundation, Inc.

Daguerreotype of Isaac Jefferson, former slave and trusted Jefferson companion, who left the most vivid and insightful descriptions of the private Jefferson and his wine and food habits, MSS 2041, courtesy of Tracy W. McGregor Library of American History, Special Collections, University of Virginia Library.

The young red-headed planter Jefferson as portrayed by John Trumbull, courtesy of Monticello/Thomas Jefferson Foundation, Inc.

Sophisticated bachelor Jefferson in his forties in a powdered wig in Paris in 1788, painted by John Trumbull for Jefferson's paramour, Maria Cosway, courtesy of White House Historical Association (White House Collection) (54).

Michel Sokolnicki's engraving of a free-spirited Jefferson in his fifties from a watercolor painted in 1798 by close friend Thaddeus Kosciusko, the Polish general and American patriot, courtesy of Yale University Art Gallery/Mabel Brady Garvan Collection and Monticello/Thomas Jefferson Foundation, Inc.

The mature, ambitious Jefferson while a candidate for president in 1800 by Rembrandt Peale, courtesy of White House Historical Association (White House Collection) (55).

Jefferson in retirement at age seventy-eight when he wrote his most elaborate and eloquent letters on wine based on a lifetime of experience by Thomas Sully, courtesy of Monticello/Thomas Jefferson Foundation, Inc.

Watercolor of Monticello depicting Jefferson's grandchildren during Jefferson's retirement years by Jane Braddick Peticolas, c. 1825, courtesy of Monticello/Thomas Jefferson Foundation, Inc.

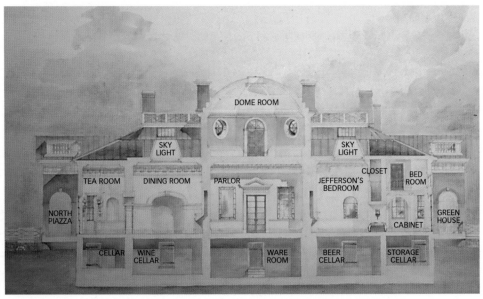

Watercolor sideview of Monticello, showing relative locations of Jefferson's wine cellar, dining room, etc., by Floyd Johnson, 1986, courtesy of Monticello/Thomas Jefferson Foundation, Inc.

Jefferson's "Wine Room" under the dining room at Monticello as formerly reconstructed, courtesy of Monticello/Thomas Jefferson Foundation, Inc.

Madeira wine decanter recently unearthed from a dry well under Monticello, courtesy of Monticello/ Thomas Jefferson Foundation, Inc.

Seau Crénelé or Scalloped Porcelain wine cooler which was filled with ice by Jefferson to chill his wineglasses, courtesy of Monticello/Thomas Jefferson Foundation, Inc.

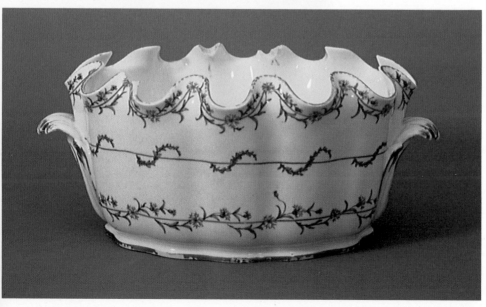

Silver wine tumblers inscribed "GW to TJ" and "TJ," courtesy of Monticello/Thomas Jefferson Foundation, Inc.

Thomas Jefferson's corkscrew on his "Swiss Army" style pocket knife, courtesy Smithsonian Institution and Monticello/Thomas Jefferson Foundation, Inc.

Jefferson's silver with his abbreviated signature "Th:J." thereon in his own handwriting, courtesy of Monticello/Thomas Jefferson Foundation, Inc.

Silver askos (Greek wine-serving vessel) which Jefferson had made from an original bronze found under a temple in Nîmes. His grandchildren called it the "duck," courtesy of Monticello/Thomas Jefferson Foundation, Inc.

Jefferson's traveling "spirit chest," courtesy of Monticello/Thomas Jefferson Foundation, Inc.

Serving table or "dumbwaiter" designed by Jefferson, which was placed between guests at dinner both at Monticello and at the President's house, courtesy of Monticello/Thomas Jefferson Foundation, Inc.

Aerial view of the restored southwest and northeast vineyards at Monticello, adjacent to the orchards, from which wine is at last being made, courtesy of Monticello/Thomas Jefferson Foundation, Inc.

Poplar Forest, near Lynchburg, ninety miles from Monticello, where he built a larger, deeper, cooler wine cellar under the dining room for use during his retirement, courtesy of Thomas Jefferson's Poplar Forest, Les Schofer photographer.

Famed Vineyards of Hermitage, above the Rhone, home of Jefferson's favorite white wine in his mature years. Courtesy of the Thomas Jefferson Foundation, Monticello Digital Archive, photograph by Charles Suddarth Kelly, one of thousands of wonderful photographs of Jefferson's travels given to Monticello by Kelly and soon to be available digitally via the Jefferson Memorial Library.

Chateau Haut-Brion, near Bordeaux, which Jefferson toured at length in 1787. His bust now stands in the cellar of the Chateau. Courtesy of the Thomas Jefferson Foundation, Monticello Digital Archive, photograph by Charles Suddarth Kelly.

Canal du Midi at the village of Castelnaudary, on which Jefferson traveled by barge across the wine country of southern France in 1787, courtesy of the author.

The vineyards of Pommard in October 2005, showing why they are called the "Golden Slope" (Cote d'Or), courtesy of the author.

ESTATE 1964 BOTTLED

POMMARD

Les Chaponnières

APPELLATION D'ORIGINE CONTROLÉE

DOMAINE PARENT, PROPRIÉTAIRE A POMMARD, COTE-D'OR

FRANCE

MIS EN BOUTEILLES AU DOMAINE

Modern wine label for Jefferson's favorite affordable red Burgundy, Pommard, from the Domaine Parent, direct descendants of Jefferson's Burgundy guide and supplier, Etienne Parent.

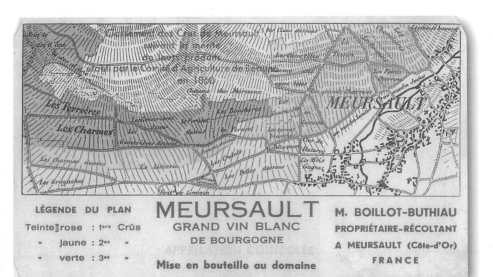

LÉGENDE DU PLAN

Teinte rose : 1ᵉʳˢ Crûs

» Jaune : 2⁰⁰ »

» verte : 3⁰⁰ »

MEURSAULT

GRAND VIN BLANC

DE BOURGOGNE

Mise en bouteille au domaine

M. BOILLOT-BUTHIAU

PROPRIÉTAIRE-RÉCOLTANT

A MEURSAULT (Côte-d'Or)

FRANCE

Modern wine label showing Jefferson's favorite affordable white Burgundy from the tiny Gouttes d'Or vineyard in the village of Meursault. The Gouttes d'Or vineyard can be found to the left of the word *Meursault* on the label's map.

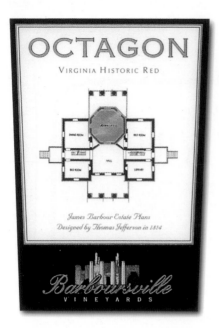

Wine label from the spectacular Barboursville Vineyards, located beside the ruins of a mansion designed by Jefferson for former Virginia governor James Barbour. The Zonin family of Italy now produces tens of thousands of cases of world-class vinifera-based wines at Barboursville, which also features an outstanding Italian restaurant named for Jefferson's favorite architect, Andrea Palladio.

Author (right) with current Monticello winemaker Gabriele Rausse in the restored Monticello vineyards, courtesy of the author.

Jefferson was asking, in essence, for an early form of what we now call estate bottling. And he was correct in his guess about ownership, as he learned when he received the (translated) reply:

January 7, 1788

Son-in-law of M. D'Yquem, and holder of all his possessions, I have the honor of answering the letter which you addressed to him.

I have had drawn off and bottled, with the greatest care, the wine which you desired. I hope you will be happy with it.

Every time that you might have need of it, I should be very happy to receive your order directly and will give it the most careful attention in order that you will be served with all possible perfection. I am sending my letter to Mr. Bondfield to be certain that it is addressed correctly [salutations omitted].

THE COUNT OF LUR-SALUCES[47]

The very next week Bondfield wrote that he had received the wine and was forwarding it by boat rather than wagon.[48]

Jefferson immediately notified his agents at Rouen to be on the lookout for the Château d'Yquem.[49] His agent, however, had never heard of the wine, and so notified Jefferson on February 4, 1788.[50] It was not until March 10 that Jefferson learned his Yquem had gone to a different freight forwarder. Nevertheless, the wine came on through, a M. Monfort writing Jefferson that his five cases of wine were coming down the Seine on a barge from Rouen.[51] On April 23 his cellar list was amended to show "248 bottles Sauterne de Comte de Lur-Saluce. 312/10/28 at Bord. bottle includ."

On November 3, 1788, Jefferson acknowledged receipt of the wine to Bondfield: "The Sauterne sent me by the Marquis de Saluces turns out very fine."[52]

Throughout 1788, Jefferson busily wrote about Bordeaux, sending some to America and trying to obtain more for himself from Bondfield. In February 1788 he resumed his wine correspondence with Alexander

Donald of Virginia, and received the following letter, which also enclosed one from Donald dating back to December 15, 1787:

FROM COLLOW FRÈRES, CARMICHAEL & CO.

Havre, 5 Feby. 1788.

SIR

We are informed by Mr. Donald that you have been kind enough to promise to procure for him a Groce of fine Claret and he has directed us to receive the same, and to pay for it, which we shall do with much pleasure when we know the Cost.[53]

Jefferson's reply has also been preserved:

February 15, 1788

Gentlemen

Mr. Donald's order for wine not leaving me time to have it brought from Bordeaux, I send him two hampers from my own stock, containing 124 bottles, for which I shall charge him only what I paid in Bordeaux. This indeed is dear, being three livres a bottle, but it is Chateau Margau, of the year 1784, bought by myself on the spot and therefore genuine: and Mr. Donald observed to me he would not limit my price.[54]

Two thoughts come to mind upon reading this letter: either Donald was a *really* good friend that Jefferson thought enough of to give him 124 bottles of 1784 Château Margaux out of the 180 he had or, more cynically, Jefferson did not like the wine enough to pay such a high price, and was glad to get it off his hands for what he paid for it.

Jefferson's letter showed an intention to have close dealings with Donald in the future, including in Virginia hams and cider, which he asked Donald to pass through to him surreptitiously as "sea-stores," since they could not be legally imported into France for Jefferson's own use. Both he and his two daughters probably missed those elements of their Virginia diet, or perhaps he wanted to give his French friends a taste of Virginia at its best.[55]

On the same day he wrote Donald:

Paris Feb. 15. 1788.

Dear Sir

You say you had tasted at Mr. Eppes's some wine I had sent him, which was good, but not equal to what you have seen. I have sent to him twice; and what you say would correspond to the first batch. The second was of Chateau Margau of the year 1784 bought by myself on the spot, and a part of the very purchase from which I now send you. It is of the best vintage which has happened in nine years, and is of one of the four vineyards which are admitted to possess exclusively the first reputation.

I may safely assure you therefore that, according to the taste of this country and of England there cannot be a bottle of better Bordeaux produced in France. It cost me at Bordeaux three livres a bottle, ready bottled and packed. This is very dear; but you say you do not limit me in price.

I send you a note of the principal wines of this country, their prices &c. and shall be happy to have you furnished with any of them which you may wish for your own use, only giving me notice enough before hand to have them provided and lodged at Havre or Bordeaux.

Your attention to forward plants, hams, cyder &c. is very obliging. The last two articles being prohibited, must pass as the captain's sea-stores.

TH: JEFFERSON[56]

Unfortunately the "note of the principal wines" has never been found, but several similar ones have, as discussed later. For one of the rare times in his life, Jefferson cited *English* opinion as having some worth on a question of importance, in this case the relative merits of various Bordeaux Châteaux and vintages.

Having severely depleted his stock of claret, Jefferson set out to replenish it, but not with the 1784 Château Margaux he praised to Donald, but with Château Lafite of the same vintage. Just a week later he wrote to Bondfield for it, enclosing a personal letter to the proprietor of Lafite, M. Pichard, president of the Bordeaux Parlement, a quasi-judicial body whose members formed the basis of much of the titled nobility of Bordeaux society, especially as it related to wines.

To Bondfield, Jefferson first mentioned the Yquem, moving on then to the Lafite:

> February 22, 1788
>
> The inclosed letter to the President Pichard is to ask of him 250 bottles of his wine de la Fite of 1784, and to begin a correspondence for receiving my supplies regularly from him. Will you be so good as to supply any defect in the address of the letter before you deliver it?[57]

In his letter to Pichard, Jefferson got right to the point, reminding the Frenchman that he had visited him at Bordeaux:

> Paris, 22d February 1788
>
> Mr. President:
>
> While passing through Bordeaux in May of last year, I had the honor of appearing at your house to pay my respects and to thank you for all the kindnesses you showed to Mr. Barclay, our Consul (in Paris) in the unpleasant affair that happened to him in Bordeaux. In hastening to renew my thanks, I take the liberty of adding thereto the request of a favor.
>
> The excellent wines named de la Fite are of your vineyard. If you have any of the 1784 vintage, and would accommodate me with 250 bottles, I would be infinitely obliged to you.
>
> If it would be possible to have them bottled and packed at your estate, it would doubtless be a guarantee that the wine was genuine, and the drawing-off and so forth well done. If not, Mr. Bondfield will be good enough to have it done, and in any case to receive the wines and have them forwarded to me at Paris.
>
> Would you also be so kind as to permit me Sir, during my stay here, and even after my return to America, to contact you directly each time I have need of wines from your house? It would be for me a valued privilege, and would also give me from time to time occasions to renew to you my assurances of sentiments of respect and attachment.[58]

On March 7, 1788, Bondfield responded, saying he had forwarded Jefferson's letter to Pichard.[59] On April 19 Bondfield forwarded Pichard's answer, in which he regretted having no more 1784 Lafite, but hoped to serve Jefferson better in the future, noting that he did have some "vin de la fitte" of the 1786 vintage, but it was not yet ready to drink.[60]

Bondfield's covering letter suggested to Jefferson that the 1784 wines of Haut-Brion, "belonging to Monsr. Le Cte. De Fumel" were thought at Bordeaux to be second-best after the Lafite of 1784. Bondfield said a few hogsheads were still available if Jefferson was interested.[61] Jefferson was indeed interested:

> Paris May 17, 1788.
>
> The vin de Sauterne safely arrived. . . .
>
> I will also ask the favor of you to purchase for me from Monsieur le Comte de Fumelle 125 bottles of his vin d'Hautbrion of 1784, of which you say he has some hogsheads still, and to forward it by the way of Havre to the care of M. Limozin, or Rouen to the care either of Mr. Garvey or M. Montfort.[62]

Bondfield replied:

> Bordeaux 28 Juin 1788
>
> The 125 Bottles of Haut Brion shall be shipt by the first Ship that sails from hence for Rouen or Havre. This part of the Kingdom ferments but has not committed any Act, restraind by respect for the Cheifs.[63]

Thus did Bondfield note the portents of the French Revolution which was to unfold the next year. He did not recognize certain other ominous portents of a more personal nature, which were eventually to deprive him of his lucrative position as American consul at Bordeaux. In May of 1788, the powerful George Mason wrote to Jefferson that his son John was going into business at Bordeaux with one Joseph Fenwick, who later replaced the faithful Bondfield as consul and became Jefferson's primary supplier of Bordeaux wines.

Mason, in a long letter also expounding the reasons why he was vot-ing *against* the proposed U.S. Constitution, began his letter with the most important thing on his mind, his son:

Virginia, Gunston Hall May 26th. 1788.

Dear Sir

My Son, John Mason, having entered into Partnership with Messrs. Joseph Fenwick & Compy., Merchants in Bourdeaux will sail from Potomack River, about the last of June.

This Letter will be forwarded by my Son, immediately upon his Arrival in Bourdeaux; and he will pay his Respects to you, in Person, as soon as he can conveniently go to Paris. The Firm of the House will, I expect, upon his Arrival in Bourdeaux, be changed to Fenwick Mason & Compy.—Any good Offices which you may do the said House, or any Advice which you may be pleased to give my Son, I shall esteem as the highest Mark of your Friendship.[64]

Mason's son failed to deliver the letter in person, enclosing it instead with one of his own in August:

Bordeaux 23d. Augt. 1788

Sir

Herewith I take the Liberty to cover you a Letter from my Father, Colo. Mason of Virginia, which I had promised myself the pleasure of delivering, but a Want of the Language and Engagements in Business have obliged me to defer my Trip to Paris untill some period during the Winter; when I shall do myself the Honour of paying my Respects to you in person.[65]

Bondfield then made a major blunder: he sent Jefferson's long-awaited Haut-Brion to someone else.

Bordeaux 6 xber 1788

A Shipment I made in August is the cause of your not having receiv'd the two Cases of hautBrion. My Coopers thro inattention Shipt them with a considerable number I then sent off to the Isle of france and which I did not discover of some Days after, too late to have them landed.

The Vintage and a Wedding we have had in our family Capivatived me most of this fall In the Country that in truth I had lost sight of the Comte. The Comte has only four hhds of 1784 on hand. I offer'd him Six hundred Livres for one of them which he refused. I am to have two Cases of the first hhd he draws off. It is urging and too much to pay three Livres in Bordeaux for a Bottle of Bordeaux Wine, but so great has been the demand for that Vintage that the holders obtain that exorbitant price.[66]

On December 14, 1788, Jefferson acknowledged Bondfield's letter, sounding almost relieved that he did not have to pay for the expensive 1784:[67]

Paris Dec. 14. 1788

Sir

Your favor of the 6th. (October) has been duly received. The accident of the wine of Haut-brion is of no consequence, and if you should not already have received or engaged for more to replace it, I can do without it, because I have asked leave to take a trip to America which will occasion my absence from hence during the next summer.

My hope is to sail in April and return in November. You will therefore be so good as to send me the bill for the Sauterne.

This proves a most excellent wine, and seems to have hit the palate of the Americans more than any wine I have ever seen in France.[68]

His account book for February 2, 1789, shows that he paid Mr. Grand, who had paid Bondfield, for the Sauternes. It was the last Bordeaux he ever noted buying in France.

In April 1789 Jefferson had his baggage packed, not realizing it would be October before he got permission and an American ship going his way. Of the 363 bottles of wine he carried to America with him, not a single one was claret. He did take 72 bottles, or 6 full cases, of the Yquem Sauternes they all liked so well.

Thereafter, Jefferson would have to rely throughout his life on American consuls and merchants to supply his Bordeaux, both red and white.

One supplier was Alexander Donald, who had every reason to be grateful and obliging to Jefferson, as he said in his letter of November 1788 to Jefferson at Paris:

Richmond 24th Novemr. 1788

DEAR SIR

The wine you were so kind as to spare me from your own stock is very excellent. It is universally admired, and whenever it is produced (which is only on particular occasions) I am prompted either by my gratitude or vanity to declare from whence it came, and give me leave to add, that we never fail to take a toast to your health.

By the way, I do not believe that you have yet been paid for it. Do me a favour to send me the amount of it, which shall instantly be paid to any person here, or I will order payment of it in London, as is most agreeable to you.[69]

Knowing he would be absent from Paris for at least six months, Jefferson ordered no more fine wines during 1789 except for one lot of Meursault he paid for on April 1.

He also showed a payment by Petit of 150/19 for white "wine of Rochegude" on July 2, less than two weeks before the Bastille was taken. Seventy-two bottles of it were among the baggage he took back to America.

JEFFERSON'S CLASSIFICATION OF THE WINES OF BORDEAUX

For connoisseurs of the esoteric, it is of interest to trace what happened to the Bordeaux wine estates ranked in 1787 by Jefferson against how they fared in the "official" classification recognized in 1855 and thereafter. Many survived more or less as they were, although in Bordeaux an "estate" may not include the same parcels of land in one generation that it did in another. As one family prospers, another declines; lands are sold and others bought; estates are split while others are consolidated by marriages. Readers seeking details of these byzantine transactions, which read like a Russian novel or a good evening soap opera, are referred to several works on Bordeaux minutiae listed in the notes.[70]

The listings which follow trace the ratings of Bordeaux wine estates Jefferson knew from his day to where they stand now. Growths which changed ranking from Jefferson in 1787 to the official classification in 1855 are indicated by their 1855 ranking shown in parentheses after the name.

THE RED WINE ESTATES OF THE MÉDOC

FIRST GROWTHS PER JEFFERSON IN 1787	FIRST GROWTHS AS CLASSIFIED IN 1855
Château Margau	Château Margaux
La Tour de Segur	Château Latour
Hautbrion	Château Haut-Brion
Château de la Fite	Château Lafite-Rothschild

JEFFERSON SECOND GROWTHS	1855 SECOND GROWTHS
Rozan	Château Rausan-Segla
	Château Rauzan-Gassies
Dabbadie	Château Beychevelle (4th)
Lionville	Château Leoville-Las-Cases
	Château Leoville-Poyferre
	Château Leoville-Barton
La Rose	Château Gruaud-Larose
Quirouen	Château Kirwan (3rd)
Durfort	Château Durfort-Vivens

JEFFERSON THIRD GROWTHS	1855 THIRD GROWTHS
Calons	Château Calon-Segur
Brane-Mouton	Château Mouton-Rothschild (2d in 1855, 1st since 1973)
Gassie	Château Rauzan-Gassies (2d)
Arboete	Château Lagrange
Pontette	Château Pontet-Canet (5th)
de Terme	Château Marquis de Terme (4th)
Candale	Château d'Issan

Several proprietors that Jefferson knew were guillotined during the Revolution soon after he left France, including Pichard, M. de Filhot, and the Comte de Fumelle. Others became exiles or émigrés, some returning later with the restoration of the monarchy. What is most interesting in tracing the Médoc classifications is the degree of stability there has been in the groupings of parcels of land under a particular estate name, across two hundred years of wars, revolutions, depressions, and devastating vine-disease epidemics.

MOUTON SUIS, MAIS UNE TROISIEME?
(I AM MOUTON, BUT A THIRD GROWTH?)

Most striking of all rankings given by Jefferson is that of the famous Château Mouton, now Mouton-Rothschild, which he said was judged a third growth based on what it sold for in 1787. In 1855, shortly after banker James Rothschild, ancestor of the late Baron Philippe, bought it, the estate was ranked a second growth. Thinking it worth better, Baron Rothschild mounted a campaign to have it elevated to a first. Taking the motto "premier ne puis, Second ne daigne, Mouton suis" ("Can't be first, won't deign to be second, I am Mouton"), Rothschild at last succeeded, in 1973, an almost superhuman feat. Never during the entire campaign did I hear any-one mention that in Jefferson's compiling of the rankings in 1787 Château Mouton was only a third growth, not a second.

There have long been movements to amend the 1855 classification to fit current market realities, since the old classing is obviously outdated. A few châteaux on it no longer even exist; others no longer make wine; still others have dramatically risen, while several have precipitously declined.[71] Numerous proposals for change have been made, but resistance has been stronger than if the French were amending their Constitution.[72]

As much has changed in the realm of Bordeaux whites since Jefferson's time as it has for the reds. Graves, for example, has been much encroached upon by the suburbs of Bordeaux. Also, since it is now known almost equally for its red wines and its whites, the whites are less prominent and have an image at least in the U.S. that is less clear than it once was.

Edmund Penning-Rowsell said that the Pontac family owned so many properties and parcels that it is very difficult to tell at this late date just which estate was referred to when someone talked of "Pontac" in the eighteenth century. Often anything sold under that name was passed off by distributors as white Haut-Brion. Jefferson of course visited Haut-Brion, as well as a different estate he called Pontac, belonging to a M. Lamont, and contrasted the quality of their different soils. Most books say that the property purchased by Lamont from Pontac was the white-wine portion of Haut-Brion, so perhaps that is what Jefferson saw.

Sauternes is still more interesting. Jefferson only mentions four estates there, but all are still among the top Sauternes today. Surprising is the allegation that the wine we know today as Sauternes, a golden, lusciously sweet dessert wine with overtones of honey, allegedly did not exist in Jefferson's time. The natural process known as "noble rot," or botrytis, which attacks and shrivels the grapes, dehydrating them and intensifying their aromas and sugar levels, is alleged by many not to have been used in Jefferson's time. The process was supposedly brought there from Germany, after Jefferson died, where it makes the great late-picked Riesling wines. The process is now highly successful all over the modern wine world, including California, New York, Australia, and even the Okanagan Valley of British Columbia, using every wine grape from Chardonnay to Pinot Blanc, and not just the Semillons and Sauvignons of Sauternes. Sauvignon Blanc grapes at the Monticello Cellars winery in the Napa Valley have made an outstanding Sauternes-like wine, called "M." Probably the best in America is Dolce.

In Bordeaux Château d'Yquem now makes a dry wine called Château "Y," which might taste more like Jefferson's version, if it really was not botrytised. But not all experts agree. Richard Olney, who "wrote the book" on Yquem, argued strongly that Yquem in Jefferson's time *was* botrytised, and thus tasted much as it does today (*Yquem* 1985, pp. 24, 45–47, 119). Olney's book on Yquem is beautifully illustrated and one of the most interesting consulted in this entire Jefferson and wine project. It was written before the Lur-Saluces family, which had owned Yquem since Jefferson's time, finally lost it to corporate interests in the 1990s.

In his classification of 1787 Sauternes, Jefferson selected without exception those estates that endured. His favorite, Yquem, is still by acclamation the greatest white of Bordeaux, and perhaps of the world. It is the only Bordeaux of any kind to have its own separate category first "great" growth, as opposed to a mere first growth, with which even Lafite and Mouton have to content themselves. If Jefferson had chosen a substitute, as most of us Sauternes lovers now have to do because of the staggering prices of Yquem, he could well have chosen what he called the Cru du Roy and we call Château Suduiraut, a hard name to pronounce in English, but a beautiful wine. The old name used by Jefferson still appears on the label, in small letters and in parentheses. The name does not mean it once belonged to the king of France, however much it sounds like that. The du Roys were simply one of the families who once owned the estate.

The main change from Jefferson's nomenclature is that the names of other towns near Sauternes, such as Preignac, have largely been absorbed into Sauternes, by which name all are now entitled to call themselves on labels. Only Barsac châteaux, which still have a distinctive character, still bottle most of their wines as Barsac rather than Sauternes. Two of the best Barsacs, Filhot and Coutet, were among the handful mentioned by Jefferson, and are still excellent and well known today.

SAUTERNES ESTATES (SWEET WHITE WINES)

PER JEFFERSON IN 1787[73]	CURRENT NAME, CLASSIFICATION
1. Diquem, Yquem de Fillotte	Château d'Yquem (1st great)
	Château Filhot (2d)
2. President du Roy	Château Suduiraut (1st)
3. Pichard	Château Coutet (1st)

GRAVES ESTATES (DRY WHITE WINES)

1. Pontac	Château Haut-Brion
	or
	Château Pontac (a principal growth, 1959)
2. St. Brise	Château Saint-Bris (a principal growth)
3. De Carbonius	Château Carbonnieux (a classified growth)

MIXING WINE AND POLITICS:
THE "AFFAIRE MOUSTIER"

Jefferson did not wait long after his return to Paris to put his new wine knowledge to practical use. The newly named French minister to the United States, the Count de Moustier, was known to be a wine lover. Jefferson wanted to give him a good first impression of Americans and to help him make a good impression himself. Wine seemed the perfect vehicle for both, so Jefferson wrote him a long letter detailing his experience with the Muscat wines of Frontignan, which he thought would please American palates:

Paris July 24, 1787

The bearer brings you a bottle of the Frontignan wine of which I spoke to
you. It has the etiquette [label] of Monsieur Lambert, the person who makes
it, with whom I made acquaintance and passed some hours in his house. He is
a good and sensible physician, depending more on the productions of his vineyard than of his profession.

There are made at Frontignan 600 peices of this wine, of which 260 are
bought by two particular merchants so that there remain 240 peices only for
market. Yet they export from Cette (about half a league from Frontignan)
30,000 peices of wine under that name.

The only persons who raise the genuine Frontignan of the first quality
are Madame de Soubeinan 200 peices, M. Reboulle 90., M. Lambert médecin,
60., M. Thomas 50., M. Argilliers 50., M. Audibert 45., and some other small
proprietors.

If any of these persons are among your acquaintance you may be sure
of genuine wine from them; if they are not, I will ensure it from Lambert, of
whose I send you a specimen. I bought it in his house. He delivers it bottled at
24s the bottle included, on the spot. With transportation and duties on the road
it costs me here 40s. but he will send it for you to Bourdeaux.[74]

Moustier, receiving the letter the same day, immediately replied:

I know no one among the proprietors of the wines of Frontignan; thus I
trust myself entirely to you, Sir, to obtain it. I suppose that it will not be altered

in crossing the sea and that it will bear the climate of America. It would be preferable I think to make a trial of 60 bottles; if it is successful both as to transportation and as to the welcome given it, I shall take thereafter as much of it as I can
procure.

THE COUNT OF MOUSTIER[75]

Jefferson received in the meantime an amusing letter from
Dr. Lambert, wherein he apologized for not realizing that Jefferson was
the American minister and not just an anonymous traveller. Excusing the
excessive frankness of his comments while Jefferson visited him, Lambert
offered to do anything he possibly could to "make it up" to the minister.[76]
Jefferson was pleased by the whole proceeding, since his purpose in travelling incognito was to receive unguarded comments such as Lambert's.

Lambert continued in his most Cartesian French that he had filled
"with the most severe exactitude" the wine order Jefferson had given him,
just before telling Lambert his real name and title. Lambert explained
that he had sent 250 bottles of his best white Muscat of Frontignan and
33 bottles of his best red, both of which Jefferson had personally selected
after tasting in Lambert's cellars.

Lambert described the wines he was sending as "extremely liquorous,"
i.e., naturally. Noting proudly that a wine so *perfumed* as this was rarely
produced, Lambert suggested Jefferson keep it in his cellar and let it age.
Lambert concluded by saying that if Jefferson believed in his good faith
and competence, and would in future years honor him with orders for his
wine, Lambert would gladly comply. He asked only that Jefferson let him
know by September or October of each year how much wine he wanted
so he could reserve it for him. The letter is a tour de force of an enthusiastic merchant wooing a rich customer. Jefferson replied July 6 in some
of his most proper French, which he had probably been speaking almost
exclusively during his incognito trip through the countryside, away from
his circle of American friends. He had received the 283 bottles and "found
in them all the good qualities for which your wines are so reknowned;
and I am perfectly content with them."[77] For those familiar with French,
at whatever level, Jefferson's letter is a classic example of just how well he

handled himself in that language, and it's worth checking out that volume of his *Papers* from a library.

Happily for Dr. Lambert, his dealings with Jefferson did not end there. As he told Jefferson in a letter from Frontignan on October 10, 1787, his banker, Mr. Cabanis, had called on Jefferson to collect the bill for his wines. While there, Jefferson had heaped praise on Lambert's wines, for which Lambert profusely thanked Jefferson. He also informed Jefferson of the bad quality of the 1787 vintage in Frontignan.[78] Jefferson's reply to Lambert, translated from his French in its pertinent parts, was as follows:

> at Paris this 13 November 1787
>
> The person of whom Mr. Cabanis spoke to you on the subject of your wine was The Count of Moustier, who has left for America, where he has been named Minister Plenipotentiary of your court at our Congress. I had proposed to him to try to introduce a taste for your wine in America. He charged me to ask you for a hundred bottles of the same vintage as mine, of which I furnished him a sample.
>
> TH: JEFFERSON.[79]

In the interim, Moustier wrote to Jefferson requesting one hundred bottles of Lambert's Frontignan to take to America on October 9, the evening before he was to sail to America from the port of Brest. Noting it was for the American ladies in particular that he wanted these wines, Moustier asked Jefferson to have them sent on to him in America.

Despite Jefferson's attempts to make things smooth for the new French minister to the U.S., it was not to be. When Moustier went to America, he took with him his sister-in-law, Jefferson's friend Madame de Bréhan. Apparently they thought that Americans were as liberal in their sexual mores as in their politics, and they carried on an affair in the old French fashion, to the shock and chagrin of the Americans. Both Jay and Madison so notified Jefferson, who was mortified at the conduct of his protégés.[80]

Nor was that all. Moustier did not appreciate either American food or manners, especially the incessant toasting. It was just too different from what he was used to. He had thought all Americans were going to be like Jefferson; Madame de Bréhan said as much. In what later became known as the "affaire Moustier," the French minister openly complained about the food and wine served to him by Alexander Hamilton. Under the flimsy pretext of a stomach disorder, he brought his own cook to Hamilton's house to prepare Moustier a separate dinner rather than eat Hamilton's food. Hamilton later said angrily that Moustier "quarreled with the eatables."[81]

It was one of those trivial incidents that tend to build either a lasting friendship or a lasting enmity, entangling others who were not even present. Moustier, sent to the U.S. as a friend of Jefferson, even though they barely knew each other, became the first cause for conflict between Hamilton and Jefferson, who at that time had never even met. Obnoxious to the end, Moustier avoided being officially recalled even when Washington gave him "leave" to return to France. He never saw Jefferson again, missing him because he was en route to his new post in Prussia as Jefferson returned to America. But the damage was done. Hamilton had gotten a bad first impression of Jefferson as a friend of snobs and libertines, an impression never wholly dissipated. He was ready to dislike Jefferson before he even met him.

The famous hundred bottles of Dr. Lambert's Muscat of Frontignan were not an unqualified success with the American ladies either. But Jefferson still believed in them. In 1791 he wrote to Lambert from the U.S. requesting more of his wines for George Washington,[82] obviously believing the wine was good, and perhaps deciding it was a "man's" wine after all, whatever that is.

In his reply, dated February 10, 1791, Lambert mentioned a visit he had made to Jefferson's house in Paris in 1788. Choosing his words carefully, Lambert said that he hoped General Washington would like his wines, and that he had taken into account in selecting them "the taste of your country as de Moustier made it known to me," in particular that he had sent this time wines which were less liquorous and sweet. Lambert closed with effusive expressions of friendship and noted that there were 60 bottles for Jefferson and 120 for Washington as he had requested, with their initials marked on the cases.[83]

Jefferson Misses Home Cooking

While stocking his cellar with French wines and having his cook trained in French cuisine, Jefferson still missed the food of Virginia. In September of 1787, he wrote Donald:

> I have taken the liberty of desiring Colo. N. Lewis of Albemarle to send a dozen or two of hams, which the captain who brings them must pretend to be a part of his private stores, or they will be seised.
>
> I have it in contemplation to write to Mr. Eppes for some of a particular kind of cyder which he makes, and in like manner to trouble you with it.[84]

In November of 1788, Jefferson learned the fate of his hams from Donald:

> Last winter Colo. N. Lewis sent down here (Richmond) two large cases of hams. I took the first opportunity of forwarding the whole to Mr. Nickolls of Portsmouth and requested him to forward them, but he has not been able to prevail on any of the Captains to take the hams. They all alledged that their ships would be liable to seizure if they had taken them, as the importation of all hams they say is prohibited in France.[85]

This shipment may well have been especially for his daughter Maria, who had not wanted to come to France, and was very homesick for everything in Virginia, especially the Eppes family. She later married their son Jack.

It is likely that Jefferson himself sorely missed these Virginia specialties too. While in the White House he used to have Mrs. Lewis's hams and his own cider brought specially to Washington to serve at his White House table. In his retirement years he called Virginia cider his main "table drink," and the closest thing to Champagne he had ever tasted. To my knowledge he never mentioned either French beer or cider, only Virginia's.

Ironically, it was the German prisoners of war he had known in the Revolution who reminded him of home the most. Nor had he seen the last of them.

Jefferson Tours and Tastes in the Vineyards of the Rhine, the Mosel, and Champagne

(1788–1789)

Jefferson's interests in Paris were not confined to French wines and cuisine. German wines, those he had chosen to drink on his sea voyage over to France, were not far away. And he had friends in the German wine country. Among his favorite people during the American Revolution were his supposed enemies, the Hessian mercenaries hired by George III to suppress his rebellious colonists. Some Hessians taken prisoner early in the war had been interned by Governor Patrick Henry near Charlottesville at Jefferson's request. One group, under General Riedesel and his aide-de-camp Baron Geismar, a major, stayed at Colle, Philip Mazzei's farm near Monticello.

The Germans, most of them officers, were not at all what one would expect "mercenaries" to be like. Due to the nearly feudal system then existing in the small princedoms which made up Germany, younger sons of noble families often had to become professional soldiers to support themselves. Their rulers, strapped for cash, could "rent" them out to whomever they liked. The rules of eighteenth-century warfare were considerably more sporting than now, so it was also a way for young officers to travel, gain adventure, and prove themselves in the field.

Many of the officers were educated and well read. Several were musical and played chamber music with the Jeffersons at Monticello. Some knew English and several had been educated at French schools. Jefferson avoided accusations of fraternizing with the enemy by asking the Virginia legislature and Continental Congress to co-opt these talented foreign officers by offering them land and cash to desert the English and join the American cause. Some did, but not enough to influence the outcome. Most came from Hesse, where the great wine country known as Rhinehesse is located, but there is no specific mention of any German wines accompanying them to Monticello. They were, after all, prisoners of war, and during that time Virginia's normally ample supplies of Hock and other German wines were scarce. From what Jefferson said while in Europe, however, wine was often discussed, German wines in particular.

As early as March 1785, while recovering from his "seasoning" of illness, Jefferson sought to revive his friendship with Major Geismar:

Paris Mar. 3. 1785.

Dear Sir

An unfortunate change in my domestic situation by the loss of a tender connection who joined me in esteeming you, occasioned me to wish a change of scene and to accept an appointment which brought me to this place and will keep me here some time. Since your departure from America I have been altogether uninformed of your subsequent history.

A vague report of your death which was never so authenticated as to command belief, but which has not been authentically contradicted, has particularly occasioned me to wish the pleasure of a line from yourself.[1]

From Geismar's reply it was apparent he was still a strong friend of Jefferson and America:

Hanau this 28 March 1785

I was most flattered by your remembering me My Dear Friend. I knew from the Gazettes that there was in Paris a Minister from the United States who bore your name, but did not know it was you.

I must admit that I was so proud as to believe, and I was not wrong, that if it was you, you would send a word to the one to whom you showed so much friendship and goodness in America. I hope you know how sincerely I join in the loss you have suffered. I have every reason to believe that she was my friend as well, and miss her as such.

But you are silent about my little lady [Martha]. It will soon be time that I exercise my rights. Is she with you, or have you left her in Virginia?

I was astonished that you had not heard from me, since I wrote to you from New York and again after arriving here. I thought you perhaps were too busy with politics to spend time over here with those who made so much trouble for you over there.

At present I dare say that I was always a great Republican, and especially a good American, although my situation there prevented me from saying it. If ever the Montgolfiere [hot-air balloon] is perfected to permit a voyage to the other part of the world, I shall descend upon Monticello. But I will have nothing more to do with the Atlantic Ocean.

In our present situation we need neither to get us together. A carriage and post horses are better. My purse, my dear friend, does not allow me a trip to Paris at this time, and since you are in Europe, I imagine you would like to see a part of Germany. Come spend some time with us. We will travel the best parts of Germany.

GEISMAR MAJOR[2]

Pleased as he must have been at this offer, and at a friendship renewed, especially with one of the few men in Europe who had been a friend of his wife, Jefferson did not contact Geismar again for three years. But when the opportunity to tour the Rhine did present itself, Jefferson did not hesitate.

A Tasting Tour of the Rhine and Mosel in 1788

In early 1788 Jefferson got the chance to make his third major European tour, this time for business and with no mixed motives—at least on the way out. His trip back through the Rhineland was another story. The occasion of his trip was the departure of Adams from London for the U.S. to become vice president. At the time, the young United States was still deep in debt from the Revolutionary War. Its major creditors, France and Holland, doubted the ability of the new nation to repay its loans. The United States was what we would call a third world nation, albeit a promising one.

In the hardest times of the Revolution it was Franklin and Adams who always somehow convinced the French or the bankers of Holland to finance them a little longer. Adams, at The Hague, had the necessary connections and a special skill for that sort of thing. Jefferson found such business "the most disagreeable to me of all others, and for which I am the most unfit person living. I do not understand bargaining, nor possess the dexterity requisite for that purpose."[3]

When Jefferson received notice from Abigail that John Adams had to go to The Hague, Jefferson saw his last chance to get Adams's help in obtaining new credit from the Dutch to pay America's war debts. Writing that "[o]ur [financial] affairs at Amsterdam press on my mind like a mountain," Jefferson set out in haste to the Netherlands to meet Adams and have a joint try at getting a new extension of credit.[4] Neither man had time to get authorization from Congress to undertake the mission, and had to trust Congress to ratify their actions later.

On March 4, 1788, Jefferson left Paris, again incognito, but this time taking his faithful number-two servant, Espagnol. The trip up, via Brussels, was "little entertaining." The weather was miserable: raining, snowing, and sleeting. Their business venture, however, was successful, and by

March 13, the Dutch bankers had agreed to finance the U.S. for the next two years.[5]

Relieved, Jefferson gave himself a little vacation. From Amsterdam he wrote to the painter Trumbull in London:

> I wrote you a line just as I was taking wing from Paris to this place. I expected to
> have staid there a week, & have been here three already. I intend to make my return
> somewhat circuitous, in order to see what I have not yet seen. This renders the
> moment of my arrival in Paris uncertain.[6]

In 1786 Trumbull had made a trip down the Rhine and written Jefferson glowing letters about it. He had visited the cellars and vineyards of Champagne, saying, "At Epernay I saw one of the great wine cellars and tasted the finest wine I ever saw."[7] These remarks were not lost on Jefferson. Before leaving Amsterdam he wrote Geismar to expect him. He bought ten maps of the Rhine and spent two weeks touring it. He travelled along the river in his carriage, renting post horses as he had in southern France. To Geismar he made it clear this was no business trip:

> Amsterdam Mar. 18. 1788.
> Having been called hither, my dear friend, by business, and being some-
> what at liberty as to my return, I propose to go along the Rhine as far as
> Strasburg before I turn off to Paris. I shall be at Frankfort probably between the
> 1st. and 5th. of April. If your residence is still at Hanau, I know you will meet
> me at Frankfort. I shall be at the Rottinhouse tavern.
> TH: JEFFERSON[8]

Geismar answered Jefferson on the sixteenth that he would indeed meet him at the "Red House," forwarding a note to the owner to send for him by courier when Jefferson arrived.[9] Nor was the Rhineland the only wineland he planned to visit. As he said in a letter to Short:

> Unless I find there [at Strasburg] any thing from you which may call me to Paris
> directly, I shall probably go a little circuitously, perhaps by the way of Reims in
> Champagne, so that I am unable to say exactly when I shall be at Paris.[10]

He wrote few letters during this voyage, so it is worth noting one other observation he made to Short in this one, especially since my own paternal ancestors came from there:

> The neighborhood of this place is that which has been to us a second mother country. It is from the palatinate on this part of the Rhine that those swarms of Germans have gone who, next to the descendants of the English, form the greatest body of our people.
>
> I have been continually amused by seeing here the origin of whatever is not English among us. I have fancied myself often in the upper parts of Maryland and Pennsylvania.[11]

Jefferson's account book has few wine entries for this trip, perhaps because Geismar was buying, but does record that he spent 2/15 for a hundred vine cuttings at Hocheim on April 9, and the same for fifty vines at Rudesheim on April 11. He visited vineyards from Erbach to Hattenheim, in the heart of the Rheingau. He and Geismar engaged Arnaud, a French-speaking *valet de place*, to guide them through the vineyards.

Making a Rhine tour was somewhat surprising for Jefferson. He disliked everything Gothic, and had little to say for the castles and cathedrals of Germany. He saw the whole place as "romantic and ruinous." Had it not been for Geismar and Trumbull, he would not have gone. Once there, the subjects that interested Jefferson most were the vineyards and the wines. As will be seen from his journals, he took great and detailed interest in how they were made.[12] In Jefferson's time, as in ours, the white wines of Germany were the basis of its reputation.

The wines he took greatest interest in were the Mosels, which he discussed in detail, even classifying them by villages, vineyards, and proprietors. His discussion of Mosels has a sort of textbook quality to it, probably because he did not get to visit the vineyards; the weather when he reached Koblentz was simply too foul. As he later told Rutledge and Shippen, however, he did taste and discuss many of them with knowledgeable experts while there. Based on later comments, a case could be made that Jefferson liked the Mosels better than the Rhines. In a letter to a Philadelphia wine merchant, quoted in full in the succeeding chapter, he called one Mosel, Brauneberg, "a *really* good wine."

There have always been trends and fads in wine, and the status of Brauneberg is a classic example. Jefferson was adamant that the wines of that village were the best of all the Mosel, better than Wehlen, Bernkastel, Piesport, Zelting, or others now considered superior. Jefferson was no eccentric, however. In 1806 Brauneberg *was* classed first of all Mosel vineyards. His opinion agreed with the prevalent one among experts until the nineteenth century, when Brauneberg began to fall from favor. Since its land and sun exposure have not changed, this swing of opinion must be due to human factors, whether a change in work habits or quality of plantings in the different villages, or perhaps all those factors. In any event Brauneberg, a rich and soft wine as Mosels go, is still fine, and deserves to be better known in the U.S. today.[13]

Jefferson did touch upon the basic truth of winemaking in that difficult region: when the vines don't get enough sun, the wine is too acidic. The finest wines are nearly always the ones which grow on the north hillsides of the river facing south or southwest. The vineyards cited by Jefferson as best all meet this definition. Recognizable phonetically with their eighteenth-century spellings, the wine villages of the Rhine and Mosel described by Jefferson as great then are basically the same ones so recognized today.

Jefferson's appetite for colorful and specific detail was also at work. He noted what flowers bloomed, what foods people ate, how much workers were paid, what everything cost. Without his little chorus of side comments, his discussions of wines would be off-key and out of context. Here then, excerpted concisely but without removal of all his asides about what the local pigs and birds look like, is Jefferson's Rhine journal.[14]

March 30. (1788).

After passing Utrecht, the hills northeast of the Rhine come into view.

The Rhine is here about three hundred yards wide. The Rhine and Waal are crossed on vibrating boats, the rope supported by a line of seven little barks.

The view from the hill at Cress is sublime. It commands the Waal, and extends far up the Rhine.

The chateau here is pretended to have lodged Julius Caesar. This is giving it an antiquity of at least eighteen centuries, which must be apocryphal.

April 1st. The transition from ease and opulence to extreme poverty is remarkable on crossing the line between the Dutch and Prussian territories. The soil and climate are the same; the governments alone differ. With the poverty, the fear also of slaves is visible in the faces of the Prussian subjects.

There are no chateaux, nor houses that bespeak the existence even of a middle class. Universal and equal poverty overspreads the whole. In the villages, too, which seem to be falling down, the overproportion of women is evident. The cultivators seem to live on their farms. The farm-houses are of mud, the better sort of brick; all covered over with thatch.

April 2nd. Passed the Rhine at *Essenberg*. It is there about a quarter of a mile wide, or five hundred yards. It is crossed in a scow with sails.

At Cologne, where he crossed the Rhine on a pendulum boat again, Jefferson the gourmet stopped to describe the still-famous ham of Westphalia, rivaled only by that of his native Virginia:

I observe the hog of this country (Westphalia), of which the celebrated ham is made, is tall, gaunt, and with heavy lop ears. Their principal food is acorns. The pork is smoked in a room which has no chimney. Well-informed people here tell me there is no other part of the world where the bacon is smoked. They do not know that we do it. They find that the small hog makes the sweetest meat.

At Cologne, Jefferson at last reached the wine country:

Here the vines begin, and it is the most northern spot on earth on which wine is made. Their first grapes came from Orleans, since that from Alsace, Champagne, etc. It is thirty-two years only since the first vines were sent from Cassel, near Mayence [Mainz] to the Cape of Good Hope, of which the Cape wine is now made. Afterwards, new supplies were sent from the same quarter. That I suppose is the most southern spot on the globe where wine is made, and it is singular that the same wine should have furnished two wines as much opposed to each other in quality as in situation.

The grape from the city of Orleans, in the Loire Valley of western France, was possibly the Chenin Blanc, from which today's great Loire Valley whites are made, including, for example, Vouvray, Coteaux du Layon, Quarts de Chaume, and Savennières. It was also a white grape which thrived well in South Africa, there known as Steen. Whether the *first* vines were thus Chenin Blancs, Pinot Gris, or perhaps others which Jefferson discussed later is subject to dispute.

When Jefferson noted how opposite "Cape" wines then were from German wines, he was perfectly correct. The difference, however, was not in the climates but in the winemaking techniques. German wines were natural wines, light gold in color, with an alcohol content of about 10 percent. In South Africa wines were then made largely for export to England and the Empire, mainly as fortified dessert wines, more akin to Port or Sherry, bearing nearer 20 percent alcohol due to the addition of brandy. These wines, the best known of which was Constantia, were from medium amber to deep brown, and thus in no way resembled the light-gold Rieslings of Germany.

Some say that the powerful Sercial of Madeira is made from Riesling as well, and the same is possible in the case of another Jefferson favorite from his White House years: Pedro Ximénez. That wine, a sweet deep brown dessert wine from southern Spain, is said likewise to be from Riesling vines brought to Spain by a German soldier name Pieter Siemens, hence "Pedro Ximénez."

On April 4, passing from Cologne to Koblenz, Jefferson observed:

> The hills are generally excessively steep, a great proportion of them barren; the rest in vines principally. In the plains, though rich, I observed they dung their vines plentifully; and it is observed here, as elsewhere, that the plains yield much wine, but bad. The good is furnished from the hills.

At Koblenz he obtained information about the wines of the Mosel:

> *Coblentz.* The Wildman ou l'Homme sauvage. A very good tavern. The tavern keeper furnished me with the Carte des postes d'Allemagne [map of German post

roads]. He accompanied me to a gentleman well acquainted with the vineyards and wines of the Moselle, about which I wished to inform myself.

Here call for Moselle wine, and particularly that of Brownberg and of the Grand Chambellan's crop of 1783 that you may be acquainted with the best quality of Moselle wine.

Remarkeably fine bread here, particularly the roll for breakfast, from which the Philadelphians derive what they call the French roll, which does not exist in France, but has been carried over by the Germans.

Stop on the road at the village of Rudesheim, and the Abbaye of Johansberg to examine their vineyards and wines. The latter is the best made on the Rhine without comparison, and is about double the price of the oldest Hoch. That of the year 1775 is the best.

On April 5 Jefferson passed on from Koblenz to Nassau, noting that the country "abounds with slate," as the best Mosel wine country does today. Even now, each autumn, baskets of slate are hauled by hand up steep hillsides and laid around the vines to reflect the heat of the sun onto the vines in this coolest of wine-growing regions.

Jefferson surveyed the best Mosels and their prices in various currencies. It is difficult to translate another century's currency values into our own, particularly from an age of independent feudal domains and frequent wars, as Germany was in Jefferson's time. Under any standard, however, these were expensive wines and, as always, Jefferson insisted on the best:

The best Moselle wines are made about fifteen leagues [45 miles] from hence, in an excessively mountainous country.

1. The first quality (without any comparison) is that made on the mountain of Brownberg (Brauneberg) adjoining to the village of Dusmond. The last fine year was 1783, which sells now at Fifty louis the foudre, which contains six aumes of one hundred and seventy bottles each, equal to about one thousand, one hundred and ten bottles.

2. Vialen (Wehlen) is the second quality, and sells new at one hundred and twenty ecus the foudre.

3. Crach-Bispost (Graach-Piesport) is the third and sells for about one hundred and five ecus. I compared Crach of 1783 with Baron Burresheim's [Brauneberg] of the same year. The latter is quite clear of acid, stronger, and very sensibly the best.

4. Selting [Zelting], which sells at one hundred ecus.

5. Kous-Berncastle [now Bernkastel], the fifth quality, sells at eighty or ninety.

After this, there is a gradation of qualities down to thirty ecus. These wines must be five or six years old before they are quite ripe for drinking. One thousand plants yield a foudre of wine a year in the most plentiful vineyards. In other vineyards, it will take two thousand or two thousand and five hundred plants to yield a foudre.

The red wines of this country are very indifferent, and will not keep. The Moselle is here from one hundred to two hundred yards wide; the Rhine three hundred to four hundred.

Leaving the Mosel, Jefferson passed on up the Rhine, taking the road by Wiesbaden and Hochheim to Frankfurt:

April 7, 1788. *Frankfort.*

The stork, or crane, is very commonly tame here. It is a miserable, dirty, ill-looking bird. The Lutheran is the reigning religion here, and is equally intolerant to the Catholic and Calvinist.

Passing to Geismar's Hanau, Jefferson noted the lot of the Hessians:

April 8th.

In Frankfort all is life, bustle, and motion; in Hanau the silence and quiet of the mansions of the dead. Nobody is seen moving in the streets; every door is shut; no sound of the saw, the hammer, or other utensil of industry. The drum and fife are all that is heard. The streets are cleaner than a German floor, because nobody passes them.[15]

Thanks to Trumbull, Jefferson knew where to stay in Frankfurt, which was said to have the finest hotels in Germany, and the Red House was said to have the best wine list of any hotel in Frankfurt, and in English, too.

As he told Short, he stayed four days tasting what English wine writer George Saintsbury called "senior" Hocks:

April 9, 1788

My old friend the Baron de Geismar met me here and has been my Cicerone. Yesterday we made an excursion up the Maine to Hanau. Tomorrow we shall go to the vineyards of Hocheim, and perhaps to Rudesheim and Johannesberg, where the most celebrated wines are made.[16]

In his Travelling Notes he elaborated:

The Wine List At The Red-House Hotel

Frankfurt. The Rothen house, or Red House chez Monsr. Dick. The son of the Tavern keeper speaks English and French, has resided some time in London, is sensible and obliging. Messrs. Dick pere et fils, are great wine merchants. Their cellar is worth seeing. You may taste at their tavern genuine Hoch, and of the oldest.

April 10th. Frankfort. Hocheim. Mayence.

We cross the Rhine at Mayence on a bridge one thousand eight hundred and forty feet long, supported by forty-seven boats. It is not in a direct line, but curved up against the stream; which may strengthen it.

In the winter the bridge is taken away entirely, on account of the ice. And then everything passes on the ice, through the whole winter.

April 11th. Mayence. Rudesheim. Johansberg. Markebronn. In a small but dull kind of batteau, with two hands rowing with a kind of large paddle, and a square sail, but scarcely a breath of wind, we went down the river at the rate of five miles an hour, making it three and a half hours to Rudesheim.

The Rhine yields salmon, carp, pike, and perch, and the little rivers running into it yield speckled trout. The plains from Maintz to Rudesheim are good and in corn; the hills mostly in vines.

Though they begin to make wine, as has been said, at Cologne, and continue it up the river indefinitely, yet it is only from Rudesheim to Hocheim that wines of the very first quality are made. The river happens there to run due east and west, so as to give its hills on that side a southern aspect. And even in this

canton, it is only Hocheim, Johansberg, and Rudesheim, that are considered as
of the very first quality.

Johansberg is a little mountain (berg signifies mountain), whereon is a reli-
gious house, about fifteen miles below Mayence, and near the village of
Vingel [Winkel]. It has a southern aspect. This wine used to be but on a par with
Hocheim and Rudesheim; but the place having come to the Bishop of Fulda,
he improved its culture so as to render it stronger; and since the year 1775, it sells
at double the price of the other two. It has none of the acid of the Hocheim and
other Rhenish wines. There are about sixty tuns made in a good year, which sell,
as soon as of a drinkable age, at one thousand franks each. The tun here contains
seven and a half aumes of one hundred and seventy bottles each.

Rudesheim is a village of about eighteen or twenty miles below Mayence.
Its fine wines are made on the hills about a mile below the village, which look
to the south, and on the middle and lower parts of them. They are terraced
[and] excessively steep.

The vignerons of Rudesheim dung their wines about once in five or six
years, putting a one-horse tumbrel load of dung on every twelve feet square.
One thousand plants yield about four aumes in a good year.

These wines begin to be drinkable at about five years old. The proprietors
sell them old or young, according to the prices offered, and according to their
own want of money. There is always a little difference between different casks,
and therefore when you choose and buy a single cask, you pay three, four, five or
six hundred florins for it. They are not at all acid, and to my taste much preferable to Hocheim, though but of the same price.

Hocheim is a village about three miles above Mayence, on the Maine,
where it empties into the Rhine. The spot whereon the good wine is made is the
hillside from the church down to the plain, a gentle slope of about a quarter of
a mile wide, and extending half a mile towards Mayence. It is of southwestern
aspect.

Dick, keeper of the Rothen-house tavern at Frankfort, a great wine merchant, who has between three and four hundred tuns of wine in his cellars, tells
me that Hocheim of the year 1783 sold, as soon as it was made, at ninety florins
the aume, Rudesheim of the same year, as soon as made, at one hundred and
fifteen florins, and Markebronn seventy florins.

But a peasant of Hocheim tells me that the best crops of Hocheim in the good years, when sold new, sell but for about thirty-two or thirty-three florins the aume; but that it is only the poorer proprietors who sell new.

Markebronn (bronn signifies a spring, and is probably of affinity with the Scotch word, burn) is a little canton in the same range of hills, adjoining to the village of Hagenheim, about three miles above Johansberg, subject to the elector of Mayence. It is a sloping hillside of southern aspect, mulatto, poor, and mixed with some stone. This yields wine of the second quality.

April 12th. Mayence [Mainz]. Oppenheim. Worms. Manheim. On the road between Mayence and Oppenheim are three cantons, which are also esteemed as yielding wines of the second quality. These are Laudenheim, Bodenheim, and Nierstein.

Bodenheim is a village nine miles, and Nierstein another about ten or eleven miles from Mayence. Here, too, the river is northeast and southwest, so as to give the hills between these villages a southeast aspect; and at Nierstein, a valley making off, brings the face of the hill round to the south.

With respect to the grapes in this country, there are three kinds in use for making white wine (for I take no notice of the red wines, as being absolutely worthless).

The Klemperien, of which the inferior qualities of Rhenish wines are made, and is cultivated because of its hardiness.

2. The Rhysslin (Riesling) grape, which grows only from Hocheim down to Rudesheim. This is small and delicate, and therefore succeeds only in this chosen spot. Even at Rudesheim it yields a fine wine only in the little spot called Hinder House.

3. The mass of good wines made at Rudesheim, below the village, being of the third kind of grape, which is called the *Orleans* grape.

The Great Tun of Heidelberg: Over 280,000 Bottles of Wine in a Single Cask

April 14th.

Heidelberg is on the Neckar just where it issues from the Bergstrasse mountains, occupying the first skirt of plain which it forms. The château is up the hill a considerable height. This château is the most noble ruin I have ever seen, having been reduced to that state by the French in the time of Louis XIV., 1693. Nothing remains under cover but the chapel.

The situation is romantic and pleasing beyond expression. It is on a great scale much like the situation of Petrarch's château, at Vaucluse, on a small one. The climate, too, is like that of Italy. The apple, the pear, cherry, peach, apricot, and almond, are all in bloom.

The famous [wine] tun of Heidelberg was new built in 1751. It is said to contain two hundred and thirty-six foudres of one thousand two hundred bottles each. I measured it, and found its length external to be twenty-eight feet ten inches; its diameter at the end twenty feet three inches; thickness of the hoops seven and a half inches; besides a great deal of external framing. There is no wine in it now.

The plains of the Rhine on this side are twelve miles wide, bounded by the Bergstrasse mountains. These appear to be eight hundred or a thousand feet high; the lower part in vines, from which is made what is called the vin de Nichar [Neckar].

April 14th. Just beyond Kaeferthal the Elector has about two hundred sangliers (wild boars), tamed. I saw about fifty; the heaviest I am told, would weigh about three hundred pounds. At the village of Kaeferthal is a plantation of rhubarb, begun in 1769. The apothecaries of Frankfort and of England are the principal buyers.

Carlsruhe is the residence of the Margrave of Baden, a sovereign prince.

April 16. *Carlsruhe* [to] *Strasburg*.

The grape is now in blossom. At Strasburg we pass the Rhine on a wooden bridge.

The Fine Wines of Alsace

April 16th. 17th. 18th. Strasburg. The vin de paille (straw wine) is made in the neighborhood of Colmar, in Alsace. It takes its name from the circumstance of spreading the grapes on straw, where they are preserved till spring, and then made into wine. The little juice then remaining in them makes a rich sweet wine, but the dearest in the world, without being the best by any means. They charge nine florins the bottle for it in the taverns of Strasburg. It is the caprice of wealth alone which continues so losing an operation. This wine is sought because dear; while the better wine of Frontignan is rarely seen at a good table because it is cheap.

April 19th. Asparagus to-day at Moyenvic. On the hills about Fenestrange, Moyenvic, and Nancy, are some small vineyards where a bad wine is made.

April 19, Nancy. The women here, as in Germany, do all sorts of work. While one considers them as useful and rational companions, one cannot forget that they are also objects of our pleasures; nor can they ever forget it. While employed in dirt and drudgery, some tag of a ribbon, some ring, or bit of brace-let, earbob or necklace, or something of that kind, will show that the desire of pleasing is never suspended in them. Women are formed by nature for atten-tions, not for hard labor. A woman never forgets one of the numerous train of little offices which belong to her. A man forgets often.[17]

After Nancy, Jefferson went straight to Champagne, spending four busy days there in vineyards and cellars. Champagne was the one great French wine for which Jefferson had no regular supplier, and he hoped to find one on the spot. Only in 1787, after he had been in France for three years, did the first purchase of Champagne appear on his cellar list, and then for only sixty bottles, a minor purchase by Jefferson standards.

The Champagne tour is unusual in that it is the only one with no explanatory letters to friends on the experience. Fortunately the notes themselves are comprehensive. In Jefferson's time and well into the nine-teenth century, the wines of Champagne were known by the names of the villages where its grapes were grown, or at least where the wine was made, like modern Burgundy. Champagne today is more like Port; the wines are identified by the company or "house" which sells them with variations for certain blends, vintages, and "super-Champagnes."

To understand Jefferson's notes, we must reaccustom ourselves to hearing village names like Ay, Pierry, and Verzenay. One proof that our ancestors knew the names of Champagne villages is the well-known Longfellow poem hailing Ohio Valley sparkling wines of Jefferson's friend

Nicholas Longworth, whose native wines Longfellow compared to Champagne in his "Ode to Catawba" (1854):

> *Very good in its way*
> *Is the Verzenay*
> *Or the Sillery soft and creamy*
> *But Catawba wine*
> *Has a taste more divine*
> *More dulcet, delicious and dreamy.*[18]

We can always hope the wine was better than the poetry.

April 21st. *Chalons sur Marne. Epernay.*

The hills are mulatto also, but whitish, occasioned by the quantity of chalk which seems to constitute their universal base. They are poor, and principally in vines. The streams of water are of the color of milk, occasioned by the chalk also.

April 22d. *Epernay.* The hills abound with chalk [and] are in vines, and this being precisely the canton where the most celebrated wines of Champagne are made, details must be entered into. Remember, however, that they will always relate to the white wines, unless where the red are expressly mentioned. The reason is that their red wines, though much esteemed on the spot, are by no means esteemed elsewhere equally with their white; nor do they merit equal esteem.

Grapes.—The bulk of their grapes are purple, (pinot noir), which they prefer for making even white wine. They press them very lightly, without treading or permitting them to ferment at all, for about an hour; so that it is the beginning of the running only which makes the bright wine. What follows the beginning is of a straw color, and therefore not placed on a level with the first. The last part of the juice, produced by strong pressure, is red and ordinary.

They choose the bunches with as much care, to make wine of the very first quality, as if to eat. Not above one-eighth of the whole grapes will do for this purpose.

The white grape [chardonnay], though not so fine for wine as the red, when the red can be produced, and more liable to rot in a moist season, yet grows better if the soil be excessively poor, and therefore in such a soil is preferred, or rather, is used of necessity, because there the red would not grow at all.

Wine.—The white wines are either mousseux, sparkling, or non-mousseux, still. The sparkling are little drunk in France, but are almost alone known and drunk in foreign countries. This makes so great a demand, and so certain a one, that it is the dearest by about an eighth, and therefore they endeavor to make all sparkling if they can. This is done by bottling in the spring, from the beginning of March till June. If it succeeds, they lose abundance of bottles, from one-tenth to one-third. This is another cause for increasing the price.

To make the still wine, they bottle in September. This is only done when they know from some circumstance that the wine will not be sparkling. So if the spring bottling fails to make a sparkling wine, they decant it into other bottles in the fall, and it then makes the very best still wine. In this operation, it loses from one-tenth to one-twentieth by sediment. They let it stand in the bottles in this case forty-eight hours, with only a napkin spread over their mouths, but no cork. The best sparkling wine, decanted in this manner, makes the best still wine, and which will keep much longer than that originally made still by being bottled in September.

The sparkling wines lose their briskness [bubble] the older they are, but they gain in quality with age to a certain length. These wines are in perfection from two to ten years old, and will even be very good to fifteen. 1766 was the best year ever known. 1775 and 1776 next to that. 1783 is the last good year, and that not to be compared with those. These wines stand icing very well.

Aij [*Ay*]. M. Dorsay makes one thousand and one hundred pieces, which sell, as soon as made, at three hundred florins, and in good years four hundred florins, in the cask. I paid in his cellar, to M. Louis, his homme d'affaires, for the remains of the year 1783, three florins ten sous the bottle.

Sparkling Champagne, of the same degree of excellence, would have cost four florins, (the piece and demiqueue are the same; the feuillette is one hundred bottles).

Auvillaij [*Hautvillers*]. The Benedictine monks make one thousand pieces, red and white, but three-fourths red, both of the first quality. The king's table is supplied by them.

Cumieres is all of the second quality, both red and white, at one hundred and fifty to two hundred florins the piece.

Epernay. All of the first quality; red and white in equal quantities.

Pierrij. M. Casotte makes five hundred pieces. M. de la Motte, three hundred pieces. M. de Failli, three hundred pieces. I tasted his wine of 1779, one of the good years. It was fine, though not equal to that of M. Dorsay, of 1783.

At Cramont also there are some wines of the first quality made. At Avisi also, and Aucy, Le Meni [Mesnil], Mareuil, Verzis-Verzenni [Verzenay]. This last place belongs to the Marquis de Sillery. The wines are carried to Sillery, and there stored, whence they are called Vins de Sillery, though not made at Sillery.

White Champagne is deemed good in proportion as it is silky [half-dry] and still. Many circumstances derange the scale of wines. The proprietor of the best vineyard, in the best year, having bad weather come upon him while he is gathering his grapes, makes a bad wine, while his neighbor, holding a more indifferent vineyard, which happens to be ingathering while the weather is good, makes a better.

The M. de Casotte at Pierrij formerly was the first house. His successors, by some imperceptible change of culture, have degraded the quality of their wines. Their cellars are admirably made, being about six, eight or ten feet wide, vaulted, and extending into the ground, in a kind of labyrinth, to a prodigious distance, with an air-hole of two feet diameter every fifty feet. From the top of the vault to the surface of the earth, is from fifteen to thirty feet. I have nowhere seen cellars comparable to these.

In packing their bottles, they lay on their side; then cross them at each end, they lay laths, and on these another row of bottles, heads and points; and so on. By this means, they can take out a bottle from the top, or where they will.

In Paris Again "Living in Splendor and Dissipation"

Jefferson left Champagne on April 23, 1788, and, travelling via Meaux, where the famous Brie cheese is now made, arrived in Paris that same night. Returned to his house on the Champs-Elysées, he found Paris in May of 1788 a "furnace of politics."[19] In America the States were debating our Constitution, and Jefferson wrote many letters to Virginians during the next year airing his views on it. His letters were often quoted (or misquoted) to support one view or another. Typical was the comment by Patrick Henry, citing Jefferson as authority for adding a Bill of Rights, all the while mocking his supposed lifestyle in Paris: "[Jefferson] thinks yet of bills of rights while living in splendor and dissipation."[20]

To Jefferson it did not look that way at all. On May 25, 1788, he wrote a private letter to Madison about his continuing money problems, indicating he was not living in splendor by any means, comparing himself to his fellow American ministers Jay, Adams, and Franklin:

Paris, May 25, 1788

Mr. Jay. Tho' appointed a minister resident at the court of Madrid. He was continually passing from Paris to Madrid and Madrid to Paris so that he had no occasion to establish a household at either. Accordingly he staid principally in furnished lodgings. He was of a disposition too to restrain himself within any limits of expence whatever, and it suited his recluse turn. He was in Europe as a voyageur only, and it was while the salary was 500 guineas more than at present.

J. Adams. He came over when all expences were paid. Of rigorous honesty, and careless of appearances, he lived for a considerable time as an oeconomical private individual. After he was fixed at The Hague and the salary a sum certain, he continued his oeconomical stile. This was the easier as the salary was at 2500 guineas then.

When he established himself [at Paris], his pecuniary affairs were under the direction of Mrs. Adams, one of the most estimable characters on earth, and most attentive and honourable oeconomists. A deficit in their accounts appeared in their winding up. The impossibility of living on the sum allowed, reputably, was the true cause of his insisting on recall.

Doctor Franklin. He came over while all expences were paid. His salary too was 2500 guineas. When Congress reduced it to less than 2000, he refused to accede to it, and asked his recall. He lived plain, but as decently as his salary would allow. He saved nothing, but avoided debt.

To him I succeeded. He had established a certain stile of living. The same was expected from me and there were 500 guineas a year less to do it on. This called for an almost womanly attention to the details of the household, equally perplexing, disgusting, and inconsistent with business.

Nor should I have mentioned it now but that the administration is passing into other hands, and more complicated forms. It would be disagreeable to me to be presented to them in the first instance as a suitor. Be so good as to reflect on it and to do, not what your friendship to me, but your opinion of what is right, will dictate.[21]

Jefferson decided in 1788 to return to America for a visit of some six months. The adoption of the Constitution and formation of a government were in a critical period. His finances needed help, a problem he could remedy better if he could talk in person with Washington and the Congress. His daughter Martha was also reaching marriageable age and he felt she should be back in America before she became unalterably attached to France. He was strengthened in this view when she announced the next spring that she wanted to become a nun, stunning the free-thinking Jefferson.

He also seems to have been homesick again. After all, he had been gone nearly five years. As he wrote to wine lover Alexander Donald:

Paris, February 7, 1788

Your letter has kindled all the fond recollections of antient times; recollections much dearer to me than anything I have known since. No attachments soothe the mind so much as those contracted in early life; nor do I recollect any societies which have given me more pleasure than those of which you have partaken with me.

I had rather be shut up in a very modest cottage, with my books, my family and a few old friends, dining on simple bacon, and letting the world roll on as it liked, than to occupy the most splendid post which any human power can give. I shall be glad to hear from you often. Give me the small news as well as the great."[22]

In Europe the changing political scene was affecting everyone. Mazzei, who had first interested Jefferson in vineyards, was in financial difficulties and sought funds in a rather strange employment, as Jefferson wrote to Madison in 1788:

The King of Poland sent an ancient Secretary here [Paris] to look out for a correspondent, a mere letter writer for him. A happy hazard threw Mazzei in his way and he is appointed. He has no diplomatic character whatever, but is to receive eight thousand livres a year as an intelligencer. I hope this employment may have some permanence. The danger is that he will overact his part.[23]

Since he planned to return to America, Jefferson ordered few wines in 1788 and 1789, but those in large lots: 250 Château d'Yquem in April 1788 and two separate orders of 250 bottles each of Meursault in February 1788 and March 1789. A February 1788 shipment of 123 Volnays completed the additions to his wine cellar for those years. It appears he was entertaining on a fine but not lavish scale, as he told Madison.

Jefferson had another reason not to leave his wine cellar too well stocked. In addition to the usual risk of stealing by servants, he had had three burglaries during 1789. When the nearby Grille de Chaillot was torn down as part of the new building program, the soldiers who guarded it went with it. This isolation left Jefferson's town house unprotected against thievery, which increased with the poverty of Paris as the Revolution approached. Under the circumstances, it is no wonder he did not wish to leave behind a cellar full of expensive wines while he was out of the country for six months or more.

Jefferson Plants Riesling Vines in His Paris Garden

That summer he wrote to Baron Geismar about the vines from the Rhine he had planted in his garden:

Paris July 15, 1788

On my return to this place I found such a mass of business awaiting me that I have never been able to write a letter of which friendship was the only motive. I take the first moment to inform you that my journey was prosperous: that the vines which I took from Hocheim and Rudesheim are now growing luxuriously in my garden here, and will cross the Atlantic next winter, and that probably, if you ever revisit Monticello, I shall be able to give you there a glass of Hock or Rudesheim of my own making.

Th: Jefferson[24]

Jefferson wrote to Governor Rutledge of South Carolina about the trip his son would be taking, saying he would "return home charged like a bee with the honey gathered on it."[25] His travelling companion, the son of Dr. Shippen of Philadelphia, wrote from Strasburg on July 31, 1788:

> Every stage of my journey has reminded me of you, and the remembrance has always been accompanied with gratitude and regard. On our way we lodged at Rudesheim and *breakfasted* the next morning on samples of Johannesberg wine. What a delicious liquor Sir it is. But I found it too expensive for us to think of importing it. The price on the spot is between 5 and 6 shillings sterg. a bottle by the *Stuck*, which holds about 41 pipes [a pipe varied from 110 to 140 U.S. gallons].[26]

Young Rutledge, writing the following day, was equally ecstatic:

> On my passage I visited the Vineyards at Johannesberg. The wines were the most delicious I ever tasted; but I fear we can never import them in America. The keeper of the Cave, if I recollect well, told me the wine would cost four shillings on the Spot.
>
> Although much pressed in time, Major Geismar prevailed on me to stay three days at Frankfort. He presented me at Court at Philipsbourg and overwhelmed me with Civilities.
>
> He said much of the friendship which you shewed him whilst he was a prisoner in Virginia and seemed happy in having an opportunity of being kind to one of your friends.[27]

Nor was Geismar disappointed. He said the young men's education was such as to do honor to the country where they obtained it, and promised to visit Jefferson in Paris when his finances allowed it.[28]

By September, Rutledge was still touring Europe, but Shippen had to return home and sought the best route across southern France. In his reply, Jefferson gave one of the first indications that he feared the French evolution toward republican government might get out of hand, saying, "The cloven hoof begins to appear."[29] Jefferson lamented that the worsening political situation forced him to remain in Paris when "I had hoped to go to Champagne to see the vintage."[30]

William Short was not so restricted. In the fall of 1788, Jefferson's secretary began a long tour of his own, exchanging letters with Jefferson as he retraced his mentor's steps through southern France and Italy. That correspondence furnished many of the details of Jefferson's activities during the winter of 1788–89, which was extraordinarily cold. The hardships of that winter helped, some think, accelerate the French Revolution. It was so cold, he later wrote Madame de Brehan, that all social life in Paris stopped for two months, as people helped try to feed the poor. Later, in his retirement when he was writing his autobiography, he recalled great bonfires being set up at street corners so that people could huddle around them to keep from freezing.[31] On December 8, 1788, Jefferson wrote to Short at Milan:

> The thermometer has been 10% of Reaumur below freezing. This is 8% of Farenheit above zero, and was the degree of cold here in the year 1740. The long continuance of this severity, and the snow now on the ground, give physical prognostications of a hard winter. You will be in a privileged climate and will have had an enviable escape from this.[32]

Short was not complaining. As he wrote to Jefferson from Lyon in October 1788, he had an excellent time at the Château de Laye, where he spent eight days watching them make Beaujolais. He also tasted the local goat cheese, pronouncing it not as good as what he was used to at Jefferson's table in Paris, where it was an ideal foil for good wines.

Short promised a treatise on the making of Beaujolais, then changed subjects, saying only: "On the whole I am persuaded we may make wine in Virginia as easily as we make cyder."[33] Short was helpful to Jefferson in obtaining the wine he compared to a kind of French Madeira—that of Mr. Rochegude:

> Toulouse April 20, 1789
>
> I forgot to mention to you that not being able to see the homme d'affaires of M. Rochegude at Avignon, I was obliged to execute your commission by chusing at his hotel the wine you desired, and leaving a memorandum for it to be sent to you to Paris.

The wine is kept in the country where it is made. That which I tasted of which kind you are to have is six years old. It costs 21s. instead of 24s as you imagined, the bottle included. It is to be paid when received at Paris together with the price of carriage and duty.[34]

Short's Rochegude does not show up on Jefferson's Paris cellar list, but there is a letter from a Daqueria Rochegude to him dated May 26, 1789, stating that six dozen bottles of his white wine had already been sent to Jefferson in two baskets by cart overland.[35] The account book for July 2 shows Petit paid 150^L - 19 for it on that date. In September of 1789, all 72 bottles of it showed up on the lengthy baggage list for America prepared in Jefferson's handwriting. It shared space with Montrachets, Yquems, Champagnes, and others, and must have been good to American tastes because he brought back to America as much Rochegude as any other wine.

GOUVERNEUR MORRIS ARRIVES
TO SHARE JEFFERSON'S WINES

In February of 1789 there arrived in France a most unusual American. A Philadelphia lawyer and former senator from Pennsylvania, Gouverneur Morris had already completed one fairly amazing career. From an old New York family, he was burdened with the un-American name "Gouverneur" from his Huguenot mother. Despite his name, Morris was on the conservative, "English" side of the great American division between Republicans and Federalists, Jeffersonians and Hamiltonians. Yet he got along very well with Jefferson, walking, dining, and riding with him in the Bois de Boulogne several times a week while they both lived in Paris.[36]

When Morris first arrived, he was probably the last person Jefferson imagined would take his place as American minister. He was too given to extravagant behavior and even more extravagant statements. Yet he had accomplished much despite his levity. He was Congress's envoy to Washington at Valley Forge and personally furnished the general his wines there, including Madeira and claret.[37] Because of his unusual skill as a draftsman, the Committee on Style chose him to phrase the final draft of the Constitution, which he completed just before leaving for France.[38] At Jefferson's request, he posed while in Paris for the Houdon bust of Washington, and some say it is his torso, not Washington's, that one sees in the statue of Washington which stands in the capitol at Richmond.[39]

Morris's most noticeable feature was his wooden leg, which biographers try to assign to a mundane accident. In Paris the accepted version, cited by Lord Palmerston, was that he lost it as a result of leaping from a lady's window after an amorous interlude.[40] The story is made more credible by his later exploits in Paris.

In Morris, Jefferson did not find a soul mate in every respect, but in wines they had a powerful common interest. A caustic critic of any wine that was less than the finest, Morris had nothing but praise for Jefferson's Paris wines. He mentions throughout his diary sitting with Jefferson before his fireplace in the Hotel de Langeac, sometimes with cups of tea in the afternoon, but often with Burgundy and Madeira in the evenings.[41] Morris noted the unpaved Champs-Elysées outside were often dusty and not as idyllic as one might picture, but he never had any complaints about the wines inside.[42]

Gouverneur Morris came to Paris as agent of Robert "the Financier" Morris, to whom he was not related. The two had a scheme to sell new settlers from Europe vast tracts of inexpensive American land. Their plan did not work out, but Morris shifted interests quickly and had five stimulating years there anyway. Succeeding Jefferson, he was the last foreign minister to remain in Paris during the terror phase of the French Revolution, leaving only after thousands of heads had rolled.

Morris brought Jefferson a glowing letter of recommendation from Washington requesting the help of the American minister with his commerce there. He may have wanted the minister's job all along, and Washington may have encouraged it. As Washington wrote to Jefferson:

Mount Vernon November 27th. 1788

Dear Sir

Notwithstanding I had the pleasure to write to you somewhat largely on the 31st. day of Augt. last, I would not dispense with transmitting a line by so

good an occasion as that which is now offered to me by the departure of
Mr. Gouveneur Morris for France.

You will find [him] full of affability, good nature, vivacity and talents. As
you will also find in him a deportment calculated to do credit to the national
character[!], I cannot hesitate to believe that you will be desirous of having
opportunities of being useful to him. Referring you to him for the state of
affairs in America, I will add no more, except the most sincere protestations of
being with very great esteem and regard Dear Sir yours &c. Go. Washington[43]

The "affability" of which Washington spoke is well illustrated in Morris's letter to the president asking for his recommendation. He began by saying that normally he didn't ask for such letters since they were merely

a kind of paper money which is only of little value, tho' perhaps a legal tender, [but]
I solicit yours as an undoubted Bill of Exchange which is Gold wherever it goes.

Permit me however to pursue the mercantile phrase (or Metaphor) and
honestly to request that you do not give me credit for more than I am worth,
lest proving a Bankrupt, you be called on by my creditors.[44]

Morris concluded with an even more mixed metaphor, part boudoir, part barnyard, which apparently was well received by the earthy old soldier and planter Washington:

I promised you some Chinese Piggs, a Promise which I can perform only by halves,
for my Boar being much addicted to gallantry, hung himself in the Pursuit of mere
common sows, and his consort, to assuage her Melancholy (for what alas can hapless
Widows do) took up with a Paramour of vulgar race, and thus her grunting
Progeny have jowls and bellies less big by Half than their Dam.

No quotation from Morris could better describe his "affability," nor better illustrate the differences in temperament between two men. Who can imagine Jefferson recounting such a tale to the father of his country?

Just after his arrival in Paris in March of 1789, Morris began writing, in the same style, his inimitable diary, which eventually reached four volumes.

In it he gave endless anecdotes of dining and wine drinking in Paris, especially of days and evenings spent with Jefferson discussing wines.

Morris joined Jefferson's circle, including Mazzei, whom he liked except that "he talked too much." He frequented the great Bordeaux wine proprietors who lived at the court, including Ségur (or rather his wife) and the Durforts. He had a close but platonic relationship with the lovely, Irish-born wife of Chastellux. He was, of course, frequently with the Lafayettes, as were most of the Americans. During the darkest days of the French Revolution, he even helped save Madame Lafayette from the guillotine.

Not all of Morris's relations were platonic, and that was one reason Jefferson could never imagine that this playboy would be his successor. On Saturday night, March 21, 1789, having been in Paris hardly a month, Morris met the Countess of Flahaut, a beautiful young woman married to an older man. Calling her a "pleasing woman," Morris dryly noted in his diary that night that "If I might judge from Appearances, [she is] not a sworn Enemy to Intrigue."[45] Morris was correct in his instinct, and he carried on a lively affair with Madame de Flahaut during the rest of his stay in Paris. A typical comment was his quip about her husband and how they hoped to enjoy "the pleasure of his absence."[46]

Next to good wines, Morris was most fond of the ladies in Paris, especially the young wives of aristocrats who could be both useful to him commercially and amusing socially. Nor was this libertine side of Morris unacceptable to Jefferson. Although the latter had supposedly broken off his love affair with Mrs. Cosway in 1787, he continued to write her. And it was the experienced Gouverneur Morris whom Jefferson chose to hand-deliver his letters to her.[47]

There is no question that she was very attractive, as all observers from James Boswell to Jefferson duly noted, and her portraits show it. Morris recorded visiting her often, and was interested in her personally after Jefferson left Paris, but apparently without success. She was described in typical Morris fashion as "vastly pleasant."[48]

On his visits to London, Morris kept company with James Boswell, the biographer of Dr. Johnson, and the famous "Scarlet Pimpernel," the English lord of movie fame who repeatedly slipped into France in disguise and dramatically rescued aristocrats from the guillotine.[49] Morris remarked that the claret in London was often better than in Paris, and that just as good could be had in America if you knew where to go (such as Jefferson's table).[50]

In Paris the Americans had a reputation for hard drinking. Morris did little to dispel it. On April 10, 1789, he noted in his diary: "Colonels Laumoy and Ternant dine with me. We drink like Men who had spent part of their lives in America."[51]

The following Sunday he did little to civilize the image of American evenings when he explained the use of chamber pots:

> At supper Mad. Le N. mentions the Description given by La Caze of a drinking Party in America where the Chamber Pot is set on the Table with the Bottles. I set her right as to the Chamber Pot, which is placed in a Corner of the Room.[52]

Next to Parisian ladies, the subject on which Jefferson and Morris had the most in common was wine, followed closely by food and botany. Both being of country gentry backgrounds, having grown up managing large farming estates, and each practicing law only briefly before going full-time into government, they had much in common. And Morris was the one man I found to whom Jefferson gave a set of his notes on viticulture from his tours of France, Germany, and Italy,[53] which Morris summarized in his diary:

> May 15, 1789. Take tea with Mr. Jefferson and talk with him about the culture of the vine, to which he has attended particularly in the best cantons of Burgundy, Champaigne and Bourdeaux.
>
> In conversation with a Vigneron this day he tells me that in good Seasons they make *une Piece* from three Roods, which is about twenty Gallons per Rood, and of course an Acre would give at this Rate above three thousand Gallons of Wine, & this from a Soil of very indifferent Quality.
>
> The Wine is small and of indifferent Flavor. But admitting that only one Crop be obtained in three Years and that the Culture &c. should be worth one half the Produce, it would leave five hundred Gallons which at 6d per Gallon is annually £ 12.10, a very great Produce and I suspect exagerated by the Vigneron.

It might however be worth a Trial in America & as far as I can judge, a steep gravelly Hill with a South Western Exposure would produce best. The Soil must be neither deep nor rich nor moist. Return home.[54]

Surprisingly, this is one of the rare first-person reports of a discussion of wine growing with Jefferson, the rest coming mainly from Jefferson himself or from his letters.

Throughout his diary Morris corroborates Jefferson's ideas on everything from the claret in Paris (it was not always that good) to how much better Madeira was when reimported from America. Morris also said straight out what I had always suspected: Lafayette did not have a good palate. It seemed odd that Jefferson never mentioned wine in his letters to Lafayette, even though he was the Frenchman Jefferson knew longest and best, and had plenty of money to afford the finest. Morris gave the answer, saying he agreed to dine at Lafayette's only if he could bring his own wine.[55]

Bringing his own wine was a habit with Morris. He carried it both to England and Holland on visits, admitting during the latter that he did not need it because in Holland the Burgundy was so "transcendently good" that he drank it "by tumblers and by bumpers."[56] Reading Morris is a lot like reading a wine and food guide to the eighteenth century. His diary format goes into little details even Jefferson often omitted.

In a classic entry, Morris shows the contrast in sobriety between the two men, telling how he and a couple of friends stayed up drinking seven bottles of Hungarian wine, then was awakened early by Short, who said Jefferson was waiting on him to go riding. Despite claiming diarrhea, Morris was forced to go anyway. Shortly he declared the return of his appetite when he saw "the finest roasting pigg I ever Beheld."[57] Morris's diary is a culinary voyage, filled with trout, sturgeon, ortholans, turbot, and fine beef, always accompanied by the best wines. Once when a wheel came off his carriage, he amused himself by eating a cold partridge as he watched them fix it.[58]

Morris was clearly not the moderate in his wine consumption that Jefferson was, and was living refutation of Jefferson's notion that wine drinkers are necessarily moderate. Morris often tried to reform, noting after one evening of excessive Madeira drinking that he was "as much out of humor with myself as one can easily be with so old an Acquaintance."[59]

Morris corroborated Jefferson in his views of the relaxed morals of the Parisians, despite his own notorious love affair with Madame Flahaut. Typical was his comment on Paris: "Pleasure is the great business [here]."[60] Morris tried to convince the unbelieving Count de Segur, of Bordeaux wine fame, who was thinking of emigrating to America, that marital infidelity was not the rule in revolutionary America.[61] Segur, Morris said, "seems incredulous, but is positive that it could be easily introduced" (infidelity, that is). Even Morris, while far more libertine than the puritanical Jefferson, saw Paris as debauched, and makes Jefferson seem less preachy: "Every Body agrees that there is an utter prostration of Morals, but this general Position can never convey to an American mind the Degree of Depravity."[62] His insight did not prevent Morris from joining the Parisian repartee, telling one attractive hostess that she was the best "dish" at her table and "rude not to ask one to partake of it."[63]

Despite his frivolity, Morris was a keen observer and left one of the best assessments of Jefferson in Paris:

> He commands very much respect in this Country and which is merited by good sense and good intentions. The French, who pique themselves on possessing the Graces, very readily excuse in others the Want of them, and to be an *Etranger* (like Charity) covers a multitude of sins. On the whole therefore I incline to think that an American Minister at this Court gains more than he loses by preserving his Originality.
>
> For the rest, Mr. Jefferson lives well, keeps a good Table and excellent Wines which he distributes freely, and by his Hospitality to his Countrymen here possesses very much their good will.[64]

Jefferson planned to return to France after a lengthy stay in America. He had requested and received an extension of three years on his appointment as American minister before leaving. In March of 1789 he renewed his lease on the Hotel de Langeac for another year, at a time when he assumed he would be leaving shortly for the United States. Later, when rumors began to circulate that he might not return, so certain was Short of his return that he bet a beaver hat on it.[65]

One problem with Jefferson's trip to America was the status of James and Sally Hemings, the brother and sister servants he had brought from Monticello. Sally was the beautiful, fair-skinned half-sister of Jefferson's deceased wife, with whom he was later accused of fathering several mulatto children. She had come to Paris with Maria, as her nurse. Her older brother James Hemings was invaluable to Jefferson as his French cook.

Jefferson's problem was that although he always called them "servants," they were, of course, slaves. As such, they had the right under French law to refuse to return to America. To circumvent this problem, Jefferson promised both of them their freedom later if they would return with him. James Hemings insisted on his freedom, and there exists an interesting document, executed personally between him and Jefferson, in which he agreed to continue to serve Jefferson until he had properly trained a new cook for him in the French techniques he had learned. James Hemings and Jefferson both kept their bargain, the former training his successors until 1796, when Jefferson finally freed him.[66] Sally Hemings was not freed until after Jefferson's death, by his daughter Martha, who was determined to keep her father's promise. She became a substantial embarrassment because of the many rumors that she was Jefferson's concubine and the mother of children he ignored.[67]

During his final summer in Paris, his friends in the American community gave a great festive dinner for Jefferson on the Fourth of July at the Hotel de Langeac. They had no idea that just ten days later the Bastille would fall, and that Jefferson himself would soon leave Paris forever. A written tribute to Jefferson was signed by Mazzei, Thomas Appleton, Benjamin Jarvis, and others of his best wine friends, on whom he was to rely for supplies after his return to America. Morris was present at the dinner and recorded in his diary that the conversation among the French guests was entirely too revolutionary for him.[68]

On July 14, 1789, the Bastille fell, and its governor and others were beheaded. Jefferson's carriage was stopped by a mob but cheered on and allowed to leave when they realized he was the American minister and not a French aristocrat, despite his fancy equipment. Jefferson and Morris began seeing decapitated heads being carried around on poles as the Revolution escalated. During this critical period Jefferson encouraged the liberal grouping of aristocrats led by Lafayette to meet at his house and discuss politics, over wine in the American manner, after the cloth was removed. It was during this period that he was called "a consulting attorney on revolution."

Jefferson's wine parties for Lafayette and his friends could not control the Revolution which was coming. Having toured the countryside, Jefferson seemed to sense better than his French friends just what whirlwind would be unleashed if the illiterate and hungry populace saw order break down. Their background was so different from that of the American revolutionaries that they were ill suited for an abrupt change to total democracy. Even the aristocratic-leaning Morris seemed to see it better than the French, noting in his diary: "The people complain for want of bread."[69] Being Morris, however, even in those perilous times he could not resist a note of levity. Observing on the road some pigs which the French farmers were being forced to sell, he recorded in his diary: "We meet many droves of Hogs, the worst-formed animals of the kind I ever saw. Long, narrow and meager, they seem rather fitted for the Race than the Table."[70]

Jefferson received a warm farewell from his old German wine friend Baron Geismar, who seemed to know Jefferson would not be returning from his "leave":

Hanau, April 13, 1789

How I envy your return to Monticello, recalling the peaceful and pleasant sojourn I spent there. It is certain that I enjoyed more liberty and contentment as a prisoner in that country than in my fatherland with all my so-called liberty.

Also, I ask you, my dear friend, if ever the occasion presents itself, that you help me find a place to live in your country. The more I advance in age, the more I feel out of place in my own country, and believe me, it is truly sad to be unhappy in your own country.

I hope this letter will find you still in Paris. If not, it will follow you into
Virginia, where I hope you will use a moment of leisure to send news of yourself to your friend, who will remain attached to you for life.

Geismar.[71]

Jefferson had plenty of time to receive Geismar's letter, which arrived
April 19. Departure times in the eighteenth century were uncertain to
say the least, depending as they did on favorable winds. They had packed
in July, but it was not until late September that they left Paris for Le
Havre to catch the boat. Some of the most carefully packed items were
Jefferson's wines, of which he took quite a selection to taste with friends in
America. He even shipped separate boxes of the same wines to different
destinations so they would be there when he arrived. Other boxes were
labelled "seastores"; their contents showed he planned to dine and drink
well en route.

The choicest wines he forwarded to George Washington at New
York, in care of John Jay as secretary of foreign affairs:

Paris Sep. 17. 1789.

Dear Sir

I have sent from this place, together with my own baggage, two hampers
and two boxes, which when arrived at Havre I have taken the liberty to order to
be separated from my baggage and sent by the first vessel to New York to your
address.

The marks and contents are as follows:

TJ. No. 30. & No. 31. These are hampers containing samples of the best wines of
this country, which I beg leave to present to the President and yourself, in order that
you may decide whether you would wish to have any, and which of them for your
own tables hereafter, and to offer my service in procuring them for you.

The kinds are 1. Monraché (the best kind of White Burgundy) 2. Champagne non mousseux (i.e. still) much preferred here to the sparkling, which goes
all to foreign countries. 3. Sauterne (a white Bordeaux) 4. Rochegude (from the
neighborhood of Avignon, somewhat of the Madeira quality) 5. Frontignan.
I have bought all of these from the Vignerons who made them, the 1st. 2d. and
5th. when on the spots myself, the 3d. and 4th. by writing to them.

{ 195 }

The Vigneron never adulterates his wine, but on the contrary gives it the most perfect and pure possible. But when once a wine has been into a merchant's hands, it never comes out unmixed. This being the basis of their trade, no degree of honesty, of personal friendship or of kindred prevents it. I must beg the favor of you to deliver one hamper to the President with my offers of service, and the preceding explanation.

P.S. Every bottle is marked (with a diamond) with the initial letter of the wine it contains.[72]

The foregoing was a remarkable shipment of wines, and shows that Jefferson thought Washington was enough of a connoisseur to appreciate these highly prized wines. Looked at from another perspective, it gives an insight into Washington. For Franklin and Madison, Jefferson brought no wines, but several cases of books. For Washington he brought a few books, but lots of wines.

WINES SHIPPED BY JEFFERSON FROM FRANCE AND THEIR DESTINATIONS[73]

MEURSAULT		SAUTERNES	
48	Monticello	24	Monticello
24	Seastores	24	Eppington
72		12	New York
		60	
ROCHEGUDE		FRONTIGNAN	
24	Monticello	24	Monticello
12	Eppington	12	Eppington
12	Seastores	10	Seastores
24	New York	29	New York
72		75	
MONTRACHET		CHAMPAGNE	
12	Eppington	12	Eppington
24	New York	24	New York
36		36	

The same day he wrote to Jay, Jefferson gave instructions to his agent at Le Havre to take special care with the boxes addressed John Jay and marked TJ No. 30 and TJ No. 31, Washington's wines.[74] On September 28 the Jeffersons' party arrived at Le Havre to embark. There to meet them was the agent Nathaniel Cutting, a young American businessman who spent two weeks with them waiting for passage on an American boat. After drinking many good glasses of wine with Jefferson, Cutting left in his diary a vivid portrait:

> I never remember to have experienced so much regret at parting from a Family with whom I had so short an acquaintance. I have found Mr. Jefferson a man of infinite information and sound Judgement.
>
> His eldest Daughter is an amiable Girl about 17 years of age, tall and genteel, has been 5 years in France, principally in a convent, for her Education, and though she has been so long resident in a Country remarkable for its Levity and the forward indelicacy of its manners, yet she retains all that winning simplicity, and good humour'd reserve that are evident proofs of innate Virtue and an happy disposition.—Characteristicks which eminently distinguish the Women of America from those of any other Country.
>
> The youngest Daughter is a lovely Girl about 11 years of age. The perfect pattern of good temper, an engaging smile ever animates her Countenance, and the chearful attention which she pays to the judicious instructions and advice of her worthy Father, the Pertinent queries which she puts to him, and the evident improvement she makes in her knowledge of Foreign Languages, History and Geography, afford a pleasing Presage that when her faculties attain their maturity, she will be the delight of her Friends, and a distinguish'd ornament to her sex.[75]

Cutting did not mention Sally or James Hemings. From the Isle of Wight the Jeffersons embarked on the American ship *Clermont* and crossed the Atlantic in twenty-six days thanks to Captain Colley, a native of Norfolk, whom Jefferson called "a bold and judicious seaman."[76]

Accompanying them in their baggage were some 363 bottles of wine, fully half of them fine Burgundies and Bordeaux. Amazingly, every single bottle of wine Jefferson brought back with him from France was *white*.

As he left France behind forever, although he did not then know it, his emotions were mixed. He had fine memories of his years there, but serious doubts about the value of a French education for young Americans. He wrote his doubts to John Banister, Jr. He purports to be talking of its effects on others, but the message sounds personal, and probably reflected what he thought the experience had done for him and not some anonymous future visitor:

> It appears to me then that an American coming to Europe for education loses in his knowledge, in his morals, in his health, in his habits, and in his happiness.
>
> He acquires a fondness for European luxury and dissipation and a contempt for the simplicity of his own country; he is fascinated with the privileges of the European aristocrats and sees with abhorrence the lovely equality which the poor enjoy with the rich in his own country.
>
> He is led by the strongest of all the human passions into a spirit for female intrigue destructive of his own and others happiness, or a passion for whores destructive of his health, and in both cases learns to consider fidelity to the marriage bed as an ungentlemanly practice and inconsistent with happiness. He recollects the voluptuary dress and arts of the European women and pities and despises the chaste affections and simplicity of those of his own country.
>
> He retains thro' life a fond recollection and a hankering after those places which were the scenes of his first pleasures and of his first connections; he returns to his own country, a foreigner.[77]

The passage about returning to his own country a "foreigner" was prophetic; that image followed him the rest of his life, and caused many of his future political problems. So closely was he associated with things French, especially luxuries like his fine French wines, that his position as a man of the people was suspect.

Only much later, in his 1821 autobiography, when he knew he would never return, did Jefferson give his most fitting farewell to France:

> I cannot leave this great and good country without expressing my sense of its preeminence of character among the nations of the earth. A more benevolent people I have never known, nor greater warmth and devotedness in their select friendships.

Their kindness and accommodation to strangers is unparalleled, and the hospitality of Paris is beyond anything I had conceived to be practicable in a large city. The politeness of the general manners, the ease and vivacity of their conversation, give a charm to their society to be found nowhere else.

In a comparison of this with other countries we have the proof of primacy which was given to Themistocles after the battle of Salamis. Every general voted to himself the first reward of valor and the second to Themistocles.

So, ask the travelled inhabitant of any nation in what country on earth would you rather live? Certainly, in my own, where are all my friends, my relations, and the earliest and sweetest affections and recollections of my life. Which would be your second choice? France.[78]

CHAPTER FIVE

The Return to America

(1789–1800)

We return like foreigners, and like them require
a considerable residence here to become Americanized.[1]
—JEFFERSON TO WILLIAM SHORT

On November 23, 1789, the Jeffersons landed safely in Norfolk. Their voyage was uneventful until they reached port, where a storm tore off the ship's topsails and a fire aboard ship damaged cargo, but none of Jefferson's wines. Upon arrival, they learned that Washington had proposed Jefferson to be secretary of state. The new position combined the duties of secretary of foreign affairs, which Jay had held, with domestic concerns, including everything from issuing patents to publishing acts of Congress in the newspapers as required by law.

Jefferson and his daughters first visited the Eppes family at Eppington, receiving there Washington's letter offering him the choice of returning to France or of being secretary of state. It was the most important position in the new government next to the presidency itself. As Washington kindly proposed it, the position sounded hard to refuse:

New York Oct. 13th. 1789

Sir

In the selection of Characters to fill the important offices of Government in the United States I was naturally led to contemplate the talents and disposition which I knew you to possess and entertain for the Service of your Country. —And without being able to consult your inclination, I was determined, as well by motives of private regard as a conviction of public propriety, to nominate you for the Department of State, which, under its present organization, involves many of the most interesting objects of the Executive Authority. —But grateful as your acceptance of this Commission would be to me, I am at the same time desirous to accommodate to your wishes, and I have therefore forborne to nominate your Successor at the Court of Versailles until I should be informed of your determination.[2]

Jefferson was not very pleased, saying he had "gloomy forebodings" about the job, and personally preferred to return to Paris. He waited three months before accepting.

On December 23, 1789, a full month after they got to Virginia, Jefferson and his daughters and James and Sally Hemings finally arrived at Monticello. Despite his claims in Paris about how he longed to return to Monticello, in a letter to Short he described his trip home without much enthusiasm as a "plunge into the forests of Albemarle." The tremendous reception he received there, however, seems to have changed his mind.

Preoccupied with his decision and with what to do about his daughters, since in neither case would he stay at Monticello, Jefferson wrote little about wine during this period. The wines he had sent from Paris almost beat him home. In a letter from James Brown of Richmond dated December 21, 1789, Brown noted he had sent hamper #1 by wagon and hamper #2 by riverboat to Monticello. Those lots contained the Meursault, Yquem, Frontignan, and Rochegude that Jefferson had earmarked for drinking at Monticello during his visit.[3]

Jefferson acknowledged receipt of the boxes sent by wagon, including one hamper #1, so he did receive at least some of his Burgundies and Sauternes while at Monticello to taste with his neighbors and visitors:

Monticello Jan. 3. 1790

Sir

I received duly your favor of Dec. 21 and with it the several articles noted to be sent therewith, except No. 1, a box of wines. I had observed in my memorandum that there were two No. 1s. and had desired both to be sent; and both are so marked in your letter: but the waggoners concurring in their declarations that one only was delivered, I am in hopes it was omitted by error, and that it may now come by my waggon, unless it is on the way in the canoes.

I will note at the foot of my letter some articles which I will beg the favor of you to send at present.[4]

The articles he wanted sent right away by wagon included twenty pounds of coffee, four pounds of chocolate, a pound of tea, six half-pint tumblers, and "12 wine glasses."

ABROAD AT HOME: RELUCTANT SECRETARY OF STATE (1790–1793)

After much hesitation, Jefferson accepted the position of secretary of state, which meant moving with the government to New York. His decision was probably foreordained, as Short had predicted after hearing from Jay and Hamilton on the subject:

They assure me that it is impossible you should resist the President, who has set his heart in such a manner on your accepting the place of Secretary of State as will induce him to press, sollicit and beg it of you. They add that his sollicitations and intreaties are so seldom given that they cannot be given in vain.[5]

On March 1, 1790, Jefferson left Monticello for New York, visiting the wine-loving Franklin in Philadelphia en route. From Alexandria, Jefferson wrote to Short, asking him to cancel his lease on the Hotel de Langeac and persuade Petit to come to New York as soon as possible as his maitre d', or "housekeeper," as Jefferson democratically put it.[6] Historians have struggled with what to call Petit, most using the old term "steward," and a few the British term "butler."

One enjoyable wine event which Jefferson missed on his trip to New York was an initiation into the Philadelphia Irish Society, officially known as the Sons of Saint Patrick. In a letter to his friend Judge Richard Peters, written from New York in June 1790, he informed Peters that he did not learn of his invitation until after he left Philadelphia; otherwise he would have been delighted.[7] We were thus deprived of one of the most potentially colorful events of early American history, which Jefferson would no doubt have vividly described for his European correspondents. The remaining accounts of George Washington's initiation into that society claim that a key element of the ritual was the undignified "application of a full bottle of claret" over the bare head of the general,[8] strangely akin to the Gatorade bath that follows a win in a modern football game.

Arriving in New York on March 21, 1790, Jefferson noted that as secretary of state his business was all "in the Broadway," so he leased a house nearby. A visitor later described it as a "mean little house," but Jefferson took the trouble to add a large, well-lit, glass-enclosed book room, even though he stayed in New York only six months, from March to August 1790. No mention was made of a wine cellar, nor of where or how he kept his wines. But he did keep James Hemings with him as cook, and apparently tried to eat as well as he could under the circumstances.

New York was, back then, a small place of only about thirty-three thousand people and mainly a commercial and not an intellectual center. Beside Paris, a cosmopolitan city of over a half million and the world capital of wine, New York was decidedly provincial. Jefferson began to feel out of place in his native country. Instead of the lively dinner parties of Paris, there were the stiff, formal dinners of President Washington.

There were similar differences in the area of wines. In New York the American custom of lengthy toasting and the drinking of sweet dessert wines after dinner rather than with it still prevailed. There was not even a real diplomatic corps for Jefferson to enjoy as he had in Paris. He was nevertheless among old friends, many, like Madison and Washington, established wine lovers, eager to learn from his expertise gained in Europe and to share with him the wines he had brought back.

Washington had been president only since April of 1789, but was well established in his custom of giving formal dinners at his New York mansion. The first of that spring was to honor Jefferson. It included close friends James Madison and John Page, both Virginia congressmen, as well as his fellow cabinet members and their wives: the Jays, the Hamiltons, and Secretary of War Henry Knox and his wife, both of whom weighed nearly three hundred pounds and were known to be as devoted to Champagne as they were to food.

Accounts of Jefferson's return dinner all mention the many toasts given, with Washington in the old style toasting individually every person at the table, but none that I have found mention any particular wines. From his letters later that year, it is apparent that none of Jefferson's French wines had arrived in time to test on New York society during the 1790 session of Congress.

Contributing to Jefferson's isolation during his first winter back in the U.S. were several "periodical" or migraine headaches which often accompanied his changes of climate. The job of secretary of state was no picnic either. Yet Jefferson took on the job with pride and good humor, writing in April to Lafayette: "Behold me, my dear friend, dubbed Secretary of State."[9]

That same month he wrote a long letter to Short detailing how to pack his belongings, especially his wine cellar: "The wines must be bottled before they are brought. I mean the Cahusac, Grave &c. in the cellar. Perhaps they are already bottled."[10] Otherwise he hardly mentioned wine that summer, noting only in his account book for July: "pd. Farquahr for 1 bottle claret 4/6" [and] "Pd. Colo. Griffin for 1 case Italian wine 30/6."

That same month he completed and sent to Congress his Report on Weights and Measures, which recommended standardizing the *gallon*, including abolition of the old "wine-gallon," another indication of how difficult it is to know for certain now what was meant by quantities and prices then, even when we have them.

One of his duties of 1790 was selecting American consuls (and thus wine suppliers) for a dozen Atlantic and Mediterranean ports, including Bordeaux, Marseilles, and Madeira. At Bordeaux he was forced by lobbying from George Mason to remove his reliable wine supplier John Bondfield and replace him with Joseph Fenwick, the partner of Mason's son John. To Mason he bluntly stated of the consulship "[t]hat of bordeaux is given to Mr. Fenwick according to your desire,"[11] notifying Bondfield sadly on the same subject that "another than yourself has been chosen for Bordeaux."[12] He disingenuously explained to his old Bordeaux supplier that Bondfield had lost out only because he was not a *native* American (being a Canadian). In reply, Bondfield poignantly remonstrated about his many years of service to the U.S. in France, since 1777, in fact, and how loyal he had been during the Revolution, only to be cast aside for reasons of political expediency and nepotism. It was to no avail. Jefferson corresponded no further with Bondfield, who soon fell upon hard financial times.[13]

Jefferson Orders "Necessaries": Lisbon, Sherry, Carcavellos, and Claret

Most of its business finished, Congress was to adjourn in August. With a long holiday at Monticello in mind, Jefferson placed the first substantial wine order since his return from Richmond merchant James Brown:

New York Aug. 8. 1790.

Sir

As I shall shortly set out for Virginia, and shall have occasion there for some necessaries, I take the liberty of stating them herein, and of asking the favor of you to send them to me by the first conveyance after the reciept of this. Any waggon going to Charlottesville may deliver them.

I have noted a quarter cask of wine. I would prefer good Lisbon; next to that Sherry, next to that Calcavallo; but still a good quality of the latter would be preferable to an indifferent quality of the former. If none of these, then claret. Whatever kind you can procure me, be so good as to have it bottled before sent.

If the wine you send me be either Lisbon, Sherry, or Calcavallo, then I would be glad of 3. or 4. doz. in addition of any sound weak wine, either red or white, which would be good for mixing with water, the kinds specified not being proper for that.[14]

Among other "necessaries," Jefferson ordered fifty pounds of rice, thirty pounds of brown sugar, twenty pounds of coffee, ten pounds of raisins and ten of almonds, as well as three bottles of capers and three of mustard and "1 cheese," type and size not specified.

This wine order raises questions about his drinking habits at this time. His preferences seem to be for dessert wines, with claret a distinct last. Yet he also wanted a wine suitable for mixing with water, indicating it was to be drunk with meals as a beverage. Probably, as in other areas, he was adaptable.

Four days later Jefferson made a more noteworthy order, not for himself but for President Washington, using as intermediary his old secretary William Short, still in Paris as American chargé d'affaires:

New York Aug. 12. 1790

Dear Sir

Being just now informed that a vessel sails this afternoon for a port of Normandy, and knowing that the President wished to have some Champagne and that this is the season to write for it, I have been to him, and he desires 40 dozen bottles.

The execution of this commission I must put upon you, begging the favor of you to procure it of the growth of M. Dorsay's vineyard at Ay opposite to Epernay in Champagne, and of the best year he has for present drinking.

It is to be *Non-mousseux*. M. Dorsay himself lives in Paris. I am anxious this wine should not move from Champagne till the heats are over, and that it should arrive at Philadelphia before the spring comes on. It will of course be in bottles.

P.S. call for the best possible, and they may be sure of a continuance of such an annual demand as long as it comes of the best.[15]

From the requirement that the Champagne be "*non-mousseux*," or non-bubbly, it is apparent that Jefferson was picking Washington's wines for him, since everyone was drinking sparkling Champagne except Jefferson. Congress voted to move its next session to Philadelphia, so Jefferson had Washington's wine sent on there rather than New York. The wine he ordered for Washington is still available in the United States, the house of Bollinger having acquired those choice vineyards.

The following day the president and his secretary of state left New York for a brief trip through Rhode Island, the only state which had rejected the Constitution and the last to ratify it. Washington wanted to mend political fences and cement the union, and the trip was a triumph for the president and Jefferson. Their arrival at Newport was celebrated by much toasting and an abundance of "federal salutes" in both cannon fire and wine. The trip gave the two men considerable time alone together, something Washington had wished. Jefferson had actually spent less time in person with Washington than the other Founding Fathers, first because Washington was always in the field with his army during the Revolution, and then because for five and a half years Jefferson was far away in Paris.

Returning from the Rhode Island trip late in August, Jefferson left for Monticello on September 1, 1790. En route he passed by Princeton, Philadelphia, Wilmington, Annapolis, Georgetown, Alexandria, and Mount Vernon. Young Thomas Lee Shippen of the famous German tour accompanied him briefly, along with Madison, describing how they "feasted on delicious crabs" and what agreeable, high-living company Jefferson was, adding to his father that he needed the loan of a fifty-dollar bank note due to expenses of the trip.[16]

JEFFERSON ORDERS MORE FINE FRENCH WINES
FOR GEORGE WASHINGTON

Jefferson's meeting with Washington at Philadelphia was the important event of his trip home that fall. From there he made his most publicized wine order, the one which some claim led to the famous bottles of Bordeaux that bear his initials (see epilogue). On September 6, 1790, Jefferson sent Short a long letter enclosing five others. The first was for Joseph Fenwick, the new American consul at Bordeaux, asking him to deliver the other four letters, which were to the proprietors of four great wine estates, including Yquem and Latour. The letter to Short gave a foreboding of the spending habits which later brought Jefferson to bankruptcy, asking Short in Paris to bear the expense of Washington's wines by borrowing against his own salary to pay for them.

The September 6 letters show Jefferson had been giving the president an earful about ordering wines. He had just written Short from New York on August 25 that he would be ordering no more wines until Congress returned in November,[17] but on September 6 he said:

> Philadelphia Sep. 6. 1790
>
> The President left this morning on his way to Mount Vernon. He engaged me some time ago to get him some wines from France, to wit 40 dozen of Champagne, 30 doz. of Sauterne, 20 dozen of Bordeaux de Segur, and 10 doz. of Frontignan.
>
> I write for wines for my own use at the same time. These will amount to about 550 livres. I leave the letter to Fenwick open, to the end that you may see the arrangements I take to leave you no other trouble."[18]

The enclosed letter to Fenwick stated:

> Philadelphia Sep. 6. 1790
>
> Dear Sir
>
> I trouble you with a commission to receive and forward to me some wines for the President and myself. They are written for in the inclosed letters to the respective owners of the vineyards, and are as follows.

M. le comte de Lur-Saluce	30. doz.	Sauterne for the President
" "	10 doz.	do. for myself
M. de Mirosmenil	20 doz.	vin de Segur for the President
Madame de Rozan	10 doz.	vin de Rozan for myself.
Monsieur Lambert at Frontignan	10 doz.	Frontignan for the President
" "	5 doz.	do. for myself

To these I must beg you to add 10 dozen for me of a good white vin ordinaire, or indeed something better, that is to say of such a quality as will do to mix with water, and also be drinkable alone. Such I suppose may be obtained at Bordeaux for ten sous the bottle.

I would wish you to buy it of the person who makes it, and give me his name and address that, if it suits me, I may always be sure of the same quality.

I have directed those for the President to be packed separately and marked G.W. and mine T.J. You will receive them ready packed.

Those from Frontignan cannot probably be forwarded so soon as the others. You need only send the letter to Dr. Lambert at Frontignan, with a note of your address, and he will forward them to Bordeaux and draw on you for the amount of the wine and expenses.

Th: Jefferson[19]

Enclosed in the letter to Fenwick was a letter in French to Madame de Rauzan which (translated) said:

Although I do not have the honor of being personally known to you, I have had the opportunity, during a tour which I made during my stay in Paris, to learn, in visiting the Bordeaux wine country, that those wines called *de Rozan*, of your growth, are of excellent quality.[20]

Jefferson asked if she would send him ten dozen bottles, packed and bottled at the vineyard, "of the best for serving immediately," and implied that he intended to become a regular customer.

Also enclosed in the letter to Fenwick was a similar note to the Comte de Miromenil, whom Jefferson addressed as the owner of La Tour de Ségur, now Château Latour. Noting that he did not know Miromenil personally, but had tasted his wines during the Bordeaux trip, Jefferson continued:

> I praised it to our President, General Washington, and he has consequently instructed me to ask you to be so kind as to furnish him with some twenty dozen of your finest for serving immediately.

Jefferson again stated he would probably renew the order each year, asking that the wine be bottled, packed, and marked "G.W." at the vineyard, and that Miromenil "be so kind as to warn me in advance of its coming and assure me that the wines are truly of your growth."

To his old friend Lambert he wrote:

> Although presently separated from you by a great distance, Sir, I am still close enough to receive some of your excellent wines. Please be so kind therefore as to send me ten dozen bottles for our President, General Washington, and five dozen for me, of white and red, with a good proportion of the latter.
>
> I would prefer that the five dozen for me be placed in half-pint bottles, if you have any, which would thus be ten dozen half-pint bottles.[21]

Jefferson possibly wanted half-pint bottles of these rare and expensive wines to give guests for tasting, not drinking, and hoped to make them go farther by opening fewer. Speculating as to when these exceptional wines were drunk, it is likely they were opened at the end of the meal, with cheese or nuts, the best time to taste the finest wines. The ordinary wines Jefferson ordered direct from Fenwick were probably drunk *with* the meal as table beverages.

Especially enthusiastic was Jefferson's letter to Lur-Saluces, owner of the great Château d'Yquem, the finest Sauternes then and now:

> The white wine of Sauternes, of your growth, which you were so kind as to send me in Paris at the beginning of the year 1788, was so well approved by the Americans who tasted it there, that I do not doubt that my compatriots generally will find it to their taste.

As soon as I established myself here I persuaded our President, General Washington, to try a selection. He asks you for thirty dozen, Sir, and I would like ten dozen for myself to be bottled and packed as previously stated in order to avoid the mishaps which can happen en route.[22]

Thirty cases of Yquem was not a bad beginning, even for the father of his country.

Upon arriving at Monticello in mid-September, Jefferson expected to find the "necessary" wines ordered from Richmond. James Brown had promised to bottle off a quarter cask of "Sherry wine of first quality imported by Mr. Donald 18 months ago direct from Cadiz" (August 16, 1790). Brown's brother John added August 30 that he had no cheese, but was sending twelve dozen bottles of Sherry and three and a half bottles of port.[23] More letters and wines followed, with the usual problems:

To James Brown

October 29, 1790

Your several favors of Aug. 30, Sep. 24, Oct. 7th and 8th have been duly received, together with the articles thereon noted to have been sent.

The French brandy and the Lisbon wine both tapped by the waggoners, tho' the latter was in a double cask. They knocked out the head of the outer one.[24]

There must have been some drinkable wine left, for Jefferson wrote to Brown for bottling supplies:

Monticello Nov. 4. 1790

DEAR SIR

Be so good as to send to this place for my use two gross of bottles and 6 gross of corks. They will arrive here after my departure, but orders relating to them are left.[25]

Jefferson left Monticello that day to join Washington and the Congress at Philadelphia. He had rented a fine house there, complete with bookroom, stables, a "garden house," and its own wine cellar. Jefferson made his usual expensive additions. The house was at 274 High Street, commonly called Market Street, three blocks from Washington's house, and within walking distance of the American Philosophical Society, a center of attention for Jefferson while in Philadelphia.

On November 30, 1790, his furniture, books, and eighty-six packing cases of effects arrived from Paris. Included in the shipment, called by Dr. Malone the most varied ever imported by an American at that time, was the rest of Jefferson's Paris wine cellar.[26] Jefferson moved into his new residence, which was also his office as secretary of state until January 9, 1791, when he noted in his account book: "Begin to dine at home."

Congress went into session December 6, requiring constant reports from Jefferson and halting his letter-writing on wine that winter. There was no need to write to favorite correspondents such as Madison and Monroe, who were both in Philadelphia as congressmen and dined at his house several times a week. When Jefferson's friends were accessible to him, he became less accessible to us, since he had no need to commit their wine talks to paper. But he had not forgotten the subject, especially the wines for the president. He wrote to Short to express concern about the French wines, which *still* had not arrived:

> January 24, 1791
>
> I must pray you to keep in mind and execute the commissions for the clock and [John] P[aul] Jones's medal. Also the *President's wine.* I have not received his bill yet. I hope the *wine* will arrive before the *warm* weather.[27]

The mails were slow, but the faithful Short was working on his orders for Washington:

> Amsterdam Dec. 23, 1790
>
> I have lately received from Paris your letter of Sep. 6. from Philadelphia inclosing a bill of exchange for 589. #6s. and a letter for Mr. Fenwick. I forwarded it to him with advice that I would pay at sight his bill for the charges respecting the wine. I have already advice of the Champaign you had ordered being already received at Havre, and I hope it is now on the sea.[28]

Short followed up:

December 29, 1790

Sir,

I mentioned to you in my last that the Champaigne was received at Havre. M. Fenwick I hope will soon dispatch the Bordeaux.

W: Short[29]

Jefferson also received at last the wines he had left in barrels in his Paris cellar. Sharp Delany, collector of customs at Baltimore, asked Jefferson to remit the duties he owed on "12 cases containing 56 dozen and 8 bottles wine." Jefferson's customs declaration still exists, signed in his hand, showing the duties on his wines came to $17.99.[30]

These wines were the Graves, Cahusac, and Portuguese wines from Jefferson's Paris cellar. They also included his remaining clarets, which were bottled, but not brought with him to America. By January of 1791 he had a fairly ample cellar once again.

Hamilton Sets the Import Duties on Fifty-six Cases of Wine from Jefferson's Paris Cellar

Ironically, when he needed to consult someone as to the duty to pay on his French wines, it was Secretary of the Treasury Hamilton. Later, when they were bitter political adversaries, Hamilton mocked Jefferson for his attachment to things French, especially "luxury" items like wine. They hardly knew each other before Jefferson's return from France, which may have affected Hamilton's opinion, since he never knew Jefferson without French influence on his tastes and appearance. Reliable observers have stated that when Jefferson first returned he was noticeably frenchified, wearing silk suits, ruffles, and an unusual topaz ring, none to the taste of his American compatriots. He soon dropped most of those habits, especially the French clothes, but by then Hamilton's first impression of him as a foppish Francophile may have been indelible.

In reverting to a more American appearance, Jefferson either overdid it, lost interest, or at least bungled the job of readjusting to American ideas of proper dress. Senator William Maclay, an otherwise like-minded Republican senator from western Pennsylvania, left in his diary for May 24, 1790, a disappointed portrait of the secretary of state: "His whole figure has a loose, shackling air. I looked for gravity, but a laxity of manner seemed shed about him [by] ill-fitting, much worn clothes."[31] Maclay also spoke of Jefferson's "vacant look," and how he "spoke unceasingly in a loose, rambling way." Perhaps Maclay was not an accurate observer, but has been much quoted mainly because there is little else on Jefferson's appearance in that period, and Maclay's remarks have the attraction of being mildly shocking.[32]

The Hamiltonians' reaction to Jefferson's manner was more subtle; they accused him of changing his image too rapidly, for political purposes, calling him sarcastically "plain Tom." The Hamiltonians described his attire as

> decorating himself in the modest garb of pure Republicanism a ridiculous affectation of simplicity [which] long ago excited the derision of the many, who know that the *externals* of pure Democracy afford but a flimsy veil to the *internal* evidences of aristocratic splendor, sensuality and Epicureanism.[33]

Although exaggerated for partisan purposes, it is easy to see that with his multiple cellars full of fine wines, his exotic house at Monticello, his French-trained chef, his esoteric library, and his high-minded intellectual interests, Jefferson came off a tad phony as a "mountain man from Virginia."

These contradictions, which were a natural part of his character, had much to do with creating cynicism in political opponents. Had Hamilton known Jefferson before his Paris "education," as Adams had, the two men just might have understood each other better, and left us comments about the Madeiras they drank together at Washington's table. Hamilton himself was, after all, from the West Indies, and no stranger to things exotic.

Nor were Jefferson's wines, or interests, just French. After he and Franklin and Adams had returned to America, their former secretary David Humphreys became Washington's special agent at Lisbon. From there he sent Jefferson, at the latter's request, a memorandum on *Portuguese* wines:

> Messrs. John Bulkeley & Son have engaged to send by the first vessel to Philadelphia different specimens of the dry Lisbon wines, with the prices, for the inspection of Mr. Jefferson in person. They are well acquainted with the subject and may be expected to deal with the strictest honor.[34]

On February 28 and March 30, 1791, Jefferson received letters from Bulkeley & Sons, which have been lost, but his account book entry for March 2, 1791 shows that he received wines as well: "Pd. duty & freight Lisbon, 36 bottles from J. Bulkeley & Son 2.5."

According to a letter to Humphreys dated April 11, the thirty-six bottles included six different wines from the Lisbon region, but aside from one called "Termo" and one "Torres," the only explicit reference to them was in Jefferson's letter to the Bulkeleys later that summer:

> Philadelphia July 13. 1791.
>
> GENTLEMEN
>
> I am now to acknowledge the receipt of your favor of Jan. 18 together with the samples of wine forwarded. That marked No. 2. and called Termo was exactly the quality desired. Next to this was No. 4. Torres. The other qualities not liked. I am now therefore to pray you to send me a pipe of the kind called Termo, the oldest and best you can procure.
>
> You will receive from Mr. Barclay, the bearer of this, 75. dollars on my account, which if I calculate rightly your millreas, will cover the cost of the pipe and the samples.
>
> TH: JEFFERSON[35]

While sampling Portuguese wines and awaiting his Champagnes and Bordeaux, Jefferson had not abandoned his interest in Italian wines.

On April 30 he received a letter from Pierre Guide, whose brother Jefferson had known at Nice and Turin. Jefferson lost no time in asking about the wines of those places:

Philadelphia May. 1. 1791.

Sir

I received last night your favor of Apr. 28. as well as those of your brother. I thank you for the communication of your invoice. I looked over the invoice with some eagerness in hopes of finding in it some of the kind of wine which I drank at Turin under the name of Nebiule.

Should you be able, with convenience, to order, in any of your future invoices, five or six dozen bottles of that, *du meilleur cru* [of the best growth], I will take them thankfully.

My object with respect to the wine being merely to distribute it here in the best houses, in order to recommend it from it's quality, which I know to be good, and from it's price, I will beg the favor of you to let me know at what price I may say to them that it can be procured in future.

If you could send me by the first stage (if the package will bear land-carriage) a single dozen of the Vin vieux de Nice, and the price, perhaps I may procure further orders from hence before I go.

TH: JEFFERSON[36]

Guide, who was in Baltimore, replied May 5, sending a dozen bottles of old red wine of Nice. He promised to send the other two dozen bottles of old Nice by the first opportunity.[37]

The old Nice miscarried. As Jefferson prepared to leave on May 17 for a "botanical" trip through New England with Madison (their political enemies said it was to build Republican support), he wrote Guide to check on the Nice:

Philadelphia May 16, 1791.

Sir

Being in the moment of setting out on my journey, I have just time to acknowledge the receipt of your favor of the 5th. inst. and to note your information that you had sent off by the stage of that day a case of wine and some raisins for me. On repeated enquiries at the different stage-offices, I find it has never arrived here, which I thought necessary to mention to you in order to excite your enquiries after it.

Th: Jefferson[38]

After his return from the New England trip Jefferson found the Nice had arrived.[39] From letters written later, while he was President and during his retirement, we know that the wine of Nice remained throughout his life a Jefferson favorite.

In Bordeaux "The Only Introduction and the Sufficient One Is the Cash"

Embarrassed at receiving no word of the wines ordered for Washington, Jefferson decided to try other sources for Bordeaux. He turned first to Richmond merchant Alexander Donald, enclosing a memorandum on the wines of Bordeaux:

Philadelphia May 13, 1791

My public occupations rarely permit me to take up the pen of private correspondence [but] I find as I advance in life I become less capable of acquiring new affections and therefore I love to hang by my old ones.

Enclosed was the following:

Memorandum on the Wines of Bordeaux

1. Red. There are 4. crops which are best and dearest, to wit Chateau-Margaux . . . Tour de Segur belonging to Monsieur Miromenil, 125. tons. Hautbrion, two thirds of which are engaged; the other third belongs to the Count de Toulouse at Toulouse, and De la Fite belonging to the President Pichard at Bordeaux. The last are in perfection at 3. years old, the three first not till 4. years. They cost about 1500.# the tun when new, and from 2000.# to 2400.# when ready for drinking.

The best red wines after the 4. crops are Rozan belonging to Madame de Rozan (who supplies me), Dabbadie ou Lionville, la Rose, Quirouen, Durfort. These cost 1000.# new. and I believe 1500.# to 1750.# fit for use. These wines are so nearly equal to the 4. crops that I do not believe any man can distinguish them when drank separately.

2. White wines. The wine made in the Canton of Grave are most esteemed at Bordeaux. The best crops are 1. Pontac belonging to M. de Lamont, 400.# the ton, new. 2. St. Brise belonging to M. de Pontac, 350.# the ton new. 3. de Carbonius belonging to the Benedictine monks. They never sell new, and when old they get 800.# the ton.

But the white wines made in the three parishes above Grave are more esteemed at Paris than the vins de Grave. These are 1. Sauterne, the best of all, belonging to M. de Lur-Saluce (who supplies me) 300.# the ton new and 600.# old. 2. Prignac. The best is the President du Roy. Same price. 3. Barsac. Best is the President Pichard's. Same price. Add to all these prices 5. sous for bottles and bottling.

You have no occasion for a letter [of introduction]. *The only introduction and the sufficient one is the cash* [emphasis added]. If you should apply to Madame de Rosan or Monsieur de Lur-Saluce, if their stock of good wine should be low, it may add an inducement to them to name me.

In all cases the owner is the person to be applied to. He will either send you none, or good. He never adulterates, because he would be a felo de se [suicide] to do it. All the persons live at Bordeaux where not otherwise mentioned.[40]

Jefferson left instructions with his assistant about what to do if wines arrived while he and Madison were in New England:

For Henry Remsen, Jr.

May 16. 1791.

I expect some parcels of wine from Bordeaux for the President and myself. Mr. Lear will receive the President's as also a parcel for him from Havre. I do not know the quantity of mine, which with the incertainty of it's coming at all prevents my leaving the duties. If it should arrive, as there would be danger of it's spoiling in a warehouse, perhaps Mr. Delany will let it come to my own cellars, on assurance that I will settle the duties on my return.

I expect 3 doz. of wine (as a sample) from Baltimore.[41]

The Jefferson Guide to the Inns of Old New England

The following day Jefferson left for a tour with Madison through New England, not returning to Philadelphia until June 19. Except for his wine tours of Europe in 1787–88, this was Jefferson's most pleasurable trip in a life filled with travel. He and Madison fished for trout in Lake George, hunted squirrels, and killed two rattlesnakes, but Jefferson's notes from the trip are mainly botanical. He obtained azaleas and sugar maples for making his own syrup at Monticello, a project which fell through. From the lakes he wrote on birch bark a letter to his daughter Maria.[42]

No mention of wines tasted on the trip has been preserved, but one unique document does remain. Called by Jefferson "Stages of My Journey," it marks the distances he traveled and places he stayed in New England. In it Jefferson rated, for food and lodging, every inn where he and Madison stayed. He even examined and rated several places where they did *not* stay, in a few cases rating three or four different inns in a single place.

The "Stages" manuscript, which Jefferson wrote in the June 20 entry in his account book the day after his return to New York, is a regular *Guide Michelin* for travel in New York, Connecticut, and Vermont in the early 1790s. His rating system was a simple one. Each rated inn was marked with a symbol. A key to the symbols was given at the end of the manuscript explaining them:

    * = good
    + = middling
    − = bad[43]

Not surprisingly, the better-rated inns were in prosperous areas like the Hudson and Connecticut River valleys. Federalists, particularly

Hamilton's son, accused them of "grumbling about the eatables" again, but the trip had a tonic effect on Jefferson like his best wines. For the first time in over a year his migraine headaches went away. The two Republicans had meetings with Aaron Burr in New York, but the primary purpose does seem to have been relaxation and intellectual pleasure.

Letters Arrive from the Proprietors of Chateaux Latour, Yquem, and Rauzan, with a Promise of 1786 Lafite

On June 19, 1791, Jefferson noted six different letters replying to his orders for Champagne, Bordeaux, and Frontignan sent off in August and September of 1790.

The first, from the Count of Miromenil, came from Paris, and promised him that the Château Latour he wanted for President Washington should be forthcoming:

Paris 18 Jan. 1791

I received, Sir, the letter which you did me the honor of writing on Sept. 6 last on behalf of your President, the General Washington, who wishes to have 20 dozen bottles of the fine wines called [La Tour de] *Ségur* du Medoc. The reknown of your General is too well-known in France for every good Frenchman not to desire to seize every occasion to give him proofs of our respect, and to hasten to carry out his orders.

I was in fact proprietor since 1765 of a part of these great wines, through my first wife, named Ségur, whom I lost in 1774. She left me two daughters whom I saw married in 1786, and to whom I gave all the properties of their mother. Thus the land of La Tour en Médoc, which they share in common, belongs today to their husbands.

Nevertheless, I have kept a friendly correspondence with Mr. Domenger, the manager, to whom I am sending your letter, asking that he fill your order. I shall also be sure to inform the Count de la Pallu and the Marquis de Beaumont, my sons-in-law, who will surely be as eager as I am to give their orders as well.

I can assure you punctuality and quality wine, and that your wishes will be entirely honored.

THE CT. DE MIROMENIL,

BRIGADIER-GENERAL[44]

The next letter, from the proprietor of the estate known as Rausan of the commune of Margaux, came from the proprietress herself. The price of her wine sounds high, but her letter bore indicia of sincerity and fair dealing. Perhaps for that reason Jefferson often chose her wine over higher-classified clarets.

Marg. in Médoc The 30th of Jan of 1791

I received, Sir, the letter which you did me the honor of writing dated Sept. 6th last, by which you ask of me ten dozen bottles of my wine of Margaux of first Quality. Although I am in the practice of selling it new (en nouveau), I find that I have a little lot of three casks of the 1785 vintage which, although good, is not one of the better years.

It has been drawn off in bottles for more than a year, and should have thus acquired all the bouquet that it will be able to for that year. I am sending you 4 cases of 25 bottles each for 50 S[ous] the bottle, in French glass, and a 5th case of 25 bottles of 1786 in English glass for 3 livres the bottle.

I only kept one cask of this quality, and I had it drawn off especially for you. This type of wine needs to remain some time in bottle, as you know, Sir. After waiting the time which you deem necessary to evaluate it, you can let me know if you wish more.

I will be able also to share with you a hogshead barrel which I kept of the year 1788, and another hogshead of the year 1790. But if you want to be able to judge these different years while they are in the wood, and if you think it proper, Sir, I will be very happy to keep each year a part of my harvest for you, and to maintain the correspondence which you have kindly seen fit to establish with me.

Therefore I shall be more careful than ever to see that it is well kept. In any case you can count, Sir, on the fact that there is neither fraud nor mixture in my wine, which makes it very wholesome and good for the health.

I am sending, per your intention, the 5 cases of wine to Mr. Fenwick's, Consul of the United States of New England, on the Quai des Chartrons.

BRIET DE RAUSAN

All of the said bottles are sealed with my seal like that on my letter. My address is: Madame Briet de Rausan, lodger at the Convent of Notre Dame, Dutra Street, Bordeaux.

I have, Sir, around 2 or 3 thousand bottles of the wine of 1785 at 50 S[ous], the bottle, all in cases of 25 bottles, and consequently ready to ship in case of need. As for that of 1786 for 3 livres the bottle, I have left only 3 hogshead.[45]

The Bordeaux wine estate with which Jefferson was most familiar was the Château d'Yquem in Sauternes, still the finest, and until quite recently still in the hands of the same Lur-Saluces family that Jefferson dealt with. As Jefferson said, Yquem "hit the palate" of his American friends in Paris better than any other wine. From the Countess de Lur-Saluces he received this reply:

Bordeaux 25 fevrier 1791

Having had the misfortune of losing the Count of Lur Saluces, Sir, and having consequently regained possession of my white wines of Yquem, Haut-Sauternes, Mr. Fenwick forwarded to me the letter which you had addressed to the late Count de Lur-Saluces.

I hope Sir that you will be happy with the shipment I have sent you, which consists of 10 cases of 50 bottles each, that is to say 3 making 150 bottles for you, and 7 making 350 bottles for General Washington.

The desire to serve you better convinced me to divert this portion of a shipment bound for Paris, and being shipped from here I can send you for 30 sous the bottle and 4 livres the case.

I ask you Sir to kindly send your orders directly to me and I shall fill them with the greatest care and promptness.

D'YQUEM COMTESSE DE LUR-SALUCES[46]

When one sees what the proprietors say about their wines, it is amusing to read what the American consul thought about how much they charged, not to mention the trouble he had procuring them. Fenwick's company wrote to Jefferson on February 10 and March 29, enclosing an invoice for twenty-eight cases of wine, fourteen for Jefferson and fourteen for Washington, which Jefferson received on June 21. The information on prices was not all good, but for those days of revolution, and considering how finicky he was, the wines seem as good as he could have hoped for:

Bordeaux 10 feby. 1791.

Sir

We have the honor of your favor of the 6th. Sepr. containing letters to several wine proprietors with a request to pay for and expedite the several parcels of wine you ordered, which shall be complyed with by the first vessel in Philadela.

We have received Madam de Rausan's parcel, and advice from the Countess de lur Saluce that she should immediately prepare and forward us the parcel ordered from her. M. de Miromenil has also wrote us that his Son in Law the Count de la Pallu, at present the proprietor of the Estate of Segur, wou'd comply with your order but we have since seen his homme d'affair who says he has no wine on hand proper to ship as a sample that will do justice to his estate, therefore cannot execute your order. Should this prove to be the case we shall venture to send for the president some of our own chusing.

Monsieur de Pichard is the proprietor of the Estate of *La fite* (formerly Segur) and monsieur de fumel of *Obrion* and *Chateau-margeaux*. These are three of the first four growths of wine in this province, the owners of which are residents here and generally provided to supply their friends. The Miromenil Estate *La Tour* (formerly Segur also) is the fourth, of which there are three proprietors Count de la Pallu, Marquis de Beaumont and the Count de Segur.

F. M & Co.

18 FEBY. 1791.[47]

The March 29 letter added further information:

The proprietors of the Miromenil Estate declined shipping the wine of Ségur order for the President. We therefore have replaced it out of the wines of Lafite, the Estate of Mr. Pichard (formerly Ségur), the growth of 1786, which we hope will prove perfect and will give entire satisfaction.

We think the Comsse. de Lur Saluce has charged a very extraordinary
price for the parcel shiped you. The same quality here never costs more than
600 to 800 per Tun of 4 hogshead and she, we observe, has charged you 30 sols
per bottle, glass included.[48]

The foregoing letter is of comfort to both the proponents and opponents of the authenticity of the "Jefferson" bottles. To the latter, it reinforces the idea that 1787 was not a preferred vintage, and when given the choice, Jefferson's Bordeaux suppliers avoided it. On the other hand it shows that substitutions were freely made in his orders, and it is possible that such a substitution resulted in the 1787 bottle of Lafite and others.

The final letter in the June 21 packet was from La Motte in Le Havre, and dealt with Washington's Champagne. Dated March 25, it noted that he still had the four cases of Champagne, which he had just sent by the *Henrietta* bound for Philadelphia. This was fortunate for Jefferson and Washington. The earlier ship which La Motte had said he was using, *Le Vendangeur*, sank, and although the crew was rescued, all the Champagnes sank with it. Ironically the greed of the captain of that vessel, who tried to overcharge La Motte, averted loss to Jefferson. By the time he learned of the mishap, the *Henrietta* and his wines had arrived safely in Philadelphia.[49]

On June 24 Jefferson wrote to Tobias Lear, Washington's trusted private secretary from 1786 to 1793, to confirm receipt of the wines:

June 24th, 1791.

Th: Jefferson presents his compliments to Mr. Lear. He has been endeavoring this morning, while the thing is in his mind, to make a statement of the cost and expenses of the President's wines, but not having a full account of the whole from Fenwick, he is unable to do it but on sight of the account rendered by him to the President.[50]

If Mr. Lear, the first time any circumstance shall give him occasion of doing Th: J. the honor of calling on him, will put that account in his pocket, the matter can be completed in two or three minutes.

The cloudiness of the present day renders it favorable to remove the 4 hampers of Champagne from Th: J's cellar, if Mr. Lear thinks proper to send for them. It would be well to open a case of every kind and place the bottles on their shelves that they may be settled before the President's return.[51]

This letter, apparently hand-carried down the street for delivery that day, conveys a real flavor of Jefferson the wine expert, giving directions on how to transport volatile Champagnes on sunless days and to set it up to let the sediment settle. There is no record that Lear came right over to get it, but he must have come soon, because in the account book for July 16 there appears the entry: "Rec'd of the President by T. Lear John Warder's [bill of] Exchange."

The other document Jefferson mentioned to Lear, an account given earlier to Washington, was probably the basis for a later, undated memorandum which summarizes all references to these wine shipments in letters and accounts:

DISBURSEMENTS FOR WINES FOR THE PRESIDENT

	L	S
D^r. Lambert. Frontignan. 2. cases G.W. N.°. 2		
3. 120 bottles——	155	0
——carriage from Frontignan to Bordeaux	44	11
Countess de Lur-Saluce. Sauterne.		
7. cases . . . 350	525	0
packages for	28	0
Fenwick De la Fite. 5 cases of		
240 bottles @ 3. 720^L Charges 30^L	750	
his charge for postage of letters	10	5
on the subject. one half his charges for entries, shipping Commissions & c.	195	8
Capt. Tilden. freight from Bordeaux to Charleston—one half	88	0
M^r. Short. Champagne. 4. hampers		
(supposd 451 bott. @ 3^L. no acct rendered)	1353	0
La. Motte. Transportn & other charges on the champagne from Paris to Havre . . .	226	18
Capt. Weeks. freight of Champagne from Havre to Philade.		
71 cub. feet @ 1/shil.	8	10
	3,460	12[52]

On June 27 Jefferson received an amusing letter from his old friend Richard Peters, of the Dolly's Chop House incident in England. In eighteenth-century banter reminiscent of Gouverneur Morris, Peters invited the secretary of state to visit.

[Belmont], 26 June 1791.

Dear Sir

Almost as soon as I saw you advertized in a New York News Paper, your Return was announced in one of ours. I have been in Town twice since I left the Assembly and once I called to enquire after you, but you had eloped. My Strawberries are gone and I have no Temptations to offer you. Come then from disinterested Motives when you wish for a little Country Air and you will get it here. Should it create an Apetite I will give you something to eat.

Madison I saw not thro' the Winter except now and then *en passant*. I hear not whether he is in Philada. or gone Southward. As he is said to be the *Fox* of America, I suppose he was too cunning to let our Paragraphists get hold of him. —Yours very Sincerely,

R. PETERS[53]

Jefferson lost no time in replying, not omitting his new wines:

June 30. 1791.

Call on me, in your turn, whenever you come to town: and if it should be about the hour of three, I shall rejoice the more. You will find a bad dinner, a good glass of wine, and a host thankful for your favor, and desirous of encouraging repetitions of it without number, form or ceremony.

TH: JEFFERSON[54]

Jefferson learned that month from Short that his favorite servant, Adrien Petit, would finally join him at Philadelphia.[55] The bachelor Jefferson, with heavy official duties, needed someone reliable to run his household. He had been trying for over a year to persuade Petit to come.

In the end it was not the entreaties of the secretary of state which prevailed, but life in the country. As Petit himself put it, living in a small village in Champagne with his mother, he was dying of boredom (*mourait d'ennui*) and was ready for Philadelphia, where he planned to *rester toujours* (stay forever). He lasted only until January 1794.[56]

On July 19, the day Petit arrived, Jefferson continued his reentry into the Philadelphia social world, inviting another wine lover of Washington's cabinet, Secretary of War Henry Knox, to dine with him at home:

July 19. 1791.

Dear General

    When the hour of dinner is approaching, sometimes it rains, sometimes it is too hot for a long walk, sometimes your business would make you wise to remain longer at your office or return there after dinner, and make it more eligible to take any sort of a dinner in town.

    Any day and every day that this would be the case, you would make me supremely happy by messing with me, without ceremony or other question than whether I dine at home. The hour is from one quarter to three quarters after three, and, taking your chance as to fare, you will be sure to meet a sincere welcome from Yours affectly. & respectfully,

TH: JEFFERSON[57]

Knox's reply was friendly and swift:

July 19. 1791.

My Dear Sir

    I have received your friendly note of this morning for which I sincerely thank you. I shall frequently avail myself of your kindness, and I should have done so this day, in order to evince my impressions on the occasion, had I not previously engaged to Mrs. Knox, that I would dine with her being the first time since her late confinement. -I am my dear Sir respectfully and affectionately Yours,

H KNOX[58]

From a letter to Short of July 28, we know that the Bordeaux and Frontignans had arrived, so the presence of both Petit and fine wines likely rekindled Jefferson's sociable instincts:

Philadelphia July 28, 1791

The wines from Champagne and Bordeaux are arrived. So is Petit. You have not informed me of the cost of the Champagne, and of it's transportation to Paris, so that my account with the President remains still open.[59]

Given the difficulties of eighteenth-century financial transactions, it is strong proof of the great love of fine wines among the Founding Fathers that they would subject themselves to the rigors of obtaining and paying for them.

From his letters after he returned to Philadelphia in 1791, it is apparent that Jefferson was healthy and intended to be sociable again. He had not yet had any serious conflicts with Hamilton, whom he was just getting to know. One early highlight of his relations with Hamilton was the treatment of Jefferson's tremendous shipment of wines and household goods from Paris, which amounted to eighty-six large, heavy packing cases. As the official in charge of customs duties, Hamilton was asked how much to charge. If he was hostile to Jefferson at that time, he certainly did not show it, allowing the entire hoard to pass duty free with the exception of the wines, for which he charged a pittance, and some expensive French wallpaper, which he taxed at a greatly undervalued rate.[60]

The inventory prepared by Short and Petit in Paris shows other wine-related items, including eight crystal decanters, twelve crystal goblets, and four small flasks, in addition to twelve cases containing fifty-six and two-thirds dozen bottles of wine in one crate, five dozen bottles in another, and twenty more bottles in another.

Jefferson apparently never made up a new cellar list while in Philadelphia, and no other document exists to tell us which wines he drank when or what he thought of them. There may exist somewhere a series of lists made in Paris in August of 1790 by Petit when he packed the wines. Petit told Jefferson of such lists in a letter of August 3, 1790. Jefferson's letter-list shows that he received this one July 19, 1791, the date of Petit's arrival in Philadelphia, which probably means he hand-carried it with him, delivering it in person upon his arrival. Translated, it states:

Paris This 3 August 1790

Sir I take the liberty of writing you to tell you that my parents have objected to my going to join you. Besides that, the wages you offer me are too mediocre to go so far away.

I am packing everything well. I believe you should receive it in good condition.

You say that if there is any wine to have it bottled. It has been at least three years since any wine has arrived in casks. There are 600 bottles of wine, including Cognac, as well as Graves and Paxarete and Frontignan and other wines of Spain. There is in each case a card with the names of all the wines.[61]

The wine cards have never been found, but the lists of other items in Jefferson's eighty-six crates of household goods are quoted in detail in the *Papers*. Too long to include in their entirety here, they are a fascinating catalogue of life at the top of eighteenth-century society, and may be found at pages thirty-four through thirty-nine of volume twenty, the last one compiled by Dr. Boyd, and completed only after his death. Just a sample gives some idea of Jefferson's lifestyle. His head may have been in the library, but his heart was in the kitchen, from whence came: olive oil and anchovies by the barrel; forty bottles of vinegar; thirty kitchen aprons; six kitchen stoves; nineteen copper saucepan covers and thirty-eight copper saucepans; chafing dishes; innumerable kitchen utensils and other food-related items which made up a goodly part of the entire shipment of his Paris effects available to Petit when he arrived to organize Jefferson's Philadelphia household in July 1791.

One interesting item which Petit had packed nearly a year earlier, and recorded as arriving with the lot, was a fifty-pound Parmesan cheese. Despite his protestations about the modesty of his dinners, it is apparent that by 1791 Jefferson had the elements of an elegant table and a fine cellar.

Notable in his crates were several books on cooking, most in French, but a few in Latin, of all things. There were no books on cooking in English.

Surprising was the absence of even a single book on wine. Throughout his life Jefferson does not seem to have recorded possessing a book on wine except regarding the making of wine, even though such existed. His comments sound remarkably similar to some wine books of the time, so it is possible he was familiar with them, but that is unlikely, since he usually bought and kept a copy of every book that had any real interest for him.[62]

"An Office of Infinite Labor"

In August 1791 he described to Philip Mazzei his life as secretary of state:

> I shall go to Monticello in September, and then certainly sell Colle.
>
> I am in an office of infinite labor, and as disagreeable to me as it is laborious. I came into it utterly against my will, and under the cogency of arguments derived from the novelty of the government, the necessity of it's setting out well &c. But I pant after Monticello and my family, and cannot let it be long before I join them.[63]

One observer described Jefferson during this period as a "lonely figure in a hostile cabinet," who suffered "social isolation in aristocratic Philadelphia."[64] His letters to and from Knox and Peters would seem to belie that notion, but there is no evidence that the invitations were ever accepted.[65]

On October 24, 1791, Congress reconvened, requiring Jefferson to present lengthy reports on his department. He began working closely with Washington on a favorite project: the construction of a permanent capital city on the Potomac near Alexandria and Georgetown. This work brought them closer together than ever before. Regrettable is the absence of any comment by either man on what they thought of the many wines that arrived that year, which they probably drank together.

Early that winter Jefferson wrote his longest outline ever of all the wines he preferred. Recipient of this mini-encyclopedia was Philadelphia merchant Henry Sheaff, who asked for the list in a letter dated November 23, 1791. Jefferson hoped to find in Sheaff a reliable local supplier to relieve him from writing all over creation for wines. Whatever the motives, it is to Sheaff that we owe the creation of Jefferson's most comprehensive wine compendium, reproduced here almost in its entirety:

A WINE TREATISE: THE SHEAFF MEMORANDUM[66]

Lisbon wines.	The best quality of the Dry kind is called Termo, and costs 70. Dollars the pipe at about 2 years old. At 5 years old it is becoming a fine wine; at 7 years old it is preferable to any but the very best Madeira. Bulkeley and son furnish it from Lisbon.
Sherry.	The best dry Sherry costs at Cadiz from 80. to 90. Dollars the pipe. But when old and fine, such as is sent to the London market, it costs £30. sterling the pipe. Mr. Yznardi, the son, Consul of the US. at Cadiz, at this time in Philadelphia, furnishes it.

The following facts are from my own enquiries in going thro' the different wine cantons of France, examining the identical vineyards producing the first quality of wines, conversing with their owners, and other persons on the spot minutely acquainted with the vineyards, and the wines made on them, and tasting them myself.

Burgundy. The best white wines are

1. Monrachet. Made on the vineyards of Monsieur de Clermont, and the Marquis de Sarsnet. The latter is rented by M. de la Tour. This sells @ 48 sous the bottle new, and 3 livres fit for drinking.
2. Meursault. The best quality of it is called the Goutte d'or. 6 sous the bottle new. I do not believe this will bear transportation. But the Monrachet will in a proper season. Monsieur Parent, tonnelier at Beaune, is a good hand to conduct a person through these vineyards.

The best red wines of Burgundy are Chambertin, Vougeau, Romanie, Veaune, Nuys, Beaune, Pommard, Voulenay. But it is only the Chambertin, Vougeau, and Veaune which are strong enough to be transported by sea even in the most favorable seasons. They sell therefore for 48.s the bottle new, which is 3 or 4 times the price of the others, and 3 livres old. I think it next to impossible to have any of the Burgundy wines brought here in a sound state.

Champagne.
ˣhe lives at.
Paris his
homme
d'affaires is
M. Louis at Aij

The Mousseux or Sparkling Champagne is never brought to a good table in France. The Mousseux or Sparkling is dearest because most in demand for exportation, but the Non-mousseux is most esteemed and alone drunk by every real connoisseur. The best is made at Aij by ˣ M. d'Orsay, M. le Duc, M de Villermont and M. Janson. The first gentleman makes more than all the rest. It is from him I have taken. It costs 3 livres the bottle when old enough for use, which is at 5 years old.

The best red Champaigne is made by the Benedictines at Auvillaij. They furnish the king's table, but the red Champagne is not of first rate estimation.

The wines of Burgundy and Champagne being made at the head of the
Seine, are brought down that river to Havre from whence they are shipped.
They should come down in the month of November so that they may be
brought over sea in the winter and arrive here before our warm Spring days.
They should be bottled on the spot where they are made. The bottle, bottling,
corking, and packing costs 5 sous a bottle. Capt. Cutting, Consul of the U.S. at
Havre is a good person and well informed to supply the wines of Burgundy and
Champagne.

Cote-rotie.	This is a league below Vienne on the opposite side of the Rhone. The best red is made at Ampuys by Monsieur de la Condamine in his vineyard called Monlis. The best white are at Chateau-grillé by Madame Peyrouse. They cost 12.ˢ the bottle new. Those which are strong enough to bear transportation cannot be drunk till 4 years old. These wines are not in such estimation as to be produced commonly at the good tables of Paris.
Hermitage.	This is made at Tains on the Rhone. The red is not very highly esteemed, but the White is the first wine in the world without a single exception. There is so little of the White made that it is difficult to buy it unless you will buy two or three times the quantity of red at the same time. The white improves fastest in a hot situation, and must be 4 years old before it is drank. It then costs, when it can be bought 3 livres the bottle.
Lunel.	This is a wine resembling the Frontignan, but not quite so rich. It is near Nismes.
Frontignan.	The price 20 to 24ˢ the bottle. I purchase always of M. Lambert, who is a physician, and the best person to apply to for information. There are two or three casks of red made in a particular vineyard, not differing at all in flavor from the white. Its scarceness makes it sought and higher priced. It is counterfeited by putting a little Alicant into the White.
Bordeaux.	Red. There are 4 vineyards of first quality, more famous than all the rest, viz:

1. Chateau-Margau belonging to Monsieur d'Agicourt, all under contract.
2. la Tour de Segur belonging to M. Miromenil.
3. Hautbrion belonging to M. de Fumelle and M. de Toulouse
4. de la Fite, belonging to President Pichard. This is in perfection at 3 years old, the three former not till four. When fit for use they all cost about 3 livres the bottle, but are so engaged beforehand it is impossible to get them.

The merchants, if you desire it, will send you a wine by any of those names, and make you pay 3 livres a bottle: but I will venture to affirm that there never was a bottle of those wines sent to America *by a merchant*. Nor is it worth while to seek for them; for I will defy any person to distinguish them, unless he tastes them together, from the wines of the next quality, to-wit

Rozan-Margau, which is made by Madame de Rozan.

This is what I import for myself, and consider as equal to any of the four crops. There are also the wines of Dabbadie, la Rose, Quirouen and Durfort, which are reckoned as good as Madame de Rozan's. Yet I have Preferred hers. These wines cost 40 to 50 sous the bottle, and sometimes 3 livres, when of the proper age for drinking.

Bordeaux white wines.

Grave. The best is called Pontac, and is made by Monsieur de Lamont. It costs 18 sous a bottle.

Sauterne. This is the best white wine of France (except Champagne and Hermitage). The best of it is made by Monsieur de Lur-Salus, and costs at 4 years old (when fit to drink) from 20 to 24 sous the bottle.

There are two other white wines made in the same neighborhood called Prignac (the best is the President du Roy), and Barsac (the best is the President Richards), esteemed by some. These last are more esteemed at Paris than those of Grave, and they cost from 8^s to 24^s the bottle according to their age. But the Sauterne is that most preferred at Paris, and much the best in my judgment. They cost the same. A great advantage of the Sauterne is that it becomes higher flavored the day after the bottle has been opened, than it is at first.

A general observation as to all wines is that there is great difference in those of the same vineyard in different years, and this affects the price considerably.

Mr. Fenwick, Consul of the US. at Bordeaux, is well informed on the subject of these wines, and has supplied the President and myself with them genuine and good. He would be a proper person to endeavor to get from the South of France some of the wines made there which are most excellent and very cheap, say 10 or 12 sous the bottle. Those of Rousillon are the best. I was not in Rousillon myself, and therefore can give no particular directions about them.

At Nismes I drank a good wine, stronger than claret, well flavored, the tavern price of which was 2 sous the quart. Mr. Fenwick might perhaps be able to get these brought through the Canal of Languedoc.

A good correspondent at Amsterdam might furnish the following wines:

Moselles.

The best are made about 15 leagues from Coblentz on the mountain of Brownberg, adjoining the village of Dusmond; and the best crop there is that of the Baron Breidbach Burresheim. This when fit for use costs 22^s the bottle. It is really a good wine.

There are others, to wit, Vialen, Crach, Bisport, Selting, Kous, Berncastle, which are good, but not equal to Brownberg.

Hock.   There are now three wines of this character, viz.

1. Hocheim
2. Johansberg
3. Rudesheim

Of these the Johansberg has for some years past acquired the highest reputation. It sells at a florin as soon as drinkable, which is not till it is 5 years old, and to be tolerably mild they all require a much greater age. The oldest and dearest are 5/ sterling the bottle wholesale.

It is to be observed of the Hock wines that no body can drink them but Germans, or the English who have learnt it from their German kings. Compared with the wines of more Southern climates they are as an olive compared with a pine-apple.

Observe that whenever the price of wine *by the bottle* is mentioned, it means to include the price of the bottle, &c which is 5 sous. Deduct that sum therefore, and it leaves always the price of the wine.

Reducing the Duties on Imported Wines

In addition to writing the remarkable document reproduced above, Secretary of State Jefferson was also trying to encourage wine drinking among his countrymen by getting the duties on imported wines reduced. To do so meant dealing directly with the ministers from the wine-producing countries.

In the winter of 1791–92 Philadelphia began to have a real diplomatic corps. Jean-Baptiste Ternant, who served in the American Revolutionary Army under Lafayette, arrived as French minister; George Hammond, who had formed close relations with Hamilton, represented England. Despite hopes for pleasant times amid good wines, the winter was spent in partisan rancor, described by Jefferson as a session of "labor, envy and malice." Nor did the weather cooperate. On February 20, 1792, Jefferson wrote that they had not seen the ground through the snow for two months and the temperature was sixteen degrees Fahrenheit. In the spring of 1792 a slight thaw came in commercial relations with France, especially regarding duties on French wines. Jefferson wrote to Morris in Paris that he had made progress on one of their favorite subjects:

Philadelphia April 28, 1792

In a bill which has passed the House of Representatives, the duties on every other species of wine are raised from one to three-fourths more than they were, [while] the best wines of France will pay little more than the worst of any other country, to wit, between six and seven cents a bottle; and where this exceeds forty per cent on their cost, they will pay but the forty per cent.

I consider this latter provision as likely to introduce in abundance the cheaper wines of France, and the more so as the tax on ardent spirits is considerably raised. I hope that these manifestations of friendly dispositions towards that country will induce them to repeal the very obnoxious laws respecting our commerce which were passed by the preceding National Assembly.

Congress will rise on this day sen'night.[67]

Morris was not successful in negotiating with the French, whose government changed too often and too violently to give well-reasoned attention to commercial business. Anticipating problems with his French wines, earlier that month Jefferson had procured a reserve supply, noting in his account book for April 7, 1792: "pd. duty on pipe of Lisbon $27.20."

Before leaving Philadelphia for a three-day stay at Monticello, Jefferson notified his supplier of the wines of Italy and Nice that he had found the old red of Nice ordered the previous year:

To Pierre Guide

Philadelphia July 21. 1792.

Sir

You will probably have received a letter from M.ʳ Girard on the subject of the first box of wine and the parcel of raisins you were so kind as to send me. By searching in another stage office, which I did not know of at that time, I have found them & have received the whole. I thought it my duty to mention this in order to save you the trouble of further enquiry, and take at the same time occasion to enclose you 12. dollars for the 3. dozen of vieux Vin Rouge de Nice.

Times in France were far from peaceful while Jefferson was at Monticello. In August King Louis XVI was "suspended" and moderate aristocrats like Lafayette were imprisoned. Gouverneur Morris, who never trusted the Revolution, had little sympathy for those who started it. He wrote coldly to Washington about Lafayette's imprisonment, saying he was "crushed by the wheel which he put in motion."[68]

Upon his return to Philadelphia, Jefferson noted in his account book the purchase of a cask of claret. He ordered on the same date from Fenwick a new supply. This may have been in part because of the reduced import duties on French wines, or out of pessimism about future developments in France, or perhaps he just had his palate set for some good Bordeaux:

> Philadelphia Oct. 10, 1792
>
> Having occasion for some of the best vin rouge of Bordeaux, such as is drunk at the best tables there & costs 400.# (old money of 10 d. sterl. the livre) per tonneau, permit me to ask the favor of you to send me 500. bottles of that quality, ready bottled in strong bottles and safely packed, that it may arrive before the warm weather of the ensuing spring.[69]

Jefferson Threatens an Embargo Against Portuguese Wines

Despite his political dissatisfaction with events in France, Jefferson continued to prefer French wines. When Portugal became troublesome, he wrote to Humphreys in Lisbon the threat that America might not always yield to Portuguese commercial demands. Just because Madeira and other Portuguese wines were standard in the colonies did not mean Americans would always prefer Portuguese wines to "superior" French ones:

> Philadelphia, November 6, 1792
>
> P.S. November 7. After writing this letter, your No. 59 came to hand. It seems then that, so far from giving new liberties to our corn trade, Portugal contemplates the prohibition of it, by giving that trade exclusively to Naples. What would she say should we give her wine-trade exclusive to France and Spain?

It is well known that far the greatest portion of the wine we consume is from Portugal and its dependencies, and it must be foreseen that from the natural increase of population in these States, the demand will become equal to the utter-most abilities of Portugal to supply, even when her last foot of land shall be put into culture. Can a wise statesman seriously think of risking such a prospect as this? To me it seems incredible; and if the fact be so, I have no doubt you will interpose your opposition with the minister, developing to him all the consequences which such a measure would have on the happiness of the two nations. He should reflect that nothing but habit has produced in this country a preference of their wines over the superior wines of France, and that if once that habit is interrupted by an absolute prohibition, it will never be recovered.[70]

As if to emphasize his point, Jefferson then wrote both Fenwick and Elbridge Gerry, the new American commissioner in France, about the excellence of Château d'Yquem, and kept ordering red Médoc, despite the "infernal robbers, vagabonds and miscreants" who interfered with wine shipments along the U.S. coast.[71]

He was also laying in supplies at Monticello for what he thought would be an early and permanent retirement from his job as secretary of state. According to Judge Dumbauld, who calculated Jefferson's use of his days, he spent 197 days at home during his four years in that office. If that sounds like a lot, he spent 876 days at Monticello during his four years as vice president, some 60 percent of his time.[72] With that much time at home, Jefferson no doubt needed a considerable cellar there.

During late 1792 and 1793 Jefferson foresaw his tenure as secretary of state drawing to a close. Political animosities had erupted into scathing public insults between opposing partisans of Hamilton and Jefferson, who was accused of being too much a Francophile. His French wines and demeanor had come back to haunt him. Jefferson on the other hand accused Hamilton of similarly unhealthy leanings toward the aristocratic and monarchical notions of the English.

Ironically, France had since turned too radical for Jefferson, who believed the French populace he knew was totally unprepared for a democratic republic. In September 1792, the French Republic was created.

As Jefferson had feared, its first act was to declare war on Austria and Prussia. In 1793 the situation dramatically worsened. Louis XVI and Marie Antoinette were publicly guillotined and France declared war on England as well. Hamilton pressed Washington to join England in the war, but the old general ordered Secretary of State Jefferson to announce U.S. neutrality. When radical French minister "Citizen" Genet heard of this act, he became so obstreperous that Jefferson had to have him recalled to France.

Jefferson finally moved out of the city to a lovely cottage in the country overlooking the Schuylkill River near Gray's Ferry, shipping his books and furniture on to Monticello. His daughter Maria joined him, along with friends from the American Philosophical Society. He wrote to Martha at Monticello of their life in the well-situated little house, a watercolor of which still exists:

> Philadelphia June 17, 1793
>
> Maria writes to you today. She is getting into tolerable health, though not good. She passes two or three days in the week with me under the trees, for I never go into the house but at the hour of bed.
>
> I never before knew the full value of trees. My house is entirely embosomed in high plane-trees, with good grass below; and under them I breakfast, dine, write, read, and receive my company. What would I not give that the trees planted nearest round the house at Monticello were full-grown.[73]

Jefferson would be pleased to know how the poplars, lindens, and other trees he planted beside Monticello are thriving today and furnish magnificent shade for visitors.

Despite his enjoyment of country life on the Schuylkill, dissension in the cabinet deterred him from staying longer. On July 31, 1793, he told Washington that he was leaving for good at the end of September. Then in August an epidemic of yellow fever broke out. Hamilton and his wife both caught it, but survived. Not wanting to desert an already shaky government, nor appear fearful by taking flight, Jefferson stayed on at Philadelphia, moving his office to his house in the country.

Naturally he wrote little on wine during the yellow fever period. But there did occur one untoward culinary incident at his country house which bears mention. While wining and dining too richly under the plane trees in the open air, his good friend Dr. James Hutchinson took a chill and died. His other friend, the surgeon of the Continental Army Dr. Benjamin Rush, blamed the outcome on Jefferson's "unhealthy habit of dining too heavily in open air."[74]

Just before Congress recessed in September 1793, Washington visited Jefferson at Gray's Ferry, asking him either to stay as secretary of state or return to Paris and replace Morris. Jefferson refused both offers. Shortly thereafter both men went home to Virginia, and Jefferson did not return to Philadelphia until November 1. With the first frost, the yellow fever epidemic ended and Jefferson completed his work, presenting extensive position papers on foreign affairs before resigning on December 31, 1793. Petit left his service, not wanting to follow him to the mountains of rural Virginia.

Despite the time of disease and turmoil, Jefferson still found time to think of wine, and ordered Sherry for Monticello just before the recess of Congress:

> To Joseph Yznardi (at Boston)
>
> Philadelphia Sept. 7, 1793
>
> I shall be obliged to you for a pipe of good dry sherry, ready for drinking, such as you have perhaps seen at the house of Messrs. Viar and as you I think informed me was of the quality frequently sent to London.
>
> P.S. The wine to be sent to Richmond in Virginia.[75]

Fittingly, Jefferson's last letter as secretary of state concerned wine, in particular the London-quality Sherry he ordered from Yznardi. On December 31, 1793, his last day in office, he wrote Yznardi at Boston, thanking him for sending the wine and asking him to forward all future correspondence, and the bill for the Sherry, to Monticello, to which he thought he was retiring permanently. As he wrote to Madison: "The little spice of ambition which I had in my younger days has long since evaporated."

First Retirement at Monticello (1794–1796)

On January 16, 1794, Jefferson arrived at Monticello, a private citizen for the first time in over a decade. Behind him, he thought, were the "inquietudes, envy and malice" of public office. What he found at Monticello, however, was not rest, but a different kind of labor. As he wrote to Washington in April 1794:

> I find, on a more minute examination of my lands than the short visits heretofore made to them permitted, that a ten years' abandonment of them to the ravages of overseers has brought on them a degree of degradation far beyond what I had expected.[76]

To repair the damage, which reduced his income from farming nearly to zero, Jefferson took over personally a new system of cropping designed to restore his lands. He had some ten thousand acres, over one thousand of which were in cultivation within riding distance of Monticello. It was a monumental task to restore it all, allowing little time for concerns like wines. Jefferson wrote to Horatio Gates in February 1794 that "[t]he length of my tether is now fixed for life between Monticello and Richmond."[77]

He told Adams his life had dramatically changed from the clerical drudgery of Philadelphia: "I live on my horse from an early breakfast to a late dinner, and very often after that till dark."[78]

He went on:

> I return to farming with an ardor which I scarcely knew in my youth, and which has got the better entirely of my love of study. Instead of writing ten or twelve letters a day, which I have been in the habit of doing as a thing of course, I put off answering my letters now, farmer-like, till a rainy day.[79]

At first he appreciated the peace and quiet, but soon began to miss company, being attached to sitting over good wine hearing and telling stories. Wine has always been known as the "oil of conversation," and it

certainly was for Jefferson. As he later told his daughter Maria when she
seemed to be withdrawing from normal social life:

> I think I discover in you a willingness to withdraw from society more than is pru-
> dent. I am convinced our own happiness requires that we should continue to mix
> with the world, and to keep pace with it as it goes; and that every person who retires
> from free communication with it is severely punished afterwards by the state of
> mind into which he gets, and which can only be prevented by feeding our sociable
> principles.
>
> I can speak from experience on this subject. From 1793 to 1797 I remained
> closely at home, saw none but those who came there, and at length became very
> sensible of the ill effect it had on my own mind, and of its direct and irresistible
> tendency to render me unfit for society and uneasy when necessarily engaged
> in it.[80]

Nor was he able to correspond with his old French friends. Lafayette
was put in prison for not being radical enough, and most of Jefferson's
French friends were thinking more of guillotines than of the bouquets of
clarets.

His neighbors did not all take well to his taste for French wines either.
Henry Randall, his first biographer, told a story which illustrates his reception at Monticello. Noting that "claret" was Jefferson's favorite "summer"
wine, Randall recounted an anecdote about a guest who did not care for
the wines at Monticello. It appears it was Jefferson's choleric neighbor,
Colonel Carter, with whom Jefferson had a falling out. To reconcile them
Madison contrived to get them together at Monticello. Both were cool to
each other at first, but as Randall told the story:

> When they sat down to the dinner-table, he was placed by the side of Mr. Jefferson.
> The ice soon broke, and C_____ began to talk with great animation. Jefferson
> reminding him that he remembered his tastes, had some old and particularly fine
> Madeira placed before him. But no; C_____ declared he would stick to claret with
> his host. They sat a couple of hours, the guest growing more and more delighted.

When they rose from the table Jefferson retired for a few moments. C_____ took our informant aside and very seriously asked, "Do you suppose I could get a glass of good brandy here? I have been so amused by Jefferson that here I have been sipping his [d . . . d] acid, cold French wine, until I am sure I shall die in the night unless I take an antidote."

His travelling companion knew all the ways at Monticello. He directed the faithful Burwell (Mr. Jefferson's favorite servant) to take a bottle of brandy to a private room, as C_____ was willing to throw no imputations on his host's tastes, and so the movement must be concealed from him! Next day he returned to Montpellier, lauding Jefferson to the skies, but sorely puzzled to understand "why a man of so much taste should drink cold, sour French wine!"

He insisted to Mr. Madison that it would injure Jefferson's health. He talked himself warm on the topic. He declared it would kill him—that some night he would be carried off by it! Finally, he insisted that Madison write and urge him to change his wine. His altered tone towards Jefferson, and his warm solicitude in the particular just named afforded great amusement to Madison and Jefferson. The trio thenceforth remained fast friends.[81]

The foregoing anecdote, for which no date is given, reveals several things about Jefferson's wines. First, he drank them chilled, at least in the summer, and he often drank wines different from the ones his guests drank, which may explain why he had wines in his cellars that he professed in his letters not to care for. It also shows that Jefferson liked drier wines than many of his contemporaries, who found his wines "sour," the eternal neophyte's word for a wine which is not sweet.

The mention of "claret" is equally ambiguous. The reference to its being chilled may mean that the wine was not *red* claret, as we are used to, and may confirm what some have long suspected: in early Virginia, many French wines sold as "claret" may have been rosé or even white rather than red.[82] If not, then Jefferson chilled his red wines, at least in the summer.

In August 1794, perhaps from his violent change of lifestyle, Jefferson had a "paroxysm" of rheumatism which kept him "in constant torment." In September Madison arrived with a personal request from Washington to return to government and help quell the Whiskey Rebellion. This series of riots by farmers in Pennsylvania was to protest an excise tax on whiskey proposed by Hamilton to use in paying off war debts. Jefferson had opposed the tax as too hard on farmers, but declined to return for health reasons. Washington finally led an army of twelve thousand militia from four states into Pennsylvania and quashed the "insurrection," but then repealed the tax.[83]

The ironic part of the incident was that Jefferson had always urged high taxes on whiskey to discourage its consumption. Like Washington and Madison, he thought low taxes on wine would encourage the consumption of it as opposed to whiskey, to the benefit of public health. Yet in this case all three men were realistic. Washington knew what his own soldiers would have said if he had taken their rum away, no matter that he and his officers drank mainly wine, and very good wine at that. Hamilton, who thought wine a luxury item for the rich, wanted it taxed more than whiskey.[84] Yet when the crunch came, Jefferson came out for whiskey for political reasons, and the hard-drinking mountaineers of the West were his supporters in all elections thereafter.

In September 1795, at the proper season, Jefferson wrote a long letter to Monroe, who had replaced Morris as American minister in Paris, showing he had not lost interest in French wines:

Monticello Sept. 6, 1795

Wines to be procured & shipped by Mr. Fenwick from Bordeaux. They will come at my risk.

250 bottles of the best vin rouge ordinaire used at the good tables of Bordeaux, such as Mr. Fenwick sent me before.

120 bottles of Sauterne, old & ready for use.

60 bottles of Frontignan.

60 bottles of white Hermitage of the first quality, old & ready for use.[85]

From the records which survive, it appears Jefferson never received the wines ordered via Monroe. The account books for the period are intact and make no mention of any payment for such wines or duties or shipping on them, which Jefferson always recorded. We may therefore assume that his entire stock of French wines in late 1795 and 1796 was limited to those left from his Paris and Philadelphia days.

The mainstay of Jefferson's everyday wines during 1796, the last year of his first retirement, was the Termo he was obtaining through Humphreys from Lisbon. On May 21, 1796, he noted in his account book broaching a new pipe because the one broached in January 1794 was finally "out." Thus the 1794 pipe, which held around 140 gallons, had lasted him nearly two and a half years. That is not a lot of wine by Jefferson standards, even with his household and visitors reduced. Of course he supplemented the Lisbon with the French wines he brought back from Philadelphia.

At the time he had no salary or good cash crops, and French wines were both expensive and hard to get.[86] There was also the matter of his fancy French image. His neighbors apparently were not fans of his French wines. Nor were they able to afford them. As he wrote his French friend Demeunier, in Albemarle County people lived modestly because "even the richest are but a little at ease."[87] At that time Jefferson himself could hardly afford the finest in French wines. He opened a nail-making factory to raise cash, and paid for his servants' brandy in nails.

Another reason for not laying in a cellar of fine wines in 1796 was that Jefferson was renovating Monticello to incorporate new ideas he got in Europe. Nearly doubling its width, he had the roof off all that year, and had 140 laborers working at once. Looking at the tens of thousands of bricks stacked everywhere, he described the whole place as a "brick-kiln." The wine cellar was less disturbed than most of the house, being under the old part, but none of the place was in any condition for one of his wine dinners.

By chance it was in that year that two of the most famous accounts by Monticello visitors were written. The first was by Jefferson's old Paris friend the Duc de la Rochefoucauld-Liancourt, whose book dwelt mainly on Jefferson's gifts as a statesman, and on his lesser talents as a farmer.[88] Probably for the reasons already given, he says not a word about a wine cellar, just as the French general Chastellux had not mentioned the subject during his visit fourteen years earlier.

The young Irishman Isaac Weld published an excellent description of Jefferson's situation in that summer of 1796:

> It [Monticello] is most singularly situated, being built upon the top of a small mountain, the apex of which has been cut off, so as to leave an area of about an acre and a half. At present it is in an unfinished state; but if carried on according to the plan laid down, it will be one of the most elegant private habitations in the United States.
>
> The house commands a magnificent prospect on one side of the blue ridge of mountains for nearly forty miles, and on the opposite one, of the low country, in appearance like an extended heath covered with trees, the tops of which alone are visible. The mists and vapours arising from the low grounds give a continual variety to the scene. The mountain whereon the house stands is thickly wooded on one side, and walks are carried round it, with different degrees of obliquity, running into each other.
>
> On the south side is the garden and a large vineyard, that produces abundance of fine fruit.[89]

The thriving vineyard referred to by Weld looked healthy, but was not yet producing wine, as he explained in the continuation of his published letter:

> Several attempts have been made in this neighbourhood to bring the manufacture of wine to perfection; none of them, however, have succeeded to the wish of the parties. A set of gentlemen once went to the expence even of bringing six Italians over for the purpose; but the vines which the Italians found growing here were different, as well as the soil from what they had been in the habit of cultivating, and they were not much more successful in the business than the people of the country.
>
> We must not, however, from hence conclude, that good wine can never be manufactured upon these mountains. It is well known that the vines, and the mode of cultivating them, vary as much in different parts of Europe as the soil in one country differs from that in another. It will require some time, therefore, and different experiments, to ascertain the particular kind of vine, and the mode of cultivating it, best adapted to the soil of these mountains. This, however,

having been once ascertained, there is every reason to suppose that the grape may be cultivated to the greatest perfection, as the climate is as favourable for the purpose as that of any country in Europe. By experiments also it is by no means improbable that they will in process of time learn the best method of converting the juice of the fruit into wine.

The thoughts on vineyards expressed by Weld sound so much like those of Jefferson that it is likely he obtained them from Jefferson. If so, he was far from giving up his hopes for winemaking at Monticello.

Weld also talked on Jefferson's favored topic of the evils of "ardent spirits." Weld's comments corroborate those made throughout his life by Jefferson:

> The common people in this neighbourhood appeared to me to be of a more frank and open disposition, more inclined to hospitality, and to live more contentedly on what they possessed, than the people of the same class in any other part of the United States I passed through. From being able, however, to procure the necessaries of life upon very easy terms, they are rather of an indolent habit, and inclined to dissipation.
>
> Intoxication is very prevalent, and it is scarcely possible to meet with a man who does not begin the day with taking one, two, or more drams as soon as he rises. Brandy is the liquor which they principally use, and having the greatest abundance of peaches, they make it at a very trifling expence. There is hardly a house to be found with two rooms in it, but where the inhabitants have a still. The females do not fall into the habit of intoxication like the men, but in other respects they are equally disposed to pleasure, and their morals are in like manner relaxed.

Considering how interested Weld was in vineyards, it is curious that he never mentions Jefferson's wines or wine cellar.

Another event occurred in 1795–96 which injured Jefferson financially and aroused him politically: Jay's Treaty. Negotiated by John Jay with the British in 1795, it took effect in 1796. The treaty gave such favorable terms to the British as to convince the French to consider war against America. It was also highly damaging to Jefferson personally, forcing him to repay a second time British creditors for debts of his wife incurred before the Revolution. It made Jefferson realize he could not avoid public life after all, since it had such dramatic impact on his personal life. He therefore decided that when Washington retired, he would run for president, opposing his old friend Adams.

After a fairly bitter campaign, the first contested election for the presidency in America, Adams defeated Jefferson by seventy-one electoral votes to sixty-eight. Under the rules then prevailing, Jefferson became vice president. He had been ambivalent about the whole thing, staying at Monticello and not really campaigning much. It was a time of political intrigue, but Jefferson actually seemed to have little trouble being a good loser. As he wrote to Edward Rutledge, father of the young traveller for whom he wrote the famous Travelling Notes, it was "no time to covet the helm."[90]

THE "HONORABLE AND EASY" OFFICE OF VICE PRESIDENT (1797–1800)

Jefferson was known by all to dislike open personal conflict, and his letter to Elbridge Gerry bore almost a note of relief: "[T]he second office of this government is honorable and easy, the first is but a splendid misery."[91]

To Dr. Benjamin Rush he admitted more candidly that he did not see exactly what use a vice president was supposed to be, but was not complaining:

> A more tranquil and unoffending station could not have been found for me, nor one so analogous to the dispositions of my mind. It will give me philosophical evenings in the winter and rural days in the summer.[92]

The latter image was not wrong as far as it went.

On March 3, 1797, the day before his inauguration as vice president, Jefferson was sworn in to an office for which he had much more enthusiasm: president of the American Philosophical Society. Founded by Franklin, the society was one of Jefferson's most enjoyable hobbies for the rest of his life, second only to founding the University of Virginia. He held the office until 1815, a remarkable tenure considering all the other things he had to do, and a monument to the energetic leadership that the other members obviously thought he provided. Through that society he met the foremost advocates of grape growing and winemaking in America while he was president and thereafter.

Another positive element in the job of vice president was the salary, which was five thousand dollars. While holding that office Jefferson actually made more in salary than he laid out in expenses for the only time in his life.[93] One item on which he cut back was wines. He lived for the entire four years at an inn called John Francis' Hotel, run by an old Frenchman. His fellow lodgers were almost entirely Republicans, and the place was referred to by the Federalist press as a "nest of Jacobins." No formal wine list of that establishment has appeared.[94] But the French proprietor served French wines, as reflected in Jefferson's *Memorandum Books* and certain tavern lists.

As vice president, his hours were not so long nor the work so arduous as when he was secretary of state. While presiding over the Senate, he had time to write the lengthy Manual of Rules still in use today, and which has been called better than that of the British Parliament.

After the inauguration, Washington gave a dinner for Adams and Jefferson, thinking he could reconcile the two old friends, but he was mistaken. After the dinner—the wines were not recorded, other than mentions of "usual toasts"—Jefferson and Adams left together, walking down the street. As Jefferson later recalled it:

> When we came to Fifth street, where our road separated, his being down Market Street, mine off along Fifth, we took leave; and he never after that consulted me as to any measures of the government.[95]

The Infamous "Mazzei Letter"

Philip Mazzei, oldest of Jefferson's wine friends, was not forgotten during Jefferson's first retirement, but might better have been. In what is now known as the "infamous Mazzei letter," the only reference to Mazzei in many books on Jefferson, the future president made the worst blunder of a lifetime in politics. That year, while political battles raged between Jefferson's Republicans and Hamilton's Federalists, Jefferson wrote an indiscreet personal letter to Mazzei, who then resided in faraway Pisa. Dashed off in a moment of anger, in a cutting, vindictive style unusual for Jefferson, the letter was highly critical of Washington, who was in his final term as president. Washington had badly wanted to retire, and Jefferson was one of those who insisted he stay on, then deserted him by refusing any post in the government. Mazzei, receiving the letter, had the lack of judgment to translate Jefferson's letter into Italian and turn it over to a newspaper in Florence. In its most aggravated and memorable parts, it read:

April 24, 1796

The aspect of our politics has wonderfully changed since you left us. In place of that noble love of liberty and republican government which carried us triumphantly through the war, an Anglican, monarchical, aristocratical party has sprung up, whose avowed object is to draw over us the substance, as they have already done the forms, of the British government.

It would give you a fever were I to name to you the apostates who have gone over to these heresies, men who were Samsons in the field and Solomons in the Council, but who have had their heads shorn by the harlot England.[96]

From Italian the letter was translated into French and published in Paris, then sent on to Philadelphia where it was retranslated into English, appearing after Washington retired. Mazzei's blunder caused a scandal in America. For one Founding Father, the Francophile Jefferson, to describe the hero Washington as a shorn Samson in service of England caused an uproar in the press. Popular journalists like "Peter Porcupine" constantly assailed Jefferson. Noah Webster, publisher of a Federalist newspaper, called the letter "treasonable." Jefferson asked Madison and Monroe for advice on a reply, but finally remained silent. The damage was done.

When Washington learned the contents of the letter, he never wrote or spoke to Jefferson again before his death in December 1799. He had considered Jefferson one of his most trusted partners since before the Revolution when they formed The Wine Company with Mazzei. The letter wounded the sensitive old General in a way he could never forgive. When Jefferson returned to public life, it was without the support of Washington.

With the historic break viewed from a decidedly more narrow perspective, it also kept us from knowing what Washington thought of all the wines Jefferson had procured for him, and on what occasions they drank them together.

Isolated from the government and its members both politically and socially, and living in a hotel, Jefferson had little need for wines at Philadelphia beyond what his French hotelkeeper provided. After the inauguration he stayed only ten days before returning to Monticello, arriving on March 20. On March 24, he noted in his account book: "The pipe of Termo broached May 21, 1796 is out. Broached a new one, 1/3 ullaged [evaporated]."

An excellent portrait of social life and wine-drinking habits in Philadelphia during John Adams's administration, while Jefferson was vice president, is provided by a letter from a member of Congress to his wife describing a White House dinner in early 1797:

> We did not adjourn untill after 4 o'clock (the hour at which we were to dine.) We, therefore, went straight from the house of Representatives to the President's, and were introduced by name to the President.
>
> We then sat down and the waiter handed round a glass of punch, which, permit me to say, was very agreeable, after having sat for five long hours, hearing a very dry debate on a very clear subject. In a few minutes, dinner was announced, and one of the gentlemen handed Mrs. Adams into the dining room. The President followed, and the company followed him.
>
> Mrs. Adams sat at the head of the table, and the Secretary at the foot, and the President sat at one side near the middle.—The company took their seats altogether promiscuously.
>
> There were about 20 persons at table. The utensils were only common blue china plates, glass tumblers and *wine-glasses* [emphasis added].
>
> The dishes were nine or ten in number, viz., at the head a piece of beef a la mode; at the foot a large roasted pig; then, alternately, fish, a leg of mutton,

tongue, boiled fowl, ham, corned beef, a dish of small birds, chicken pie, and
perhaps two dishes more. All these, however, were preceded by soup, not calf's-
head, but common. The vegetables were peas, salad, potatoes—new ones but
very small, cranberry sauce. The desserts: tarts, custards, jelies, ice cream, blanc
mange, strawberries, cherries, (very poor) raisins, almonds, &c.

And the wines: Madeira and Port.

After a few glasses, Mrs. Adams withdrew with her daughter, Col. W. S.
Smith's wife, who said nothing that I heard all the time she sat at table. We
drank the United States, and then no toasts or sentiments, but did just as we
pleased, and took a French leave when it suited.[97]

More interesting than the wines themselves were the order of serving
and the glassware. Many books say that wines at that period were always
drunk after the meal was over and the cloth removed. That may have been
generally true, but not always, as this account shows. It appears that cock-
tails were usual and expected before the meal, in this case in the form of
punch. For Jefferson, when he became president, it would have been only
a modest change to substitute appropriate wines as the cocktail instead of
punch, just as white wine has now partly displaced mixed drinks on patios
around the United States.

The presence of both wineglasses and glass tumblers on the cloth when
the meal *began* is interesting. Did it mean that guests had the choice of
drinking wine with their meal if they liked? If not, why were the glasses there
at all if they had to be removed and replaced when the cloth was removed?
The wines themselves, being Madeira and Port, may give the answer: the
closest the Adamses' guests probably came to drinking wines with their
meals was during whatever toasts were offered and during dessert. As
will be seen in the chapter on Jefferson's presidency, he changed these old
toasting customs, adopting a more modern, modified-French system.

Although he was at Monticello from July to December of 1797, there
is not a single entry in either his *Garden Book* or his *Farm Book* for that
year, nor any mention of wines. On December 12, 1797, he returned to
Philadelphia. He had hoped that partisan bitterness might dissipate that
year. He noted in his *Anas* on February 15, 1798, that he dined with a large

company at President Adams's house, sitting next to him and conversing pleasantly on many subjects.

Later however, when his infamous letter to Mazzei denigrating Washington and Adams was read officially to Congress by a Federalist delegate, it reopened the old wounds, and Jefferson was again ostracized from political society. Then yet another French-English conflict worsened his situation further. Adams, up to then less of an Anglophile than the Hamiltonians wanted, had sent John Marshall, Elbridge Gerry, and Charles Pinckney to Paris to negotiate with the French. The envoys were met instead with contempt by three French representatives, referred to as "X, Y, and Z," who demanded cash bribes for an agreement with France, which caused the outraged Americans to sail straight home.

A war fever began in the United States over the XYZ Affair. French-born residents began leaving the country, and even Jefferson thought a war with France was likely. He had long since lost his faith in the stability of French governments as allies, much as he loved the people and their wines. Yet so closely was he associated in the public mind with France and all things French that he was mercilessly lampooned in the press.

One example was at a dinner given later for Monroe when he returned from France as minister. The hosts were Jefferson and Gallatin, who had become Republican leader in Congress in the absence of Madison, who had not stood for reelection. At the Monroe dinner many festive toasts were offered. In the Federalist press "Peter Porcupine" referred to the toasts as being hoisted by "Monsieur" Jefferson and "Citizen" Monroe. Even worse was a toast offered at a Federalist rally on the Fourth of July, which went: "To Adams: may he like Samson slay thousands of Frenchmen with the jawbone of Jefferson."[98]

He described the poisoned atmosphere in Philadelphia in a letter to his daughter Martha:

> Your letters serve, like gleams of light, to cheer a dreary scene, where envy, hatred, malice, revenge, and all the worst passions of men are marshalled to make one another as miserable as possible.[99]

When the xenophobic Alien and Sedition Acts were read in the Senate, Jefferson rode out of Philadelphia and back to Monticello, six weeks before Congress was due to adjourn. Calling 1798 the "reign of witches," he determined to run for president in earnest, and to unseat the Federalists from control.

In such circumstances, good wines were the least of his worries. Yet life went on. His five-thousand-dollar salary was paid in quarterly installments, and he was in Philadelphia so little that he left a power of attorney there with John Barnes to receive his salary and pay his bills. The account book for July 27, 1798, shows that "Barnes pd. bill of Bulkeley 69.45 millreas" for Lisbon wine, which he seems to have drunk almost exclusively at Monticello during this period. His second wine entry of the year, for November 27, 1798, showed that he broached still another new pipe of Lisbon, that of 1797 being "out."

The latter half of 1798 was spent mainly in reroofing Monticello. He wrote few letters on anything, let alone wine, blaming the "infidelities of the post office," which was under dominance of Federalist postmasters and appointees. The year 1799 was even more devoted to building at Monticello. Jefferson stayed at Philadelphia only from December 25, 1798, to March 1, 1799, spending all but two months of 1799 at home. He did not return to Philadelphia until December 26, 1799, apparently missing by design the memorial services for Washington, who had died earlier that month without ever again speaking to him.

In January of 1800 he recorded in his *Anas* (a sort of political diary he called "scraps," later published in three gossipy volumes) that the Senate was only meeting for a half-hour a day. He left the session in May, not returning until November. All during the summer of 1800 there was a constant stream of political visitors at Monticello, but to avoid image problems Jefferson neither ordered nor served French wines. Remarkably, no entries or letters written by him for wines of any kind have been preserved for 1799. In 1800 only one letter, from old friend Samuel Smith dated October 8, 1800, did arrive, announcing that two pipes of good Sherry from Cadiz had been forwarded to Jefferson by U.S. Consul Yznardi.[100]

Regardless of the outcome of the election, some good Sherry would await him at Monticello.

The Great Wine Lover Is Elected President

Jefferson expected to win his election, but in February 1801 found himself instead in an electoral stalemate with his ostensible vice presidential running mate, Aaron Burr of New York, each having seventy-three votes to Adams's sixty-three. As Burr schemed to have himself declared president, Hamilton spoke out for Jefferson as the lesser of two evils, describing Burr in chilling and prophetic terms: "a Bonaparte, profligate and voluptuary, unprincipled, as true a Catiline as ever met in midnight conclave."[101]

After threats that the middle states might arm themselves if chicanery prevailed, Jefferson at last won by a narrow vote in the House of Representatives. His old friend Adams took the loss hard, telling Jefferson to his face: "[Y]ou turned me out, you turned me out," and saying that if he had his life to live over, he would be "a shoemaker."[102] The two friends reconciled much later in life, by mail, and created an invaluable correspondence, but never again did they share in person a glass of Madeira or any other wine.

Whatever the political consequences of Jefferson's victory, and they were profound, it had a vast impact on the wine cellar of the President's House, then under construction in the new capital at Washington. The United States had elected the greatest wine lover ever to hold the office. One of the first letters he received was from Thomas Newton, ancestor of the famous Madeira wine house Cossart Gordon, who wrote that some of the finest Madeira ever seen in the United States was on its way to him, and he wondered if Jefferson might be interested. The new president replied forthwith that he would "gladly take a pipe."[103]

CHAPTER SIX

Wine in the President's House

(1801–1809)

His wine was truly the best I ever drank, particularly
his champaign. It is delicious indeed.

—WILLIAM PLUMER, Federalist congressman from New Hampshire, 1802[1]

President Jefferson's wines were in general very
indifferent, though he had a great variety of them.

—SIR AUGUSTUS JOHN FOSTER, secretary to the English minister, 1805–1807.[2]

Thomas Jefferson was president for eight years, his two four-year terms
running from March 4, 1801, through March 4, 1809. The White House,
then called merely the President's House, has never seen as many good
wines since. While paid only $25,000 a year for salary and all expenses,

Jefferson spent an average of $3,200 a year *just on wine* during his first term, and well over $16,500 during his two terms. Interestingly, his spending dropped dramatically after he was reelected—to only $1,000 in 1805, and to just over $200 during 1808, his last full year in office.

In addition to providing a copious flow of Champagne, Jefferson treated his many guests to the finest Sherries and Madeiras, classified-growth Bordeaux reds and Sauternes, white and red Hermitage, Chambertin of Burgundy, Tokay from Hungary, and a variety of the finest wines of Italy and Portugal, including Port and Chianti and many less-known wines. Jefferson wanted to introduce Americans to good wines and make America a nation of wine drinkers as opposed to whiskey and spirit drinkers.

He served a few American wines from the Ohio Valley, but little comment exists as to what was thought of them. American wines were not served at the White House in any quantity until the presidency of Lincoln, whose wife took a special interest in them.[3] In the months just before and after his inauguration, however, Jefferson did carry on extensive correspondence with John Adlum, Jean-Jacques Dufour, Peter Legaux, and other pioneers of vine culture and winemaking in America, particularly in the Ohio Valley, Pennsylvania, and the District of Columbia. These related wine interests are treated separately in chapter eight.

Not all of the wines Jefferson recorded having bought were great wines, and one question usually asked is: what *types* of wines did Jefferson serve at the White House? Were they sweet or dry? Red or white? What did he drink them with? *Who* did he drink them with? How good were they, *really*?

Counting them as best one can, and considering there may be duplications and omissions, it can be said with some assurance that at least half were sweet wines, or what we would call dessert wines. Of course some wines can be either sweet or dry, depending on the season, winemaker's choice, or techniques employed. And Jefferson persistently sought out unusual types of wine, such as dry, unbrandied Port and "natural" pale Sherry. He also selected different wines for his personal use from those he served guests. There is little evidence, if any, that he took much interest in the current hot topic of wine-food matching.

We know that in French wines he liked the richest vintage years, when the grapes were picked very ripe, even late. He had a sweet tooth, yet he also ordered a considerable number of unmistakably dry dinner wines. And in Jefferson's time some wines were often dry that now are usually sweet, the best example being one of his favorites, Sauternes, and its first cousin, Barsac.

Some historical variables can never accurately be traced with precision. Jefferson was a wine drinker for over a half-century, and wine tastes changed even during his lifetime. As a foremost English wine expert of his era wrote in 1824, just two years before Jefferson's death:

The taste of the English in wine has varied considerably during the two last centuries. For five or six hundred years, the light growths of France and of the banks of the Rhine were imported in largest quantity, while the rich sweet wines of the Mediterranean and the islands of the Archipelago (Greek Isles) were held in highest estimation.

Then came the dry white wines of Spain, which for a time were preferred to all others on account of their strength and durability. At the close of the seventeenth, and beginning of the eighteenth centuries, the red growths of the Bordelais were in most frequent demand: but the wars in which the country was then involved put a stop to their importation, and led to the substitution of the rough vintages of Portugal.

From the long continued use of these strong dry wines, which are made doubly strong for the English market, the relish for sweet wines, which was once so prevalent, has gradually declined; and several kinds, such as Canary, Mountain, &c., which, as several of my readers may be old enough to remember, were drunk very generally by way of "morning whet," are now scarcely ever met with. Since the peace of 1814, the renewal of our intercourse with the continent has tended to revive the taste for light wines, and to lessen materially the consumption of the growths of Portugal and Spain.[4]

Even more dramatic changes and evolutions have occurred since Jefferson's time and in our own time. When this project began, few Americans knew of the Montepulciano and Carmignano wines of Tuscany, so praised by Jefferson. Now they are again among the highly rated wines of Italy, among a select few entitled to their own guaranteed place-name certificates.

Predictions about what specific Jefferson wines were like in his time are risky unless Jefferson personally described them. Fortunately, on many occasions he gave written opinions of his wines, usually in renewing or declining to renew an order. His opinions seem reliable when checked against the standard books of his time and against modern experience. His White House wines are treated as nearly as possible in chronological order, letting Jefferson's judgments speak for themselves, modified only by opposing or corroborating opinions from his guests and correspondents where available.

Immediately after entering the President's House, Jefferson began an extraordinary series of dinner parties at which wine drinking and talk of wine were major features. Like his contemporary, the devious French minister Talleyrand and his "Champagne diplomacy," Jefferson tried to warm his guests with fine wines, then used the convivial atmosphere to create better political and diplomatic relations, both with foreign powers and his own domestic friends and foes. As in Philadelphia and Paris, he tried to "mitigate business with dinner." His purchases for these politically useful but enjoyable dinners were staggering in their variety and cost.

Jefferson insisted somewhat lamely that his dinner parties were strictly social affairs without political implications, calling them "private dinners, for of official dinners we have none." Although he professed to keep his public and private lives separate, the dinner parties which he gave at the mansion he democratically referred to as the president's "house" illustrate a subtle talent for using a contrived domestic setting as a tool to gain political ends.[5] It is interesting that it was Jefferson, who styled himself as quiet and retiring, who gave the most effective dinner parties, far outstripping Washington and Adams.

Jefferson rarely mixed conservative Federalists with liberal Republicans at his dinners. Just as the guest lists were carefully planned, so was great attention given to physical surroundings. To encourage conviviality and a feeling of equality, round tables were generally used, with no head to compete for. No one was below the salt.

To insure confidentiality, portable dumbwaiters were used wherever possible in place of servants. A French chef, imported wines, and Jefferson's rather informal wardrobe completed the picture. Politics were less often the topics of conversation than might be expected, and discussions usually remained on subjects of general interest, including wines. The good will and sense of camaraderie thus created were useful instruments both for bonding political allies and for conciliating opponents.

When Congress was out of session, Jefferson invited members of the local community to share his hospitality as well. They were not disappointed, for frugality was never the rule at Jefferson's table. Etienne Lemaire, Jefferson's steward and head of household, once said he sometimes spent fifty dollars a day just on food. Computed over eight years in office ($50 × 365 × 8 = $146,000), such extravagance would have claimed nearly three-fourths of his $200,000 in salary. Seen in that light, his wine expenses don't seem quite so profligate. When you consider that today a normal ratio of wine cost to food cost for a fine dinner is often one-to-one, Jefferson's wine expenses were at least in line with his food expenses, however excessive the latter may have been.

But dinners for politicians and diplomats were clearly not all pleasure. Jefferson once described his fall dinners to his daughter Martha as his burdensome "winter campaign," their planning occupying large parts of his days. To his daughter Maria he said his entertaining "[s]erves only to get rid of life, not to enjoy it."[6] The dinners usually began about three-thirty or four in the afternoon and continued until between six and eight in the evening.

It was in his first term that Jefferson bought and served the most expensive wines and entertained most lavishly. His hospitality was no doubt much appreciated by the legislators, most of whom lived in boardinghouses and did not bring their wives. Washington was then a rough country town with unpaved streets and no fine buildings. It was only in June of 1800, at the end of the Adams administration, while Jefferson was vice president, that the capital was moved from the older and more urbane city of Philadelphia to the country village of Washington. Less than a year later, Jefferson was sworn in as the third president. He once commented that what Washington needed most was a gravelled road from the White House to the Georgetown Bridge. The irrepressible Gouverneur Morris described social life in early Washington more sarcastically: "We only need here houses, cellars, kitchens, scholarly men, amiable women, and a few other such trifles, to possess a perfect city."[7]

Morris was not alone in his view of Washington. Augustus John Foster, secretary to the British minister, who was critical of Jefferson's wines, said four years later that Washington still did not have "a single street or a single shop."[8] Nor was the established port of Georgetown much better, however fashionable it has since become. The usually positive Abigail Adams referred to Georgetown at the time of Jefferson's first term as "a dirty little hole."[9]

Jefferson was considerably more charitable, calling Washington "a very agreeable country residence [with] good society and enough of it."[10] He set out to create the elements Morris had specified as lacking, furnishing the White House with the best wine cellar and finest food, and inviting the most entertaining people in the new capital to his frequent dinners. There being no theaters, operas, or other diversions, good dinners, fine wines, and lively conversations were the heart of social life in his administration.

For his entire White House years, Jefferson left detailed sets of records of his wine purchases and consumption. His *Memorandum Books* usually reveal not only how much wine was received and what was paid for it, but how it was packed, if any bottles were broken or spoiled, from whom it was received, by what ship it sailed, under what captain, and an incredible amount of similarly specific data. He always noted the costs for freight, customs duties, ports shipped to and from, and the name of the customs-tax collector. He often calculated how much *per bottle* the incidental costs were on each wine.

Typical were his summaries of how much Champagne was drunk per person, and how long each 110-gallon barrel (pipe) of Madeira lasted. Such summaries tell much about which wines he drank and in what quantity.

But in the White House years, as in most periods, it was his letters which tell *why* he drank what he did, and what he thought of it.

Unfortunately, the presidential letters not edited by Dr. Boyd are only now being completed by the able Dr. Barbara Oberg of Princeton, which will be a huge help to future scholars. For now the sources are fragmented, rough, and in places only partly legible. They are a disorganized embarrassment of riches awaiting thorough study in the areas beyond politics and official history, such as wine. The *Memorandum Books*, on the other hand, serve well for now. There are also far more comments by other observers on Jefferson's wines while he was in the White House than for any other period.

The best analysis of Jefferson's wine notes was done by Jefferson himself late in life, during his retirement, in a list he headed up "Wine Provided at Washington." It is a messy document, like a real cellar book but prepared after the fact.

Its preparation was likely as a refresher for the recollection of an old man who knew his memory would soon be failing. Being the storyteller he was, Jefferson probably also wanted a reliable written record to refer to when regaling visitors about the old days, as several visitors to Monticello record him doing. It appears he prepared the list in either 1822 or 1823, because he says:

> The Index having been made from 13 to 22 years after the articles were entered, the Christian names (of brokers, etc.) there omitted were most of them forgotten. Some are inserted in the index from memory. More might have been if done sooner.[11]

It is plausible to believe that Jefferson also intended to leave "Wine Provided at Washington" as a historical document for future wine lovers to study and learn about the great wines of his period, and we are perhaps doing now just what he hoped we would do. Whatever its purpose, this memorandum is easily one of the most fascinating of his records, and is reproduced here in its entirety. Modern readers will readily recognize the Chambertin of Burgundy and the Châteaux Margaux, Rausan, and Yquem of Bordeaux. Yet the list also includes some surprises, especially the numerous wines from Spain and Italy, which are discussed in detail in conjunction with his letters explaining them.

Just as the old abbreviation "do." for "ditto" once confused me, so did the word "Montico" on this list puzzle me when I first saw it in Jefferson's handwriting. For a fleeting moment it seemed odd that I'd never heard of what sounded like a Spanish wine. Of course, I soon realized it was an abbreviation for Monticello, where Jefferson actually sent some of the wines that he suggested in the list were "provided" at Washington. When the list is compared to his letters, it is apparent that over a third of these wines were sent home and not provided at Washington at all. Because Monticello was always filled with official and unofficial guests of the president, however, the distinction is probably not a meaningful one, and they might just as well have been served at the White House as at Monticello.

With that brief introduction, here then is the most extensive single wine list of Jefferson's long and wine-filled life.

JEFFERSON'S GREATEST CELLAR BOOK: THE LIST OF "THE WINE PROVIDED AT WASHINGTON"[12]

			D[OLLARS].
1801			
	May 3.	A pipe of Brazil Madeira from Colo. Newton	350.
	20.	A pipe of Pedro Ximenes Mountain from Yznardi,	
		126. galls. @ 2. D.	252.
		Feb. 1803.	
		A Quartr. cask of Tent from do. 30. galls. @ 1.50	45.
		A keg of Pacharettti doux, from do. doz. of claret from do.	
		15. doz. Sauterne from H. Sheaff @ 8.D.	120.
		148 bottles claret @ 10. D. pr. doz.	
		6. doz. do. @ 12. D.	
	June 12.	2. pipes of Brazil Madeira from Taylor & Newton.	700.
		148. bott. claret @ 10. D. pr. doz. 123.33	
		<u>72. do. @ 12. D. 72.</u>	
		220 195.33	195.33
	Sep. 28.	2. pipes of Brazil Madeira from Taylor & Newton.	700.
	Nov. 28.	30. doz. =360. bottles of Sauterne from Sheaff.	240.

D[OLLARS].

1802

Jan. 7.	A tierce (60. galls.) Malaga from Mr Yznardi.		
	Lacryma Christi (Lagrima ?).		106.
	The above is 46. years old, viz. vintage of 1755.		
	2 doz. bottles of claret from Mr. Barnes @ 8. D.		16.
Feb. 24.	1. pipe dry Pacharetti from Mr. Yznardi		202.
	1. pipe Sherry of London quality 10. y. old		188.
	1/2 pipe of Sherry of a different quality		94.
	278 bottles of it sent to Monticello.		
	Feb. 1803		
	1/2 pipe of white Sherry		84.
		D	
	Insurance on the wines of Feb. 24.	22.72	
May 6.	Duties pd. Yznardi on do.	156	
		178.72	178.72
	Claret from J. Barnes		
Nov.	A half barrel of Syracuse from Capt. McNiel		
Dec. 1.	100. bottles Champagne from the Chevalr. Yrujo		

1803

Jan. 10.	100 do. @ .86 1/2 viz. .75 first cost + 11 1/4 duty		172.50
	2. half pipes of wines of Oeyras from		
	Mr. Jarvis at Lisbon. Sent to Monticello.		98.17
Mar. 3.	2 pipes of Brazil Madeira from James Taylor, Norfolk.		700.
21.	12. doz. Sauterne from Sheaff @ 8 2/3 D.		104.33
Oct. 21.	50. bottles white Hermitage @ 73 1/3 cents + 8 3/4		
	duty = 82 cents + 9 1/2 freight = 91 ½.		45.80
23.	150. bottles Rozan Margau @ 82 1/2 c. + 8 3/4		
	duty = 91 1/4 cents + 8 3/4 = 1. D.		150.00
	150. do. Sauterne @ 64 1/6 + 8 3/4		
	duty = 72 9/10 + 8 3/4 frt. = 81 3/4 c.		122.57

Dec. 1.	400 do. Champagne d'Aij	cost	duty	frt	
	(153. broke)	.68 3/4	.07 1/2	.19 = .95	484.
	100. do. Burgundy	.59 1/2	.07 1/2	.19 = .95	
	of Chambertin				

10.	A quarter cask Mountain of crop of 1747. from		
	Kirkpatrick of Malaga frt. 10.		
30.	2 pipes Termo one the crop of Carrasqeira,		
	the other Arrunda. Jarvis. 170		196.35
	1. butt of Pale Sherry from Yznardi.		194.85

DOLLARS].

1804

Mar. 19.	A pipe of Brazil Madeira from Taylor		354.07
	A box Champagne from do. 5. doz. @ .62 1/2 cents		37.50
June 20.	138. bottles of wines from Florence		
	(123 Montepulciano) frt. & duty 25 1/2 c. costs 26 c.		33.12
July	400. bottles Champagne from N.Y. same as Mar.		
	19. @ 1. D. (23 broke)		400.
July 20.	98. bottles claret from Sheaff		82.
Nov. 28.	240. bottles of Hungary wine		
	@ 1.70 36. do. Tokay	3.31 from (Eric)	546.43.
	12. do. other wines	4.36 Bollman	
Dec.	1 pipe dry Pacharetti prime cost		194.85
	1 Sherry 15. y. old		
	147. bottles Port		152.25
	(for) Montico 53. Bucellas. 10. y. old		
	1. pipe Arrudae wine from Jarvis. Lisbon.		
	36. bottles Chateau Margaux of 98. @ 7"		
	72. do. Rozan Margaux of 98. @ 4 – 10s.	778f-5 [Lee]	
	72. do. Salus Sauterne @ 2" – 5s		

1805

Apr. 17.	38. bottles Aleatico. 3 do. Santo.		
	3. do. Artemino. 19. do. Chianti		
	10. do. Montepulciano.		
May 30.	100. bott. vino del Carmine [from the estate of a		
	convent near Florence]. Appleton 1 hhd.		
	(I.e. half pipe) Marsalla. Preble.		
Oct. 19.	1. Qr. cask old Termo from Jarvis 26.20		
	+ frt. duties & c.	73.83
	1 do. Bucellas from do.	28.60	
Nov. 9.	473 bottles Montepulciano. Cost Leghorn		
	.25 = 118.50 = .25 pr. bottle duties 35.60		
	freight 46.38 port charges 6.08 = 88.06 – =		
	18 1/2 pr. bottle		
	100 bottles hermitage		

1806

Jan.	2. pipes Marsalla wine. Higgins 212. D. cost + 69.60 duty		

D[OLLARS].

Apr. 22.	100. bottles white Hermitage cost		76.62
	at Marseilles	duty, frt. +	21.
	6. do. vin de paille do.		7.82
		+	1.22

June 7.   100. do. White Hermitage costs at Marseilles
76.62 + frt. 8.91 + duty 12.835 = 98.365
barrique 45 galls. Cahusac. cost @ Bordeaux
22.85 + frt. 14.725 + dut. 22.275 = 60 D.

July   50. bottles Nebioule shipped by Thos. Storm for Kuhn.
200. bottles Nebioule from Kuhn. Cost delivered
at Genoa .54 cents pr. bottle.

1807

Feb.   200. bottles Hermitage from Marseilles.

June 4.   350. bottles (80. galls.) Montepulciano
from Leghorn 91.55 D. + frt. 40.42 +
duties 29.85 + port charges 2.25 =
164.07 or .47 pr. bottle.

13.   A cask Cahusac (23. galls.) cost at Bordeaux
29.51 + frt. 4.88 + duties 7.36 + port charges
D.C. 4.83 = 46.58 or 2.02 pr. gallon.
120 bottles St. George sent to Monto.

	cost at Cette @ .24 pr. bottle	42.875
	charges .15	26.847
		69.722

Oct. 8.   Do. from Mr. Barnes. 60 bottles.

Dec. 2.   3. kegs Nebioule yielding 134. bottles.

D

1808

Apr. 4.   100 bottles wine of Nice costs there

100 bottles wine of Nice costs there	30.84
freight to Marseilles	1.96
freight to Phila.	24.42
duty & permit	17.69
postage	.67
	75.58

In his index to the "Wine Provided at Washington," Jefferson listed thirty-nine wines from five countries:

France	12
Italy	11
Spain	10
Portugal	5
Hungary	2+

The most striking point about the list is the relative importance of Spanish wines, considering that Spain was a country Jefferson never visited, and one whose wines he had previously taken little interest in. Why the sudden interest in Spanish wines? Politics possibly had a little to do with it. Spain was a great power and in conflict with England. Yet viewed objectively, Jefferson's wine list is even more eclectic than his politics. Probably the best answer to why he had such an assortment of types of wines was that he simply liked to experiment with wines as he did with other subjects. In the America of his time, the taste of his countrymen ran to heavier, more alcoholic wines like those of Spain, and that may have been one reason for his experiments with them. They were also popular with the English, and more politically prudent to drink with them than French wines, and more prudent to drink with the French when the Portuguese were there, and so on.

One wine which was definitely political in character was Madeira, which symbolized to Americans a common patriotism and spirit of independence, whatever their other differences. It is apparent that Jefferson turned back to Madeira partly for reasons of domestic political appearances. The majority of foreigners at his inauguration may have been French,[13] but for his preferred wine he chose Madeira, the one wine Americans agreed upon as their virtual national beverage after the Revolution.

Madeira had been the favorite of both Washington and Adams. Washington had always ordered his Madeira direct from the island itself, and was very particular about which "house" provided it, but Jefferson had often ordered his locally, in contrast to his method of ordering French wines.[14] Indeed, Jefferson rarely left much discussion in prepresidential years of where he got his Madeiras, or of what he thought of them. That was to change.

Almost immediately upon being sworn in as president, Jefferson received a letter from Thomas Newton of Norfolk, advising him that some unusually fine Madeiras were available. Newton had been George Washington's Madeira supplier, and had relatives on the island of Madeira who helped found the great wine house today known as Cossart Gordon, so it is certain that his Madeiras were some of the finest obtainable. Newton's letter, dated March 12, 1801, stated in relevant part that

> I have just received a consignment of old Madeira wines, Brasil Quality and London Particular, from a Portuguese house who ships my own wine for drinking. The Brasil kind is superior to any other sent here and is such as is seldom imported; if you should want a supply, I will direct it to be saved for you.[15]

Jefferson replied promptly on March 23 that he would "gladly take a pipe of the Brasil quality." The pipe was received at Alexandria on April 14.

On April 8 Newton wrote to urge Jefferson not to neglect the London Particular either, noting that

> the Brasil wine is highly esteemed here; it is superior to the London Particular [but] the latter is fine three years old & you will find it clear, let the cask be ever so shaked.

Jefferson's follow-up letter has not been found, but it is clear from a letter from James Taylor for Newton dated June 4 that he had ordered two more pipes of the Brazil Quality Madeira and paid for them on August 28.[16] In the meantime, Newton was instructing the new president on the proper times for serving these wines and on their accompaniments. He acknowledged receipt of payment for the first pipe of Brazil via Jefferson's practice of tearing in half bank bills and mailing the halves separately to avoid what he called "the infidelities of the post office":

> Norfolk, May 13, 1801
>
> I duly received yours of the 7th inclosing 4 half bills of the U.S. bank. It gives me pleasure to know you approved of the wine; it is highly approved of here. The London Particular wine is also of very good quality, & very proper for using at dinner.
>
> The Brasil is a fitt cordial after dinner. This is the custom here, as we consider that wine of inferior quality while eating is as good to the taste as best.

On May 16, Newton wrote to Jefferson that he had sent some of the "London Particular for table use" to Richmond, probably for forwarding to Monticello. The account books show that the various pipes of old Brazil Madeira purchased that year by Jefferson cost $350 per pipe of about 110 U.S. gallons.

On September 25 Newton noted that Jefferson's agent John Barnes had paid Taylor for two more pipes of Brazil and that

> two more pipes of the same quality of wines are forwarded for you, which I obtained from a Gentleman that had bought them. Mr. Taylor has left some very fine London Particular wines three years old & very little difference between it & the Brasil + fifty dollars lower in price. I can safely recommend it as good wine. Very few would know any difference in the taste. I expect more Brasil quality if the British will permit it to come from Madeira, & shall be glad to supply you.

Jefferson was ready, noting on November 3 that his first pipe was out. On November 4 Newton wrote that he had sent two more pipes of Brazil. In January of 1802 Jefferson paid for what he called his fourth and fifth pipes of Madeira, again with U.S. bank notes cut in half and mailed separately.

On July 22, 1802, Newton wrote that his "correspondent in Madeira has wine superior to any that has yet been shipped. I intend to direct a pipe or two for trial."

On February 6 of 1803, Jefferson ordered still more Madeira. Newton had unfortunately sold all of his finest, and responded on February 16 that "two pipes of Brasil wine shall be sent you, the first *good* only. If you would say how many you would take yearly, I would order them with my own, of superior quality."

Jefferson did not neglect Newton's advice, and asked to make his yearly Madeira order automatic. Newton acknowledged it on August 10, 1803: "Agreeable to your desire, I wrote for two pipes best wine for you."

The history of his White House purchases and consumption of Madeira is noted with compulsive precision in his *Memorandum Books*, which tell everything about the wine except why he stopped drinking it:

1802

June 6. My second pipe of Madeira is out this day, broached Nov. 3. has lasted 6. months.

1803

Apr. 10 the 3d. pipe of Madeira broached June 6, 1802, is out. it has lasted 10. months, of which I was absent 3.

1804

May 28. the pipe of Madeira broached Apr. 10.03 is out. it has lasted 13M(onths)—18D(ays), of which I have been absent 3M(onths)—2D(ays).

1805

May 15. drew off the remains of the 5th pipe of Madeira, 76 bottles & sent them to Monticello, and broached the 6th pipe. the 5th broached May 28, 1804.

1807

Nov. 25. the last pipe of Madeira is broached this day, & is to be bottled. the preceding one was broached July 06.

Thus ended the last Madeira in the White House cellars of Thomas Jefferson. Whether he could no longer afford it, or had temporarily lost his taste for it, or thought his guests had, is unknown. Perhaps shipping had become too difficult because of hostilities between France and Portugal, which was allied with England. Whatever the cause, Jefferson drank less of it in his later years than before.

In a letter to him of June 23, 1808, his daughter Martha noted that "the Madeira gave out" at Monticello as well. At that time apparently all the Monticello wine stocks were low, because she also noted that "[c]ooking wine will be wanting" and that there was "no white wine therefore but what was in the octagon cellars." The latter reference is the only mention of another possible cellar at Monticello other than the presently restored "wine room." It could have existed briefly under an octagonal projection on the Monticello house, but most likely referred to a cellar under his octagonal-shaped Poplar Forest house, where he also kept wine. Perhaps excavations of further sites at Monticello and Poplar Forest, which has recently been restored, will turn up other finds like those at Monticello, where a crystal decanter marked "Madeira" and a metal Château Lafite neck label were unearthed a few years ago.

THE CHAMPAGNES OF PRESIDENT JEFFERSON

The favorite wine of Jefferson's first term was Champagne, recognized then as now as a festive beverage, suitable for giving a lively tone to a dinner party. Contrary to his own advice, Jefferson did not obtain his Champagne direct from the producer, but from the Spanish envoy to Washington, the haughty Marques de Casa Yrujo, who married the daughter of Governor McKean of Pennsylvania, a prominent Republican and Jefferson supporter.

It was Yrujo who found for Jefferson his first Washington chef,[17] the Frenchman Honoré Julien, on whom Jefferson relied heavily until he found his famous maitre d' Etienne Lemaire. Yrujo, like Jefferson's other wine friend Mazzei, proved politically unreliable and was later implicated in some of the schemes of Aaron Burr. He and Jefferson did not remain friends.[18]

It was from Yrujo, however, that Jefferson obtained the first of his famous Washington Champagnes. The written record of the event is a letter from Yrujo dated November 20, 1802, in which he noted he was sending two hampers of Champagne, containing two hundred bottles, which was "one-half my stock." Yrujo hoped it "may prove as good as in reputation."

On December 9, Jefferson thanked the Spanish minister for the two hundred bottles of his Champagne, but insisted on paying, saying: "It is sufficient obligation to me to spare me so excellent a supply."

On December 30, Yrujo said he could spare the two hundred bottles "without inconvenience," and asked Jefferson the return favor of "another dozen of your excellent Madeira." At first glance it appears Jefferson was paying Yrujo for his Champagne in Madeira, but an account book entry for January 11, 1803. shows he also paid $150 in cash for the two hundred bottles of Champagne.

Apparently Yrujo's Champagne was a big hit in Washington, as Jefferson noted in his *Memorandum Book* for 1802:

Dec. 20.   Note a hamper of champagne of 50 bottles opened Dec. 7 is finished Dec. 19th in which time 125 gentlemen have dined, which is 2 bottles to 5 persons.

At nearly a half-bottle of Champagne per gentleman, not counting any Madeiras or other wines, Jefferson's guests were doing well in the pre-Christmas dinners at the White House, and Champagne was obviously a popular wine.

It is hard to say for certain that these were stag affairs, as generally supposed, but the reference to "gentlemen" suggests they were. Many of his early dinners were such because he was a widower and had no hostess to preside except when one of his daughters or Dolley Madison was available to act as hostess. Without a proper hostess there, no lady of the early nineteenth century would have been willing to dine with a company of men. It now seems incongruous, given the current image and reputation of Champagne as the quintessential wine for women and mixed company, to have served it exclusively to groups of hard-drinking congressmen and diplomats. But Jefferson was not the only official who liked to serve Champagne. His secretary of war, General Dearborn of Maine, already had a well-stocked cellar of it, with which he too was generous.[19]

Jefferson could not continue to raid Yrujo's private stock; they had already drunk up half of it in less than two months. The next spring he wrote to Fulwar Skipwith, whom he had appointed to the lucrative post of U.S. commercial agent in Paris. Jefferson gave Skipwith a quick course in buying and shipping Champagne, and while he was at it, asked for a supply of Burgundy as well.

Washington May 4, 1803

I am about to ask from you the execution of a troublesome commission, without being able to encourage its undertaking by an assurance that it may not be repeated hereafter. The meanness of quality, as well as extravagance of price of the French wines which can be purchased in this country have determined me to seek them in the spot where they grow.

The wines of champagne can be best got by the way of Paris, where the agency of a friend becomes necessary. This agency I take the liberty of soliciting from you. The following were the places, persons, and quantities for champagne of the 1st quality when I was there in 1788 at Aij: Monsr. Dorsay made 1100. pieces, M. le Duc 400., M. de Villermont 300., M. Lanson 250. At Auvillaij the Benedictines made 1,000 pieces, & L'Abbaliste 1100.[20]

At Pierrij, M. Casotte made 500. pieces, de la Motte 300., des Failli 500., Hoquast 200., les Seminarines 150. At Devris Versonnis, the property of the Marquis de Silleri, wines of Aij made on M. Dorsay's vineyard were the best, & from him I always afterwards took my supplies. I paid always from 3″ to 3″—10′ the bottle for the best & of the best years. I am told wines have considerably risen since that.

M. Dorsay lived in Paris during winter, I believe on the Quai D'orsay. I could wish 400 bottles of the white Champagne non-mousseux of the best year now on hand for which purpose I shall enclose herein a bill of exchange for 400. Dollars.

Great care & some attention is required on their passage from Aij to Havre, that they may not be exposed to a hot sun. It is essential that they should leave Havre by the middle of July, or they will not be here in time to save me from the necessity of buying here bad & dear.

The wines of burgundy would be very desirable & there are three kinds of their red wines, Chambertin, Voujeau, & Veaune, & one of their whites, Monrachet, which under favorable circumstances will bear transportation, but always with risk of being spoiled if exposed on the way to either great heat or cold, as I have known by experience since I returned to America.

Unless the Champagnes have risen in price more than I am informed, there may be something left of my bill, which I should like to receive in Chambertin & Monrachet in equal, & ever so small quantities, if you can take the trouble of getting it for me, merely as an experiment. If it succeeds I may ask a quantity the next year. It should leave it's cellars in Chambertin & Monrachet about the beginning of October & come through without delay at either Paris or Havre.

There was living at Beaune, near Chambertin & Monrachet a tonnelier named Parent, who being a taster & bottler of wines by trade, was my conductor through the vineyards & cellars of the Cote, & ever after my wine-broker & correspondent. If living, he will execute for me faithfully any order you may be so good as to send him.

SIGNED TH: JEFFERSON[21]

On May 9 Jefferson forwarded payment to Skipwith. When he did receive the order much later that year, it was worth waiting for: four hundred bottles of still Champagne, one hundred bottles of the great red Chambertin, but no Montrachet. On November 17, 1803, he noted with typical thoroughness the import duties:

Desired Mr. Barnes to remit to Genl. Muhlenberg for 400 bottles champagne duties $29.66, which is 7 1/2 cents per bottle—freight $40.26, which is 10 cents per bottle = $69.92 = 17 1/2 cents per bottle.

His entries on consumption were no less meticulous. He noted in 1804 the rate of consumption of Skipwith's shipment:

Mar. 20.   There remains on hand 40 bottles of the 247 of champagne recd from Fulwar Skipwith. The consumption then has been 207 bottles, which on 651 persons dined is a bottle to 3 1/7 persons. Hence the annual stock necessary may be calculated at 415 bottles a year, or say 500.

This entry, with its switch to the word "person," may indicate that more women had begun attending the dinners, but the most Jeffersonian touch is the cavalier reference to quantity. After making elaborate notations and computing the precise cost per bottle, arriving at a firm figure of 415, Jefferson then blithely concluded "or say 500." Thus he was adding nearly 20 percent to his expenditures with a sort of "what the hell, make it 500 bottles," which is typical of his spending habits.

Of course, Jefferson had no wine store on the corner, or even in the city, to resort to if he ran out of wine. And shipments from abroad were only possible at certain moderate seasons, and then risky. It was therefore wise of Jefferson to order extra and well in advance.

The wine from Skipwith was split into two shipments: the first, the four hundred bottles of non-*mousseux* Champagne, was sent to the port of Philadelphia to be forwarded to Washington. The one hundred bottles of Chambertin were sent to Norfolk to be shipped on to Monticello. It appears Jefferson wished to keep this especially rare and delicate wine entirely for his own use.

One reason Jefferson contacted Skipwith for his Champagne was the difficulty in obtaining any in the United States, whatever the quality. In January 1803 he had written James Taylor at Norfolk, who had taken over Newton's business. On January 24 Taylor wrote that he had just received "a few cases of Champaign," and would reserve Jefferson some if he liked. Jefferson, cautious, asked for a sample first, promising to take "30 dozen" bottles if it was of good quality, but insisting that Champagne, "if not fine, would be useless here."

Taylor sent him a sample to Alexandria on February 20, but by the time Jefferson replied on March 25 saying his Champagne had "been tried and is approved and I shall be glad to take eight cases more, say 480 bottles of it before the first of May," he learned that he had waited too late. On May 21, 1803, Newton informed him that Taylor had sold all the Champagne before they heard from Jefferson, and no more of *any* kind was available.

Jefferson turned to New York wine merchant Theodorus Bailey, writing on June 10, 1803, that if any good Champagne could be had for less than a dollar a bottle, he "would take 400 bottles of it." Bailey replied June

16 that he was negotiating for some, but it was selling for exactly a dollar a bottle. Taking no more chances, Jefferson replied by return mail June 21 that he would pay that price, enclosing a note for four hundred dollars on the bank of the United States. On June 26 and July 5 Bailey confirmed that he had sent to Jefferson aboard the ship *Little Jim*, bound for Washington, the four hundred bottles of Champagne. Wine merchant Bailey later visited Jefferson at one of his dinners and left very favorable comments about the sobriety which accompanied his fine wines and foods, noting that his guests drank "to the digestive point and no further."

Jefferson's interest in Champagne did not dull his appetite for other French wines during his first term, as shown by the variety listed among the "Wines Provided at Washington." Jefferson's finest dry dinner wines were still the great Bordeaux of the highest quality, obtained through the American consul directly from the proprietors. For "common use," he did turn for everyday claret to local wine merchants like Sheaff at Philadelphia. With the rise of Napoleon in 1799, shipments from France were uncertain, depending on what government was in power, and who they were at war with at that moment.

In 1801, for example, Jefferson ordered 180 bottles of Sauternes from Sheaff in May, another 360 bottles of it in November, and 220 bottles of claret in May and again in June. By 1803, however, he had settled in and was ordering Château "Rozan" and Château d'Yquem direct from Bordeaux again. He also ordered, as he said with "hesitation" because of the political situation, some white Hermitage from Stephen Cathalan at Marseilles, receiving it with no problem several times, and greatly approving certain shipments, as will be discussed at length in the retirement chapter, when he wrote enthusiastically and at length on his white Rhône wines.

PRESIDENT JEFFERSON'S PORTUGUESE WINES: "PROVISION FOR MY FUTURE COMFORT"

About the time he stopped ordering Madeira, Jefferson began ordering dry Portuguese table wines like those he drank while secretary of state and during his first "retirement" in the 1790s. His first, a quarter cask of dry Lisbon, was sent to his cellar at Monticello. His friend David Humphreys had left Lisbon, so Jefferson turned to the American consul there, William Jarvis. In January 1803 Jefferson noted receipt through Jarvis of two half-pipes (or "hogsheads" of sixty gallons each) of wine of Oeyras. This wine, from the Carcavelos region near Lisbon, was from the estate of Oeyras, better known as the Marques de Pombal.

Jarvis tried to present the Oeyras to Jefferson as a gift, but the president insisted on paying, which in addition to being more ethical for a public official, also allowed him to be more candid about what he thought of them:

> May 10, 1803
>
> The wines of that name [Oeyras] are no longer of their antient quality. The objection is just what you mention, a too great sweetness, which though age will lessen, it will never reduce to the dryness I prize. Out of the many samples of the dry wines of Portugal I prefer Termo and ask the favor of you to send me a pipe of it [and will] hereafter remit in advance for what I shall desire.

Jarvis, never one to follow instructions to the letter, sent Jefferson two pipes of Termo instead of one, but from the most popular estates, specifying the proprietors who produced them. Jefferson noted in his December 1803 *Memorandum Book* receiving: "2 pipes Termo, one the crop of Carrasqueira, the other Arruda. Jarvis. 170 milreas. 196.35."[22]

The following summer Jefferson acknowledged that he was pleased with them:

> July 19, 1804
>
> Your favor of October 26 as also the two pipes of Termo came safely to hand in the course of the winter . . . paid for them and the Oeyras and want in future a pipe per year of the best Termo always in a double case, or it is sure to be adulterated before it gets to its ultimate destination.

On November 25, Jarvis shipped Jefferson a pipe of the Termo of Arruda via New York, calling it "as fine of the dry kind as Lisbon produces." Having no reply from Jefferson for several months, on May 15, 1805, Jarvis wrote again to confirm his November letter. Apparently the wine was slow in arriving in New York, or was held up there, for it was not until June 5, 1806, that Jefferson's *Memorandum Book* showed payment for it. It appears Jefferson was sending his dry Lisbons to Monticello while he drank Champagne, Madeira, and Spanish wines at the White House.

Finally, on July 6, 1805, Jefferson noted receipt of the Arruda to Jarvis, and that it was "of very superior quality. I should be glad to receive always of exactly the same quality, adhering to the rule of putting no brandy in them."

Jarvis complied, writing on October 11 that he had sent ahead via New York 2 sample bottles drawn from two pipes of Arruda of the current vintage, which he recommended as

> a very fine wine & I think it will prove satisfactory with a year or two's age.
> [Because the] vintage was remarkably fine, I took the liberty to send two pipes, they being the product of one of the best estates in Portugal.

Jefferson noted another purchase in his *Memorandum Book* for October 19, 1805: "One Qr. cask *old* Termo from Jarvis."

It was not until the following February 9 that he gave to David Gelston, the customs collector in New York, his impressions of the Arruda, saying he would take only one of the two pipes, and that the wine "was pale, but has a reddish tinge sufficiently distinguishable to the eye." This quote was the closest Jefferson came to saying he had tasted a wine akin to the rosé wines like Mateus and Lancer's for which Lisbon has become famous in our own time. To him the appearance of a little color in a white was considered a defect. That is not surprising, since it was not until the twentieth century that the term *rosé* became popular, and it was not until the 1980s that the new name "blush" wine, for a very light rosé such as Jefferson described, caught on in America.

Jefferson must have been satisfied with the rosé of Arruda, because even though he did not take both pipes offered, he did order an entire hundred-gallon pipe, which may well have been all he needed. Gelston forwarded it, but by January 10, 1806, Jarvis still had not heard whether

Jefferson had received or approved it, and wrote to inquire. On April 16 Jefferson gave a positive but not entirely encouraging reply, saying he

> chose one of the two pipes & shall expect your bill for the amount of that and the two preceding ones (2 Qr. casks of Termo & Bucellas paid to Hooe & Co.). All wines from you are at Monticello to ripen. I need no more at the moment. [Thank you for] this provision for my future comfort.

Jefferson ordered no more wines from Jarvis while president, having apparently, as he said, sufficiently filled his Monticello cellar in preparation for his retirement.

An interesting sidelight to his acquisition of these Lisbon wines is the intermediaries. David Gelston, the collector of customs taxes at New York, was a protégé and lieutenant of Aaron Burr. It was through Burr that he received the lucrative collector's post, which paid more than twice as much per year in fees as any cabinet member made in salary.[23] The other interesting player in the scenario was Robert T. Hooe of Alexandria, through whom Jefferson arranged receipt of the last shipment. Hooe owned a grocery in Alexandria specializing in fancy imported goods, advertising "Lemons, Sweet Oranges and Lisbon Wine in Quarter Casks."[24] Earlier, under Washington, he audited the city's accounts and incorporated a marine insurance company there. But most interesting was his role as one of the "midnight appointees" of departing President John Adams.

It was the lawsuit over the appointment of Hooe and others as justices of the peace which resulted in the most important constitutional law decision in American history, Chief Justice John Marshall's opinion in *Marbury v. Madison*.[25] Despite Hooe's role in that dispute, and Gelston's even closer ties with the perfidious Burr, Jefferson seems to have held no grudge, or at least to have set it aside where wines were at stake. He bought and received wines through Gelston and Hooe just as if they had been the staunchest friends. Indeed where good wines were concerned, his principle seems to have been that *veritas* lay strictly *in vino*.

Jefferson's other source of good Portuguese wines while he was president was Dr. Oliveira Fernandez, a Portuguese-born physician and merchant living at Norfolk. On January 4, 1805, Jefferson wrote to him for some Bucellas, a wine he had also ordered from Jarvis, as well as some Port, which he had noted buying before, but with which he seemed only slightly familiar:

> Mr. Newton having been so kind as to furnish me with a sample of your Port wine, and informed me that you have also some Bucellas, old & of first quality, I presume to ask the favor of you to furnish me a quarter cask of each, to be forwarded in *double cases* to Richmond.
>
> I am not certain whether there be not some skill requisite in bottling port. If so, it would perhaps be better to have it bottled in Norfolk where, I believe, there are persons who follow the business of bottling.

Fernandez complied without delay:

> Norfolk January 24, 1805
>
> We have shipped on board the Schooner *Mary Cobb* one quarter cask of London Particular Port and a few gallons of Bucellas wine, being the last stock of that kind of 10 years old in bottles—and well cased.

Bucellas was and still is a white wine, made in the region of that name north of Lisbon. It is made primarily from the Arinto grape, believed by some to be a Riesling clone transplanted from Germany. Today Bucellas is a light, dry white wine with a delicate, unusual bouquet. With age it gains real finesse and turns gold in color. In a sense it is somewhat like a Riesling in general character, but yet has a unique and delicious Portuguese tang of its own. Bucellas is an old wine, mentioned in Shakespeare as Charneco, a village in the Bucellas region. Falstaff, who "sold his soul to the devil for a cup of Madeira," also drank Bucellas with his anchovies, a salt-with-sweet combination still popular in Portugal today. Bucellas was most popular in England late in Jefferson's life, after Wellington's returning troops brought to England a taste for it acquired in the Iberian Peninsular Wars against Napoleon.

Today Bucellas is a natural wine, with no brandy or sugar added, as they often were in Jefferson's time. Dickens mentioned Bucellas as a popular dessert wine. It was fairly cheap in those days, but so often counterfeited with South African wine that a couplet from Thomas Hood's *Public Dinner* in 1845 charged: "Bucellas made handy, / By Cape and bad brandy."

Today only about 450 acres remain of the once-extensive Bucellas vineyards and it is rarely seen now in America. When found, however, it is well worth trying, particularly a "Bucellas Velho" (old). I strongly agree with H. Warner Allen, that knowledgeable English writer on Portuguese wines, who said of it: "We could do with a great deal more Bucellas." Unfortunately no personal comments on Bucellas by Jefferson remain; we know only that he had many bottles of it in his cellars, always of the best kind, unbrandied, and old.

Jefferson must have liked Fernandez's Port, for on March 7, 1805, he noted in his *Memorandum Book* ordering more *unbrandied* Port and some "Factory" Port, plus some Teneriffe from the Canary Islands, enclosing his draft for $152.25. He noted there the receipt of his first order as:

147 bottles Port
        from Fernandez
53 Bucellas 10 y. old   152.25.

Jefferson's insistence that his Port be unbrandied probably assured that he drank very little of it, for unbrandied Port was hard to find. The fashion then, and today, was for Port to have brandy added to arrest the fermentation before all the sugar had fermented out. Making a red Port unbrandied which is smooth, yet still travels well, is a challenge today, and must have been even more so in Jefferson's day. There was little unbrandied Port on the market then and little now.

The "Factory" Port he ordered is another interesting sidelight. At Oporto, where some of the greatest Port wine lodges are located, the English mercantile agents, or "factors," set up a virtual monopoly of Port production, and most of the finest Ports came from them, colloquially called "Factory" Port, hence Jefferson's reference.[26] With his views of the English, who were treating that part of Portugal as little more than a colony, it is easy to see why Jefferson was not then more attached to Port, which was, after all, called "the Englishman's wine." Considering that status and Jefferson's politics, it is a tribute to its quality that Jefferson drank so much of it.

There is one further exchange of letters, this time with his grand-daughter Ellen Wayles Randolph, about the Portuguese wines from Jarvis. Referring to her mother, Jefferson's daughter Martha, Ellen wrote on October 20, 1808:

Mama is afraid she will not have time to write to you this post and bids me mention to you that Aunt Marks [Jefferson's sister] and myself returned to Monticello to have the wine bottled. Two pipes of Termo which were in a crazy condition were bottled. One cask Oeras wine had leaked in the summer. The remainder was drawn off in 203 bottles. Another cask of the same wine which was tumbling to pieces was drawn off in two smaller casks.

I believe we left all the wine in perfect safety if the two smaller casks, which were the best we could get, are to be depended on. Burwell thinks they will do. They had been used for water casks. Mama has sent over twice since we came away to look at them. They were perfectly sound and she intends to send every week or ten days to have them examined until you return.[27]

She followed up reassuringly on December 15, 1808:

The OERAS Wine which was in the little crazy casks is bottled off. There are not bottles enough to draw any other kind, but it is no matter, for all the rest is perfectly safe.

During his retirement Jefferson wrote to Jarvis, who had returned to the U.S., that *all* his wines had turned out, with proper aging in the Monticello cellar, to be very good.

President Jefferson's Surprise Favorites, Spanish Wines

The most surprising wine experiment of Jefferson's presidency was his sudden and continuing interest in the wines of Spain. With rare exceptions, Jefferson had never before shown much interest in those wines, for which he had no suppliers, and with which he had little experience. Yet once he was in Washington, his correspondence on Spanish wines is one of the lengthiest and most compliment filled of his life, and he describes what we would perhaps call pale Sherry his "favorite wine."

The letters actually began before the election, on October 8, 1800, when he received a note from Samuel Smith that the American consul at Cadiz had arrived in Boston, and had some fine Spanish wines with him. When Jefferson relayed the message that he was interested, Consul Don Josef Yznardi wrote to Jefferson in Spanish, as he always did, on March 18, 1801, that he had "tres medias Botas de Vino, dos de Xerex, una de color, y otra blanco, y la otra de Malaga, especiales de calidad."[28]

Cadiz, where Yznardi was stationed, was the main Andalusian port for the wines of both Malaga and the wine region we now call Sherry, and the French call Xeres, and the Spanish themselves now call Jerez. Yznardi's spelling shows just how transitory "correct" orthography can be, but we know he was talking about the same wine.

Eager to try the new wines, Jefferson answered the letter the day he received it, repeating it in English, and agreeing to take all the wines:

> To Yznardi
>
> Washington, March 24, 1801
>
> You mention having at your disposal two casks of white and red sherry and one of Malaga; If the sherry be dry, I will gladly take them, as also the Malaga. If you would order for me a pipe of dry Pacharetti and one of dry sherry of first quality to be forwarded from Spain as old as possible so as to be ready for immediate use. I should be obliged to you.

Three days later, Yznardi wrote from Boston that he would "gladly meet your needs," adding on April 7 that he had ordered a pipe of "Pacarete" as well as a barrel of Rota Tent, similar to Malaga, and that his Sherry should be coming via Philadelphia. Jefferson noted in his *Memorandum Book* that the wines received were "34 bottles Pacharetti, 55 do. Ruota Tenta."

Today we Americans tend to think of Rota more as a naval base than a wine center, but in Jefferson's time it was already a great wine port. On November 25, 1801, he noted in his *Memorandum Book* paying for a "tierce" of Malaga Lágrima of 1755.

Pacaret, or Paxarete, Pajarete, or Pacharetti, was an ancient monastery town a few miles from Jerez which was known in Jefferson's time for rich and highly esteemed wines made primarily from the Malvasia or Malmsey grape and the Pedro Ximénez, discussed earlier. Its name was also frequently "borrowed" and applied to any rich, sweet wine shipped from the region, as well as to certain Muscats. Jefferson's specific request for *dry* Paxarete is interesting, and one wonders just how dry they really were. It is notable how often he requested "dry" wines from regions where the overwhelming majority of the wines were known to be sweet. Perhaps it was his way of assuring minimum adulteration and doctoring. Certain historians do, however, say that some Paxaretes were known for their "light, delicate taste and fragrancy,"[29] and perhaps Jefferson was trying to get the driest and least brandied available.

Tent was a form of Tinta, or "tinted," and usually referred to a darker or red wine. It could come from anywhere in southern Spain, including Malaga, where it was often called "Mountain" or Alicante, or the nearby town of Algeciras. The fact that Jefferson's Tent was specified as coming from Rota probably meant it was a better quality. Some had no brandy added and was used as a beverage wine, which seems from his reference to have been how Jefferson planned to use it, in contrast to his "sherries," which he sent to Monticello to age, indicating they were heavier and not meant to be drunk young.[30]

The Malaga "Lágrima" 1755 in particular was a keeper, and possibly similar to the deep wines of Pedro Ximénez known today as Venerable, which are still available. The 1755 may indicate it was a solera wine as well. Jefferson obviously liked the wines from his new supplier, ordering more the next month, to which Yznardi replied on January 15, 1802, enclosing a bill for:

one pipe Pedro Ximenes	126 gallons	$252
one Qr. cask Rota Tent	30 gallons	$ 45
one Hhd. Malaga Lacrima Christy—45 yrs		$106

On January 30, 1802, Yznardi notified Jefferson that the following "mixed parcel" of *Vinos de Xerez* had arrived at Baltimore:

> . . . una bota de los anos seco [dry years]
>
> —media bota de calidad distinto semesante a Madera
>
> —una bota de Paxarete Seco
>
> —media bota de vino sin color.

Of this lot Yznardi recommended the pale Sherry or "wine without color," which proved prophetic, since it immediately became Jefferson's favorite. It appears to have been an almost entirely natural Sherry, with no brandy added to stop the fermentation, and perhaps without the *flor* yeast which gives modern Sherry its unique tang. Little was said by either man of the Spanish wine "resembling Madeira," which was probably a Malmsey or Malvasia from southern Spain.

On February 4, 1802, Jefferson acknowledged he owed $403 for the January 15 shipment, noting almost in passing among the wine comments: "The Senate has confirmed your appointment as Consul and you will receive the commission as soon as made out."

No doubt it did not hurt Yznardi's chances for confirmation as American consul at Cadiz that he was President Jefferson's valued supplier of Spanish wines. On February 12, 1802, he confirmed the shipment and prices of:

$188	a pipe of sherry, 10 years, equal to London market
202	a pipe Paxarete
84	a half pipe natural sherry
94	a half pipe of sherry "with" color
$568	
22.72	Insurance
$590.72	

Jefferson wrote to the new consul his enthusiastic assessment of the wines:

Washington, May 10, 1803

Among the wines you were so kind as to furnish me, the one called in your
letter Xeres sin color (pale sherry) has most particularly attached my taste to it.
I now drink nothing else, and am apprehensive that if I should fail in the means of
getting it, it will be a privation which I shall feel sensibly once a day.

Send me annually a pipe of it, old & fine. I will pay the first pipe at
short sight.

On July 19, Yznardi agreed to send "Your Excellency" the annual pipe, packed in two or three half-cases "as they are easier stowed on board."

Yznardi shipped on October 18, 1803, "one cased Butt superior Sherry wine" to Monticello. On January 19 and 26, 1804, Jefferson confirmed that he wanted a pipe of the same quality every year, as well as a pipe of dry Pacharetti of first quality each year. In a partly illegible portion of the January 26, 1804, letter, Jefferson asked that the next pale Sherry be of the same quality "but less age."

The pale Sherry remained among Jefferson's favorites as noted in his last wine letter to Yznardi:

Washington, March 29, 1806

The wines sent have been chiefly deposited at Monticello to be ripening for
use when I retire to reside there and they constitute a sufficient stock to begin upon.
Please discontinue the sending me any more until I may particularly ask it. Of all
wines received the Xeres sin color is the finest. It has a smoothness and mildness
peculiarly agreeable.

Jefferson seems to have agreed with the anonymous author of a seventeenth-century British drinking song:

Then let us drink old sacke, boyes,
Which makes us fond and merry.

The life of mirth, and joy on earth,
Is a cuppe of good old Sherry.

The only Spanish wine which President Jefferson received from someone other than Yznardi came from a Mr. Kirkpatrick, American consul at Malaga. On September 23, 1803, Kirkpatrick wrote to Jefferson, saying he was sending him some very old (1747) Malaga as a gift. The December 10, 1803, entry in the "Wine Provided at Washington" recorded on that date receipt of" [a] quarter cask of Mountain of crop of 1747 from Kirkpatrick of Malaga. frt. 10."

The June 21, 1804, *Memorandum Book* entry shows the payment of the freight on the wine by James Madison. What Jefferson thought of the wine is not certain, but it must have been one of the wines he later prescribed for his daughter Maria as "stomachic" because so old and mild.

Jefferson's White House Wine Cellar

Several interesting items about Jefferson's White House wine cellars were unearthed by William Seale, a specialist in historical re-creations. When I first interviewed him in late 1984, Mr. Seale was just completing his outstanding two-volume two-thousand-page *History of the White House* for the White House Historical Association. He kindly consented to let me read and quote from his typewritten manuscript on Jefferson's White House.

Seale is the only person I've found who knows much about the physical arrangements of Jefferson's White House wine cellar, which he describes as being dug by Jefferson just west of the original White House under what is now the West Wing. It was called the "ice house," and appears in Jefferson's original drawings, in his handwriting, as such.[31] According to Seale, the cellar was a circular, bucket-shaped affair with the top wider than the bottom, sixteen feet down in the ground, made entirely of brick, with a building over it and a covered walk connecting it to the White House itself. It had a platform floor for racking and bottling wines, and was elevated over a bed of ice packed in sawdust for further cooling. The ice was replenished each month. The ice house itself was not unusual for colonial Virginia: Jefferson himself had one at Monticello which has been restored and lies at the end of the all-weather passageway just down from the wine cellar. There is no indication yet, however, that Jefferson used his Monticello ice cellar for storing or cooling wine.

Just how he came upon the idea of using the space above an ice house to store and preserve wines at the White House is not known, and it may have been another Jeffersonian invention. He apparently tried this method after the original White House cellar, which was under the house, proved unsatisfactory. It appears to have had outside or "English basement" windows like his own cellar at Monticello which were too much exposed to the south sun. Whatever the configuration or location of the cellar, it certainly contained some magnificent wines, about which a surprising amount of comment has been preserved. We also know quite a bit about the foods served with his wines while he was president. Long lists of food purchases by his steward Lemaire have survived. Written on large folio pages, and reviewed and approved regularly in Jefferson's own handwriting, the entries in Lemaire's Day Book seem basically correct, although some historians have accused Lemaire of inflating them and stealing Jefferson blind over the seven years he was there. He left Jefferson's service a suspiciously wealthy man. It is also possible that Lemaire is a victim of historical revisionism.

Of the excellence of Jefferson's food, there is no doubt or dispute. Overseer Edmund Bacon's most enthusiastic comments on Jefferson were about what he ate during a sixteen-day visit to the White House at the end of his second term:

> He had eleven servants with him from Monticello. He had a French cook in Washington named Julien, and he took Eda and Fanny there to learn French cookery. He always preferred French cookery. Eda and Fanny were afterwards his cooks at Monticello.[32]

In recent years there has been renewed interest in Jefferson's foods. In 2005 the Jefferson Foundation published a beautiful volume, richly illustrated, entitled *Dining at Monticello*. The new volume contains a series of ten essays, complemented by over fifty pages of recipes, and its illustrations are wonderfully evocative of what a dinner at Monticello must have been like. The recipes from both his Paris kitchen, written in French in Jefferson's handwriting, and from Monticello were also published earlier by the Jefferson Foundation in a handsome very small edition edited by Marie Kimball. The first Monticello compilation was made by Jefferson's granddaughter Virginia Randolph Trist, who lived at Monticello with Jefferson and knew the food actually served there. Most of those recipes were attributed to various ladies in the family, and few to any of Jefferson's French cooks or French-trained servant cooks.

Except for the Paris "recipes," which are really more a list of dishes and ingredients than explanations of how to prepare the dishes, no White House recipe has been found written in Jefferson's own handwriting. Nor is there any mention of Jefferson himself ever taking the slightest interest in preparing food. He was a pure eater and not interested in doing any cooking. As usual, it was Isaac who confirmed this fact most aptly: "Mr. Jefferson had a clock in his kitchen at Monticello; never went into the kitchen except to wind up the clock."[33]

Like any French-trained gourmet, however, Jefferson knew the importance of fresh ingredients. Among the most enduring images of him are his rides with steward Etienne Lemaire to the market at Georgetown in their three-wheeled wagon, the two of them coming home laden with produce for White House feasts. Bacon knew Lemaire and shopped with him during his 1809 visit:

> The first thing in the morning there was to go to the market. There was no market then in Washington. Mr. Jefferson's steward was a French man named Lemaire. He was a very smart man, was well educated, and as much of a gentlemen in his appearance as any man. His carriage driver would get out the wagon early in the morning, and Lemaire would go with him to Georgetown to market and I went with them very often. Lemaire told me that it often took fifty dollars to pay for what marketing they would use in a day. Mr. Jefferson's salary did not support him while he was President.[34]

THE FOOD ACCOUNTS OF ETIENNE LEMAIRE

Very little is known, unfortunately, of Jefferson's White House chef, Honoré Julien, but his steward and maitre d', the portly Etienne Lemaire, was much discussed. Formerly butler for William and Anne Bingham, a wealthy and fashionable couple in Philadelphia, Lemaire was highly praised by White House guests. His large format Day Book for 1806–1809, which Jefferson reviewed and signed monthly, is a fascinating insight into the ingredients of the Jefferson table. It is written in a sort of franglais, typical renderings being "rocquefiche" for rockfish and "melon d'eau" for watermelon.[35]

Lemaire, who averaged five hundred dollars per month in food spending when Congress was in session, also recorded wine purchases, including Château Margaux and Hermitage, and it was he who bought the corks and bottled Jefferson's wines. In that sense he was truly a *butler*, or "bottler," as the title was originally spelled.

One memorable shopping trip was for the feast given January 13, 1806, for the Tunisian ambassador Mellimelli and his retainers. Lemaire bought 120 pounds of beef, 90 pounds of mutton, 35 pounds of veal, 27 pounds of pork, 3 turkeys, 30 "small birds," 17 dozen eggs, 25 pounds of butter, 30 pounds of rice, and a variety of vegetables.

VERBATIM SAMPLES TRANSLATED FROM LEMAIRE'S PANTRY LISTS

MEATS			
Ourse, 30 livres	= 30 pounds of bear meat	lapin	= rabbit
		ecureiull	= squirrel
		langue de boeuf	= beef tongue
perdrix	= partridges	FISH	
canards sauvages	= wild ducks	maurue	= cod
canards de ferme	= farm ducks	bremes	= bream
canards de basse cour	= courtyard ducks	sprat	= small herring
venaison	= venison	alosse	= shad
pigeon	= squab	friture	= smelts
jeune ois	= young goose	esturgeon	= sturgeon
dindin pour pattez frais	= turkey for fresh galantine (paté)	douzaine de crâb	= dozen crabs
		gallon dhuitres	= gallon of oysters

VEGETABLES				
thomattes	= tomatoes	cressan	= watercress
quarottes	= carrots	asperge	= asparagus
du omene	= hominy		
laitue de Fairfax	= Fairfax County lettuce	FRUITS	
		serisses	= cherries
arecost blanc	= white beans	paiches	= peaches
epinards	= spinach	ananas	= pineapple
pomes deter	= potatoes	fraises	= strawberries
salade de doucettes	= lamb's lettuce	poires	= pears
oseille	= sorrel	OTHERS	
percil	= parsley	chataigne	= chestnuts
artichaux	= artichokes	baril de cornichons	= barrel of gherkins
		barill de craker	= barrel of crackers

In addition to the hominy, watermelon, and squirrel, his shopping lists included *farine de mais*, or cornmeal, *farine de sarazin*, or buckwheat, *fèves*, a French word that then covered everything from lima beans to black-eyed peas, and last, what Lemaire rendered as "trois peck de sweet patates," which needs no translation.

How and When Wine Was Served at Jefferson's White House Dinners

About the service of wine by Jefferson much is known, but ambiguities remain. Wine was apparently served before, during, and after dinner. Jefferson did not, of course, have "lunch" as we know it, eating only two meals a day: breakfast between eight and nine, and dinner at three to four, depending on the season. Jefferson seldom ate a "supper" in the old sense of a light, late-evening meal, as George Washington liked to do.

Jefferson had two types of dinners at the White House while president. The first kind, the "official" official dinners, were served in the large dining room to the west, which still exists as a state dining room. These formal occasions were lamented by Jefferson, who complained about them in his letters. The dinners he preferred were the smaller, more informal ones held in the "family" dining room to the east, now the Green Room.

A good description of Jefferson's private dining room was given by Marie Kimball in her *Thomas Jefferson's Cook Book* (1933, 1976):

> The room was elaborately furnished, as an inventory in Jefferson's own hand assures us. There was an "elegant sideboard with pedestals and urn knife cases, a large Mahogany Dining Table in six pieces, a Small dining Table in three parts, a large Mahogany Square Table, two Glass Cases to contain the Silver and plated ware, an Oval breakfast Table, and fifteen chairs, black and gold.
>
> The floor was covered by a canvas cloth, painted green. In Jefferson's own words, this was "laid down on the floor of the dining room when the table is set and taken up when the table is removed," merely to secure a very handsome floor from grease and the scouring which that necessitates.
>
> Jefferson had a particular aversion to the presence of servants while he was at table, "believing," as one writer says, "that much of the domestic and even public discord is produced by the mutilated and misconstructed repetition of free conversation at dinner tables, by these mute but not inattentive listeners." To avoid this he had brought back from France the idea of the "dumb waiter," a sort of stand with shelves, containing everything for the dinner from beginning to end. This was placed between the guests and enabled them to serve themselves. There were five of these in the private dining room.
>
> Jefferson went even farther than this, as we learn from one of his guests. There was in his dining room an invention for introducing and removing the dinner without the opening and shutting of doors. A set of circular shelves were so contrived in the wall, that on touching a spring they turned into the room loaded with the dishes placed on them by the servants without the wall, and by the same process the removed dishes were conveyed out of the room.

A restoration of the large dumbwaiter is still present, in the northwest corner of the Green Room. It appears to be a handsome double-size door, but surprisingly rotates, revealing ample shelves on the other side, which accurately fits the description of Jefferson's dumbwaiter.

A word should perhaps be said here about Jefferson's dumbwaiters. The confusing thing about them is that there were at least three different kinds. The first and best-known is the pulley type used at Monticello to convey wine and other items up from the cellar to the dining room and to return the empties back down without intervention of a servant. The second kind is the revolving-door type found in the Green Room and at Monticello. The third is the French type described by Marie Kimball. It is really not what Americans would call a dumbwaiter at all. It is a kind of rolling serving tray or small sideboard with shelves, shared between guests, to hold everything, including wines, for which there was no room on the table. It is eminently practical, and it is surprising modern Americans have not adopted it. But then Jefferson had lots of ideas that we failed to adopt until much later, like the enjoyment of fine wines, so perhaps rolling dumbwaiters will yet be popular.

One of the best descriptions of a small Jefferson dinner was given by Benjamin Latrobe, architect of the Capitol. His verbal portrait of the service of wines by Jefferson and the atmosphere of his table was sent to his wife:

> To Mary Elizabeth Latrobe
>
> Washington, November 24, 1802.
>
> I went to dine with the President. His two daughters, Mr. and Mrs. Madison, Mr. Lincoln (Attorney General), Dr. Thornton, a Mr. Carter from Virginia, and Captain Lewis (the President's Secretary) were the party. The dinner was excellent, cooked rather in the French style (larded venison). The dessert was profuse and extremely elegant, and the knicknacs, after withdrawing the cloths, profuse and numberless.
>
> Wine in great variety, from sherry to champagne, and a few decanters of rare Spanish wine, presents from Chevalier D'Yrujo.
>
> The conversation, of which Mr. Madison was the principal leader, was incomparably pleasant, and though Mr. Jefferson said little at dinner besides attending to the filling of plates, which he did with great ease and grace for a philosopher, he became very talkative as soon as the cloth was removed.
>
> The ladies stayed till five, and half an hour afterwards the gentlemen followed them to the tea table, where a most agreeable and spirited conversation was kept until seven, when everybody withdrew. It is a long time since I have been

present at so elegant a mental treat. Literature, wit, and a little business, with a great deal of miscellaneous remarks on agriculture and building, filled every minute.

There is a degree of ease in Mr. Jefferson's company that every one seems to feel and to enjoy. At dinner Mrs. Randolph was asked by Mr. Carter to drink a glass of wine with him, and did so. Mr. Jefferson told her she was acting against the health law. She said she was not acquainted with it, that it must have passed during her absence. He replied that three laws governed his table—no healths, no politics, no restraint. I enjoyed the benefit of the law, and drank for the first time at such a party only one glass of wine, and, though I sat by the President, he did not invite me to drink.[36]

President Jefferson, while proclaiming freedom and democracy, found it necessary to set written rules outlawing stiffer forms of etiquette, such as the order of entry, seating, and toasts at official dinners. His prescribed informality was a sort of formality in itself. It was a contradiction in terms on the same level as his mixture of democratic ideals with aristocratic tastes.

Jefferson's Rules of Etiquette first appeared in November of 1803 and ruffled the feathers of more traditional members of the diplomatic corps. The Rules began reasonably enough, sort of like a trivial version of the Declaration of Independence:

Rules of Etiquette in Washington

    i. In order to bring the members of society together in the first instance, the custom of the country has established that residents shall pay the first visit to strangers, and, among stranger, first comers to later comers, foreign and domestic; the character of stranger ceasing after the first visits. To this rule there is a single exception. Foreign ministers, from the necessity of making themselves known, pay the first visit to the ministers of the nation, which is returned.

    ii. When brought together in society, all are perfectly equal, whether foreign or domestic, titled or untitled, in or out of office.

All other observances are but exemplifications of these two principles. To maintain the principle of equality, or of pêle mêle, and prevent the growth of precedence out of courtesy, the members of the Executive will practice at their own houses, and recommend an adherence to the ancient usage of the country, of gentlemen in mass giving precedence to the ladies in mass, in passing from one apartment where they are assembled into another.[37]

However sound in theory, the last rule did not sit well in practice with the diplomats of Europe. Even with Americans, the term "pell-mell" seemed too apt. "Chaotic" was thought by some to be more appropriate.

The Merry Affair

The loudest protest against the Rules came from the wife of Anthony Merry, the "Envoy Extraordinary of his Britannic Majesty," whose ideas on democratic etiquette are pretty well predicted by his title. The story goes that when Merry arrived in 1803 to present his credentials, Jefferson received the minister in his bedroom slippers. Ignoring this affront, Merry and Mrs. Merry attended a "formal" dinner at the president's residence shortly thereafter, expecting to be the guests of honor. To their surprise all guests, whatever their rank, were seated according to how fast they were in reaching the table, and not by any diplomatic order of precedence. Ambassador Merry bitterly protested this supposed affront to his government's dignity—he did not, however, complain of the wines served.[38] This complaint was reserved for his secretary, Sir Augustus John Foster, who said later:

President Jefferson's wines were in general very indifferent though he had a great variety of them, including some native juice of the grape from the Ohio, and some Nebioule from Piedmont.[39]

This comment is the only unfavorable one extant on Jefferson's White House wines. It is probably more telling that Merry, whose father made his fortune as an importer of Spanish wines to England, found nothing to criticize in Jefferson's wines, including the many Sherries and other Spanish wines. Merry was certainly no friend of Jefferson. In addition to their squabble over etiquette, he was also accused of plotting against Jefferson with Aaron Burr.

Foster described with relish Jefferson's rather motley and not always complementary company, and what they thought of his food. One, a congressman-butcher from Philadelphia, while dining at the president's table with his son, "a great country lout"

> could not help forgetting the legislator for a few moments to express the feelings
> of his profession concerning a certain leg of mutton of a miserably lean descention,
> noting that at his stall no such leg of mutton should ever have found a place.

More charitable were the comments of William Plumer, a political opponent and Federalist congressman from New Hampshire, who wrote to his wife in 1804 describing

> a party of about ten members of Congress who dined with the President. They sat
> down at the table at four, rose at six, and walked immediately into another room,
> and drank coffee.

Giving Jefferson a rare compliment, Plumer noted that

> he had a very good dinner, with a profusion of fruits and sweetmeats. *The wine
> was the best I ever drank, particularly the champaigne, which was indeed delicious*
> [emphasis added].

Plumer noted that eight different wines were served that evening. He also remarked, as others had, that Jefferson never mixed members of different political parties at his dinners, and dissension was minimal. But Plumer could not resist one thrust at Jefferson, stating that "I wish his French politics were as good as his French wines; but to me at least, they have by no means so exquisite a flavor."[40]

Another Federalist dinner guest was the Reverend Manasseh Cutler of Ohio, who described a meal for ten Federalists during the last stages of Jefferson's presidency as consisting of "loin of veal, cutlet of mutton or veal, fried eggs, fried beef, a pie called macaroni [and] other jimcracks, a great variety of fruit, *plenty of wines, and good*" [emphasis added].[41]

The most flattering descriptions of Jefferson's wines, and the dinner parties at which they were served, appear in the letters of Margaret Bayard Smith, wife of Samuel Harrison Smith, editor of the *National Intelligencer*. Her gossipy epic *The First Forty Years of Washington Society* (1906, 1965) noted that Jefferson usually entertained only about a dozen guests, allowing free play for general conversation:

> At his usual dinner parties the company seldom or ever exceeded fourteen, including himself and his secretary. His guests were generally selected in reference to their tastes, habits, and suitability in all respects, which attention had a wonderful effect in making parties more agreeable than dinner parties usually are.[42]

As readers will recall, the forming of little isolated cliques at Parisian dinners was one feature which Americans most criticized. Jefferson sought to avoid it and thus enliven his own dinners.

> At Mr. Jefferson's table the conversation was general; every guest was entertained and interested in whatever topic was discussed. To each an opportunity was offered for the exercise of his colloquial powers, and the stream of conversation thus enriched by such various contributions flowed on full, free and animated; of course he took the lead and gave the tone.
>
> One circumstance, though minute in itself, had certainly a great influence on the conversational powers of Mr. Jefferson's guests. Instead of being arrayed in strait parallel lines, where they could not see the countenances of those who sat on the same side, they encircled a round or oval table where all could see each others' faces, and feel the animating influence of looks as well as words.
>
> The excellence and superior skill of his French cook was acknowledged by all who frequented his table, for never before had such dinners been given in the President's House, *nor such a variety of the finest and most costly wines* [emphasis added].
>
> In his entertainments, republican simplicity was united to Epicurean delicacy. [A] lady noticed a piece of furniture of a rather singular form as she was passing through a small parlour leaning on his arm, and struck by its beauty as well as

novelty, stopped to inquire its use. [Jefferson] touched a spring, the little doors flew
open, and disclosed within, a goblet of water, a *decanter of wine* [emphasis added],
a plate of light cakes, and a night-taper. "I often sit up late," said he, "and my wants
are thus provided for without keeping a servant up."[43]

This reference that Jefferson kept a decanter of wine to drink alone in the
evening while studying or writing is the only one I've found so indicating.

Mrs. Smith recounted a favorite Jefferson story about a most unusual
dinner attended by several chiefs of the Osage Indian tribe. Jefferson
called them the most gigantic men he'd ever seen. (By a quirk of history,
the dinner was the same day that Aaron Burr killed Alexander Hamilton
in a duel.)[44] Mrs. Smith set the scene, leaving a key description of how
wine was served chilled in Jefferson's White House:

One would have supposed in a scene so novel and imposing as was that day
exhibited to these sons of the Forest, that some indication of curiosity or surprise might have been discovered but not the slightest emotion of any kind was
visible. Imperturbably as the rocks of their savage homes, they stood in a kind of
dignified and majestic stillness, calmly looking on the gay and bustling scene
around them.

During the progress of dinner, strange and incomprehensible as every object
around them must have been, and distasteful as the mode of cooking probably was,
they exhibited no emotion whatever until *the wines in coolers filled with ice* were
placed on the table.

On seeing the ice, one of the chiefs looked on the others with an expression
of doubt and surprise, to which their looks responded. To satisfy the doubt evidently
felt by all, the elder chief took hold of a piece of ice, started when he felt it, and
handed it to his companions, who seemed equally startled. It must be noticed that
it was a hot day in July.[45]

From this comment it is apparent that at least some of Jefferson's
wines were served chilled. His account books have several entries showing the purchase of wine coolers. These were a kind of decanter with
pouches or pockets to hold ice, which cooled the wine in the days before

refrigeration. As shown by his *seau crenellé*, or ribbed porcelain "bucket," he also sometimes chilled his wine glasses in ice, much as we now do our beer mugs.

Apparently the only member of Jefferson's Republican Party to leave written descriptions of his White House dinners was Dr. Samuel Mitchill, an amusing and typically Jeffersonian character. Mitchill wined and dined often with Jefferson at his small dinners in the Green Room. His wife seldom accompanied him to Washington, so he wrote her almost daily, and she had regular parties in New York City where the main entertainment was the reading of his letters from Washington. A friend said of Mitchill's love of conversation, especially his own: "Tap the doctor at any time, he will flow." Jefferson called him "the Congressional Dictionary," and his colleagues knew him as "the Stalking Library."

On January 10, 1802, Mitchill gave one of the best descriptions of Jefferson's presidential dinners:

> He has generally a company of eight or ten persons to dine with him every day. The dinners are neat and plentiful, and no healths are drunk at table, nor are any toasts or sentiments given after dinner. You drink as you please, and converse at your ease. In this way every guest feels inclined to drink to the digestive or the social point, and no further.[46]

Like an anonymous eighteenth-century commentator, Mitchell thought that by too much toasting, "gentlemen ruin their healths by drinking that of others." Dr. Mitchill's famous comment that at Jefferson's table "you drink as you please and converse at your ease" no doubt referred to the freedom *from* having to drink "healths" whether you wanted to or not.

JOHN QUINCY ADAMS ON JEFFERSON'S WINE DINNERS

Not all guests were as favorable to Jefferson and his dinner table dissertations on wines. John Quincy Adams, once a youthful friend and protégé of Jefferson's in Paris, but an opposition senator during Jefferson's presidency, left numerous barbed accounts of evenings with the wine-loving Jefferson:

> November 3d. [1807] Dined at the President's, with a company consisting chiefly of members of Congress. At dinner there was an amusing conversation between [Jefferson] and Dr. Mitchill, though altogether desultory. *There was, as usual, a dissertation upon wines; not very edifying* [emphasis added].
>
> Mr. Jefferson said that the Epicurean philosophy came nearest to the truth, in his opinion, of any ancient system of philosophy, but that it had been misunderstood and misrepresented.
>
> On the whole, it was one of the *agreeable* [emphasis added] dinners I have had at Mr. Jefferson's.[47]

Adams had been Jefferson's dinner guest on numerous earlier occasions, usually in company with other congressmen and political leaders. He mentioned briefly an evening in 1804 when he drank wine and swapped "outrageous" stories with Jefferson, Mrs. Smith, and Aaron Burr. On each occasion that Adams dined with Jefferson, wine was apparently a prime topic, just as it had been with Jefferson and Adams's father in Paris a generation earlier.

Even Adams's wife, Louisa Catherine, a harsh critic of Jefferson's politics, admired his wines and his dinners:

> The entertainment was handsome. French servants in livery, a French butler, a French cuisine, and a buffet *full of choice wine* [emphasis added]: Had he had a tolerable fire on one of the bitterest days I ever experienced, we might almost have fancied ourselves in Europe.[48]

In John Quincy Adams's memoirs there are other accounts of several dinners at President Jefferson's house which give an excellent flavor of what the evenings and company must have been like.[49] In November 1803 Adams and his wife joined "Mr. Madison, his lady, and her sister," along with Mr. Eppes and Mr. Randolph, Mr. Jefferson's two sons-in-law, both members of the House of Representatives, and other guests. Most sources say dinner usually was at four, but Adams recorded that he "came at six." In November of 1804 the main topics of conversation were, as usual, wine and the French Revolution. Adams commented acidly of his former hero that Jefferson's "genius is of the old French school. It conceives better than it combines." Other dinners attended by Adams included Aaron Burr and the exotic Tunisian ambassador Meley-Meley and his two secretaries. Although the latter dinner was to be served precisely at sunset to observe the Mohammedan strictures of Ramadan, the ambassador arrived late, then smoked and took snuff, making the others wait for dinner. Despite Ramadan, his assistants indulged excessively in Jefferson's wines, one of the rare instances of such at Jefferson's table, and from alleged teetotallers at that.

JEFFERSON'S MAMMOTH CHEESE

Little record remains of what cheeses Jefferson served with his wines except that he had many of them brought specially from Baltimore. One which excited great attention was the so-called "mammoth cheese" given to him by some Pennsylvanians. Made in Cheshire, Massachusetts, it weighed 1,235 pounds. Jefferson insisted on paying for it, which ended up costing him two hundred dollars, twice the price of normal cheese. Said to be the product of nine hundred cows, the cheese was fifteen inches thick and four feet in diameter. It was carried by boat, wagon, and sleigh to Washington in 1801 and presented to Jefferson personally by Elder John Leland, a Massachusetts Baptist.[50]

On its way to Washington, the giant cheese was paraded through towns and ports and much celebrated. People even began to refer to Elder Leland as "the mammoth priest," and to Jefferson as the "mammoth president." The cheese itself lasted far longer than even Jefferson had imagined. Reverend Cutler ate some of it at Jefferson's table on New Year's Day of both 1802 and 1803, and it was trotted out again for the Fourth of July, 1803. Contemporary observers said it was served until well into 1805, when the remains were thrown into the Potomac. No one mentioned what wines Jefferson served with the mammoth cheese.

During his first term, when he indulged in the finest Champagnes, Bordeaux, and Madeiras, Jefferson's political fortunes were reflected in his wines. He was extremely active as president, concluding the popular Louisiana Purchase, in celebration of which his rule against toasts was broken, Senator Plumer reporting that the congressmen drank so much they went home without their hats.[51] It was also during his first term that he launched the Lewis and Clark expedition to the West. Little did Jefferson suspect that in California, Frenchman Jean-Louis Vignes was planting vineyards of European wine vines near present-day Los Angeles. Jefferson apparently never knew of the winemaking experiments in California which took place during the later years of his life.

Toward the end of his first term, his personal finances began a downward slide. His high living, particularly his conspicuous consumption of expensive wines, possibly added a bit to his downfall in that regard, but wines were only a small part of a much larger picture.

Jefferson's second term, like many in our own day, was troubled and ended in less happy times than his first. What had once looked like peace later proved to be merely a lull in a general European war, in which even the United States was eventually entangled. Later, naval war and mutual blockades between England and France, with America caught in the middle, slowed Jefferson's flow of French wines.

When Napoleon declared himself emperor in 1804, Jefferson's bitterest foe headed the country whose wines he most sought. In 1805, when Admiral Nelson defeated Napoleon at Trafalgar, French sea power was broken, and Jefferson's old enemies the English became more of a menace. America's navy was too weak, partly due to Jefferson's own policies, to protect its own merchant ships. Both England and France imposed blockades on European ships, and England began the seizure, or "impressing," of American seaman. Jefferson called both countries, in a speech to Congress, "The sea pirates and land robbers of Europe."[52]

The situation so deteriorated that Jefferson recommended, and Congress adopted, embargoes against all European goods, including wines.

With his cellar nearly depleted, his famous dinner parties fell upon lean years. By the time he left Washington in March of 1809, he had so few wines left in his cellar that for once he failed even to make an inventory before returning to Monticello.

Worst of all Jefferson's misfortunes was the illness and death of his younger daughter Maria, which occurred in the heart of his contested election with Burr. While he was making a memo about how fast his Champagne was being drunk, he received word that Maria was gravely ill following complications from childbirth. This daughter, who closely resembled her mother in appearance and temperament, also suffered from the same fragile health. When Jefferson heard of her illness, he wrote to his son-in-law, Congressman Jack Eppes, prescribing wine as the best medicine under the circumstances. He then left in haste for Monticello, where she had been carried on a litter. In his letter, written at a moment when she seemed to be improving, he said of his daughter:

> Your letter of the 9th has at length relieved my spirits; still the debility of Maria will need attention, lest a recurrence of fever should degenerate into typhus.
> I should suppose the system of wine and food as effectual to prevent as to cure that fever.
>
> The sherry at Monticello is old and genuine, and the Pedro Ximenes much older still, and stomachic. Her palate and stomach will be the best arbiters between them.[53]

Jefferson made it to her bedside before she died a month later.[54]

JEFFERSON AND THE WINES OF ITALY

To distract himself from yet another grievous loss, Jefferson turned to other subjects. Ever since his friendship with neighbor Philip Mazzei before the American Revolution, Jefferson had been interested in Italian wines. During his visit there in 1787, he tasted a few of the better wines of Tuscany and the Piedmont. In 1788 he had corresponded briefly with Thomas Appleton, an American then in France. By 1803, Appleton had become the American consul at the port of Leghorn (Livorno in Italian), the main seaport for Chianti and the other wines of Tuscany. With Italy divided among various kingdoms, and less a part of the general European strife, Jefferson turned to its wines, first out of curiosity aroused by Mazzei, later as the best alternative to replace his unavailable French wines.

His first wine letter to Thomas Appleton at Leghorn was dated July 5, 1803, and requested that he

> send me a gross of the best Florence wine. I think Montepulciano is generally deemed the best. I am much acquainted with the Montepulciano and know that it is not a sweet wine.

Since he did not mention it in his travel journals, we must assume that Jefferson's knowledge of it came mainly from Mazzei. And he was correct: in his time, Montepulciano was considered by some the best of the Chianti-like reds shipped from Florence.

His letter sparked a lively correspondence lasting nearly twenty years. The following January 20, 1804, Appleton wrote: "By the same vessel you will receive, sir, a small case containing a few bottles as samples of the best wines which are the growth of Tuscany."

Jefferson's response to these wines has not been located, but it must have been enthusiastic from the comments of Appleton when he next wrote to Jefferson on March 15, 1804:

> Your opinion of the wine of Montepulciano perfectly coincides with the prevailing one in this country; for it is here held in the highest estimation among the class of dry wines. It is universally the custom in Tuscany to preserve the best qualities in flasks [fiascos], over which is put a small quantity of oil to keep out the exterior air, and the whole covered with a piece of parchment. Of so delicate a nature do they conceive them to be, as to imagine it impossible to transport by sea without a detriment, even from one port of the coast to another.
>
> I have by the same conveyance added a few samples of dry wines of Tuscany, and on each bottle is a label specifying its kind. Should either of those

be approved by you, they shall be procured from the spot on which they grow. Their prices will vary little from that of Montepulciano, except the Aleatico, which though not a dry wine, is usually sold at this time at the price of any other product of Tuscany.

I have taken the liberty to forward 225 vine-cuttings of nine different qualities, taken from the botanical garden of Florence. They were chosen and presented to me by my particular friend Propoto Lastri, Director of the same. All these plants produce dry wine (excepting the Aleatico).

The Tokay has been transplanted into Etruria with utmost success, and the wine so perfectly similar to the finest of Hungary that the most intelligent cannot discern the smallest difference. Mr. Lastri is therefore decidedly of opinion that it depends on the process observed in making the wine, and not on the soil in which it grows. To this end he scrupulously adheres to the mode which is adopted in Tokay.

Names of the plants enclosed in a barrel

> Trebbiano
> Lachrima Christi
> S. Giovetto
> Abrostine bianco
> Idem rosso
> Tokai
> Morgiano
> Maminto.

Apparently the dry Tuscan wines arrived quickly, for on July 19, 1804, Jefferson informed Appleton that

[t]he wines also came in fine order. The Aleatico is a fine wine, but certainly not in proportion to the difference in price you estimated. The Chianti, Pomina, and Verdea are good wines, the latter the least so, but best of all is the Montepulciano. I have seen no wine please more, insomuch that I must not be without it hereafter. I have therefore enclosed you a bill of exchange on London for 250 dollars, to cover the cost of the parcel before sent, and of as much more as it will cover to be sent immediately.

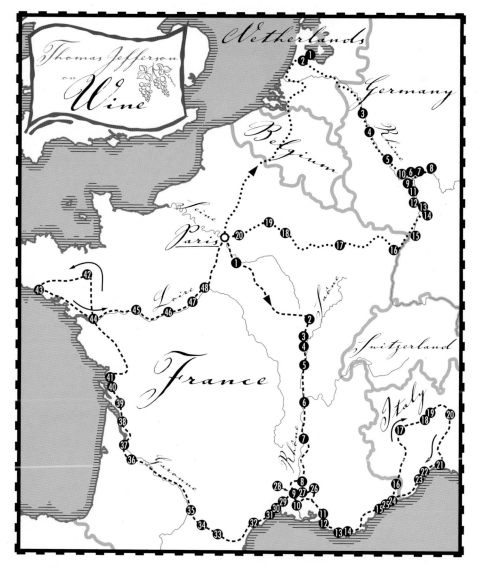

Map showing Jefferson's two lengthy trips through the vineyards of Burgundy, Italy, Provence, Bordeaux, the Loire Valley, Germany, and Champagne in 1787 and 1788.

The opulent, decadent Louis XVI, described by Jefferson as "hunting half the day, drunk the rest," courtesy of Monticello/Thomas Jefferson Foundation, Inc.

Maria Cosway, the beautiful, blonde, married Anglo-Italian paramour of the widower Jefferson in Paris, courtesy of the Huntington Library, Art Collections, and Botanical Gardens, San Marino, California.

JOHN ADAM DICK & SON

Merchants, Innkeepers & Proprietors of the
Hotel, called
The Great Red House
Frankfort ont the Mein.

Beg leave to acquaint the Nobility Gentry and the
Public in general; that they deal in all Sorts of
Genuine Hock or Rhenish Wine.
Whereof the following are mostly demanded and
to be had from them, at most moderate Rates.

Places	Vintages	pr. Tun		L. Sterl.
Hochheim	1726	262		327
	1748	164		196
	1760	72		108
	1761	72		105
	1762	72		105
	1766	66		98
	1775	59		108
	1779	59		165
	1780	50		79
	1781	50		114
	1783	50		92
Rüdesheim	1726	262		327
	1748	164		196
	1760	72		108
	1761	72		108
	1762	72		105
	1766	66		98
	1775	59		108
	1779	59		108
	1780	50		79
	1781	50		114
	1783	50		92
Johannsberg	1775	66		262
	1779	66		262
	1780	59		164
	1781	66		230
	1783	59		164
Markebronn	1726	262		327
	1748	164		196
	1760	72		105
	1761	72		105
	1762	72		105
	1766	66		98
	1775	59		108
	1779	59		108
	1780	50		79
	1781	50		114
	1783	50		92
Nierstein Lauben & Bodenheim	1760	52		82
	1761	52		82
	1762	52		82
	1766	51		82
	1775	40		79
	1779	45		79
	1780	40		59
	1781	45		79
	1783	47		79

... in Aums or Quarter Casks (42½ Gallons each;) from the Continuance of their ... Qualities, & of the very best ... render themselves worthy ... that they will exert every Care & Attention ... at proportionable Prices & of the respect. lovers of Hock ... These and all other Sorts of Hock may also be had ... Assuring the respect. above J. A. Dick & Son. ... Orders, if once favoured with them.

A Tun contains 8. Aums.
An Aum contains 42½ Gallons.

The incredible wine list from the Red House in Frankfurt, where Jefferson stayed in 1788, which lists numerous vintages of great Rhine wines still famous today, courtesy of the Library of Congress, Manuscript Division.

Original wineglasses used by Jefferson, courtesy of Monticello/Thomas Jefferson Foundation, Inc.

Ivory pocket notebook used by Jefferson to record observations and purchases (including wines), which he later erased, reusing the notebook after transferring his notes to his permanent memorandum books, courtesy of Monticello/Thomas Jefferson Foundation, Inc.

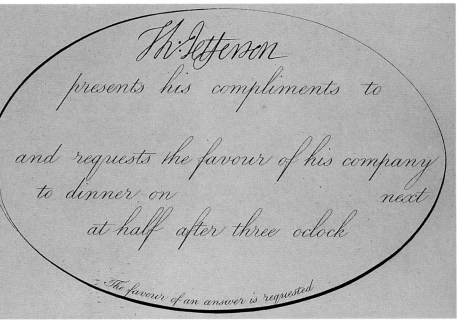

Th: Jefferson
presents his compliments to

and requests the favour of his company
to dinner on   next
at half after three oclock

The favour of an answer is requested

Jefferson's invitation to dinner at the President's house, courtesy of Monticello/Thomas Jefferson Foundation, Inc.

Key to Jefferson's Monticello wine cellar, courtesy of H. Andrew Johnson/Thomas Jefferson Foundation, Inc.

Old Chateau Lafite capsule recently unearthed beneath Monticello, courtesy of Monticello/Thomas Jefferson Foundation, Inc.

Shadow portrait believed to be of Jefferson, courtesy of
Monticello/Thomas Jefferson Foundation, Inc.

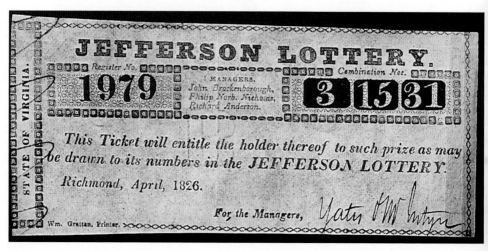

Lottery ticket for the sale of Monticello at auction which Jefferson tried unsuccessfully to use to pay
off the enormous debts he incurred during a lifetime of public service, courtesy of Monticello/Thomas
Jefferson Foundation, Inc.

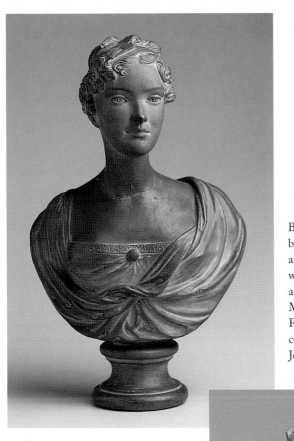

Busts by William Coffee of Jefferson's beautiful granddaughters Cornelia (left) and Anne Cary (below) Randolph, with whom he enjoyed his wines and conversation in the evenings at Monticello and on trips to Poplar Forest during his retirement years, courtesy of Monticello/Thomas Jefferson Foundation, Inc.

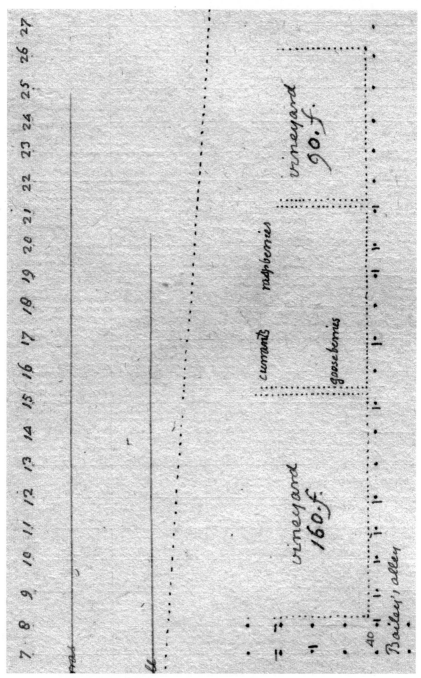

Jefferson's drawing of the vineyards at Monticello, which was used in their current replanting, courtesy of the Massachusetts Historical Society.

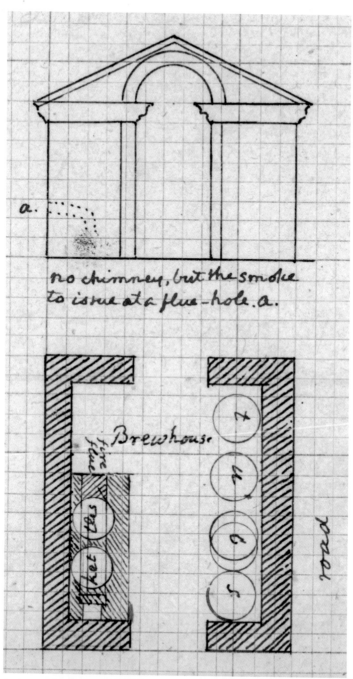

Jefferson's drawing for a Palladian-style Monticello brewery or "brewhouse," which was probably built but not yet located for restoration, courtesy of the Massachusetts Historical Society.

Monticello Dec. 16. 15.

Dear Sir

Disappointments in procuring supplies of wine
have at length left me without a drop of wine. I must the. upon
request you to send me a quarter cask of the best you have.
Termo is what I would prefer; and next to that good port besides
the exorbitancy of price to which Madeira has got, it is a wine
which I do not drink, being entirely too powerful. wine from
long habit has become an indispensable for my health, which
is now suffering by it's disuse. this urges me to request the
immediate forwarding, that is now desired to Messrs Gibson
and Jefferson of Richmond, whom I now write to, pay your
draught for the amount at sight. should you have no sound wine
of the characters I have named, my necessity obliges me to ask
the favor of you to get any person in Norfolk who has such
as you can recommend to forward me the supply, whose draught
on your letter of advice to Gibson & Jefferson will be instantly paid.
the wine should be in a double cask to prevent adulteration.

I have had the happiness of possessing here two or
three times your most learned and able countryman Correa
di Serra. he left us a few days ago; but I hope to have him
here again in the spring. it would double the pleasure were
curiosity or any other motive to induce you to visit
this part of the country & meet him here. I think you
should see something of the interior of our country.
I salute you with assurances of great esteem & respect.

Dr Fernandes

Th. Jefferson

36543

Jefferson letter of December 16, 1815, to Dr. Fernandez ordering wines ("the best you have"),
including double casks of his favorite white Termo of Lisbon or his second choice, Port, because
Madeira had become too expensive, lamenting that disrupted shipping during the War of 1812
had left him "without a drop of wine," which was "indispensable for my health," courtesy of the
Library of Congress, Manuscript Division.

Dear Sir   Monticello Apr. 11. 1823.

I recieved successively the two bottles of wine you were
so kind as to send me. the first called Tokay, is truly a fine wine,
of high flavor. and, as you assure me there was not a drop of brandy
or other spirit in it, I may say it is a wine of good body of it's own.
the 2d. bottle, a red wine, I tried when I had good judges at the table
we agreed it was a wine one might always drink with satisfaction,
but of no peculiar excellence. of your book on the culture of the vine
it would be presumption in me to give any opinion, because it is a
culture of which I have no knolege either from practice or reading.
wishing you very sincerely compleat success in this your laudable
undertaking, I assure you of my great esteem and respect.

                                        Th. Jefferson

Maj. John Adlum

Jefferson letter of April 11, 1823, to Major John Adlum, who made wine from native American grapes from his vineyards in Rock Creek Park in Washington, D.C., courtesy of the Library of Congress, Manuscript Division.

Bordeaux red wines.

There are four crops of them more famous than all the rest. these are
Chateau-Margau, Tour de Segur, Haultbrion, & de la Fite. they cost
3 livres a bottle, old; but are so engaged beforehand that it is impossible to get them. the merchants, if you desire it, will send you a
wine by any of those names, & make you pay 3 livres a bottle: but I
will venture to affirm that there never was a bottle of those wines
sent to America by a merchant. nor is it worth while to seek
for them; for I will defy any person to distinguish them from
the wines of the next quality, to wit

Rohan-Margau, which is made by Madame de Rohan. this is that I
import for myself, & consider as equal to any of the four crops.
there are also the wines of Dabbadie la Rose, Quirouen & Dunfort
which are reckoned as good as Madame de Rozan's. yet I
have preferred hers. these wines cost 40 sous the bottle, when of
the proper age for drinking.

Bordeaux white wines.

Grave. the best is called Pontac, & is made by Monsr. de Lamont.
it costs 18 sous a bottle.

Sauterne. this is the best white wine of France (except Champagne
and Hermitage) the best of it is made by Monsr. de Luz-Saluz,
and costs at 4 years old (when fit to drink) from 20 to 24 sous
the bottle. there are two other white wines made in the same neighborhood called Prignac & Barsac, esteemed by some. but the Sauterne is that preferred at Paris, & much the best in my judgement.
they cost the same. a great advantage of the Sauterne is that
it becomes higher flavored the day after the bottle has been opened, than it is at first.

Mr. Fenwick, Consul of the US. at Bordeaux, is well informed on
the subject of these wines, and has supplied the President & myself with them genuine & good. he would be a proper person to endeavor to get from the South of France some of the wines made there which
are most excellent & very cheap, say 10. or 12 sous the bottle. those of Rousillon are the best. I was not in Rousillon myself, & therefore can give
no particular directions about them.
at Nismes I drank a good wine stronger than claret, well flavored.
the tavern price of which was 2 sous the quart. mr Fenwick might perhaps be able to get these brought through the Canal of Languedoc.

A comprehensive memorandum in Jefferson's handwriting on the wines he preferred, written in 1790, for Philadelphia wine merchant Henry Sheaff, discussing great chateaux of Bordeaux, Sauternes, and Graves, Portuguese whites, Sherries, several red and white Burgundies and the Rhines and Moselles of Germany, all of which still thrive today, courtesy of Herbert R. Strauss Collection, Newberry Library, Chicago.

Lisbon wines. the best quality, of the Dry kind is called Termo, and costs 70.
Dollars the pipe at about 2. years old. at 5. years old it is
becoming a fine wine; at 7. years old is preferable to any but
the very best Madeira. Bulkeley & son furnish it from Lisbon.

Sherry. the best dry Sherry costs at Cadiz, from 80. to 90. Dollars the pipe.
but when old & fine, such as is sent to the London market it
costs £30. sterling the pipe. Mr. Ysnardi, the son, Consul of the
US. at Cadiz, at this time in Philadelphia, furnishes it.

The following facts are from my own enquiries in going thro'
the different wine cantons of France, and examining the identical
vineyards producing the first quality of wines, conversing with their
owners, & other persons on the spot minutely acquainted with the
vineyards, & the wines made on them, and tasting them myself.

Burgundy. the best wines of Burgundy are

Monrachet, a white wine. it is made but by two persons, towit Mons.º de
Clermont, & Mons.º de Sarsnet. the latter rents to Mons.º de la Tour.
this costs 48. sous the bottle, new, and 3. livres when fit for drinking.

Meursault. a white wine. the best quality of it is called Goutte d'or. it costs
6. sous the bottle new. I do not believe this will bear transportation. but the
Monrachet will in a proper season.

Chambertin, Vougeaut, Veaune are red wines, of the first quality, and are the
only fine red wines of Burgundy which will bear transportation, and
even these require to be moved in the best season, & not to be exposed to great heat or great cold. they cost 48. sous the bottle, new & 3. livres old.
I think it next to impossible to have any of the Burgundy wines brought
here in a sound state.

Champagne. the Mousseux or Sparkling Champagne is never brought to a good table in
France. the still, or non-mousseux, is alone drunk by connoisseurs.

Aij. the best is made at Aij by Mons.º d'Orsay, who makes more than
all the other proprietors of the first quality, put together. it costs 3. livres
the bottle when of the proper age to drink, which is at 5. years old.

the Red Champagne is not a fine wine. the best is made by the Benedictine
monks at Auvillay. being made at the head of the Seine, are brought down that ri-
ver to Havre from whence they are shipped. they should come down in the month of November so that they may
be brought over sea in the winter as arriving here before our warm Spring days. they should be bottled
on the spot where they are made. the bottle, bottling, corking & packing costs 5 sous a bottle.
Capt. Cutting Consul of the U.S. at Havre a good person & well informed, to supply the wines of Burgundy & champagne.

A good correspondent at Amsterdam might furnish the following wines.

Moselle. the best of these is called Brownberg, being made on a mountain of
that name adjoining the village of Dusmond, 15 leagues from Coblentz,
to which last place it is brought & stored for sale. the best crop of
Brownberg is that of the Baron Breidbach Burresheim. it costs
22. sous the bottle when old enough to drink. it is really a good wine.

Hock. there has been discovered within these 30. years, a finer wine of this
quality, called Johansberg, now decidedly preferred to Hock. they
both cost 5/ sterl. a bottle when of the oldest & best quality. it is
to be observed of the Hock wines that no body can drink them but
Germans or the English who have learnt it from their German kings.
compared with the wines of more southern climates they are
olive compared with a pine-apple.

Observe that whenever the price of wine by the bottle is mentioned, it means
to include the price of the bottle, which is 5. sous. deduct that
sum therefore, & it leaves always the price of the wine.

MONTICELLO WINE TRAIL

N

to Washington DC

Stone Mountain Vineyards

Ruckersville

Horton Cellars

Barboursville

Earlysville

Barboursville Vineyards

Gordonsville

Skyline Drive

White Hall Vineyards

White Hall

King Family Vineyards

Crozet

Oakencroft Winery

Keswick Vineyards

to Staunton

Charlottesville

to Richmond

Veritas Winery

Blue Ridge Parkway

Afton Mountain Vineyards

Cardinal Point Winery

Jefferson Vineyards

DelFosse Vineyards & Winery

First Colony Winery

Kluge Estate Winery

Wintergreen Winery

Hill Top Berry Farm & Winery

Mountain Cove Vineyards

to Lynchburg

Scottsville

MONTICELLO WINE TRAIL

Suggested Wine Trails

Northwest
- Stone Mountain Vineyards
- White Hall Vineyards
- Oakencroft Vineyard & Winery

West
- King Family Vineyards
- Veritas Vineyards & Winery
- Afton Mountain Vineyards
- Cardinal Point Vineyard & Winery
- Wintergreen Winery

Northeast
- Barboursville Vineyards
- Horton Cellars Winery
- Keswick Vineyards

Southwest
- DelFosse Vineyards & Winery
- Mountain Cove Vineyards & Winegarden
- Hill Top Berry Farm & Winery

Southeast
- Jefferson Vineyards
- Kluge Estate Winery & Vineyard
- First Colony Winery

The Monticello Wine Trail, a group of excellent wineries surrounding Monticello where world-class wines are now made as Jefferson once dreamed, courtesy of Felicia Rogan, President, Monticello Wine Trails.

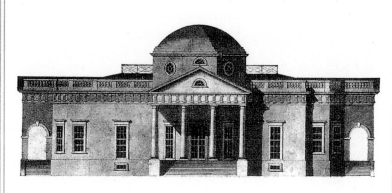

JEFFERSON CLARET

2003

Monticello

Produced and Bottled by   *Oakencroft Vineyard and Winery*

ALC. 13% BY VOL.

OAKENCROFT

CABERNET
FRANC
MONTICELLO
2002

ALC. 13% BY VOL.

Labels of wines from the beautiful Oakencroft
Winery, showing a modern blend of red varietals
typical of what Jefferson knew as everyday "claret"
(above), and a Cabernet Franc, the Bordeaux
varietal which has thus far made the best red
wines in the Monticello appellation (left).

Jefferson had not so praised a wine since Yquem and pale Sherry. Pomina is still available today in America as Pomino, both red and dry white, and can be smooth and quite pleasant. The ancient Frescobaldi family is the proprietor.

The Verdea is a grape now grown mainly in the Apulia and Calabria regions of southern Italy where it produces a rather common white wine, much of it sent to Vermouth factories in Turin. What kind of wine it produced in Jefferson's time is hard to guess, but his evaluation of it as the least good of the lot was probably accurate.

Appleton's next letters to Jefferson in 1804 apparently have been lost, the only reference to them being in Jefferson's letter of May 4, 1805:

> Your favors of December 24th and February 1st are received, and the Vin del Carmine sometime since arrived at New York, is daily expected here. I have received from Mr. Barnes 2. boxes containing 77. bottles of different wines of Tuscany. The Montepulciano was superlatively good. As I make it a point to receive no presents while in office, I must ask you to make this apology to Mr. Barnes and to pay him the price of the wine.

While enjoying the dry Tuscan wines, Jefferson also kept up his supply of the sweet dessert wine of Sicily known as Marsala, which he obtained through military rather than diplomatic channels. As he noted in a letter of May 16, 1805, to George Dyson, U.S. Naval Agent at Syracuse, Sicily: "I wrote by Mr. John Adams to Mr. Woodhouse of Marsala desiring him to send me a pipe of Marsala wine by an arrangement with Mr. Smith, the Secretary of the Navy."

That summer Jefferson received the Marsala and sent a polygraph machine (letter copier, not a lie detector) to Commodore Edward Preble of the U.S. Navy in appreciation. In a letter of July 6, 1805 Jefferson noted:

> I received the hogshead of Marsala wine you were so kind as to send me. Altho' not yet fined[55] (which operation I always leave to time), I perceive it is an excellent wine, and well worthy of being laid in stocks to acquire age.

Coming as it did in the midst of a serious quarrel with England, Jefferson's choice of Woodhouse Marsala was unusual, for that wine was almost as quintessentially English as Port.

In 1760 an English merchant from Liverpool named John Woodhouse visited Marsala, the seaport in western Sicily. Noting the terrain and climate were comparable to those of Spain and Portugal, he decided wines similar to Sherry or Port might profitably be made there. He established a company, began making wine, and in 1772 shipped some six hundred gallons of Marsala wine to England, where it was a great success. Thereafter Woodhouse's wines became popular in England as inexpensive substitutes for Sherry and Port. Soon other English families came to Marsala and commenced a trade in the local wines.

Legend has it that Admiral Nelson stopped in Marsala and "victuallized" his fleet with strong Marsala wine before his great battle with Napoleon at Trafalgar, believing it an excellent cheap substitute for their usual rum. That incident had a lot to do with Marsala's becoming a popular wine in Regency and Victorian England.

Marsala, whose name comes from *Marsah Allah*, Arabic for "God's Harbour," is less known today, but still exported in some quantity to the U.S., partly as a cooking wine. The Woodhouse firm still exists and thrives, but is now eclipsed by Italian firms, particularly Florio, which exports more Marsala to America.[56]

The late Maurice Healy, author of the amusing book *Stay Me With Flagons*, and one of the most knowledgeable palates of the last century, had kind words for it, saying that he once had "an old particular of Woodhouse's that only cost 9 d. (pence) a glass, and was undistinguishable from a very fine old Madeira."[57] Healy thought it so much like Madeira that he suspected it was mislabelled. Perhaps the "Marsala Madeira" from Woodhouse drunk by Jefferson was such a wine.

To the wine drinker eager to try a Marsala, the best advice I can give is to expect something sweet unless it is well aged, when Marsala tends to become drier. Those seeking the wine closest to what Jefferson would have liked should try Marsala Vergini, which are unsweetened, well aged, and the closest thing to "natural" one can likely find here.

Jefferson reverted to his favorite Montepulciano in a letter to Appleton dated April 29, 1806:

In November I received the 473 bottles of Montepulciano, which is truly the best I have ever yet received. I think it would be best in the future to confine our stock to this crop, which you say is from the grounds of the antient Jesuits. I will now pray you to send me about the latter part of September or beginning of October every year 400 bottles of this wine in strong bottles.

I trouble you with a letter to Mr. Kuhn, our Consul at Genoa, or to Mr. Storm, his partner, on the subject of some Nebiolo for which I wrote to him and of which he informs me he has already sent 50 bottles to your care.

Jefferson recalled Nebbiolo from his travels in Italy. On October 26 he inquired whether Appleton had received his letter:

I hope the 400 bottles of Montepulciano of the growth of the antient Jesuits are well on their way. I informed you that the 473 bottles of that growth sent me in 1805 were the best I have ever received, and I can now add that the whole of it being now used, there were not in the whole more than 3 or 4 bottles spoiled.

Appleton wrote in January and March of 1807 to inform the president that his Montepulciano was being looked after:

[March 21, 1807]

My last respects were in date of the 15th of January. I then mentioned I had purchased for you about 200 bottles of Montepulciano wine, but I have now increased the quantity to 350.

It grew on the same grounds as that which I sent you two years since, and I am assured by the proprietor that it will prove at least equal. This wine is conveyed to Leghorn over a hundred miles of land and as many of water, in thin flasks covered with oil & cotton, but I have had it carefully bottled & sealed here. I therefore believe it will be delivered to you in the most perfect order.

Jefferson then wrote to Kuhn on the Nebbiolos:

> To Peter Kuhn, Jr.
>
> Washington Mar. 30. 1807.
>
> I recieved, in April last, a letter from Mr. Thos. H. Storm written in your absence, and informing me he had sent on for me 50. bottles of Nebioule wine. These arrived safe, with the loss of only 10. of them, and were of very fine quality, answering fully to what I recollected of that wine when at Turin.
>
> Since that I have recieved your favors of Mar. 25. Apr. 25. and May 28. informing me that you had forwarded to Mr. Appleton at Leghorn 200. bottles for me, which, when arrived there were reduced to 96. These were forwarded by him, but, on their arrival here, but 1. single bottle remained unbursted. I found, from the quality of that one bottle that it had been put up too new. It had nothing of the quality of Nebioule but it's briskness, which was excessive.
>
> In your letter of May 28. you mention that a friend, Count Pavia, had promised you 200. bottles of his own growth, which you would forward. Having heard nothing further of these, nor recieved any letter from you, I very much apprehend they have been intercepted by the lawless rovers on the ocean.
>
> Not discouraged by these two failures, out of three, I will still ask the favor of you to send me a hundred bottles, and to draw on me at 30. days sight for the amount of all the parcels.
>
> Th: Jefferson

Intent on building up his cellar, Jefferson promptly ordered more "Marsala Madeira":

> To William Higgins:
>
> Washington May 23. 1807.
>
> I take the liberty of solliciting you to send me a pipe of the Marsala Madeira of Mr. Woodhouse and of praying you to draw on me for the amount through the Navy department, as on the former occasion.
>
> Th: Jefferson[58]

The Marsala letter, sent by way of the American consul on the island of Malta, bears an amusing notation, made in an unknown hand, by someone who handled it: "From that infamous hypocrite, T. Jefferson." The letter is franked as "official correspondence," which use of both the navy and the franking privilege to get personal wines may be what caused the unknown writer, probably a Federalist, to call Jefferson a hypocrite.

In Jefferson's covering letter to Captain Barron, he wishes him a "pleasant voyage." From the endorsement, one suspects that the unknown writer who called Jefferson an "infamous hypocrite" might have been Captain Barron himself.

Peter Kuhn answered Jefferson's March 30 letter, promising him the Nebbiolo:

> Genoa, June 8, 1807
>
> By the Schooner Louisiana, Capt. McFarlan of Philadelphia, who sailed from hence on the 16th of May, I had the honour to put on board for your Excellency three barrels of Nebiole wine properly embaled as received from Turin.
>
> My motive for sending the wine in barrels proceeded from the failure of several attempts in the transportation of it in bottles. After it will be settled, bottled, well-corked and the bottles laid upon their sides for the term of three or four months, the quality and taste of the wine will be infinitely improved as I know from the tryal I made of a barrel prior to shipping those on board of the Louisiana.

Appleton also sent more Montepulciano and a selection of Italian liqueurs:

> Leghorn, June 10, 1807
>
> By the ship Jane, Capt.ⁿ M.ᶜCarthy, I sent three hundred & fifty bottles of Montepulciano wine. I hope it has been found excellent of its kind, as the last vintage in that part of Tuscany was uncommonly good; and it was shipped for America at a season, when it could neither suffer from the heat or the cold.
>
> You will observe, Sir, that there was a balance due you of Doll. 24. & C.ˢ 50. for this amount I have thought it would be agreeable to invest in the best liquors of Italy, which I have accordingly done in purchasing 50 bottles. They

consist of the following

						Pacoli
10 bottles of	Monte peposito	@	4.	—	40
10	d°	Canolla	@	4.	—	40
10	d°	Caffe	@	4.	—	40
10	d° ..	Latte di Vecchio	@	4.	—	40
10	d° .	Cedrate	@	4.	—	40
8	d° .	d'Alkarmes	@	5.	—	40
						240 Pacoli

I am told by judges of liqueurs that they are exceedingly fine and which I believe on trial will prove so.

It is remarkable how Jefferson's experiments parallel our own. Just as Italian grappas and liqueurs like Amaretto have swept the U.S., so was Jefferson experimenting with them, despite his claimed aversion to brandy.

Before receiving Appleton's last letter, Jefferson had already sent another of his own, dated July 9, 1807:

A very sudden dispatch of a vessel to the Mediterranean with orders from the Navy department gives me time only to acknolege the reciept of your letter of Apr. 1. as also of the 350. bottles of Montepulciano, which is come in good order, and the quality entirely approved.

I avail myself of this opportunity, perhaps the last which may happen for some time, to request you to send me this autumn 300. bottles of Montepulciano of the same crop with the last cargoes and 50. lb. of Maccaroni.

On October 22, 1807, Jefferson notified the collector of customs that

[t]he three small casks of wine from Leghorn, are, I presume, what is called Nebioule, as I expected from Mr. Kuhn a wine of that name. I will ask the favor of you to send it by the first vessel bound to this place, Alexandria or Georgetown. If it be not already in double casks, I would thank you to have each cask put into an outer one.

Th: Jefferson

The next mention of Italian wines was not until July 28, 1808, in a letter from Jefferson, then at Monticello, to his steward Etienne Lemaire, who stayed behind to run the household at the White House. In it Jefferson noted that Nebbiolo was popular at Monticello and he wanted more of it sent there, as he was looking to his retirement just a few months away:

> I find several pipes of wine here in so decayed a state as to render it prudent to bottle them off. This will give me occasion for all the bottles I can muster up. Will you be so good as to pack in crates or barrels all you can possibly spare from Washington and send them by the first vessel.
>
> P.S. Send also all the Nabioule wine. It is much esteemed here.

Lemaire answered on August 4, 1808, in French as always, sending Jefferson seventy-eight bottles of Nebbiolo by boat by way of Richmond.

On the same day Jefferson wrote to Lemaire, he also addressed his last letter to Appleton for eight long years. Jefferson, about to retire, was wary that war would cut him off, perhaps forever, from the Italian wines he so much enjoyed, and asked for the first time for a supply of white Montefiascone, also known today as Est!Est!!Est!!! Clearly he had not lost his habit of experimenting:

> I am this moment and at this place called on to sign and send off a passport for the Leonidas bound to Algiers with naval stores on public account. She as a public vessel may pass unmolested, [so] I avail myself of the occasion of desiring you to be so good as to send me a supply of wines by her, that is to say 100. bottles of Montepulciano, 100. bottles of Montefiascone, and 100. bottles of a white wine which Dr. Ridgeley tells me he drank at your table, and as he thinks by the name of white Florence.
>
> He describes it as extremely pleasant, cheap, and so light that it may be drank as cyder. I am satisfied this is a wine which Mr. Mazzei brought over when he first came to America, which I well recollect to have been much pleased with, and to which I misapplied the name of Verdéa when I wrote to you for a sample of that wine.
>
> I presume the difficulties proceeding from the British orders and French decrees have prevented you from sending my annual supply of Montepulciano, and as I shall on the 4th of March next retire to private life, I must request a discontinuance except when specially desired. Mr. Madison will indubitably be my successor.

This letter is a classic of its kind, devoting most of its length to wine, and passing over the succession to the presidency as worth only one sentence.

Jefferson's Letters on the
Wines of Southern France

Jefferson's most unusual correspondence about French wines while he was president was not to anyone in Bordeaux or Burgundy but in Marseilles. Stephen Cathalan, the American consul whose home Jefferson visited in 1787, was Jefferson's supplier for wines of the Rhône and southern France and his primary wine source overall during retirement. Their correspondence lasted some thirty-two years, from 1786 through 1819. In scores of letters, many of them previously unedited, the two men discussed in great detail the wines of the Rhône, the Midi, and Languedoc, as well as Gaillac, Roussillon, and other regions only recently becoming known again in America.

The finest wine Cathalan obtained for Jefferson was the great white Hermitage, whose vineyards he had visited by climbing to the top on a mule in 1787. On November 2, 1805, Cathalan notified the president that he had located a reliable grower-supplier of Hermitage and was sending him via William Lee, consul at Bordeaux, a "sample" of a hundred bottles. The growers were Messrs. Jourdan of Tains.

Jefferson was pleased with the wine, and on April 28, 1806, wrote to thank Cathalan for a second shipment of two hundred bottles which he described as "the very best I have ever received; it is exactly to our taste, neither too dry nor too sweet." He seems to have liked less six bottles of Hermitage *vin de paille*, a late-harvest wine from Roussanne and/or Marsanne grapes partially dried on straw mats in the manner of the *vin santos* which he had tasted in Italy.

The next shipment did not go so well. On June 29, 1807, Jefferson wrote to Cathalan grumpily about the latest white Hermitage, but still asked for one hundred more bottles of it the next season:

> M. Jourdan's last supply of wine is of quite a different quality from those of the two preceding years; they were what we call soft, or silky, and what I believe you express by the terms *doux et liquoreux* [sweet and luscious]. What he last sent is dry and

hard, more resembling Sauterne or Barsac, and will not be drank here. I would wish that when the year and seasons have given this quality to the wines, he would rather leave my orders unexecuted, and in short to recieve his wines only when they are of the quality of the two preceding supplies. I have asked at this time for only 100 bottles of his wine.

Cathalan forwarded Jefferson's critique of the Hermitage to the Jourdan family. Their response, while polite and respectful, implied criticism of the president's palate as inferior to their British clients, who appreciated drier wines. They pointed out that the First Lord of the British Admiralty had very much liked the same lot of wine that Jefferson disliked, and that white Hermitage was a dry wine and had the touch of sweetness Jefferson preferred only in rare years. The Jourdan letter, as translated from the Library of Congress microfilm, read as follows:

Mr. S^n Cathalan

Tain 1st 8ber, 1807

We have received in its time your favor of the 20th past to which we were unable to respond earlier due to our harvest. The first Lord of the Admiralty, being an old acquaintance of our father who wishes us very well, and to whom we sent last year, as to other Lords, some of the same white wine, with which they were very well satisfied, for they have since asked us for more of the same.

This is no reason for also finding them so in America, and the criticisms that you made of our wine on the part of your President cause us to conclude that in America you desire a wine having a touch of sweetness, which is rather rare in the said wines. That is why, not finding any of that sort at this moment, we shall suspend the order for 100 bottles which the President desires until next year, being persuaded that those grapes we have just harvested will have all the sweetness that is desired in America.

We learn with regret that Mr. Jefferson wishes to retire from public life, and we believe that the United States of America will suffer a great loss by this retirement. If he comes to France, we hope that by your intervention he will do us the favor of accepting our soup, which would flatter us very greatly.

JOURDAN & SONS.

Jefferson purchased no more white Hermitage while president. He did, however, obtain several rare wines of the south of France, including red Bellet from Nice, which he later called in his retirement years "the finest everyday wine in the world," and one lot of Cahusac of Gaillac, the wine he had first shared with John Adams twenty years earlier in Paris. He had bad luck with the Cahusac, explaining to William Lee, American consul at Bordeaux:

June 25, 1807

> The second cask of Cahusac which you were so kind as to send me arrived a few days ago. The vessel in which it was shipped from Bordeaux had been driven to the W. Indies in distress, unloaded her cargo there, refitted and is just returned. After such a voyage and into such a climate it was to be expected that the wine would be the worse. In fact it was too much pricked for any use but that of vinegar.
>
> Knowing the superior excellence of the Cahusac sec, and that it is a wine of as much body as those of Lisbon, and will consequently bear transportation, I must trouble you again to apply to M. Caillier, Regisseur of Made. de la Rochefoucault at Cahusac near Bergerac, Dordogne, for another barrel of his oldest vin sec de Cahusac but could [you] not prevail on him to send it ready bottled.

Little did Jefferson know when he sent this letter that he would receive no more wines, or even letters, from Cathalan for eight long years. As embargo turned to war, Jefferson was cut off from his best source of wines from southern France. For nearly a decade American trade with France was minimal, but it was good for Jefferson while it lasted, and he took it up again as soon as possible following the conclusion of the War of 1812.

Jefferson on Lowering Import Duties on Wine

One of Jefferson's pet causes was the lowering of import duties on wines. He favored simplifying import duties on wine and making them uniform. He knew from personal experience the need for reform; the duties were so uncertain that collectors had to consult *him* while he was president to set the amount of duty on his more unusual wines. On May 28, 1807, the collector at Baltimore, Gabriel Christie, confirmed such a request:

> I yesterday shipped to Washington the 4 cases of wine, in very good order. We have charged the duties on the gallon which as near as we could ascertain will be found to be about 80 gallons. I forward you the bill of lading and also return agreeably to your request the paper you sent me for the ascertainment of the duties.

This incident moved Jefferson to write one of his more important wine letters to Albert Gallatin, his secretary of the treasury:

Jefferson's Proposal for a New Wine Tariff

I gave you, some time ago, a project of a more equal tariff on wines than that which now exists. But in that I yielded considerably to the faulty classification of them in our law. I have now formed one with attention, classing them more rigorously. Were the duty on cheap wines put on the same ratio with the dear, it would wonderfully enlarge the field of those who use wine, to the expulsion of whiskey.

The introduction of a very cheap wine (St. George) into my neighborhood, within two years past, has quadrupled in that time the number of those who keep wine, and will ere long increase them tenfold. This would be a great gain to the treasury, and to the sobriety of our country. I will here add my tariff, wherein you will be able to decide whether it will not, on a fit occasion, be proper for legislative attention. Affectionate salutations.[59]

The St. George referred to by Jefferson was not, of course, the great Nuits-Saint-George of Burgundy, but what is now Saint-Georges-d'Orcq (or d'Orcques) of Provence, near Montpellier, which has been popular with English tourists for decades.

St. Lucar is a port town in the Sherry region, and the place from which Columbus set sail for America. Its fine wines today are known as Manzanilla.

JUNE 3, 1807

	COST PER GAL.	15 PER CENT	20 PER CENT	25 PERCENT BEING THE AVERAGE OF PRESENT DUTIES	30 PER CENT	35 PER CENT	PRESENT DUTY PER CENT
Tokay, Cape, Malmesey, Hock	4 00	60	80	1 00	1 20	1 40	Tokay 45 cents, which is 11 1–4 Malmesey 58 " " 14 1–2 Hock 35 " " 25
Champagne, Burgundy, Claret,* Hermitage	2 75	41 1–4	55	68 3–4	82 1–2	96 1–4	Champagne 45 " 16 1–2 Burgundy 45 Claret Hermitage 35 " " 12 1–2
London particular Madeira	2 20	33	44	55	66	77	58 " " 26 1–2
All other Madeira	1 80	27	36	45	54	63	50 " " 27 1–2
Pacharetti, Sherry	1 50	22 1–2	30	37 1–2	45	54	Pacharetti 23 " " 15 Sherry 40 " " 26 1–2
†The wines of Medoc and Grave not before	1 25	18 3–4	25	31 1–4	37 1–2	43 3–4	35 " " 28

mentioned, those of Palus, Coterrotie, Condrieu, Moselle									
St. Lucar and all of Portugal	80	12	16	20	24	28	St. Lucar	40	" " 50
							Other Spanish	23	" " 28 3–4
Sicily, Teneriffe, Fayal, Malaga, St. George, and other western islands	67	10	13	16 3–4	20	23	Sicily	23	" " 34
							Teneriffe, &c. in bottles	28	" " 35
All other wines							in casks	23	often 400%
									41

*The term Claret should be abolished, because unknown in the country where it is made, and because indefinite here. The four crops should be enumerated here instead of Claret, and all other wines to which that appellation has been applied, should fall into the ad valorem class. The four crops are Lafitte, Latour and Margaux, in Medoc, and Hautbrion in Grave.

†Blanquefort, Calon, Leoville, Cantenac, &c., are all wines of Medoc. Barsac, Sauterne, Beaume, Preignac, St. Bris, Carbonicu, Langon, Podensac, &c., are of Grave. All these are of the second order, being next after the four crops.

It is interesting that Jefferson decided the term "claret" should be abolished, after ordering so much of it during his first term as President. His tax proposal is in line with most wine lists of the period. Perusing it, one notes he recorded possessing or tasting every single wine on it at one time or another.

On June 2, 1807, Jefferson sent Gallatin an addendum regarding "Florence" wines such as Chianti and Montepulciano, as well as Nebbiolo, suggesting they were so rarely imported that they could

> remain in the nonenumerated or ad valorem wines. The Montepulciano, which is the best of the Florence wines, costs .75 per gallon, from whence the prices of the others descend very low. It might be named in the class of .67.

MOVING TO MONTICELLO

"All my wishes end, where I hope my days will end, at Monticello."

As far as his wine cellar was concerned, Jefferson was prepared to retire. He had notified his suppliers that his Monticello wine cellar was full and he was canceling all standing orders. He made no cellar list when he left Washington, it being evident from his letters that he had already shipped most of his wines ahead a few at a time until the famed White House cellars were nearly empty when he was ready to retire.

His overseer Bacon came to Washington several days ahead to supervise the packing and moving, and went shopping nearly every day with Lemaire to prepare for the daily farewell dinners. From his descriptions, Jefferson may have cut down on his wine purchases, but not on his dinners:

> He was perfectly tired out with company. He had a very long dining room, and his table was chock-full every one of the sixteen days I was there. There were Congressmen, foreigners, and all sorts of people to dine with him. He dined at four o'clock, and they generally sat and talked until night. It used to worry me to sit so long, and I finally quit when I got through eating and went off and left them.[60]

From his letters home it appears that Jefferson did not enjoy these costly departure dinners much more than Bacon did, but he considered them obligatory and helpful to his friend and successor Madison in establishing his government. Jefferson expressed fears, however, that he would not be able to enjoy the retirement he had so long looked forward to because he would be too poor to take advantage of it.[61]

To a degree he was right; at the end of his life he was virtually bankrupt. But his retirement was in many ways a happy one, and it was certainly filled with fine wines, for throughout his final seventeen years as the patriarch of Monticello, he continued his extensive correspondence about wines, and continued to have perhaps the finest, and certainly the most eclectic, wine cellar in the United States.

CHAPTER SEVEN

Retirement at Monticello

(1809–1826)[1]

I find friendship to be like wine: raw when new; ripened with age the true old man's
milk and restorative cordial.

—TO DR. BENJAMIN RUSH (1811)[2]

Throughout the seventeen years of his retirement, Jefferson found comfort in old friendships and old wines. Among the highlights was a resumption of his correspondence with John and Abigail Adams, to whom he wrote wistfully that old age was sometimes to "taste the tasted . . . o'er our palates to decant another vintage."[3]

Later there was a lengthy visit from Lafayette, during which so much wine was drunk that Jefferson's wine cellar was nearly empty when Lafayette left. Much of his time and energy went into founding the University of Virginia. During Lafayette's visit in 1824, a great dinner was given in the still-unfinished rotunda, during which thirteen straight toasts were drunk, one for each of the original states. It is said that Jefferson relaxed his rule against toasting and downed two glasses when Virginia was being honored.[4]

Despite financial problems and the trauma of the War of 1812, the first years of retirement were in general happy ones. Jefferson never wavered in his belief that one of the first goals in life was to be happy, as he had written in the Declaration. He described himself to Maria Cosway, his former love in Paris, as living "like a patriarch of old," surrounded by grandchildren and admiring visitors.[5] Locally he was called the "sage of Monticello," no doubt sarcastically by a few, but seriously by most.

Some visitors left comments which imply that his wine-drinking habits changed with age, and that he began drinking wine more after dinner than with it. Perhaps it was in deference to local custom since he became a very local man, never again leaving the state of Virginia. He rarely went anywhere except to his "retreat" house at Poplar Forest, some ninety miles from Monticello, and then mainly to escape the hordes of admiring but tiring visitors who came to ogle the great man. It is also possible that his change of diet—he began to eat more vegetables in old age—changed his wine-drinking habits, since wines go less well with vegetables, and that he saved his wines to savor after dinner.

Whatever his habits, Jefferson kept a well-stocked cellar right up to his death, even though he suffered financial ruin, causing him to sell his entire library to Congress to pay debts, and ending three years after his death with the sale of Monticello itself. Mostly gone during his retirement years were the great Bordeaux, Champagnes, and Burgundies of his affluent days, replaced by good but less expensive wines from southern France and Italy. Names like Roussillon, Rivesaltes, Limoux, Bellet of Nice, Ledanon, and Paillerols filled his letters. Even the name he had said while president should be abolished, "claret," began to appear again in quantity on his cellar lists.

Only one native American wine, the Scuppernong of North Carolina, a white kind of muscadine, began to appear. He tried to obtain it from the best proprietors, just as he did his best foreign wines, and on occasion complimented it.[6]

In old age he seemed to drink more red wines, but there were so many variations that it is difficult to generalize meaningfully, so it is better to let Jefferson's letters speak for themselves. In a sense it is a benefit for us that he had such long distances from suppliers: they caused him to be more detailed and explicit in his wine correspondence.

Among the first visitors to Monticello after Jefferson retired was Margaret Bayard Smith, who noted that as of 1809 he still served his good wines *with* the meal:

> The table was plainly, but genteely and plentifully spread, and his immense and costly variety of French and Italian wines gave place to Madeira and a sweet ladies' wine.[7]

The transition to retirement was not at first a major change according to Mrs. Smith, who was thoroughly familiar with the wines in Jefferson's White House.

A second account, from Elijah Fletcher in 1811, noted Jefferson serving wine as a cocktail: "I was introduced to him and shook hands. We went into the drawing room—wines and liqueurs were soon handed us."[8]

With his cellar nearly full, he had less reason to write to his old wine correspondents. He did order and receive in 1809 some unusual Spanish wines. In a letter written from "Washington City" dated July 16, 1809, one John Martin Baker announced that

> I have the honor to make known to you that in the present month I shall embark with my family for the Balearick Islands (via Algiers). Immediately on my arrival at Majorca, I shall have the satisfaction Sir, to select and ship per the very first opportunity the Two Pipes Albaflor wine, and address them, as you were pleased to direct me.[9]

Unfortunately there is no *Memorandum Book* entry for them, so it is possible Jefferson never received them.

If Jefferson did receive the Albaflor, it was one of the most unusual wines in his cellar. In his day Albaflor was a white dessert wine made in great stone vats in the style of old Greek wines, even though it came from the Spanish island of Mallorca in the Mediterranean. Henderson described it in the 1820s as resembling Sauternes. Today it is considered a rather ordinary white, referred to in many books as being made on the nearby island of Minorca rather than Mallorca.[10] While working in Calaratjada on Mallorca as a bartender, I never encountered it either place.

As Jefferson began to draw on the wines in his cellar, he found aging had improved them. Learning that his old friend William Jarvis had retired, Jefferson wrote to thank him:

> December 5, 1810
>
> You may remember some wines you were so kind as to procure for me in 1803: Carrasqueirra, Arruda and Oeyras. The first of these is now abroach, and is among the best wines I have ever had. The Oeyras, with the age it has, 12 years, has become also a fine wine. It did not promise at first. Altho' sweet, it is not too much so, & is highly flavored. Come however and judge for yourself, that you may bear testimony to others.

Surrounded by his grandchildren, Jefferson was as content as he had ever been in his life, and so wrote to his old friend General Thaddeus Kosciusko:

> Monticello, February 26, 1810
>
> I am retired to Monticello where, in the bosom of my family, and surrounded by my books, I enjoy a repose to which I have been long a stranger. My mornings are devoted to correspondence. From breakfast to dinner I am in my shops, my garden, or on horseback among my farms. From dinner to dark I give to society and recreation with my neighbors and friends; and from candle light to early bed-time, I read. My health is perfect; and my strength considerably reinforced by the activity of the course I pursue. Perhaps it is as great as usually falls to the lot of near sixty-seven years of age.[11]

Later, when his financial situation became desperate, Jefferson turned to Kosciusko for loans to tide him over the worst passages, and to repay Kosciusko he had to sell both lands and possessions. But for the moment his life was pleasant and his wine cellar full.

The following year Jefferson reopened communication with southern France, writing to Peter Walsh at Cette to request some St. George wines:

> Monticello, March 27, 1811
>
> Sir
>
> I some time ago received from you through m Coles, who is known to you, some St George wine which was much approved. The object of the present letter is to ask the favor of you to send me annually a supply of a pipe (about 120 gallons) of the same quality.

Walsh replied, promising to try an end run of the English blockade of southern French ports:

> Cette, October 10, 1811
>
> Your order for wine is duly noted, but our vessels being for a long time excluded by the English from these Seas, obliges me to try the means of getting it shift from Bordeaux, for which purpose I have written to Mr. Lee our Consul there.

The War of 1812: A Long "Dry" Spell

From 1812 through 1815, as war raged in Europe, then spread to America, resulting in the capture of Washington and the burning of the President's House and the Capitol, Jefferson wrote no letters to import wines. He reverted to his former idea that America had to become self-sufficient in wine, writing several letters on the subject in 1811 and 1812.[12] In 1813 he wrote no letters at all about wines, but did try to obtain cork oak trees to plant at Monticello to make his own corks for bottling his wines.[13]

The highlight of this dark period was the rekindling of his friendship with John Adams. The reconciliation was accomplished by their mutual friend Dr. Benjamin Rush. In January 1811 Rush mentioned to Jefferson his regret at the long break between the two old friends. In reply, Jefferson recalled how Washington had written him from Mount Vernon and asked him to gather the cabinet members, including himself and Hamilton, with Vice President Adams, which was the sole time in his administration that such a meeting took place. Recalling the event to Rush, Jefferson said he had the meeting at his own house in Philadelphia, and how it was "after dinner, sitting at our wine," that he realized he had much more in common with Adams than he ever would with the others.[14]

Rush followed up with both men. On December 5, 1811, Jefferson wrote to him that his neighbors, the Coles, had recently met John Adams by chance in Boston and spent a day at his home in Braintree during which Adams professed continuing friendship for Jefferson. A letter soon followed from Adams. Jefferson replied at once:

January 21, 1812

You and I have been wonderfully spared, and myself with remarkable health and a considerable activity of body and mind. I am on horseback three or four hours of every day; visit three or four times a year a possession I have ninety miles distant [Poplar Forest], performing the winter journey on horseback.

I walk little, however, a single mile being too much for me; and I live in the midst of my grandchildren, one of whom has lately promoted me to be a great-grandfather. I have heard with pleasure that you also retain good health, and a greater power of exercise in walking than I do.[15]

Other letters quickly followed, culminating in one of the great correspondences in American history. The subject of wine was little discussed. Adams did introduce Jefferson to George Ticknor, a young man who later drank many fine glasses with him, and who helped Jefferson restock his wine cellar.

A young Bostonian who later became a writer and Harvard professor, Ticknor visited Monticello in February of 1815. Following the visit, Ticknor helped Jefferson buy books to replenish his cherished library, which he had sold to Congress to replace its own library, which was destroyed by the British during the War of 1812. Rather than using the proceeds of the sale solely on books, however, after paying his most pressing debts, Jefferson set aside nearly half his proceeds to buy wines. Replenishing his wine cellar was apparently as important to him as replenishing his library.

Times being what they were, everyone seemed to be out of wine. Even his nephew and favorite Peter Carr, son of his sister and his deceased best friend Dabney Carr, wrote to him for wine. Once a young protégé whom Jefferson had advised on European travel and the study of law, Peter Carr in 1815 was middle-aged and wrote to Jefferson for a supply of Port or claret to ease the pains of his rheumatism.

The chain of events began on December 14, 1814, with a letter from Adams confirming that young Ticknor would be coming to Virginia.[16] On February 4, 1815, a rainy Saturday morning, Ticknor and his friend Francis Calley Gray, whom historians always call a "proper young Bostonian," arrived at Monticello. They stayed only until Tuesday, but in their brief stay wrote two of the most celebrated accounts of Jefferson in retirement.[17]

En route from Richmond by stagecoach, they saw the results of the War of 1812: hordes of ill and underfed militiamen released from service without pay. The roads were bad and a dead horse lay beside one creek they had to ford on the way. In contrast was the road up to Monticello. A great forest of primeval oaks, larger than any they had ever seen in New England, made an "extremely grand and imposing" approach to Jefferson's home. As Ticknor recalled his first sight of Jefferson, then aged seventy-two, he was as impressive as his famous home:

> Mr. Jefferson entered; and if I was astonished to find Mr. Madison short and somewhat awkward, I was doubly astonished to find Mr. Jefferson, whom I had always supposed to be a small man, more than six feet high, with dignity in his appearance, and ease and graciousness in his manners.[18]

Gray likewise was surprised at Jefferson's appearance:

> He is quite tall, six feet one or two inches, face streaked and speckled with red, light gray eyes, white hair, dressed in shoes of very thin soft leather with pointed toes and heels ascending in a peak behind. His figure bony, long and with broad shoulders, a true Virginian.

Both young men thought Jefferson's mode of dress eccentric and that he should change it. The Monticello chair bottoms were worn with "the hair sticking out in all directions," yet the inlaid floor of cherry and beech was "kept polished as highly as if it were of fine mahogany."

Each young man described in detail Jefferson's drinking habits. Gray said that on the first afternoon, a cold rainy one, "a toddy was brought us, which neither of us took, and which was never after handed again." Whether this was a hot toddy of whiskey or brandy, made to warm the cold travellers, we may never know for certain. Gray continued:

> The drinking cups were of silver marked G.W. to T.J. The table liquors were beer and cider, and after dinner wine. In the same room we took tea and at ten in the evening retired.

Ticknor recalled in a letter to his father that

> [a]t half past three the great bell rings, and those who are disposed resort to the drawing-room, and the rest go to the dining-room at the second call of the bell, which is at four o'clock.
>
> The dinner was always choice, and served in the French style, but no wine was set on the table till the cloth was removed. The ladies sat until about six, then retired, but returned with a tea-tray a little before seven, and spent the evening with the gentlemen; which was always pleasant, for they are obviously accustomed to join in the conversation.

Jefferson's granddaughter Ellen Randolph Coolidge corroborated this pattern, saying in the same year that "we dined about three, and he liked to sit over his wine (he never took more than three glasses, and these after and not during dinner)."[19] One wonders if the thirty minutes in the drawing room were for those who wanted a preprandial wine cocktail. Jefferson seems to have followed that practice in the White House.

On the night before they were to leave, Jefferson's grandson brought news from Charlottesville that General Andrew Jackson had defeated the British at New Orleans, effectively ending the threat to American commerce (and to Jefferson's flow of good wines). The next day, as they were leaving, Jefferson promised Ticknor introductions to his friends in Europe for Ticknor's upcoming grand tour. The young men left impressed that they had met "an extraordinary character." Most impressive of all to them was what Jefferson called his "canine appetite for books." He remarked that he could not live without them, a fact his old servant Isaac stated just as forcefully and much more colorfully:

> Old Master had abundance of books; sometimes would have twenty of 'em down
> on the floor at once—read fust one, then t'other. Isaac has often wondered how Old
> Master came to have such a mighty head; read so many of them books; and when they
> go to him and ax him anything, he go straight to the book and tell you all about it.[20]

Later that same year, moved by Congress's loss of its entire library by fire, and himself desperate for money to pay his debts, Jefferson sold Congress his entire library, his most cherished possession.

When Ticknor heard of Jefferson's generous act, he responded in kind, offering to purchase for Jefferson any books he wished to replace, whether in Boston or Europe. On June 10, 1815, Jefferson informed Adams of Ticknor's generosity in "reprocuring" his favorite volumes. In July Jefferson sent Philadelphia banker John Vaughan $550, of which $350 was to go to Ticknor for books. The other $200 was to go to banker Stephen Girard, "who has correspondents in France," to purchase wines. On July 4 he wrote Ticknor himself, accepting his "aid in replacing some of the literary treasures which I furnished to Congress," asking mainly for "the classics." Jefferson devoted much more correspondence to the two hundred dollars' worth of wines than he did to the three hundred fifty dollars in books. On the other hand, he was never totally without books, but it had been several years since he had tasted a new wine.

DEPRIVED OF WINE, JEFFERSON MAKES "A SMART CASK OF CIDER"

During the long, dry years of the War of 1812, Jefferson turned to cider and beer. There were no markets where one could buy a quick six-pack of beer or gallon of cider. Most beverages beyond water were homemade. The household at Monticello was no different, except for the meticulous care with which Jefferson required his cider and beer to be made.

Virginia remains today the home of fine apple cider. In Jefferson's time it was New England that was known for cider, and his friend and rival John Adams, despite his love of wines, swore by cider as his favorite beverage. Jefferson too, while a master of wine lore, knew his cider, and always kept a separate cellar full of it. As his Monticello overseer Edmund Bacon described it:

> Then every March we had to bottle all his cider. Dear me, this was a job. It took us two weeks. Mr. Jefferson was very particular about his cider. He gave me instructions to have every apple cleaned perfectly clean when it was made.[21]

Jefferson insisted on a certain blend of particular varieties of apples, each picked and pressed at the correct stage of ripeness. He noted in his *Garden Book* on September 4, 1776:

> Mr. Epps examines my North orchard and says it consists of Clark's pear-mains, Golden Wilding & red Hughes. He says the Golden Wilding must not be mellowed before pressed; it will yeild nothing. It must be pressed as soon as gathered. Mixed with the red Hughes they make the best cyder & yeild best.

On February 28, 1797, he wrote to his daughter Martha:

> It will be worth his (Mr. Randolph's) while to have the making of his crab cyder well attended to hereafter, as I learn that good cyder of the qualities commonly at

market sell for a quarter of a dollar the bottle, wholesale, including in that the price of the bottle. Crab-cyder would probably command more.[22]

For nearly fifteen years, including his busy years as president, Jefferson left no comments on cider, or at any rate they have not survived. The War of 1812 changed all that. On June 29, 1814, in response to a letter from James Mease of Philadelphia, Jefferson wrote a remarkable letter on cider in which he no longer discussed clean apples or gallons per bushel, but described the "body" of his favorite cider, comparing it to a "silky champaigne":

> Maj[r]. Taliaferro made a cask of cyder which, in the estimation of every one who tasted it was the finest they had ever seen. He grafted an orchard from it, as did also his son in law, our late Chancellor Wythe. The cyder they constantly made from this was preferred by every person to the Crab or any other cyder ever known in this state. It has more body, is less acid, and comes nearer to the silky Champaigne than any other.[23]

Not all Jefferson's cider was homemade. On December 13, 1816, he wrote to Joseph Dougherty in Washington:

> The cyder which I used to procure from Norfolk was obtained thro' the channel of Col° Newton, member of Congress from that district. He always purchased and shipped it to me. The difficulty I experienced was in getting it brought without being watered by the sailors.

Even after the War of 1812 ended, and the wine tap was turned back on, cider remained a favorite "table drink." Each year it was back to cider making, as he directed overseer Bacon on November 15, 1817:

> We have saved red Hughes enough from the North orchard to make a smart cask of cyder. They are mellow now & beginning to rot. I will pray you therefore to have them made into cyder immediately. Let them be made clean one by one, and all the rotten ones thrown away or the rot cut out. Nothing else can ensure fine cyder.[24]

Just months before his death on July 4, 1826, the eighty-three-year-old connoisseur still wrote in praise of his special cider, telling his grand-daughter Ellen Randolph Coolidge:

> Your letter of the 8th was received the day before yesterday, and as the season for engrafting is passing rapidly by I will not detain the apple-cuttings for Mr. Gray (until I may have other matter for writing a big letter to you), but I send a dozen cuttings, as much as a letter can protect, by our 1st mail.
>
> They are called the Taliaferro apple, being from a seedling tree discovered by a gentleman of that name near Williamsburg, and yield unquestionably the finest cyder we have ever known, and more like wine than any liquor I have ever tasted which was not wine.[25]

While he wrote mainly of cider, and preferred fine wines, it appears that Jefferson was, like his contemporaries, experimenting with fruit brandies. In his account books there are references to "peach mobby" and "perry," as the British still call light pear brandy even today.[26]

Jefferson's Plan for a Palladian Brewery at Monticello

Of all beverages except wine and Virginia cider, Jefferson preferred his home-brewed beer. His preference for beer is not surprising. For more than three hundred years, most Americans have agreed with Dr. Samuel Johnson when he said: "Beer . . . is bliss." Many of our greatest leaders were beer drinkers, and William Penn was one of our first successful commercial brewers. Matthew Vassar, when he founded his college in Poughkeepsie, did so with funds made from brewing beer. What a pity the beer didn't survive as well as the college or we could now order a "cold Vassar."

Yet the beer we drink is different from that of the Founding Fathers. In Jefferson's day beer was darker, sweeter, heavier, and had more alcohol and less bubble. Some didn't sound too palatable, being laced with molasses, horseradish, sassafras, and "rheumatism weed." An early one with limited success was uninvitingly called "gas beer."[27] Patrick Henry was a beer drinker and proselytizer, and as one of his biographers suggested, in a passage reminiscent of Jefferson, Henry

> thought that the introduction of a harmless beverage as a substitute for distilled spirits would be beneficial. To effect this object he ordered from his merchant in Scotland a consignment of barley and a Scotch brewer and his wife to cultivate the grain and make small beer. To render the beverage fashionable and popular, he always had it upon his table while he was governor during his last term of office.

Jefferson did profit from one side effect of the War of 1812. An experienced English brewer, Captain Joseph Miller, was taken prisoner, and Jefferson managed to have him interned at Monticello to teach his servants how to make beer. Just as Jefferson never cooked despite his great love of food, there is no indication that he personally ever made beer. While his wife was living, she always made the beer from a recipe in her own handwriting. Later, he was always interested in other people making the best beer for him.

On September 17, 1813, he wrote to his friend William D. Meriwether for return of a book on the subject:

> I lent you some time ago the *London & Country Brewer* and Combrun's book on the same subject. We are this day beginning, under the directions of Capt. Miller, the business of brewing malt liquors, and if these books are no longer useful to you, I will thank you for them, as we may perhaps be able to derive some information from them.

That winter Jefferson wrote to Richard Randolph for jugs for his beer:

> January 25, 1814
>
> Will you be so good as to send me two gross of your beer jugs; the one gross to be quart jugs, and the other pottle [1/2 gallon] do. They are to be delivered to Mr. William Johnson, a waterman of Milton, who will apply for them in about a week.

Later that year he reported to Captain Miller the progress of their brewing experiments:

June 26, 1815

Our brewing of the last autumn is generally good, altho' not as rich as that of the preceding year. The batch we are now using is excellent. That which Peter Hemings did for Mr. Bankhead (grandson-in-law) was good, and the brewing of corn which he did here after your departure would have been good, but that he spoiled it by over-hopping.[28] A little more experience however will make him a good brewer. My absence in Bedford [Poplar Forest] in the spring prevented our preparing some malt then, which I now regret.

The War of 1812 having ended that year, Jefferson hoped that Captain Miller would remain in Virginia. The following year it appeared he would, and Jefferson wrote to Colonel Charles Yancey about the need for a local brewery.

While waiting for the legislature to act, Captain Miller kept up his correspondence with the influential former president on the subject.[29] By 1820 Jefferson was able to report progress to Madison, sounding like as much of an expert in beer as he had become in wine:

April 11, 1820

About the last of Oct. or the beginning of Nov. we begin for the ensuing year, and malt and brew 3. 60 gall^n casks *successively*, which will give so many successive lessons to the person you send.

Inasmuch as you will want a house for malting, which is quickest made by digging into the steep side of a hill, so as to need a roof only, and you will want a haircloth also of the size of your loft to lay the grain on.

I will give you notice in the fall when we are to commence malting, and our malter and brewer is uncommonly intelligent and capable of giving instruction if your pupil is as ready at comprehending it.

Ever & affectionately yours.

By 1821, Jefferson could write to his neighbor, Governor James Barbour, that one of his servants had become an expert brewer, and that his homemade beer was superior to the "meagre" and "vapid" beers of the public breweries.

Today nothing remains of the Monticello brewery. There is, however, one drawing, in Jefferson's careful hand on lined architect's paper, showing a simple plan for a Palladian-style "brew-house" at Monticello. Where it was built, or even if it was built, we do not know for sure. But that Jefferson knew how to build it and drew the plans for it is clear beyond dispute.

Jefferson Rebuilds His Cellar of French Wines

Whatever his successes with beer and cider, there was no question as to his preference for wines. As soon as the War of 1812 ended, and he had a little money left over from what Ticknor used to restock his library, Jefferson wrote a long letter to his friend Cathalan in Marseilles:

July 3, 1815

My good and antient friend

It is so long since I have heard from you that this letter seems almost as if written to the dead, and you have the like grounds for receiving it as from the same region. The fine wines of your region are not forgotten, nor the friend thro' whom I used to obtain them. And first the white Hermitage of M. Jourdan of Tains, of the quality having "un peu de la liqueur" as he expressed it, which we call silky, soft, smooth, in contradistinction to the dry, hard or rough. What I had from M. Jourdan of this quality was barely a little sweetish, so as to be sensible and no more, and this is exactly the quality I esteem.

Next comes the red wine of Nice, such as my friend Mr. Sasserno sent me, which was indeed very fine. That country being now united with France will render it easier for you I hope to order it to Marseilles.

There is a 3d kind of wine which I am less able to specify to you with certainty by its particular name. I used to meet with it at Paris under the general term of Vin rouge de (red wine of) Roussillon; and it was usually drunk after the repast as a vin de liqueur. There is a name of Rivesalte which runs in my head, and almost identifies itself with the red wine of Roussillon. Should the wine of Rivesalte, from what you know of it, answer the description given, you may conclude it is that I mean.

Having occasion to place some money in Paris for other purposes, I have added to it 200 Dollars subject there to your orders. Taking from it first the 50. lb of Maccaroni, I would wish about a fifth of the residue to be laid out in Hermitage, and the remaining 4/5 equally divided between the wines of Nice and Roussillon.

Be assured of my constant friendship & respect.

In August of 1815 Jefferson wrote to his old wine supplier Henry Sheaff of Philadelphia, who replied on October 16:

Yours of the 11th August I duly received, and until this day it was not in my power to answer it owing to indisposition. I have retired from all kinds of Business. I can procure you a Quarter Cask of Sherry Wine. The price will be $2.75 per gallon, and Lisbon 2.50 & 2.60 of a Superior Quality. If that will answer, I will send you a Quarter Cask. I have had a paubic [?] stroke which has deprived me of the use of my right side entirely.

Jefferson replied sympathetically:

October 26, 1815

I regret that I troubled you with an application so improper. I was led to suppose your continuance in business by the Philadelphia Directory in which I found your name as still a wine-merchant, and at the old stand. I learn with more regret the bodily affliction under which you labor, and hope it will add to the examples we have seen of entire recovery from so distressing a disease. I conclude it better to get a supply of wine from Richmond as being nearer, and my stock out.

Jefferson's letter to Richmond was addressed to Patrick Gibson, partner of his distant cousin George Jefferson:

October 28, 1815

My grandson is desired to procure for me in Richmond a quarter cask of Lisbon which he will desire you to pay about 75 D. This will render necessary the sale of 35 barrels of flour mentioned in my last letter.

The grandson was Thomas Jefferson Randolph, eldest son of Martha and Thomas Mann Randolph, who became Jefferson's cellar keeper in his old age.

JEFFERSON IS LEFT "WITHOUT A DROP OF WINE"

Apparently his sources in Richmond were out of wine also, for in December he wrote a despairing letter to his old Portuguese friend Fernandez at Norfolk.

December 16, 1815

Dear Sir

Disappointments in procuring supplies have at length left me without a drop of wine. I must therefore request you to send me a quarter cask of the best you have. Termo is what I would prefer, and next to that good port. Besides the exorbitance of price to which Madeira has got, it is a wine which I do not drink, being entirely too powerful. Wine from long habit has become an indispensable for my health, which is now suffering by its disuse.

On January 18, 1816, Fernandez replied that he had

sent a quarter cask of the best Port wine. Judging, after your information, that you prefer for your own common use a sound, genuine, old but not brandied wine, and having received on the 16th from the same country a small parcel of Teneriffe wine of which 2 bols. & 4 Quart. casks are very old & of the best quality.

Fernandez awaited Jefferson's instructions. He did not have to wait long.

Monticello, January 24, 1816

I thank you for thinking of me on the receipt of your Teneriffe, which tho of a place whose wines are not generally of high estimation, yet I know there are some crops of it of excellent quality.

You mention that yours is sound, unbrandied, and old, the two first of these qualities are indispensable, and the last a high recommendation. I will therefore gladly take a quarter cask & request you to send it to Richmond, but either in a double cask or box, to prevent watering by rascally boatmen of our river.

I am much indebted to you for the Port you have been so kind as to spare me. I am in daily expectation of light wines (which I mostly use myself) from France and Italy, for which I wrote some time ago, and hope not again to be left entirely without as lately.

The wine arrived from Patrick Gibson:

Richmond, February 22, 1816

I send you a cask Teneriffe wine recd. of Dr. Fernandez. I have by your directions enclosed it in a rough cask to secure it from the watermen.

The Gauger's mark is twenty-nine gallons. Majr. Gibson has judged of the wine and Mr. Richardson informs me that the Major says it is the best Teneriffe he has ever tasted.

Even though he had regressed to the kinds of wines available in Virginia before the Revolutionary War, Jefferson was happy to get any wine at all after having recently been "without a drop":

March 26, 1816

The Port you were so kind as to send me is indeed excellent. I certainly would not wish to be indulged a second time from your private stock, but if you have among that which is for sale any of as good quality, I should be much gratified with another quarter cask to be forwarded as before.

Later he reiterated his request:

August 18, 1816

The supplies of wine which I had ordered from different parts of Europe & which have now begun to arrive, have greatly relieved my wants, but a quarter cask of unmixed port will be a very acceptable addition.

Fernandez's reply was apparently the last letter on wine exchanged between the two men:

> Norfolk, August 27, 1816
>
> Your much esteemed favour, dated 18th Inst. came to hand but yesterday, after the departure of the mail. I am sorry that letters within our state take sometimes longer to reach their destination than those from Boston or Savannah. I will not forget to forward the quarter cask of choice Port wine, as soon as a small parcel, recommended for my use, will arrive.

In 1822 Fernandez was named American chargé d'affaires in London, and there is no evidence that the two men ever met again.

From 1815 on, Jefferson again took up correspondence with old suppliers of French and Italian wines. As he told Caesar A. Rodney on March 16, 1815, in inviting him for a visit: "You will find me in habitual good health, great contentedness, enfeebled in body, impaired in memory, but without decay in my friendships."[30]

Another old friendship began to "bear fruit," so to speak:

> From Stephen Cathalan
>
> Marseilles, January 6, 1816
>
> I have ordered to M. Jourdan of Tains the white Hermitage wine, and to the successors to M. Sasserno the old wine of Nice, & to Mr. Durand of Perpignan the Red wine of Roussillon that you have ordered to me.

Jefferson began notifying customs officers at American ports that his wines would soon be arriving again. He wrote to David Gelston, Aaron Burr's former lieutenant, who was still customs collector for New York:

> January 20, 1816
>
> On the return of peace I have written to Marseilles, Leghorn &c. for some wines, and as their opportunities do not give them a choice of ports, I have taken the liberty of desiring them to be addressed to the Collector of whatever port a vessel may be coming to. The extensive commerce of New York will probably subject you at times to some of these addresses. In this case I must throw myself on your friendship for notice of the case.

The reference to Leghorn was of course to the wines of Italy and his old friend Appleton. In a series of letters which have apparently been lost, Jefferson had written to his friend late in 1815 seeking his favorite Italian wine, Montepulciano. In January 1816 Appleton informed him that he was not sending the wine requested, but wines from two other Tuscan towns:

January 14, 1816

The wine of Montepulciano, owing to an uncommon season, is greatly inferior to that usually made in that part of Tuscany. Of course, I shall defer sending you the wine you request until the next vintage.

In the meantime, I am promis'd some of the villages of Carminiani and Ama, and should they prove of the quality I am assured they are, I purpose to send you a hundred bottles on trial. The sample I have tasted appears to me very little inferior to the wines of Montepulciano.

On the same day Jefferson addressed a letter to Appleton. It bore for the first time an inkling of his financial distress. Rather than ordering a certain quantity of wine and paying whatever it cost, Jefferson told Appleton how much he could afford, and to buy only as much wine as he could pay for:

January 14, 1816

I must confine myself to the physical want of some good Montepulciano; and your friendship has here-to-fore supplied me that which was so good that I naturally address my want to you. In your letter of May 1. 05. you mention that what you then sent me was produced on grounds formerly belonging to the order of Jesuits and sold for the benefit of the government in 1773 at the time that institution was abolished.

I send this letter to my friend John Vaughan of Philadelphia and enclose with it to him 50. D. to be remitted to you and I pray you to send me its amount in Montepulciano, in black bottles, well corked & cemented, and in strong boxes. The warm season be so fast advancing when you receive this that no time will be lost. Perhaps I may trouble you annually for about the same amount, this being a very favorite wine, and habit having rendered the light and highly flavored wines a necessity with me.

Appleton's reply brought news of the death of Mazzei. Later he learned that the death was in character, being "hasten'd by an injudicious connection" with a young and "comely" wife precisely half a century younger than himself.[31] Appleton's letter advised there was no Montepulciano fit to send, and discussed briefly the bad political conditions which later produced Garibaldi and the Italian revolution.

Leghorn, May 30, 1816

My last letter to you, Sir, was in date of the 10th of the present month envoying duplicates of the legal attestations of Mr. Massei. Owing to the failure in quality of the wine of Montepulciano of the last vintage, I should defer sending of the growth of that place until the next season.

In the meantime I have procur'd from a friend a barrel of Carmigniani wine which, though not equal to that of Montepulciano, is one of the best-flavored wines of Tuscany when well made and carefully bottled and sealed with pitch. One barrel contains fifty serving bottles, which are in one case.

I have the promise of a barrel of Ama wine, to which none is superior except Montepulciano; and in the estimation of many they are on a level. These wines can always be procur'd at a much less price than that of Montepulciano, as they are convey'd by the Arno River while the latter is transported 150 miles over land.

Today the competition between Montepulciano and Carmignano continues. Both have controlled place-name status. Montepulciano, producing over 2 million litres a year, is still better known than Carmignano, which produces only some 130,000. Yet the respected American expert on Italian wines Burton Anderson has sometimes preferred the quality of the Carmignanos, so Appleton may have been offering Jefferson a bargain.[32] The Ama was likewise well thought of. Today with the reorganization of the red wines of Tuscany into zones, Ama is a Chianti, and one of the finest is called Castello di Ama.

In his *Memoirs* Mazzei told of holding a blind tasting for the Abbot Ricasoli in London where only three wines were served: a Bordeaux, a Burgundy, and a Carmignano. The tasters allegedly preferred the Carmignano over the great French wines. Of course they were all Italians, but it was a blind tasting.[33]

Jefferson disregarded both Mazzei and Appleton and held fast to his insistence on his beloved Montepulciano, refusing to consider substitutes:

> July 18, 1816
>
> I remark the temporary difficulty you mention of obtaining good Montep-ulciano, and prefer waiting for that, when to be had, to a quicker supply of any other kind which might not so certainly suit our tastes. It might not be amiss perhaps to substitute a bottle or two as samples of any other wines which would bear the voyage, and be of a quality and price to recommend them. You know we like dry wines, or at any rate not more than silky.

Before receiving Jefferson's instructions, however, Appleton had already sent him fifty-seven bottles of Chianti and a like number from the village of Artiminiano, now called Artimino. The site of a famous Medici hunting lodge, Artimino can now sell its wine either as a Chianti or, if it is willing to submit to a rigorous tasting, as Carmignano.

Appleton persisted in his recommendations:

> July 30, 1816
>
> I have now shipp'd two cases of Tuscan wine: No. 1. contains 57 bottles of Artiminiano; No. 2. contains an equal number of bottles of Chianti wine, this latter is of a very high flavour; and both are directed to the care of The Collector for that port. By the next vessel I am in hopes to be able to forward the Ama, a wine of a very superior quality, indeed.

On September 27, Appleton reaffirmed his shipments, adding:

> I have now shipped two cases of Ama wine, No. 1 containing 57 bottles & No. 2. 30. The last mentioned wine is esteem'd the first quality of all I have sent and the next after Montepulciano.

It seems odd to us that this is one of the few times Jefferson used the name Chianti, so familiar to us. But in Jefferson's day the red wines of

Tuscany were called either "red Florence" or by the name of a particular region or estate like Ama or Artimino. The name Chianti comes from a military league in the region which came to prominence around the time of the extravagant Medici prince Lorenzo the Magnificent. Its symbol, a black cock or rooster called gallo nero, now appears on neck labels as the official symbol of Chianti Classico, the finest region.[34]

Appleton was trying to steer Jefferson to wines of quality which were cheaper and more accessible than Montepulciano. Artimino, for example, still exists, and at a tasting of red wines of Tuscany a few years ago, Burton Anderson judged a wine called Fattoria di Artimino, legally classified a Carmignano, as the best wine in the tasting.[35]

Fortunately we now see more Carmignano and Ama wines in the United States. The best to date from Tuscan areas other than Montepulciano have been the Carmignanos of Tenuta di Capezzana of Ugo Contini Bonacossi. Appleton must have felt the same, for on October 20, 1816, he shipped Jefferson another eighty-seven bottles.

In the last extant letter from Jefferson to Appleton, he made one last try for Montepulciano:

> August 1, 1817
>
> The wines you were so good as to send me were all received exactly as you described them. The Ama was the best, but still not equal to the Montepulciano, and as I learn from your letter of Sep. 27 (1816) that the crop of wines for that year was desperate, I have not applied to you for any this year.
>
> If however it has proved that any good Montepulciano (of the growth formerly sent me) has been produced, contrary to your expectation, the little atom of balance of the 400 D. remaining after payment of the interest might be invested in that. It will give us a taste.

Jefferson may have never received his last taste of Montepulciano. But there is listed in the letter index of the State Department Bureau of the Rolls a summary of a four-page letter from Jefferson to Appleton in 1819, about wine, and there is also an invoice dated April 30, 1819, for eighty-one pounds for shipment of 1 1/2 Tuscan barrels of *white* Pomina wine from

Leghorn to Monticello. This was possibly Jefferson's last Italian wine, but due to the lack of editing of many records of that period, there may have been another or two, possibly even one last taste of Montepulciano.

"MORTIFICATION OF THE PALATE"

In March of 1816, Jefferson had not received any of Cathalan's letters of that year and was beginning to despair. In a lengthy letter, he repeated his opinions about the wines of Hermitage, Nice, and Rivesaltes of Roussillon, reverting in places to French, as he did more and more in retirement, after he was out of politics and didn't care about being called a Francophile:

> March 19, 1816
>
> I received yesterday your favor of Nov. 29, from which I learn with much mortification (of the palate at least) that my letter of the 3d of July has never got to your hands. It was confided to the Secretary of State's office. The material part was a request of some particular wines which were therein specified.
>
> God bless you and preserve you many years in health and prosperity.

In a pair of letters sent together in June of 1816, Cathalan told the thirsty Jefferson that the wine tap was turned back on and that the Rivesalte was good; he had tasted it himself. He also included a different red Gaillac from a village now called Peyrole, and gave him further information on where the Ledanon came from. The letters also brought news of the death of yet another old friend and wine supplier, Henri Bergasse.

> June 4, 1816
>
> I have shipped one cask containing one barrel of about 38 gallons de Roussillon wine, which Mr. Louis Durand of Perpignan has at last sent to me assuring it to be the exact quality you wished, & by the bottle he sent me and [having] time to taste it, I took it, at first, for its flavor & taste for old Madeira wine, however with some difference hastily perceived thereafter.
>
> P.S. June 19, 1816

I have shipped two cases of 12 bottles each red wine of Paillerols & 1 basket maccaroni & one box containing 30 bottles Red wine of Ledanon.

The quality of the wine of Paillerols is not yet generally known, but I beg your reference to the printed paper inserted in the said copy.[36]

The wine of Ledanon is from a village at 5 miles distant of the famous antick Pont du Gard, about 11 miles from Nismes going to the South du Saint Esprit tout du bas du [far down in] Languedoc. You tasted of that lot of wine at dinner at my house in the year 1787, which I called *Vin Santo*.[37] The sister of my Father had the best vineyards on that & when alive used to send it yearly. You found it good, and being more . . . than the claret I had, you preferred it.

She died in the year 1794 at 88. of age, by which event we lost with her our yearly stock of this wine. Her landed property was sold and now a switz has vineyards in Ledanon & purchased the 1st. qualities of the wine of Ledanon. It is from him that I procured that wine, mentioning that I wanted the best & genuine as it was for you. Hoping he has (tho' wine salers are not genuinely to be trusted, many being called *Monsieur Mélange*) [Mister Mixer] acted faithfully. He has hope if these wines prove satisfactory to your palate, they will be demanded by the commerce of the United States.

I beg you to accept these two samples of wine to be drinked with your family and friends, if it turns out to your taste.

In talking about wines with you, you remember what I dared say of the famous chaix of Mr. Henry Bergasse at Marseilles where we dined together in '87. He left this place soon after the 23d. April 1789 when the populace of Marseilles rised a riot on that day, asking lower prices for bread & wine, pretending that since Bergasse had improved the quality of the wines of Provence, very near as good as Bordeaux claret, they had to pay [more] in price, & they threatened to destroy his chais. It was fortunately prevented, but he never returned here and died some years ago at Lyons.

This letter introduces not only the famous phrase "*Monsieur Mélange*," but wines which Jefferson apparently knew in France but had not previously mentioned in his orders: Ledanon and Paillerols. Taking them in reverse order of importance, Paillerols, which only appeared this once, was the old spelling for another wine of the region around Gaillac. Like the white

Gaillac called Cahusac which Jefferson got through Adams, the wine still exists, now called Peyrole.[38]

Of more interest is the Ledanon, which has fallen upon hard times, but in Jefferson's day was considered one of the best wines of France. Located in the modern department of Gard, in Languedoc, Ledanon is also spelled Ledenon. Jacquelin, in his exhaustive study of wine villages, called the wines rather harshly "tank wines," but also says that the local red *ordinaire* is "fairly fruity."[39] Cathalan's description of Ledanon is one of the better ones, with its stress on the Roman bridge over the Gard river near Nîmes. Today Nîmes has given its name to a much better-known product: the cloth once called "serge de Nîmes," now abbreviated in French and English to "denim."

The wine most known from the Ledanon region today is a lighter wine called Costières du Gard, meaning it is grown in hillside vineyards. Full-bodied but not heavy or Port-like as Jefferson described Ledanon, Costières has a good bouquet. Redding said it had "a very agreeable bouquet," and was once even "distinguished" enough to be "served pure at tables of the first rank in France," phraseology that sounds like Jefferson. It was also shipped to Burgundy for blending in weak years. Perhaps one day some of the best will again be served here at "tables of the first rank."[40]

More important in both Jefferson's time and ours is the third wine mentioned by Cathalan: Roussillon. Actually the name of the old southwest French province next to Spain, Roussillon is the home of several good wines, two of the best of which Jefferson liked. Still made on the same sheltered seaside hills around Perpignan from which Jefferson obtained them, the reds of Roussillon have been called by Hugh Johnson "formidable, the biggest and most highly colored of the Carignanes" (grape variety). The best of them have received A.C. or controlled place-name status under the titles Côtes du Roussillon and Côtes du Roussillon-Villages. Johnson compared them favorably to Châteauneuf-du-Pape, which is high praise.[41]

Jefferson's other Roussillon was a much different wine, but more esteemed then and now. Rivesaltes is a picturesque fishing village in Roussillon at the foothills of the Pyrenees, facing the Mediterranean, about five miles north of Perpignan on the highway to Narbonne. At Rivesaltes are Muscat and Malmsey vines said locally to have been brought from Cyprus by returning Crusaders. Mainly produced by small, farmer-owned co-ops, the Muscat of Rivesaltes is a very fine *vin doux naturel* (natural sweet wine) of relatively low alcohol (about 15 percent), similar to some of our own California late-harvest dessert wines. Jacquelin calls them "delicate, yet full of fire and bouqueted; with age the wine becomes sweet, perfumed and agreeable." That description is nearly identical to those given in Jefferson's time.[42]

During the previous month, John Martin Baker, who had promised Jefferson the Albaflor wine from Mallorca, wrote to say that he had ordered for him on the spot at Bordeaux some Barsac, from one of the best châteaux. It was the only Bordeaux, white or red, in Jefferson's cellar during his retirement. We know he received it, because it appeared on his cellar list for January 1820 and was still there, without a bottle having been drunk, in January 1824. By the following January it was gone, presumably drunk during Lafayette's visit in November 1824.

From John Martin Baker

May 15, 1816

I am sending to the care of D. Gelston, Esquire, New York, a case of Barsac white wine, growth of the Estate called Durancour. It is genuine and two years old. I have seen it drawn and bottled in my presence while there. I hope it may meet your approbation.

Whether this was the "dry" Barsac Jefferson earlier disliked or the delicious dessert wine we know and that he praised in the late 1780s is uncertain, but Jefferson appears to have waited a long time before drinking it.

In 1817, Jefferson's neighbor and protégé James Monroe became president. In a most unusual letter of congratulations to a new president from a former one, Jefferson devoted only the first and last sentences to the presidency, all the rest being confined to what wines Monroe should procure. Monroe, having lived in Paris as Jefferson had, seems to have been more of a wine lover than Madison, with whom Jefferson rarely mentioned the subject in writing. And when he was bringing back wines and books to Washington and Franklin, for Madison he chose exclusively books and no wines. It appears that Monroe's was a wine-loving administration, and Jefferson's letters on the subject peaked during this period.

Monticello, April 8, 1817

DEAR SIR, —I shall not waste your time in idle congratulations. You know my joy on the commitment of the helm of our Government to your hands.

I promised you when I should have received and tried the wines I had ordered from France and Italy to give you a note of the kinds which I should think worthy of your procurement; and this being the season for ordering them, so that they may come in the mild temperature of autumn, I now fulfil my promise.

Vin blanc liquoureux d'Hermitage de M. Jourdan à Tains. This costs about eighty-two and a half cents a bottle put on shipboard.

Vin de Ledanon (In Languedoc) something of the port character but higher flavored, more delicate, less rough. I do not know its price, but probably about twenty-five cents a bottle.

Vin de Roussillon. The best is that of Perpignan of Rivesalte of the crop of M. Durand. It costs seventy-two cents a gallon, bears bringing in a cask. If put into bottles there it costs eleven cents a bottle more than if bottled here by an inexplicable and pernicious arrangement of our tariff.

Vin de Nice. The crop called Bellet, of Mr. Sasserno, is the best. This is the most elegant every-day wine in the world and costs thirty-one cents the bottle. Not much being made, it is little known at the general markets.

Mr. Cathalan of Marseilles is the best channel for getting the first three of these wines and a good one for the *Nice,* being in their neighborhood and knowing well who makes the crops of best quality. The *Nice* being a wine foreign to France occasions some troublesome forms.

There is still another wine to be named to you, which is the wine of Florence called *Montepulciano,* with which Mr. Appleton can best furnish you. There is a particular very best crop of it known to him and which he has usually sent to me. This costs twenty-five cents per bottle. He knows, too, from experience how to have it so bottled and packed as to ensure its bearing the passage which in the ordinary way it does not. I have imported it through him annually ten or twelve years and do not think I have lost one bottle in one hundred.

I salute you with all my wishes for a prosperous and splendid voyage over
the ocean on which you are embarked, and with sincere prayers for the continuance of your life and health.[43]

His last attempt to use the State Department to forward wine letters having failed, Jefferson renewed his contacts with the administration,
hoping once more to use political clout to satisfy his wine needs. In a letter
to the State Department he wrote:

To Daniel Brent

June 8, 1817

Long indulgence by your predecessors in the direction of the department
of State in the privilege of getting my letters to Europe put under the same
cover with their official dispatches of the department has encouraged me to
ask the same Favor of you. My increasing aversion to writing will be a security
against any abuse of this Favor. On this ground I take the liberty of inclosing a
letter to Mr. Gallatin, and requesting of your goodness to give it a *safe* passage
with the dispatches of your office to that legation.

Jefferson tried later that year to ease the son of his old wine supplier
Sasserno into the position of American consul at Nice. He wrote to his former protégé, then rival, John Quincy Adams, who was serving as secretary
of state:

I was intimately acquainted with his father, the late Mr. Sasserno, one of the most
worthy & respectable merchants of Nice. The son being destined for commerce,
was sent to London where he staid some years in a commercial house, and learnt to
speak and write English well. He has now succeeded to the business of his father, &
I receive satisfactory assurances.

Our commerce with Nice is not inconsiderable. Its productions are the
same as those of the rest of Italy, fruits, oils, wines &c., but its wines are the
very first of that country, being of remarkable flavor & good body.

Many Americans pass their winters there, as do the English, & have hitherto been obliged to put themselves under the patronage of the English Consul.

As he told President Monroe, Jefferson liked nearly all of the wines received from Cathalan. In a proud grandfatherly letter, Jefferson wrote Cathalan in June to request wines for his grandson, whom he always referred to as "Jefferson," and who seems to have taken the place of the son he never had. Clearly he hoped the young man would follow in his footsteps as a wine lover, and sought to establish a cellar for him:

June 6, 1817

Dear Sir

My last to you was of Feb. 1. 16, since which I have received your several favors & the several parcels of wine & maccaroni came safe to hand. All of them were good, but those particularly esteemed for daily use were the Nice, Ledanon & Roussillon. The Nice de Bellet is superlatively fine.

The vin de Ledanon too is excellent, and the Roussillon of M. Durand very good. This last will be most sought for from this quarter as being lower priced & more adapted to the taste of this country, artificially created by our long restraint under the English government to the strong wines of Portugal and Spain. The Ledanon recalled to my memory what I had drunk at your table 30 years ago, and I am as partial to it now as then.

The return of the first swallow, just now seen, reminds me that the season is now arrived when the provision of another year should be attended to. I therefore am now directing a remittance to m Vaughan, at Philadelphia, requesting him to transmit 200 Dollars of it for myself and 65 Dollars for my grandson Thomas Jefferson Randolph. When you shall have received it, I will pray you to procure for me the wines and other articles stated in the invoice inclosed and to extend your kindness to my grandson also.

If you will have the goodness to have my parcels marked T. J. & his T. J. R. they will be taken care of by the way as if they were all mine, and will still be easily separated when they come to our hands.

There is a number of my friends who have tasted these wines at my table, and are so much pleased with their qualities and prices that they are about forming a company, and engaging an agent in Richmond to import for them once a year what each shall direct.

Our new President, Col. Monroe, has asked from me some information as to the wines I would recommend for his table and how to get them. I recommended to him the *vin blanc liqoreux* [rich white wine] d'Hermitage de M. Jourdan, the Ledanon, the Roussillon de M. Durand, and the Nice de Bellet of M. Sasserno, and that he should get them thro' you, as best knowing the particular qualities to which I refer.

I am anxious to introduce here these fine wines in place of the alcoholic wines of Spain and Portugal; and the universal approbation of all who taste them at my table will, I am persuaded, turn by degrees the current of demand from this part of our country that it will continue to spread *de proche en proche* [from friend to friend]. The delicacy and innocence of these wines will change the habit from the coarse & inebriating kinds hitherto only known here.

My own annual demand will generally be about what it is this year; the President probably the double or treble. The wine of M. Jourdan being chiefly for a *bonne bouche* [fine palate], I shall still ask for it occasionally.

In my letter recommending wines to our President, I propose to him the naming young m Sasserno our Consul at Nice.

Wishing all possible happiness to yourself & family, I salute you with unchanging friendship and respect.

Memorandum Enclosed
Vin de Perpignan de M. Durand.
100 gallons *en double futaille* [cask].
Vin de Ledanon. 100 bottles.
best olive oil. 5 gallons in bottles
Maccaroni 100 lb.
Raisins. 50 lb. those of Smyrna, sans pepins, would be preferred.
Anchovies. 1 doz. bottles.
  the above are for Th: Jefferson
The following articles are for Thomas J. Randolph.
60 gallons of Vin de Perpignan of M. Durand, in double casks.
100 bottles vin de M. Bergasse of the Quality of Bordeaux claret.

Jefferson began recommending his newly available wines to other Virginia friends, sometimes sounding a bit carried away with it all. He even began saying that the Montepulciano was "equal to the best Burgundy," and that Roussillon was "considered on a footing with Madeira." He was not a maverick, however, since many experts of the period agreed with him.[44] The wines received from Cathalan whetted his appetite for more:

January 18, 1818

The maccaroni, anchovies, oil, and vins rouges et blancs de M. Bergasse, announced in your letter of Aug. 27, are all received and approved, and I am in daily expectation of hearing further from you and of receiving the wines of Rivesalte, Ledanon & Nice. I find from consumption of the stock sent in 1816 that that asked in 1817 will not carry me thro' the present year. I must therefore request you to send me without delay 200 bottles of the vin rouge de M. Bergasse of the Bordeaux quality such as you sent my grandson.

By April 4 his shipment had arrived:

The Rivesalte & Nice wines arrived in Richmond 2 days ago. The Rivesalte will require time to settle before it can be fairly tasted. The Nice is good, but it is not exactly that of the preceeding year, which was a little silky, just enough to be sensible, & to please the palate of our friends beyond that of any wine I have ever seen. That now received is dry but well flavored. The Ledanon is arrived at Alexandria, but not yet got to Richmond. [Received]:

64	bottles of Rivesalte
300	bottles of Nice wine
5	gallons best olives of Aix
12	bottles of anchovies
50	lb. raisins of Smyrna, *sans pépins* [seedless]
100	lb. maccaroni

On the Library of Congress microfilm there appears an unusual invoice, undated, but from its placement dates from this time period. Its provenance is uncertain, but it probably came from Cathalan, judging from the contents. For now it is one of the few documents which mentions wines not corroborated by other Jefferson records, especially as to red Hermitage and Côte Rôtie of the Rhône, which Jefferson had visited, as well as some unusual white "Barjolais," or Beaujolais, not to mention the only "champain" of his retirement and some Blanquette of Limoux, which he listed in his cellar a few years later.

The presence of wines from Bergasse, whom only Jefferson seems to have imported from, indicates it was his, but it is curiously unrelated to his other wine records with which it was found.

No. 1. Blanquette de Limoux at 2 livre per bottle

    2. Muscat of Frontignan f. 1.50

    3. Champain f. 4.75

    4. Hermitage rouge of 1814 f. 3.

    5. red Cote-rotie f. 2.50

    6. white wine of Barjolais f. 1.25

Cost of the boxes & shipping expenses Here f. 13.85.

24 bottles in each box.

    Red Bergasse at f. 1. per bottle. white wine vinegar.

    Keg containing 23 olives a 50 ce[(ntimes)] 11.50.

Wine and Health

Without doubt the subject on which Jefferson issued the greatest number of contradictory statements was his health. As shown in great detail by the medical chronology compiled at Monticello, he was constantly telling one group of correspondents how healthy he had been all his life while at nearly the same time telling another group he was at "death's door" and had little more of what he called the *tedium vitae* to bear. He often pronounced distrust of doctors and "physick," yet often resorted to them anyway.

He once believed to some extent in the positive effects of mineral springs. As in France, when he went to Aix to heal a broken wrist whose swelling would not go down, he accepted an invitation to Warm Springs, Virginia, to try the waters. Arriving there feeling well, he left ill, and regretted the visit the rest of his life.

As he recalled his visit in 1825:

> Being at that period in the neighborhood of our Warm Springs, and well in health, I wished to be better and tried them. They have destroyed in a great degree my internal organism, and I have never since had a moment of perfect health.[45]

Jefferson stayed at Warm Springs from August 8 to August 27, 1818, writing to Martha on the fourteenth that he was bathing three times a day for fifteen minutes each. On the twenty-first, however, he developed boils on both buttocks, and left on the twenty-seventh in bad health, with the visit reducing him "to death's door" and apparently having a long-term effect on his digestion.

Jefferson continued to write letters, and although for a while he could eat little, one letter he wrote to a fellow Warm Springs visitor shows he had not lost his taste for wines, providing samples the moment he felt better.

> To Col. William Alston, Clifton, S.C.
>
> October 6, 1818
>
> While I had the pleasure of being with you at the Warm Springs, I took the liberty of recommending to you some wines of France & Italy, with a note of their prices & of the channels thro' which they may be got. But instead of calling for them on my recommendation only, I have thought it better that you should have some samples to direct your choice, for in nothing have the habits of the palate more decisive influence than in our relish of wines.
>
> I have therefore made up a box of a couple of dozen bottles, among which you will find samples of the wines of white Hermitage, Ledanon, Roussillon (of Rivesalte), Bergasse claret, all of France, and of Nice & Montepulciano of Italy. Some of them I hope will be found to your taste.

Whatever he was telling others about being at "death's door" that fall, wine was still on his mind.

One of Jefferson's favorite topics in later life was how wine promoted sobriety. Having disagreed with Hamilton on the point, and having mostly lost his fight to have taxes on imported wines lowered, he nevertheless kept coming back to the point. In November of 1818, when the wine-loving Monroe was president and Alexander Dallas of Pennsylvania was secretary of the treasury, Jefferson tried again. Rejecting Hamilton's argument that wine was a luxury drink for the rich, Jefferson argued the contrary to Monroe, who had seen the role wine played in French life while minister there. He also wrote to Dallas and to the new American minister to France, William H. Crawford of Georgia, to urge lower import duties on wine.

Originally from Virginia, Crawford emigrated to Georgia, and in 1824 was a leading candidate for president with Andrew Jackson, Henry Clay, and the eventual winner, John Quincy Adams. At one time it was rumored that Jefferson planned to support Crawford, but the latter cancelled a visit to Monticello in 1823, possibly losing Jefferson's endorsement and the election.[46] Whatever his politics, Crawford interested Jefferson because he was in a position to argue for lowering the import duties on French wines:

November 10, 1818

I think it a great error to consider a heavy tax on wines as a tax on luxury. On the contrary it is a tax on the health of our citizens. It is a legislative declaration that none but the richest of them shall be permitted to drink wine, and in effect a condemnation of all the middling & lower conditions of society to the poison of whisky, which is destroying them by wholesale, and ruining their families.

Whereas were the duties on the cheap wines proportioned to their first cost, the whole middling class of this country could have the gratification of that milder stimulus, and a great proportion of them would go into its use and banish the baneful whisky.

Surely it is not from the necessities of our treasury that we thus undertake to debar the mass of our citizens the use of not only an innocent gratification, but a healthy substitute instead of a bewitching poison.

The following month he wrote to a friend in France a letter which is better known than the one he wrote to Crawford, perhaps because it has so many quotable passages.

To M. de Neuville

December 13, 1818

I rejoice, as a moralist, at the prospect of a reduction of the duties on wine by our national legislature. It is an error to view a tax on that liquor as merely a tax on the rich. It is a prohibition of its use to the middling class of our citizens, and a condemnation of them to the poison of whiskey, which is desolating their houses.

No nation is drunken where wine is cheap, and none sober where the dearness of wine substitutes ardent spirits as the common beverage. It is, in truth, the only antidote to the bane of whiskey.[47]

The following year a physician asked Jefferson to explain how he remained so vigorous and healthy at his relatively advanced age. Not mentioning his recent health problems, Jefferson replied:

To Doctor Vine Utley

Monticello, March 21, 1819

I live so much like other people that I might refer to ordinary life as the history of my own. Like my friend the Doctor (Benjamin Rush), I have lived temperately, eating little animal food, and that not as an aliment so much as a condiment for the vegetables, which constitute my principal diet.

I double however, the Doctor's glass and a half of wine, and even treble it with a friend; but halve its effects by drinking the weak wines only. The ardent wines I cannot drink, nor do I use ardent spirits in any form.

Malt liquors and cider are my table drinks, and my breakfast, like that also of my friend, is of tea and coffee. I have been blest with organs of digestion which accept and concoct, without ever murmuring, whatever the palate chooses to consign to them, and I have not yet lost a tooth by age.[48]

This letter, much quoted by those wishing to prove that Jefferson was nearly a vegetarian, in context shows only that he ate less meat *late* in life, especially after his Warm Springs debacle. Nor does it mean that beer and cider were his only table drinks for *all* of his life, since during most of it he drank wine with his meals.

Most interesting of his wine comments in the Utley letter, however, is his reference to quantity. He customarily drank three glasses at dinner, and four and a half with a friend. Depending on the size of the glasses, that could well mean half or most of a modern 750 millilitre bottle.

In what was to be his last letter to Cathalan, Jefferson summarized his mature tastes in wine. His vocabulary is that of a finished connoisseur. Scraps of French protrude everywhere:

May 26, 1819

I will explain to you the terms by which we characterize different qualities of wine. They are

> 1. *Sweet* wines, such as Frontignan & Lunel of France, Pacharetti doux of Spain; Calcavalla of Portugal, le vin du Cap, &c.
> 2. *Acid* wines, such as Vin de Graves, du Rhein, de Hocheim etc.
> 3. *Dry* wines, having not the least either of sweetness or of acidity in them, as Madère, Pacharetti sec, vin d'oporto and the Ledanon, which I call a dry wine also.
> 4. *Silky* wines which are in truth a compound in their taste of the *dry* wines dashed with a little *sweetness*, barely sensible to the palate. The Silky Madeira which we sometimes get here, is made so by putting a small portion of Malmsey with the dry Madeira.

There is another quality of wine which we call *rough* or *astringent*, and you also I believe call it astringent, which is often found in both the dry & silky wines. There is something of this quality in the Ledanon, and a great deal of it in the vin d'oporto, which is not only dry, but astringent approaching almost bitterness.

I will now say why I go into these details with you. In the first place you are not to conclude that I am become a *buveur* [drinker]. My measure is a sober one of 3. or 4. glasses at dinner, & not a drop at any other time. But to these 3 or 4 glasses *Je suis bien friand* [I am very attached].

Congress, at their last session, still continuing the fixed duties on certain enumerated wines, reduced that on all *non-enumerated* from 15 to 6 cents the bottle. Mr. Bergasse should take care that his wines not be invoiced or shipped under any enumerated names, and particularly his claret, or red wine qualité de Bordeaux.

I have added to my list of wines this year 50 bottles of vin muscat blanc de lunel. I should have much preferred a wine which should be *sweet* and *astringent* but I knew of none. If you know of any, not too high priced, I would thank you to substitute it instead of the Lunel:

60	gallons Rivesalte
150	bottles vin de Bellet de Nice
150	bottles of Ledanon
150	bottles vin rouge de Bergasse qualité de Bordeaux
50	bottles vin muscat blanc de Lunel
5	gallons oil of Aix
100	lb. of maccaroni
12	bottles anchovies
50	lb. raisins de Smyrne sans pépins, if to be had, if not then others.

The long friendship of Jefferson and Cathalan ended with the latter's death in 1819, probably before he even received Jefferson's letter of May 26. Jefferson learned of the event by reading about it in the paper. He called it in a letter of July 28 to his daughter Martha "an important loss to me."[49]

The death of Cathalan did not deter Jefferson from importing. Two years later he wrote to a wine merchant in Richmond:

To William Wallace

August 19, 1821

Sir

I thank you for your attention in offering me a supply of claret, & if I were in want I should be induced by it to try its quality, but importing my wines myself, I am sufficiently in stock at present, and expect in autumn a year's supply written for some time ago.

This letter was the first one I found on the Library of Congress microfilm indicating that Jefferson had another European supplier after Cathalan. Soon, however, I was to find that his flow of wines had remained constant.

It was once thought that in the last seven or eight years of his life, Jefferson was so poor that he was reduced to drinking Scuppernong. He did of course suffer financial reversals after the Panic of 1819. Yet visitors to Monticello, notably Daniel Webster in 1824, said that Jefferson had fine wines in his cellar right down to his death in 1826, even though the names of the wines were hard to decipher from the manuscripts and were often misspelled in published editions. Now we know for certain that Webster was right.

First, careful editing of the Jefferson *Memorandum Books* by James Bear and Cinder Stanton shows that he did have many good wines in his cellar throughout his late years. Recently, copies of his letters, down to his very last, have been deciphered by Dr. Jefferson Looney, editor of the Retirement Series of the *Papers*. The letters explain and correspond exactly with the wine entries in his *Memorandum Books*. The letters, written mostly in Jefferson's own elderly but unmistakable hand, show that his curiosity about wine, and his taste for experimenting, remained active until the end.

On September 27, 1819, Cathalan's representative Julius Olivier wrote to say he would "fulfill your order," but having no Muscat wine, would substitute some "old vin cuit" from Bergasse instead. On October 9 Olivier wrote again, saying Cathalan's successor as consul, Joshua Dodge, would be getting the Bellet wine of Nice from Sasserno, but that

> Bergasse would not broach one of his large casks of *vin cuit* for so few bottles, so I have put 4 bottles for you to taste. I have put in 18 bottles vin cuit & 6 bottles claret of Limoux for a trial.

The enclosed invoice from Olivier also included the usual macaroni, olive oil, and anchovies. That summer Jefferson placed his annual wine order, writing to the new American consul at Marseilles:

> To Joshua Dodge
>
> July 13, 1820
>
> The Nice wines you were kind enough to find came safe. It is time for the order of my annual supply. The 6 bottles that Olivier sent of Clairette wine of

Limoux from M. Chevalier we found so much to our taste that I have asked 150 bottles of it this year if you would please get it exactly of the same quality.

Jefferson concluded by listing his request for 1820:

I gross (say 12 doz. bottles) Bergasse's claret, taking care not to call it by that name on account of the high duties here on all *clarets*.

150	bottles of Ledanon
150	bottles vin clairette de Limoux from Mr. Chevalier
30	gallons vin sec de Rivesalte de M. Durand
24	bottles virgin olive oil of Aix
50	lb. Maccaroni (those of Naples preferred)
6	bottles of Anchovies.

It is hard to say just what the "claret" of Limoux was, whether simply a light-red wine from near the town of that name, or whether a wine from the *clairette* grape, which alternate spelling Jefferson used, and which Redding said was one of the most popular Limoux wines in their day.

In his account book entry for February 23, 1820, Jefferson recorded receiving precisely the wines and quantities on Olivier's invoice. Only the Muscat of Rivesaltes, which he noted was a "cask of 31 velts" was still en route from Richmond when the others arrived. A *velt* was about two gallons.[50]

The *vin cuit*, or "cooked wine," similar to Italian *vino cotto* today, was highly prized in Jefferson's time, but mostly unknown in America. Cyrus Redding described it as originally coming from Greece and being most popular in Italy and deep southern France. It was generally made from Muscat grapes, of the richest and finest, gathered only in the hottest part of the day when there was no dew, then exposed to the sun on mats for five or six days, after which the pressed juice and pulp were cooked down to about two-thirds of their original volume, making a rich and concentrated wine, deep amber and "pleasant to the taste," according to Redding. When old it was often "passed off" as Muscat wine of Cyprus.[51]

Today *vins cuits* are rarely seen in the U.S. under that name, but perhaps that will change as Muscats become more popular. Late-harvest Muscats and moscatos now regularly win gold medals at U.S. international wine competitions. These wines, while a far cry from the lavish ones of his presidency, were very good, and excellent for the price, which was some 75 percent lower.

Satisfied with this order, Jefferson placed a nearly identical one with Dodge the next year on April 19, 1821, again paying two hundred dollars for it. The only change was the substitution of a cask of sweet Muscat of Rivesalte for the dry Rivesaltes he had ordered in 1820. The 1821 wines were shipped in the cool months of fall. The wines from Boston arrived and that same week he made an inventory of his wine cellar:

JANUARY 7, 1822—STOCK OF WINES ON HAND—

	BOTTLES
Rousillon of Rivesalte dry, a cask of 62 gal. plus	25
Muscat de Rivesalte	6
Ledanon	145
Claret of Bergasse	55
Limoux	25
Old Muscat 18; vin cuit 3; vin cuit de Provence 17	38
Barsac	20
Scuppernon 45 + 26 + 1	72
	386
Received this day from Marseilles as follows:	
Muscat de Rivesalte	150
Ledanon	150
Claret of Bergasse	144
Vin blanc de Limoux	150
	594

Whole stock on hand 62 gall + 980

Despite his financial problems, Jefferson had at age seventy-eight a cellar of nearly a thousand bottles.

During his last years, much of Jefferson's energy went into founding the University of Virginia, which he thought should rival Harvard as the great center of American learning. But raising the money and convincing the right people that such a project was necessary was no easy task. Once, thinking he would quit, he suggested, again using a wine metaphor, that Virginia students should be sent to Transylvania College in Kentucky, since that former part of Virginia had "more of the flavor of the old cask."[52]

Jefferson's greatest task in retirement was letter writing. As his granddaughter later wrote, he was one of the most prolific correspondents in American history:

> [T]he letters received by him that were preserved amounted to twenty-six thousand at the time of his death; while the copies left by him, of those which he himself had written, numbered sixteen thousand. These were but a small portion of what he wrote, as he wrote numbers of which he retained no copies.[53]

Jefferson put much thought into his letters, even the simplest. His talent for epigram was well suited to letter writing, and he obviously relished it. Yet he certainly had too much of a good thing, and a constant lament of his retirement years was about his endless correspondence, which he called his "epistolary corvée" (chore). To Adams he described his feelings in 1816: "My greatest oppression is a correspondence afflictingly laborious." The following year he pictured to his friend his routine:

> January 11, 1817
> From sunrise to one or two o'clock, and often from dinner to dark, I am drudging at the writing table. All this to answer letters into which neither interest nor inclination on my part enters, and often from persons whose names I have never before heard. Yet, writing civilly, it is hard to refuse them civil answers.[54]

This letter tells volumes about what sort of man Thomas Jefferson was: diligent to a fault, compelled to do what was right and proper despite personal cost. No one ever said he could not complain about it to his friends, however:

To John Adams

I happened to turn to my letter-list some time ago, and a curiosity was excited to count those received in a single year. It was the year before the last. I found the number to be one thousand two hundred and sixty-seven, many of them requiring answers of elaborate research, and all to be answered with due attention and consideration. Take an average of this number for a week or a day, and I will repeat the question suggested by other considerations in mine of the 1st.

Is this life? At best it is but the life of a millhorse, who sees no end to his circle but in death. To such a life that of a cabbage is paradise.[55]

The metaphor of living like a cabbage was frequent in Jefferson's old-age letters. He did not like being sedentary. He also occasionally referred to himself, when his memory faltered, as "an old, half-strung fiddle."[56] Like most people his age, he noticed that too many of the memorable events of his current life involved the illness and death of old friends. As he wrote to Adams:

June 1, 1822

The papers tell us that General Stark is off at the age of 93. Charles Thompson still lives at about the same age—cheerful, slender as a grasshopper, and so much without memory that he scarcely recognizes the members of his household. Is this life? It is at most the life of a cabbage.[57]

In November of that year Jefferson broke his left wrist, adding to the pain and stiffness of rheumatism in his fingers and the lasting effects of breaking his right wrist in Paris, which never totally healed. Together, his infirmities made writing almost impossible, and his granddaughters began copying his letters from dictation. As he wrote to Lafayette the next year:

November 4, 1823

My dear Friend—

Two dislocated wrists and crippled fingers have rendered writing so slow and laborious as to oblige me to withdraw from nearly all correspondence—not however, from yours, while I can make a stroke with a pen.[58]

Despite his sore fingers and aching wrists, Jefferson wrote to order his annual wines from Marseilles. In a letter of June 11, 1822, to Dodge and his partner Oxnard, he noted without further elaboration that the "articles" he had ordered the previous year were all "received and approved." He also noted he was sending $180 for that year, $137.44 for himself and the rest for his grandson Thomas Jefferson Randolph. At the bottom of the letter were his wine requests in his own handwriting, and in Randolph's handwriting his separate requests, as follows:

For TJ

100 b[ottles] Ledanon

240 b. vin rouge de Bergasse

125 b. Muscat de Rivesalte

100 b. vin blanc de Limoux

For TJR

4 boxes claret 96 b. = $18

1 box Muscat 24   9

1 box Limoux 24   9.

When Jefferson received these wines in November of that same year, he made an inventory which tells us exactly what he and his guests were drinking:

STATEMENT OF WINES ON HAND   NOV. 26, 1822

	JAN. 7	NOV. 25	REC'D NOV. 25	TOTAL ON HAND
Ledanon	295	216	100	316
Claret	199	none	144	144

Limoux	175	114	75	189
Muscat Rivesalte	156	66	100	166
Scuppernon	72	31	–	31
Barsac	20	20	–	20
	955	447		866

In a letter dated June 23, 1823, Jefferson noted that in the interim Joshua Dodge had made a voyage to America and visited Jefferson at Monticello. His 1823 order seemed to lean a little more toward red wines than before:

100	Ledanon
100	red Bergasse
50	Muscat de Rivesalte
25	white wine of Limoux
30	Gal. brandy.

It was unusual to find Jefferson ordering brandy, although he had kept spirits for servants, workmen, and such guests as wanted it. He left no comment as to whether any of it was for himself to relieve the discomforts of rheumatism and other old age pains. The total cost of this order, $71.39, was half that of the previous year. It was a good thing Jefferson received wines that year, for he would need them in 1824, when the Marquis de Lafayette came for a long and festive visit.

Jefferson made no inventory in 1823, but he did in 1824, so we know what his cellar was like when Lafayette arrived. From that record, it appears that consumption had remained stable, and that the entertaining at Monticello went on apace.

On January 9, 1824, the day his 1823 order arrived, Jefferson made this entry in his account book:

	OLD STOCK NOW ON HAND	TOTAL NOW REC'D	ON HAND NOW
Ledanon	83	100	183
Claret	0	100	100

Limoux	4	100	29
Muscat	53	50	103
Scuppernon	11	–	11
Barsac	20	–	20
	171	275	446

On June 6, 1824, Jefferson placed his annual order with Dodge and Oxnard. The only new item, or rather the reintroduction of an old item, was to

> have added to my usual bill a 30 gal. cask of your vin ordinaire such as you drink with water at your own tables. I found the wines of that description so cheap, even at Paris, that they would make a cheaper table drink here than even our cyder & beer.

At the bottom of the letter he listed his wants, and the amounts, redefining, however, the name of the white wine of Limoux:

150	red Bergasse
100	red Ledanon
100	Blanquette de Limoux
50	Muscat de Rivesalte
30	gal. cask vin ordinaire
3 1/2	doz. b. virgin oil of Aix
12	b. anchovies
80	lb. maccaroni.

The reference to the venerable wine called Blanquette de Limoux is notable. Both in Jefferson's time and ours, this name, older than Champagne, referred to a white, sparkling wine. Today the California winery colorfully named Toad Hollow imports an excellent, lightly sweet sparkling Blanquette de Limoux "methode ancienne" available across America, but whose French origin is barely recognizable in tiny print at the bottom of the label.[59]

Jefferson hoped his 1824 wines would arrive early because Lafayette was coming. In August of 1824, learning that Lafayette was visiting John Adams in Massachusetts, Jefferson wrote to him, encouraging a visit to Monticello.[60] His cellar, even in January 1824, right after he received his 1823 order, had less than half as many bottles as it had just two years earlier, and at the rate the Jeffersons seemed to drink wine, it was probably down to a quarter of its normal capacity when Lafayette arrived in November of 1824.

Lafayette Visits Jefferson, Drinks Up His Wine Cellar

When Lafayette visited Adams, he found him scarcely able to rise from his chair, and unable to feed himself, but with his mind unimpaired. Lafayette was much younger at sixty-nine, and while in America from August 15, 1824, through September 3, 1825, visited every state, at one stretch covering over five thousand miles in four months by riverboat, canal, and coach.[61] He arrived at Monticello on November 4, 1824, and stayed until November 15, spending most of his time talking with Jefferson, whom he found "much aged" after thirty-five years, but "marvelously well" for eighty-one. Lafayette himself had put on so much weight that Madison did not even recognize him.[62]

The public highlight of Lafayette's visit was a dinner for four hundred under the rotunda of the new University of Virginia. Both Jefferson and Madison were present, and there was much toasting. Also present was George Ticknor, who had become a close friend. With him was his friend Joseph Coolidge of Massachusetts, there to woo Jefferson's granddaughter Ellen Randolph. He later married her and took her north, where by missing the ravages of the Civil War the Coolidges were able to preserve many of Jefferson's papers, including many of his letters on wine.

No mention of what Lafayette thought of all Jefferson's wines now remains. On May 9, 1825, the riverboat on which he was travelling the Ohio sank in the middle of the night. The vigorous Lafayette swam safely to shore, but said every letter and memo he had of his famous voyage through America was lost, and with them no doubt his recollections of Monticello and its wines. It is certain that Lafayette still liked wine, however, because two of the main items he mentioned saving from the wreck were a cask of claret and a cask of Madeira. Or perhaps they were just floating and easy to save.[63]

In any case someone in his party, which included his son George Washington Lafayette and secretary Auguste Levasseur, liked wine, for right after they left, Jefferson wrote to Bernard Peyton that he had to replenish his supply of red wine, which was almost entirely consumed during the visit.[64]

Fortunately for us it was not all gone, because the next month one of Jefferson's most famous and observant visitors, Daniel Webster, came to dinner. With him were Ticknor and two of the new professors from Europe that Jefferson had recruited for the University of Virginia. Webster added a better description of the wines and Jefferson's taste in foods than anyone had in several years:

December 1824

His diet is simple, but he seems restrained only by his taste. His breakfast is tea and coffee, bread always fresh from the oven, of which he does not seem afraid, with sometimes a slight accompaniment of cold meat. He enjoys his dinner well, taking with his meat a large portion of vegetables.

He has a strong preference for the wines of the continent, of which he has many sorts of excellent quality, having been more than commonly successful in his mode of importing and preserving them. Among others, we found the following, which are very rare in this country, and apparently not at all injured by transportation: L'Ednau, Muscat, Samian, and Blanchette de Limoux.

Dinner is served in half Virginian, half French style, in good taste and abundance. No wine is put on the table till the cloth is removed.[65]

Webster, a politician and orator, and not the author of the famous dictionaries, couldn't spell Jefferson's wines. Whether he did not write them down, or simply tried to guess at them phonetically we don't know, but from our knowledge of Jefferson's cellar lists and letters we know that Lafayette had not drunk all of Jefferson's wines, for Webster has identified for us at least three of them: L'Ednau is obviously Ledanon; the Muscat that of Rivesalte; and the Blanchette the Blanquette of Limoux. The Samian is more curious, but the most famous Samian wine was the Muscat of Samos, made with sundried grapes by the ancient Greek method. Webster's "Samian" probably referred to Jefferson's *vin cuit* Muscat from Provence. It was made by similar methods and with similar results, and was first suggested to Jefferson by Bergasse as a substitute for old Muscat of Samos.

Ticknor and Webster noted Jefferson's continued delight in after-dinner conversation over wine, seeing that the University of Virginia had joined Europe as his favored topics. Ticknor, who had earlier noted Jefferson's "discursive manner and love of paradox," and that he loved "old books and young society," found him little changed in his temperament, spirit, or relish of wines. It seems that, from the reactions of these visitors, Jefferson still had enough of the "oil of conversation" in his cellar at the end of 1824 to entertain them in the style everyone had expected, however near bankruptcy he actually was.

After the departure of Lafayette and Webster, Jefferson directed Bernard Payton in December 1824 to pay for his wines from Dodge that had just arrived in New York.[66] He noted in his account book for January 4, 1825, that the "wines rec'd from Dodge & Oxnard Dec. 14 & this day" were:

	FOR MYSELF	FOR T.J.R.	TOTAL
vin rouge de Bergasse	150	100	250
red wine of Ledanon	100	–	100
Blanquette de Limoux	75	25	100
Muscat de Rivesalte	50	25	75
	375	150	525

In the same entry, without specifying any figure, Jefferson noted cryptically that at this time, which was just after Lafayette and his party left, "My preceeding stock was all but out."

No order for wines in the year 1825 has been located, perhaps because Jefferson was too ill during that period to write it himself, and therefore did not keep a copy. When Lafayette made his farewell visit in August of the previous year, Jefferson was too ill to leave Monticello for Charlottesville for the farewell dinner for his old friend at the University of Virginia. The medical chronology shows Jefferson was already taking laudanum (liquid opium) for the pain of what was to be his final illness.

We do know, however, that a wine order was placed for 1825, because his January 21, 1826, account book shows an entry for Bernard Peyton to pay the collector of the port of New York the duties and freight on another three hundred bottles of wine and the usual cases of virgin olive oil, anchovies, and macaroni from Dodge.

JEFFERSON'S LAST WINE CELLAR

There is also his final cellar list, made just six months before his death, which is nearly identical to those for the last several years, but had nearly 150 *more* bottles of the same types of wines than he had when Lafayette arrived, showing continuing interest in his wine cellar.

FEBRUARY 1, 1826—STOCK OF WINE

	OLD STOCK ON HAND	NOW RECEIVED	TOTAL
vin rouge de Bergasse	142	–	142
red Ledanon	37	150	187
blanquette de Limoux	49	–	49
Muscat de Rivesalte	36	150	186
Claret from Richmond	22	–	22
	286		586

Scuppernon quant. suf.

In his final days, apparently suffering painful complications of an enlarged prostate or related illness, Jefferson was probably temporarily beyond the analgesic powers of the light wines he loved. Too ill to receive visitors or to write much himself beyond the essential, he left few comments on his last cellar except that he didn't care to count how many bottles of Scuppernong he had, apparently judging that he had a "quantity sufficient" for him. But the old man had clearly not lost his palate.

The most striking evidence regarding Jefferson's last wine cellar is the last letter of his life, written on June 25, 1826, less than a month before he died. In it he directs that his agent Bernard Peyton pay eighteen dollars for duties and shipping to the collector of the port where his 1826 wines were to arrive:

> Monticello June 25 [18]26.
>
> Dear Sir,
>
> I have had no information from Dodge & Isnard [Oxnard] but of the time of shipping the wine, the vessel and port. The papers the collector was so kind as to send, never came to my hand, but as he ascertained the duty &c. I have this day desired Colo Peyton to remit him 18 D. and I will give you the further trouble of requesting him to ship the wines to Peyton's address who will pay all charges. I salute you with great affection and respect.
>
> TH: JEFFERSON

These wines were the annual supply from southern France he had been ordering throughout the 1820s. Hoping to live at least until July 4, and perhaps well beyond, he was restocking his cellar with wines for all occasions: Blanquette de Limoux as an aperitif before dinner; white *vin ordinaire* and light red clarets from Bergasse to drink with dinner; and some classic Muscats and Port-like Ledanon to savor after dinner, as they chose.[67]

At Jefferson's last illness, his wine cellar was filled with nearly fifty cases of good wines with a new shipment en route. Had he survived, as he clearly hoped he would, he and his family and friends would have had many more long and happy Monticello evenings, with wine, to enjoy.

CHAPTER EIGHT

Vineyards at Monticello

(1770–1826)

The great desideratum of making at home a good wine.

—JEFFERSON TO LEVIN GALE (1816)[1]

Throughout his long life, Thomas Jefferson tried to make wine from his own grapevines. An avid gardener, he planted and studied the progress of hundreds of plants of every kind, including dozens of species of wine-grape vines. His massive *Garden Book* shows the magnitude of this favorite hobby and how fervently he pursued it. Yet he was modest about his knowledge, admitting in one of his most famous quotes: "Though an old man, I am but a young gardener."[2]

Jefferson was unsuccessful as a farmer, apparently never making a profit from any of his plantations. It was much the same with his vineyards: he planted many, but never succeeded in making a drop of wine because he never managed to grow enough grapes to make wine. Despite his reverses in grape growing, his enthusiasm for plants and planting never waned:

I have often thought that if heaven had given me choice of my position and calling, it should have been on a rich spot of earth, well watered, and near a good market for the productions of the garden. No occupation is so delightful to me as the culture of the earth, and no culture comparable to that of the garden.

Such a variety of subjects, some one always coming to perfection, the failure of one thing repaired by the success of another, and instead of one harvest a continued one throughout the year. Under a total want of demand except for our family table, I am still devoted to the garden.[3]

He exaggerated his beliefs on the subject only slightly when he said: "The greatest service which can be rendered any country is to add an useful plant to its culture."[4] Among the plants Jefferson most wanted to encourage in America was the wine vine. After his stay in Europe he became discouraged about its commercial possibilities, but he always favored home winemaking, and during the wine embargoes of the War of 1812, he even began to rethink whether a commercial wine industry was not a good idea after all.

Although his vineyards at Monticello failed, either from neglect during his absences or from vine diseases, Jefferson never gave up the idea. In the process he cultivated at Monticello not only every native American vine he could obtain, but also vines from the finest vineyards of France, Germany, and Italy. Despite his failures, he died with the belief that his experiments were a useful encouragement to others, and even his own failure to make wine never dissuaded him from his idea that America would one day become a great winemaking country.

In the year Jefferson moved to Monticello, 1770, the first mention of vine-planting appears in a letter from George Wythe:

> March 9, 1770
> I send you some nectarines and apricot graffs and grape vines, the best I had; and have directed your messenger to call upon Major Taliaferro for some of his.[5]

No notation exists indicating whether Jefferson planted Wythe's vines, but the following spring he planted grapes obtained from his neighbor Nicholas Lewis, who later had charge of Monticello while Jefferson was in Europe. In the *Garden Book* for March 28, 1771, appears the entry: "planted 5 grapes from N. Lewis's on S.E. edge of garden."[6] On April 2, 1773, he noted: "planted 50 vines of various kinds from The Forest."[7] The Forest was the family home of Martha Wayles Skelton, Jefferson's wife. The spot where Jefferson planted the fifty vines from the Forest has never been exactly determined.

That same year Jefferson acquired a new neighbor, the Italian Philip Mazzei, who rapidly became the major influence on his grape-growing attempts. Mazzei brought with him several *vignerons*, or vineyard workers, all well schooled in the arts of vine growing and winemaking. Descendants of some of them still live near

Monticello, and one is even said to teach at the University of Virginia. In addition to the *vignerons*, Mazzei also brought with him thousands of vine cuttings from Italy, France, Spain, and Portugal to plant in Virginia.

Jefferson soon put to use the skills of the Tuscan wine growers, noting in the *Garden Book* for April 6, 1774:

> Planted 30 vines just below where the new garden wall will run, towards the westernmost end. 8 of them at the western-most end of the row were Spanish Raisins (Muscats) from Colo. Bland's. Next to them were 16 native vines from Winslow's in New Kent [County] and at the easternmost end were 6 native vines of Monticello. They were planted by some Tuscan vignerons who came over with Mr. Mazzei. the manner was as follows:
>
> A trench 4.-f. deep and 4.-f. wide was dug. at the bottom were put small green bushes, and on them a thin coat of dung and earth mixed, which raised the bed to within 2 1/2 feet of the surface. the cuttings which were from 3 1/2 to 6. f. long, and which had been hitherto buried in the earth, were then produced, about 18. I[inches] on their butts were dip into a thick paste made of cowdung and water and then planted in the bottom, the Raisins, 3.-f. apart, the rest about 2. f. having a stick stuck by each to which it was bound with bear grass in order to support it while the earth should be drawn in.
>
> The earth was then thrown in, the mould first, and afterwards the other earth in the same order in which it was dung, leaving the bottom clay for the last. the earth was thrown in very loose & care was taken to avoid trampling in it. the trench was not quite filled, but left somewhat hollowing to receive & retain the water, & the superfluous earth was left on each side without the trench. then the supporting sticks were drawn out and would have served for the other rows had the plantation been to be continued. in such a case, the rows are to be 4 f. apart, so that in fact the whole surface is taken up to the depth of 4 f.
>
> The best way of doing it is to dig every other trench, and leave the earth which is thrown out exposed for a twelve month. then the vines may be planted at any time from the middle of November to the first week in April. afterwards dig the other alternate trenches, and leave the earth of these also exposed for a twelvemonth. when the latter trenches are planted, leave the superfluous earth in ridges between the rows of vines till by the subsidence of the earth it becomes necessary to pull it into the trenches. if any of your grapes turn out illy, cut off the vine & ingraft another on the stock. an acre in vines where they are 2 1/2 f. apart in the row will admit 4316. in all. [8]

The success of these vines was short lived. On May 5, 1774, Jefferson noted in his *Garden Book* that the preceding night there had been a killing "frost which destroyed almost every thing."[9] The frost also froze all the vines and saplings previously planted at Colle by Mazzei,[10] and they remained without leaves throughout the summer until the following spring. In Williamsburg the frost was so severe that it "hath destroyed all the Grapes in the public vineyard, which was in a very Flourishing State before."[11] Mazzei described the events thus:

> The spring after my arrival, something occurred which I was told had not happened before within the memory of man. On the night of May 4, 1774, a frost, caused by a northwest wind, ruined the corn and the wheat just above the ground, froze the small oak and other young trees, and caused all other trees to shed their leaves, which did not bud again until the following year. It was horrible to see the woods entirely stripped of leaves in summer, as if it had been midwinter. The bunches of grapes were already quite large, but they froze with the new crop. The old part of the vine, from which the branches had sprung, suffered too.
>
> But the vines put out new shoots, which produced about half the amount of grapes of the preceding years, and ripened at the usual season in the woods and gardens. Dr. Bland, the nephew of Mr. Richard Bland, who had been in Europe and had studied medicine at Edinburgh, said to me: "I assure you that in this country only fire could destroy the vines".

Undaunted, Mazzei commissioned the entry of six more Tuscan *vignerons* from Lucca during the summer of 1774.[12] Mazzei later wrote with great optimism of his activities and hopes in that year:

> Every now and then I went to my estate to see how my orders were being executed, to give new instructions, and to discuss public and private matters with Mr. Jefferson.
>
> I learned from my men that, in their wanderings through the woods in search of varieties of wild grapes, they had seen no less than 200. I examined 36 varieties on my own estate, and among them were some good, some mediocre, some bad, and some downright worthless ones. I chose 6 of the best to make two casks of wine, one of which I kept for myself, giving the other to my men, who did not drink it, because they found they could sell it at a shilling—the equivalent of one lira—a bottle.
>
> I believe that in no other country are conditions so favorable to the culture of grapevines as there. I measured two vines, the stems of which were

more than a yard and a half in circumference. July grape cuttings came up in such abundance that my men urged me to make wine. The first year, the various kinds that reached me in good condition produced shoots of such length that Vincenzo Rossi remarked: "Master, don't write home about it, because nobody there would believe you and they would call you a liar".[13]

THE VIRGINIA WINE COMPANY

With his land and labor force complete, Mazzei began drawing up plans in November of 1774 which he entitled "Proposal for Forming a Company or Partnership for the purpose of raising and making Wine, Oil, agruminous Plants, and Silk."[14] This was the famous Wine Company that many Jefferson buffs have heard of. The original partnership document is lost, but two copies remain. The one at the Library of Congress sounds like pure Mazzei, giving nearly total discretion to the "factor" of the enterprise, Mazzei, to plant vines and make wines as he saw fit. Thirty-seven subscribers are shown, including Jefferson, Washington, Peyton Randolph, and George Mason. Each had to put up at least fifty pounds sterling to buy one share.[15]

An executive committee of eight members had full power to act for the others. Interestingly, Jefferson was not a member, although his close friend John Page was. Royal governor Earl Dunsmore was a member, and owned more shares (four) than any other member except Mazzei himself. Obviously Dunsmore did not think at that time that divisions between these educated planters and the king would ever reach open revolution and war. The colonial subscribers probably did not either.

For nearly four years, despite the war, Mazzei's vineyards went very well. On January 27, 1779, he wrote enthusiastically to General Washington: "This country is better calculated than any other I am acquainted with for the produce of wine."[16]

That same year two events destroyed Mazzei's. First he was sent to Europe as commercial agent for Virginia. Then a group of Hessian prisoners of war were quartered at Colle. General Riedesel and Captain Geismar of Hesse became good friends of Jefferson and he later visited Geismar in Germany.[17] Jefferson later described what he believed happened to Mazzei's vineyards at Colle:

To Albert Gallatin

January 25, 1793

We made up a subscription for him of 2000 pounds sterling, and he began his experiment on a piece of land adjoining to mine. His intention was, before the time of his people should expire, to import more from Italy. He planted a considerable vineyard, and attended to it with great diligence for three years. The war then came on, the time of his people soon expired, some of them enlisted, others chose to settle on other lands and labor for themselves; some were taken away by the gentlemen of the country for gardeners, so that there did not remain a single one with him, and the interruption of navigation prevented his importing others. In this state of things he was himself employed by the State of Virginia to go to Europe as their agent. He rented his place to General Riedesel, whose horses in one week destroyed the whole labor of three or four years; and thus ended an experiment which, from every appearance, would in a year or two more have established the practicability of that branch of culture in America.[18]

Others describe what happened differently, blaming the destruction of Mazzei's vineyards not on the wine-loving Germans, but on the horse-loving English:

> Major Irving and his friends had paid a fancy price for the rent of Colle. They particularly liked it because there was forage for their horses, they said. The horses were already pastured there, and a long correspondence ensued while they wrangled over terms with Riedesel. . . . General Riedesel was an ardent gardener. From his correspondence with the English major, it looks as though it must have been Major Irving's horses, not Riedesel's, that ruined Mazzei's vineyards.[19]

Although he came back to Virginia after the war, Mazzei was never able to summon the workers, money, or local interest to begin a new Virginia vineyard company. In 1785 he left Virginia for good, spending the rest of his days in Europe, on several occasions sending Jefferson cuttings of the best Italian wine grapes for planting at Monticello.

As always, the most vivid and direct account comes from Isaac. He recalled not only Mazzei and his Tuscan *vignerons*, but even the Hessian prisoners of war, and correctly pronounced phonetically the names of both the Italians and the Germans:

> He [Jefferson] talked French and Italian. Madzay talked with him. His place was called Colle. General Redhazel [Riedesel] stayed there. He [Mazzei] lived at Monticello with Old Master some time . . . Mazzei brought to Monticello Antonine, Jovanini, Francis, Modena, and

Bellegrini, all gardeners. My Old Master's garden was monstrous large: two rows of palings, all 'round ten feet high . . .

Isaac knowed General Redhazel. He stayed at Colle, Mr. Mazzei's place, two miles and a quarter from Monticello—a long wood house built by Mazzei's servants. The servant's house built of little saplin's of oak and hickory instead of laths then plastered up. It seemed as if de folks in dem days hadn't sense enough to make laths. The Italian people raised plenty of vegetables; cooked the most victuals of any people Isaac ever see.[20]

Isaac and Bacon never mentioned any wine being made at Monticello, and, being reliable sources, probably would have if there had been any. Only one writer has said that any wine was ever made from the vineyards at Monticello. In his work *The Young Jefferson*, published in 1945, Claude Bowers asserted that

> several of the [Mazzei] Tuscans found employment at Monticello, and they appear to have attended the native vines with such success that Jefferson was able to send his friends at Williamsburg some wine from his own vintage.[21]

While Bowers appears to be referring to some particular correspondence as authority for saying Jefferson actually made wine from native grapes at Monticello, no evidence currently supports this statement. It more likely refers to some of the wine Mazzei made from wild grapes from Jefferson's woods, which could have been sent to Williamsburg to create interest in the Wine Company.

In 1778, the Monticello vineyards are mentioned for the first time since the disastrous frost of 1774. In the plan of the orchard, a considerable area of vines was shown, beginning some eighty-six feet below the garden wall. The horizontal, or east-west, dimension was one hundred feet, and the north-south measurement appears to be one hundred feet. There were 561 vines from unknown sources, probably Mazzei, growing two feet apart.[22]

After the Revolution ended five years later, Jefferson noted in the *Garden Book* entry of September 3, 1783: "white frosts which killed vines in this neighborhood."[23]

There also exists a brief, intriguing *Garden Book* entry on October 22, 1782: "seventeen bushels of winter [wild] grapes (the stems first excluded) made 40 gallons of vinegar of the first running, & pouring water on, yielded . . . gallons of a weaker kind."[24] The entry reinforces the idea that Jefferson never made any wine at Monticello, for if he recorded vinegar making, it is unlikely he would have omitted all mention of his winemaking.

There are no further references to vines or vineyards until Jefferson had gone to Paris as American minister. During his five years in Paris, from 1784 to 1789, Nicholas Lewis and Francis Eppes managed Monticello, and Jefferson kept no *Garden Book*. From France, he did begin writing about the European vines he could acquire and wanted to grow in his Monticello vineyard. On October 28, 1785, he wrote to the Reverend James Madison:

> I am tomorrow to get to M. Malsherbes . . . He is making for me a collection of the vines from which the Burgundy, Champagne, Bordeaux, Frontignac, and other of the most valuable wines of this country are made.[25]

Three months later, Jefferson asked Giannini about the wine project at Monticello, writing him from Paris:

> February 5, 1786
> How does my vineyard come on? Have there been grapes enough to make a trial of wine? If there should be, I should be glad to receive here a few bottles of the wine.

On September 2, 1786, Giannini sent this explanation:

> As for the vineyard, the vines are improving marvelously but no wine has been made because each year the grapes are picked before they are ripe, which is very harmful to the vines. I have begged Mr. Lewis to stop people from taking grapes. When the grapes are ripe I will make wine and send it to Paris in the autumn. The vineyard now extends all the way to the fishpond, that is to say, to the right of the figs. The location is well adapted to a vineyard, as I have already told you.[26]

On December 26, 1786, Jefferson responded to a letter from the Frenchman Ferdinand Grand, whom Benjamin Franklin had asked for some grapevines. To Grand's question whether America did not already possess abundant vines of its own, Jefferson replied: "[T]ho' we have some grapes as good as in France, yet we have by no means such a variety, nor so perfect a succession of them."[27] This letter is typical of Jefferson's occasional theme that native American grapes were as well suited to winemaking as European varieties. Despite what he said about the promise of native American grapes, Jefferson almost always drank wines made exclusively from European *vinifera* grapes.

Jefferson's 1787 tour of the vineyards of Italy and southern France impressed him tremendously. At first, seeing the poverty of most of the vineyard workers, and even owners, he was utterly discouraged about the wine industry having any *financial* promise for America. As he wrote to William Drayton, chairman of the South Carolina Society for Promoting Agriculture, of which Jefferson was a member:

> July 30, 1787
>
> The culture of the vine is not desirable in lands capable of producing anything else. It is a species of gambling, and desperate gambling, too, wherein whether you make much or nothing, you are equally ruined. The middling crop alone is the saving point, and that the seasons seldom hit. Accordingly, we see much wretchedness among this class of cultivators.
>
> Wine, too, is so cheap in these countries (of Europe), that a laborer with us, employed in the culture of any other article, may exchange it for wine, more and better than he could raise himself.[28]

He wrote to Wythe in a similar vein the same year:

> The vine is the parent of misery. Those who cultivate it are always poor, and he who would employ himself with us in the culture of corn, cotton, &c., can produce, in exchange for them, much more wine, and better, than he could raise by its direct culture.[29]

Jefferson remained interested in grape growing as a personal hobby, however, and obtained vines from several regions of Europe to plant in his Monticello vineyards on his return to America. On February 3, 1788, Parent wrote Jefferson from Beaune that he was sending vines from the finest vineyards of Montrachet, Clos de Vougeot, Chambertin, and Romanée, an incredible assortment. In 1788 he obtained some cuttings of the finest Riesling vines at Hochheim and Rudesieim and planted them in his garden at Paris, where they thrived, as noted in the chapter on his travels in Germany.

In the same year he urged young John Rutledge to study during his travels the growing of the plant which produced the "dried raisin" as possibly a profitable item of agriculture for America.[30] The "dried raisin" appears from his letters to be made from the Muscat grape. On May 7, 1789, he wrote to William Drayton of South Carolina that Cathalan had sent to Drayton: "43 pièces de vignes' [vine cuttings] of the Muscat of which the dried raisins are made."[31]

Thomas Jefferson and the Cork Oak Tree

Another European plant in which Jefferson became very interested was the cork oak tree, from whose bark wine corks are cut. Even after Jefferson became discouraged about vineyards, he still needed corks for his imported wines, many of which arrived in cask. Throughout his life as a wine drinker, he was always running out of corks or bottles, and sometimes both. As his daughter Martha once wrote to him: "It was corks and not bottles that we're wanting to bottle the rest of the wine."[32]

While in Paris, he decided that the cork oak tree from southern France and Portugal would grow well in the southern United States and wrote to his friend Drayton in South Carolina, urging him to see if it would be profitable for southern agriculture:

> May 6, 1786
> By Colonel Franks, in the month of February last, I sent a parcel of acorns of the cork oak, which I desired him to ask the favor of the Delegates of South Carolina in Congress to forward to you.[33]

Jefferson sent Drayton still more acorns the following year via his botanical friend the Abbé Arnoud.[34]

> When the nurseryman whom you have been so good as to employ to prepare the olives & olive plants to be sent to Charleston shall be executing that Commission, I shall be glad if he will at the same time prepare a few plants only of the following kinds:
> Figs. the best kind for drying. a few plants.
> Raisins. do.
> Cork trees, a few plants.
> Pistaches. a few plants.
> Capers.[35]

In his remarkable baggage list prepared that September, Jefferson catalogued in Box #9 of his plants for Virginia: "2 cork oaks."[36]

For the next twenty years, while he held public office, no further mention of the cork oak appears in the *Garden Book* or correspondence. Shortly after his retirement, however, he wrote to Bernard McMahon of Philadelphia, whom

Betts referred to as a "seedsman" and the publisher of *The American Gardener's Calendar*, asking for cork oaks:

> January 13, 1810
>
> The Cedar of Lebanon & Cork Oak are two trees I have long wished to possess. But even if you have them, they could only come by water, & in charge of a careful individual, of which opportunities rarely occur.[37]

In March of 1811 the opportunity seemed to have arrived with Jefferson's neighbor Harmer Gilmer, a medical student studying in Philadelphia, who tried to carry the cork oak plants or acorns to him in a box.[38] A colleague wrote, however, that the naval blockades preceding the War of 1812 had once again frustrated his plans:

> From James Ronaldson
>
> November 2, 1812
>
> It was very unfortunate the Cork seeds I ordered from Bayonne were on board the Amanda, taken and condemned last spring under the British orders of Council. This plant should be procured from Portugal, now that so much intercourse exists with that country.
>
> The Cork thrives on poor sandy land, and I think is suited to all the coast land from Delaware to cape Florida. It would be more profitable than pine trees.[39]

Modern foresters would no doubt be surprised to learn that the cork could be more profitable than pines, but at least Jefferson had support from the experts of his own time, and was not just off on a quixotic quest in pursuing the elusive cork oak. Ronaldson's letter also provoked from Jefferson the first account still existing of what happened to his previous experiments:

> To James Ronaldson
>
> January 12, 1813
>
> I have been long endeavoring to procure the Cork tree from Europe, but without success. A plant which I brought with me from Paris died after languishing some time, and of several parcels of acorns received from a correspondent at Marseilles [Cathalan], not one has ever vegetated.

I shall continue my endeavors, although disheartened by the noncha-
lance of our Southern fellow citizens, with whom alone they can
thrive.[40]

Another decade passed before Jefferson took up the subject again one last
time just before his death in 1826. In a remarkable letter, he outlined an exotic,
experimental grove for the botany students at the University of Virginia:

April 27, 1826
The trees I should propose would be exotics of distinguished useful-
ness, and accommodated to our climate; such as the Larch, cedar of Leba-
non, Cork Oak, the Marronnier, Mahogany, the Catachu or Indian rubber
tree of Napul, (30%) Teak tree, or Indian oak of Burman (23%) the various
woods of Brazil, etc. . . .
The Marronnier (chestnut) and Cork Oak I can obtain from France.[41]

During His First "Retirement," Jefferson's Interest in Vineyards Is Renewed

Following his initial discouragement about vineyards upon his return from
France, Jefferson gradually warmed to the subject. In 1792 he received from Pierre
Guide of Nice some more "raisins," apparently Muscats, thinking to plant them
successfully from seeds.[42] Nor had he yet given up on his South Carolina friends
and their interest in grapes. On December 2, 1792, he asked Stephen Cathalan of
Marseilles to send *every year* some dried raisins, which Jefferson called *des panses*
in French, to Drayton in South Carolina, still hoping to help him establish their
culture in that state.[43]

His interest in wine-grape vineyards slowly returned as well. On January
25, 1793, he wrote to Gallatin about how the horses of the Hessian prisoners
had trampled Mazzei's vineyards at Colle during the Revolution. In the letter
Jefferson sounded as if he was considering whether winemaking might not yet be
feasible at Monticello, at least for his own family's use, since the climate seemed
to him to be suitable; he had seen how harsh the winters could be in France. He
was not one to give up on a pet project, no matter what difficulties or expenses
seemed to prevent its completion.

He received news later that year from his son-in-law Randolph that some
of Mazzei's hard-working *vignerons* were still in the neighborhood and available

and eager to work. As shown by several account book entries, Jefferson later hired them.[44]

By 1796, the year he was elected vice president, his vineyards were again a subject of interest, and he was trying to reestablish them, as he informed Benjamin Hawkins:

> March 22, 1796
>
> The vines you were so kind as to send me by Mr. Chiles were delivered to me alive. Every one budded after it was planted. Yet every one died immediately after. It was certainly not for want of care. Yours is certainly the most valuable collection in America, and I must keep it in view, & pray you to do the same, to have a complete assortment of them, by the first opportunity which may occur.
>
> I have also a grape from Italy, of a brick dust color, coming about a fortnight later than the sweet water & lasting until frost, the most valuable I ever knew.[45]

In 1798 he wrote to his daughter Martha from Philadelphia reiterating that the land at Monticello looked excellent for a vineyard, comparing it favorably to the vineyard lands he had seen in Burgundy.[46]

While president, Jefferson was bombarded with requests, particularly from new American citizens from France and Switzerland, that the government finance the establishment of vineyards in the new territories of the West. On February 1, 1801, Jean-Jacques Dufour wrote Jefferson from the optimistically named town of First Vineyard, Kentucky, enclosing a petition to Congress for a large grant of free land. The six-page, handwritten petition, in both French and English, has been preserved at the Library of Congress, but is too long to reproduce here. Dufour tried again on January 15, 1802. Jefferson never ceded any lands for the project, but similar projects flourished for a while under French-Swiss management at places like Vevay, Indiana.[47]

On March 4, 1801, Frenchman Peter Legaux wrote Jefferson in French with a similar proposal from his new home at Spring Mills, some thirteen miles northwest of Philadelphia. According to Betts, Legaux was perhaps the most intelligent and public-spirited of the new grape growers, and the person most responsible for introducing the strain of labrusca grape from which the distinctive wines of northeastern America were derived. On March 24, Jefferson thanked Legaux for his offer of vines for Monticello, but said it was too late in the season to put them out, and asked Legaux to send him some the next year instead.[48]

Legaux wrote again the next day, asking Jefferson to join a group of subscribers to promote the culture of the vine, enclosing a copy of the proposal in French. The whole idea must have reminded Jefferson of Mazzei's attempts a quarter century earlier in Virginia. There is no record that Jefferson sent the twenty-dollar membership fee requested by Legaux, but the documents at the Library of Congress show that Benjamin Latrobe, architect of the Capitol and another wine lover, was a subscriber, as well as some sixty-four other prominent citizens. The proposal went to the Pennsylvania legislature, where it was apparently well received.[49]

As if to remind Jefferson of the dismal outcomes of such experiments in the past, a violent hailstorm struck Monticello in June 1801, breaking most of the glass windows at the house and damaging what remained of the vineyards.

On May 11, 1802, during a visit to Monticello, Jefferson proudly wrote in his *Garden Book* the beginning of a new chapter of the Monticello vineyards:

> Planted grape vines received from Legaux in the S.W. Vineyard in vacant spaces of rows in the upper or
>
> 1st row.   Very large white eating grapes.
> 2nd row   30. plants of vines from Burgundy and Champagne with roots.
> 4th row   30. plants of vines of Bordeaux with roots.
> 5th row   . . .
> 6th row   10. plants of vines from Cape of Good Hope with roots.[50]

The above reference was the first mention of a *southwest* vineyard, probably the best exposure at Monticello because it catches more afternoon sun. During 1802 Jefferson was ill again, suffering from deafness and a ringing in the ears, possibly from his old "periodical" headaches. His indisposition seems to have prevented any further vineyard visits that year.

On February 13, 1803, Nathaniel Macon wrote to Jefferson enclosing a note from William Hawkins dated February 4. It apparently was written in response to a request for more vines by Jefferson, and stated:

> There are but two kinds of grapes remaining, one oval, purple, early ripe. the other round, white. Dr. Brichon is supposed to have taken cuttings of all the various kinds which Colo. Hawkins had. Enquiry shall be made.[51]

According to Monticello Director of Grounds Peter Hatch, who is now in charge of restoring the Monticello vineyards, during 1804 Jefferson also obtained many grapevine cuttings from Georgetown nurseryman Thomas Main, which he set out at the White House and replanted at Monticello in 1807.[52] In 1805 Thomas Appleton informed Jefferson that he and Mazzei had contrived to send him "one case of vine cuttings." Jefferson apparently replied not only to Appleton but also to Mazzei. Later that year Mazzei mentioned that letter, and gave vague references to which vines he had sent to Jefferson:

> From Philip Mazzei
>
> September 12, 1805
>
> Upon my return from Florence and Rome . . . I found your welcome letter of May 4. I gather that you had not as yet received . . . the large case containing 322 root cuttings of several varieties of grapes, 23 of them of Smyrna seedless grapes, which left Leghorn on March 13 of this year.[53]

Jefferson did receive the Mazzei vines in good order and sent them to Monticello for planting.[54] During the next two years he was too busy as president to tend any vineyards at Monticello, but kept the vines from Mazzei in the gardens at the President's House.

Planting of the Vineyards at Monticello in 1807

It was in 1807, as he thought almost constantly of retirement, and hostilities in Europe made him wonder if his supplies of European wine might be cut off, that Jefferson began to work on his most extensive vineyard plans for Monticello. All that year he kept up a busy correspondence about his revitalized vineyards, and made several entries about them in his Weather Memorandum Book. On February 25, Timothy Matlack of Lancaster, Pennsylvania, in the "Dutch" country, sent him cuttings of a "purple Syrian grape from Twitman." On April 21 Jefferson noted: "planted . . . 6. plants of Purple Syrian grape from Twickenham, upper row of S.W. vineyard at N.E. end."[55]

A *northeast* vineyard of seventeen *terrasses*, the eighteenth being "occupied chiefly by trees," was first mentioned on March 25, 1807. This vineyard is shown on the 1811 orchard plan, seemingly in the same area, next to the first vineyard, but separated from it by the berry squares. The only dimensions given are 90 feet on an east-west axis for the east vineyard and 160 feet for the west. Most of the vines in it were planted in 1807.

On March 25, 1807, Jefferson noted plantings encompassing both the Italian vines from Mazzei and the transplanted vines from Main of Georgetown that had been at the President's House in the southwest vineyards, which had grown from six *terrasses* in 1802 to eleven *terrasses* in 1807:

Mar. 25.   S.W. vineyard. at S.W. end of 1st terras planted 2. Malaga grape vines. Maine. at N.E. end. 1st terras 12 black Hamburg grape vines from Main planted only in vacancies.

> 2nd. . . . .12. red do.
>
> 3rd. . . . .10. white Frontignac.
>
> 4th . . . .20. Chasselas.
>
> 5th . . . . 3. Muscadine.
>
> 6th . . . .11. Brick coloured grapes.
>
> 7th . . . .10. Black cluster grapes.

N.E. vineyard. beginning at S.W. end of it, & planting only in vacancies.

> 1st terras. 6. plants of Seralamanna grapes II. cuttings from them.
>
> 2nd. . . . .15. cuttings of the same, or Piedm^t Malmsy.
>
> 3rd. . . . .13. Piedmont Malmesy or Seralamana.
>
> 4th. . . . 1. Smyrna without seeds.
>
> 5th. . . . 7. Galetlas.
>
> 6th. . . . 7. Queen's grapes.
>
> 7th. . . . 5. Great July grapes.
>
> 8th. . . . 6. Tokay.
>
> 9th. . . .13. Tokay.
>
> 10th. . . .13. Trebbiano.
>
> 11th. . . .17. Lachrima Christi.
>
> 12th. . . . 6. San Giovetto.
>
> 13th. . . .15. Abrostine white.
>
> 14th. . . .21. do. . .red or Aleaticos.
>
> 15th. . . .15. Aleatico. or Abrostine red.
>
> 16th. . . .13. Margiano.
>
> 17th. . . .15. Mamsnole.

S.W. vineyard. N.E. end. 9th terras + Tokays, same as 9th of N.E. Vineyard.

> 10th. . . . 6. Trebbianos. same as 10th of N.E.
>
> 11th. . . . 3. Lachrima Christi, same as 11th of N.E.[56]

With Malaga grapes, black Hamburg (red) Muscat, Frontignac (white) Muscat, French Chasselas, and Italians: Trebbiano, Lachrima Christi, San Giovetto (the grape of Chianti), and red Aleatico Muscats, Jefferson could have produced a considerable variety of wines. Most interesting was the Black Cluster, now identified as probably the famous Cabernet Sauvignon, grape of the greatest red Bordeaux and today the finest reds of California's Napa Valley.

To care for this large vineyard, Jefferson sent a memorandum dated May 13, 1807, to his trusted Monticello overseer, Edmund Bacon, which stated: "Directions for Plantation Affairs. Wormley must be directed to weed . . . the vineyards . . . when they need it."[57]

How well Wormley weeded has not been recorded, but on October 19, 1807, Jefferson wrote to Timothy Matlack again, asking for more grapevines for planting in February 1809, when Jefferson would have retired as president, indicating he looked forward with eagerness to the day when he would "be able to carry and plant them myself at Monticello."[58]

In 1808 Jefferson wrote a Frenchman, C.P. Lasteyrie du Saillant, his old ideas on the impracticality of cultivation of the vine in America:

> July 15, 1808
> We could, in the United States, make as great a variety of wines as are made in Europe, not exactly of the same kinds, but doubtless as good. Yet I have ever observed to my countrymen who think its introduction important, that a laborer cultivating wheat, rice, tobacco, or cotton here will be able with the proceeds to purchase double the quantity of the wine he could make.[59]

It now appears Jefferson was wrong on this point, with vineyards beginning to replace tobacco fields in Virginia and North Carolina.

That same year William Tatham of Newbern, North Carolina, wrote Jefferson encouragingly about his own success in winemaking and predicted that North Carolina would become a winemaking center:

> I have found the culture of grapes throughout this country a subject of more importance than is in general imagined, & the annual production of home made wine is greater than in any other part I have visited in the U. States. I have a small quantity of wine, made by my own direction, which is very similar, & perhaps not inferior to the Rota Tent (Vino Tinto de Rota) of Spain.[60]

In 1809 Jefferson renewed his correspondence with Major John Adlum, former Revolutionary War soldier, judge, and enthusiastic amateur winemaker. Adlum had a two-hundred-acre estate near Georgetown in what is now Rock Creek Park. On October 7 Jefferson wrote to him from Monticello for cuttings from native grapevines Adlum was growing. Apparently discouraged about successfully growing European vines, Jefferson tried growing native hardier vines. He even insisted at times that the native Labrusca-made wines were equal in quality and taste to the best of Europe, comparing them, incredibly, to Burgundies:

> While I lived in Washington, a member of Congress from your state presented me with two bottles of wine made by you, one of which, of Madeira colour, he said was entirely fictitious, the other, a dark red wine was made from a wild or native grape, called in Maryland the Fox grape, but very different from what is called by that name in Virginia.
>
> This was a very fine wine, & so exactly resembling the red Burgundy of Caumartin (one of the best crops) that on fair comparison with that, of which I had very good on the same table imported by myself from the place where made, the company could not distinguish the one from the other. I think it would be well to push the culture of that grape, without losing our time & efforts in search of foreign vines, which it will take centuries to adapt to our soil & climate.[61]

Adlum acknowledged Jefferson's letter and sent him a bottle of wine of his own making from grapes which he had grown in his own vineyard:

> February 15, 1810
> It will give me great pleasure at any time to furnish you or any of your friends with cuttings that I have to spare for I think with you it is best to propagate the culture of our native grapes in preference to foreign. They are already adapted to our climate, and I have little doubt but that grapes of a good quality for making wine may be found in every state in the Union. . . .
> I have drank a very decent wine at Mr. Thomas Gauls who lived at Spring Mill and at Isaac Kolb at the Valley Forge made out of what they called the fall grape and they both told me that they made about a hogshead every year from grapes that grew in their fields and along the fences.[62]

Similar letters to and from Adlum and others about planting native grapes occupied Jefferson throughout the rest of his retirement.[63]

March 13, 1810

With this day's mail I send you a number of cuttings of the vines from which I made the wine I had the honor of sending you by Mr. Christie. I also enclose a bottle of wine, made last season.

Mr. Gale, who lives a few miles from me, got a number of cuttings from me, and trains them in the manner mentioned by Forsyth in his book on fruit trees, and it is astonishing to see what strength the shoots grow, but he has not yet made any wine from them. It is his opinion that they ought to be planted a rod apart (that is) 16-1/2 feet.[64]

For the remainder of the year 1810 and most of 1811 Jefferson left no record of vineyard activity, but did leave a "Planting Memorandum for Poplar Forest: 11 grapes of one kind; 21 ditto of another," but nothing for Monticello. The plan of the orchard and garden made in 1811 still shows two vineyards, the southwest and the northeast, side by side on the same location as the original vineyard in 1778.

Jefferson also wrote to James Monroe for *vinifera* vine cuttings the latter had brought from France:

January 16, 1816

I have an opportunity of getting some vines planted next month under the direction of Mr. David, brought up to the business from his infancy. Will you permit me to take the trimmings of your vines, such I mean as ought to be taken from them next month. It shall be done by him so as to ensure no injury to them.[65]

Unfortunately, it appears Monroe's European vines faired no better than Jefferson's and the latter went back to discussing native American vines.[66]

In 1817 Jefferson became interested in the Scuppernong, which was once the wine for which Virginia was best known. Jefferson may have learned of Scuppernong from General John Cocke, whose diary for March 27, 1817, shows:

Sent to Monticello for some Marseilles figs and Paper Mulberry, and at the same time sent Mr. Jefferson some wine made from the Scuppernong grape of North Carolina, a fruit which must be well worthy to be cultivated. The wine is of delicious flavor, resembling Frontinac.[67]

On April 4, 1817, Jefferson noted in the *Garden Book*, perhaps after being impressed with Cocke's sample of Scuppernong: "planted 15. scuppernong vines in lowest terras of vineyard."[68]

His wine-loving son-in-law John Wayles Eppes also wrote to Jefferson on the Scuppernong, the hot new subject:

In a letter from Colo. Burton he informs me that he has procured a cask of the Scuppernong wine two years old. He says it is greatly superior to what you tasted at my house and that he has made arrangements for forwarding it to Mr. Gibson at Richmond.[69]

On May 10 Jefferson wrote an interesting letter to Judge William Johnson in Washington, which showed enthusiasm for Scuppernong:

May 10, 1817

[Thanks for pamphlet on] agriculture, the employment of our first parents in Eden, the happiest we can follow, and the most important to our country. I am not without hope that thro' your efforts and example, we shall yet see it a country abounding in wine and oil. North Carolina has the merit of taking the lead in the former culture, of giving the first specimens of an exquisite wine, produced in quantity, and established in its culture beyond the danger of being discontinued.

Her Scuppernong wine, made on the south side of the Sound, would be distinguished on the best tables of Europe for its fine aroma, and chrystalline transparence. Unhappily that aroma, in most of the samples I have seen, has been entirely submerged in brandy. This coarse taste and practice is the peculiarity of Englishmen, and of their apes, Americans.[70]

Jefferson did not discuss Scuppernong again in writing, as far as we know, until February 28, 1819, when he wrote to Nathaniel Macon:

Doctor Hall, a friend of mine, one of the representatives of N. Carolina, brought with him to this place a few bottles of Scuppernong wine, the best American that I have tasted. I asked for two to send you which he willingly gave.[71]

On August 11, 1821, Samuel Maverick of Montpelier, South Carolina, wrote to Jefferson about the rot, the spot, and other perils of the scuppernong grower. In March 4, 1822, letter, Maverick added that

The Cultivation of the Vine has commenced on the Black Warrior River by the Settlement of Frenchmen, but with what success I am unable to say, as I did not go so low by 70 miles. I saw several of the Frenchmen. They appear confident of success of the vine . . . any ideas respecting or on the Culture of the Vine, will be thankfully received.[72]

On May 12, Jefferson replied, revealing the sad state of the Monticello vineyards, but also that he was still adamantly in favor of wine, especially American wines:

Age, debility and decay of memory have for some time withdrawn me from attention to matters without doors. The grape you inquire after as having gone from this place is not now recollected by me. As some in my vineyard have died, others have been substituted without noting which, so that at present all are unknown.

That as good wines will be made in America as in Europe, the Scuppernong of North Carolina furnishes sufficient proof. The vine is congenial to every climate in Europe from Hungary to the Mediterranean, and will be bound to succeed in the same temperatures here whenever tried by intelligent vignerons.[73]

JEFFERSON RECEIVES MUSCAT CUTTINGS FROM JOSEPH BONAPARTE

On April 5, 1822, James W. Wallace wrote to Jefferson:

I have obtained some cuttings for you which I obtained in New York under the name of bland grape. . . . To these I add some, given to me on the Delaware in the Steam boat, said to have been introduced by Joseph Bonaparte from France, called Muscatel—the account of their qualities so exactly resembles the one I heard you give that I am induced to believe 'tis a favorite grape with you, but, have no recollection of the name you gave it.[74]

Jefferson's reply to this letter apparently has not been preserved.

On June 5, 1822, Major Adlum informed Jefferson that he was still in the business of making wine, in Georgetown, with as much enthusiasm as ever. On June 13 Jefferson answered in the same vein,[75] and his family and friends continued to seek out the very best Scuppernongs for the aged expert. His grandson Francis Wayles Eppes wrote:

October 31, 1822

My Dr. Grand Father

I obtained from Col. Burton the address of several gentlemen who make the Carolina wine. He was much opposed to giving the information, but upon my insisting, told me that Thomas Co & Co. Commission Merchants, Plymouth, would be more likely to please than any others. In case however, that you might still prefer the winemakers themselves, he informed me that Ebinezer Pettigrew, of Edenton, and George E. Spruel, of Plymouth, make it best. The former will not always sell, being very wealthy, the latter is not in as good circumstances, and owns the famous vine covering an acre of ground. Col. B. informed us that the vine does not grow from the slip, which accounts for the failure of yours.[76]

On March 14 and 24, 1823, Adlum sent Jefferson samples of an American "Tokay" and "Burgundy," showing that abuse of European wine terms was already rampant. The "Burgundy" apparently was made from the Catawba grape, of which Adlum later supplied cuttings to Nicholas Longworth of Cincinnati, who made the grape and its wine world famous.[77]

Jefferson replied in his final letter to Adlum with a humility befitting a man who had tried for fifty years and never made a drop of wine:

April 11, 1823

Dear Sir

I received successively the two bottles of wine you were so kind as to send me. The first, called Tokay, is a truly fine wine, of high flavor, and, as you assure me, there was not a drop of brandy or other spirit in it. I may say it is a wine of a good body of it's own. The 2d bottle, a red wine, I tried when I had good judges at the table. We agreed it was a wine one might always drink with satisfaction, but of no peculiar excellence.

Of your book on the culture of the vine it would be presumption in me to give any opinion, because it is a culture of which I have no knowledge either from practice or reading.

TH: JEFFERSON

The Adlum book Jefferson referred to was retained in his library, and recently has been reprinted in a new edition.[78]

Apparently Jefferson obtained the Scuppernong mentioned by Francis Eppes, from the winemaker, for on June 3, 1823, he wrote to Thomas Cox of Plymouth, North Carolina, thanking him for the Scuppernong, and at age eighty, ever the connoisseur, asked: "What is deemed the age of perfect ripeness of this wine, and the proper one for drinking it?"[79]

Current Restoration of the Monticello Vineyards

In 1977 expert professional horticulturist Peter Hatch was hired to be director of grounds at Monticello. One of his tasks was to restore Jefferson's vineyards, orchards, and gardens. Through extensive archeological digs, the original northeast and southwest vineyard sites were positively located. Diligent analysis was done of Jefferson's letters and entries in his *Garden Book* and other original sources, and the vineyards were replanted as accurately as possible. Jefferson's handwritten 1807 diagram was used, and the northeast vineyard originally planted by Mazzei was replanted in 1985 with twenty-one *vinifera* varieties obtained from the University of California at Davis. By 1990 the northeast vineyard was producing three hundred bottles of wine per harvest.

Among a host of perplexing problems, the naming of grapes was especially challenging. In viticulture as in spelling, the people of the eighteenth and early nineteenth centuries were somewhat arbitrary. Jefferson's famous "Black Cluster" was said by one vine supplier to be the Cabernet of Bordeaux, by another the Pinot Noir of Burgundy. Despite its name, which clearly implies a red grape, a third Jefferson supplier thought the grape was the Pinot Gris of France, known to Italians (and now Americans) as Pinot Grigio. Solving those problems as logically and accurately as he could, Hatch replanted the northeast vineyard with the most verifiable Jefferson grapes, including: Pinot Noir, Cabernet Sauvignon, Chardonnay, Pinot Blanc, Sangiovese, Trebbiano, Pinot Meunier, Chasselas (both rosé and doré), White Muscat, Red Muscat, Aleatico, Picolit, Pedro Ximénes (Malaga), Malvasia of Tuscany, Tocai of Friuli and Furmint (Tokay of Hungary).

In 1993 Hatch replanted the southwest vineyard. Because the various grapes planted in the northeast vineyard matured at different times, it proved difficult to blend them effectively. To avoid that problem, the southwest vineyard was planted entirely in Sangiovese. By 1995 it too was producing three hundred bottles per harvest. What appear to be small harvests are explained by the small size of Jefferson's vineyards. The northeast vineyard was and is a mere nine thousand square feet; the larger southwest vineyard contains only sixteen thousand square feet. Together his entire vineyard area covers less than one acre.

Hatch's book *The Fruits and Fruit Trees of Monticello* contains an outstanding chapter on Jefferson's vineyards entitled "Grapes: The Species of Utopia," in which he explains in detail how Jefferson was at heart a plant collector and experimental gardener rather than a winemaker. His restored vineyards are therefore more like a lively outdoor museum than a working vineyard intended to produce wine commercially. Jefferson left, surprisingly, no harvest dates and few notes on the state of his vineyards, in contrast to his elaborately detailed notes on English peas and apples. With his vineyards, as with so many areas of Jefferson's life, there are many unanswerable puzzles, which Hatch aptly summarizes: "A study of viticulture at Monticello is a study of the ambiguities, contradictions and even the elusiveness of Jefferson himself."[80]

The current winemaker at Monticello is Gabriele Rausse. Born in Italy, he is a fitting successor to Philip Mazzei. A mellow, philosophical man of the earth, he has ably assisted Peter Hatch in restoring the vineyards and, unlike Jefferson, has lost only one vine in twenty-one years. Rausse also has his own private winery just six miles from Monticello and there makes some excellent wines from his own vinifera grapes. A natural raconteur, Rausse tells great stories about the successes and frustrations of the Monticello vineyards. When they planted clover to prevent erosion in the vineyards, it lured groundhogs wholesale. When they built a fence to keep out pests, it broke and raccoons devastated the vines. In 1996 they lost their entire crop to storms spun off from a hurricane. One year they made over a thousand bottles; another year bad weather limited the harvest to a mere ninety-seven bottles. In 2004 the entire crop was lost to the weather.

One possible contribution of the many animal pests at Monticello is their ability to judge the ripeness of grapes. As Rausse explains it, when the sugar level, or Brix, is seventeen degrees, deer begin to eat the grapes. Then come the groundhogs, who are so avid for fruit that they climb peach trees and tear down fences. Most fastidious of the four-footed pests of Monticello are the foxes, which will not steal grapes unless they are over twenty-one degrees in sugar on the Brix scale.

WHY JEFFERSON FAILED TO MAKE ANY WINE

As perhaps the leading pioneer of early American amateur grape growers, Jefferson faced a multitude of problems, solutions for some of which were not found until the twentieth century. Growing European vinifera grapes in the harsher climate of the Piedmont region of Virginia subjected them to a host of new vine diseases. The best known, phylloxera, devastated the vineyards of Europe in the late nineteenth century and was cured only when it was discovered that grafting European shoots onto native American roots gave grapevines resistance to the disease. It is ironic that Jefferson grafted nearly every other fruit in his vast gardens, but somehow apparently never thought to graft his grapevines, even though others in Virginia, such as John Cocke, were already trying such grafts.[81]

Even if Jefferson had grafted his vineyards, however, they faced other problems probably insoluble in his era. Most of his vines died, before they could even develop phylloxera, from severe frosts, various mildews, and black rot. Monticello was also famously lacking in water. The springs and wells ran dry in some months, a problem which Jefferson finally solved partially by an elaborate system of cisterns to catch rainwater. Never, however, was there likely enough water to irrigate his vineyards. Conversely, even though he terraced the vineyards, the soil at the site was rather heavy and probably did not drain well.

Worst were the four-footed predators, from deer and rabbits to the prolific groundhogs of Monticello mountain. Jefferson noted that servants also ate his grapes, and he believed that Hessian prisoners of war also accidentally trampled some of the vineyards with their horses. Later studies show that his grandchildren and their friends probably ate many as well.

The modern restorers of the Monticello vineyards have faced all of these problems, plus a new one that Jefferson luckily never knew: bureaucratic regulation of alcohol. Nevertheless, the modern Jeffersonians, using new technology, have succeeded in making wine at Monticello where Jefferson failed. My favorite to date by far is Gabriele Rausse's 1999, of pure Sangiovese, from the southwest vineyard. Wines from his own vineyards, both Cabernets and Chardonnays, are among the best of the region. The success shows that Jefferson's dream of a Virginia wine industry was not misguided. Jefferson was, in this area as in so many others, simply much ahead of his time.

EPILOGUE

The Latest Jefferson Controversy:
The Mysterious Case of Bordeaux

The last thing one would have imagined about Jefferson is a controversy over his wines. For nearly two centuries, including the Prohibition era, the only possible controversy about Jefferson and wine was the fact that he was not a teetotaler, as Founding Fathers were sort of expected to be. Even as his love of wine came to light, however, his insistence on sobriety and moderation, and his frequent denunciations of whisky and strong spirits, supported his positive image more or less without controversy.

Then, in 1985, wealthy German wine collector Hardy Rodenstock announced that he had purchased, from a source he steadfastly refused to reveal, a case or more of eighteenth-century wines which either belonged to, or were intended for, Thomas Jefferson. Although details have come out piecemeal, the wine trove apparently consisted of over a dozen bottles, all Bordeaux, including reds from Châteaux Lafite, Margaux, and Mouton, and the mutual favorite of Jefferson and Rodenstock, Château d'Yquem, the only white and only dessert wine of the group.

The bottles are said to have been found in an old cellar bricked up for protection during the French Revolution, an image reminiscent of Edgar Allan Poe's story "The Cask of Amontillado." On December 5, 1985, famed wine auctioneer Michael Broadbent of Christie's, a premier expert on old wines, presided in London over the sale of the first "Jefferson" bottle, which was engraved "1787 Chateau Lafitte," followed below by the initials "Th.J.," resembling a standard Jefferson shorthand signature. Handblown and dark amber-green, the old bottle had pitted sides and a striated neck. The wine itself was said to be of a "remarkably deep" color and its level "just 1/2 inch below the cork," which appeared to be original with even its large, original wax seal still intact.[1]

As reported in a dramatic story in *The New Yorker* in a column entitled "A Piece of History," an unnamed "eyewitness of the historic events" reported that a standing-room-only crowd attended the auction, recorded by a film crew worthy of the set of a major motion picture. The bottle itself stood on green felt in its own glass case. Seven active bidders, including *Wine Spectator* publisher Marvin Shanken, bid on the bottle. In the end, Christopher Forbes, son of the late publisher Malcolm Forbes and brother of former presidential candidate Steve Forbes, bought the bottle for what was then a record price of $156,450 (105,000 British pounds sterling). The bidding, which lasted just one minute and 39 seconds, far outdid the previous high price ever paid at auction for any bottle of wine from any source.[2]

Owner Rodenstock agreed, pronouncing himself "staggered." Publisher Malcolm Forbes described himself as "stunned" that his son had spent so much on one bottle, saying, "I wish Jefferson had drunk the damn bottle himself and saved me the expense." The bottle was flown back from London to New York on Forbes's corporate jet, in its own separate seat, and placed in the Forbes art gallery on Fifth Avenue, where it was displayed in its own glass case. Forbes later began to mellow toward it, saying the bottle was "spiritual" and would go well with his other Jefferson memorabilia, including a table and original Jefferson letters.[3]

Then misfortune struck. The bottle became too warm from the lights in the case, causing the ancient cork to shrink and fall into the wine.[4]

Controversy began to haunt the bottles after this mishap. From the beginning there had been questions about the origins of the mysterious bottles. In an October 1985 article in *The New York Times*, wine journalist Howard Goldberg had questioned their origins, saying researchers at Monticello had found no support in Jefferson's meticulous records that he had ever ordered, received, or referred to any Bordeaux of 1787, and had received 1784s only from Yquem and Margaux, although he had ordered 1784 Lafite but the owner had had no more available. Monticello researchers also found the initialing "Th.J." abnormal, since Jefferson habitually labeled his personal property with the old style initials "T.I," and used a colon differently, situated between and above and below the "Th" and the "J" in his abbreviated signatures.[5]

Mr. Broadbent stoutly defended the bottles, saying Christie's had had them "authenticated" and that experts vouched for the engraving date and that both the cork and its wax seal were "original." Mr. Rodenstock, known to connoisseurs as "Herr Yquem" because of his love for the great Sauternes, told Goldberg in a telephone interview most of what is still publicly known about the origin of the bottles, saying he had purchased "more than a dozen" of them earlier in 1985, including three 1784 Yquems, three 1787 Yquems, three 1787 Lafites, three 1787 Moutons (called Branne-Mouton in the eighteenth century), as well as "others" from those châteaux and three additional bottles with "no identifying marks." Mr. Rodenstock explained that he had already opened and tasted at Château d'Yquem one of the bottles in May of 1985 and that a laboratory had dated the cork to between 1780 and 1790.[6]

Mr. Rodenstock offered to take one of the 1787 bottles to Monticello to celebrate its two hundredth anniversary, but the experts there continued to express scepticism, suggesting that the enthusiastic and dedicated Mr. Rodenstock, who appeared sincere in his belief in the authenticity of the wines, might himself have been deceived. Mr. Rodenstock continued to defend the wines vigorously, however, offering documentary evidence from records of châteaux in Bordeaux as to how Jefferson's orders for Bordeaux wines in 1791 might have been filled with these bottles as substitutes for the ones he had ordered, as was done on several other occasions.[7] Mr. Rodenstock wrote several letters to *Wine Spectator* editors vouching for the bottles, to which he obviously was quite attached. In a public response, the magazine ran a brief editorial entitled "Unanswered Questions," calling on Mr. Rodenstock to "lay his cards on the table" by revealing how and from where and from whom he had obtained the bottles so that their authenticity could be determined once and for all.[8]

In September 1986, Mr. Broadbent replied in a column in the British wine magazine *Decanter* entitled, tellingly, "No More Doubts."[9] The column described a tasting in June 1986 of one of the bottles of alleged 1787 Mouton at the current Château Mouton-Rothschild. It was attended by all the top brass of Mouton and a glass was tasted by the since-deceased Baron Philippe, who was then too ill to leave his bed. Mr. Broadbent, supported by respected English wine writer Jancis Robinson, master of wine and BBC television commentator on wine, pronounced the 1787 bottle to be "pure Mouton."[10] *Wine Spectator*'s review of the same June 3, 1986, tasting at Mouton took a measured tone, quoting almost entirely from the *Decanter* article in a short, unsigned piece entitled "Historic Mouton 'Delicious to Drink.'"[11]

On the same page of the same issue, however, the *Spectator* ran pictures of the 1787 "Lafitte" and of Mr. Broadbent with the 1787 Mouton with the heading "Did Cork Fall Into Forbes' Lafite Bottle?" Referring to the debacle mentioned earlier, and quoting Mr. Broadbent, the article noted that the 1787 Lafite cork had fallen down into its old bottle, apparently dried out by the heat of the lights in its special display case. The bottle, however, was still on display, but was too dark for anyone to see inside without handling it. The museum declined to answer the *Spectator*'s questions, its corporate communications director saying only, "If I knew anything about this, I wouldn't tell you anyway." After that misfortune, the controversy seemed about to die down.

Then, on December 4, 1986, a bottle bearing the inscription "1784 Chateau d'Yquem Th.J." was auctioned by Christie's in London. Two bidders competed to the end. One, Barbara Wall, a wine retailer from Syracuse, New York, kept upping her bid until her only competitor, a mysterious, teetotaling Jordanian named Iyad Shiblaq, began to walk toward the exit. Just as the auctioneers thought the man was leaving, Shiblaq suddenly made the winning bid of $56,628 (39,600 English pounds as of that date). Before rushing out, Mr. Shiblaq stated that he had bought the wine for a person in New York he would not reveal, but he hoped that the bottle would remain in England, unopened and undrunk, as a collector's item.[12]

It was later reported in *Wine Spectator*, quoting *The New York Post*, that the true buyer was none other than Dodi al Fayed, producer of *Chariots of Fire*, who later died in the tragic and notorious automobile accident in Paris with Princess Diana. According to the *Spectator*, Shiblaq called Mr. Broadbent to ask how to store the ancient bottle. Broadbent allegedly told him, "The cork is the problem. The bottle is as tough as old boots, but the cork could fall in if it is not kept properly." An unsigned separate sidebar on the same page continued to stress that among Monticello experts there were still "Historical Doubts" about the authenticity of all the bottles.[13]

Wine Spectator later seemed to have had its questions about the Jefferson bottles answered, and its skepticism seemed to abate. At the June 1987 VinExpo in Bordeaux, a half-bottle alleged to be 1784 Margaux with Jefferson's initials was put up for auction by Mr. Rodenstock, with Mr. Broadbent of Christie's once again taking part. The "uniquely shaped" .375 milliliter bottle, "squat and long-necked," sold for $30,000, fifth-highest price ever paid for a bottle of wine. A mysterious telephone bidder, whom Broadbent identified only as "an Arab gentleman bidding for a friend," made a final bid of $28,300.

The presiding French auctioneer countered with a sealed, secret bid from yet another unidentified bidder. There were no live bidders present. The unidentified Arab bidder declined to go higher. To the surprise of many, the winning bidder was none other than Marvin Shanken, owner and publisher of *Wine Spectator*. Mr. Shanken stated that he did not plan to drink or even open the bottle, but to put it on display at the New York headquarters of M. Shanken Communications as "an important part of American history."[14]

In 1988 British wine writer Jancis Robinson published an account of a fabulous Yquem tasting at the château on September 30, 1987, with all the wines furnished without charge by Mr. Rodenstock. The elite of the wine world was there, including the late Richard Olney, author of the eloquently written, beautifully illustrated definitive "biography" of the Château d'Yquem, as well as famed Los Angeles wine collector Bipin Desai and the grandson of the late Baron Philippe Rothschild of Mouton, plus several owners of other Bordeaux châteaux. Mr. Rodenstock produced undisputable Yquems from 1858, 1848, and 1811 to go with a 1921 and a 1937 as well as sixteen vintages of *dry* Yquem known as Ygrec.

The scene seemed to establish that a man who loved Yquem that much, and could afford such rarities, could not and would not be fooled into embracing a "Jefferson" Yquem that was anything but authentic. Jancis Robinson seemed to agree. The star wine of the tasting, not a Jefferson bottle, but allegedly from the cellars of a Russian tsar in St. Petersburg and even older than the Jefferson bottles, was by an analysis of the glass in the bottle said to be from approximately 1750. Robinson opined that the wine was perhaps not as good as another 1784 "Jefferson" bottle of Yquem tasted in Germany in 1986, but was worth enduring a thirteen-hour meal/tasting of countless other famous wines, all of which were swallowed. A French taster, Jo Gryn of the *Gault-Millau* French wine magazine, agreed.[15]

Just as it seemed peace had settled over the latest Jefferson controversy following the Yquem tasting, there came a slapstick, Marx Brothers–like sequel. As reported in *The New York Times* under the heading "A $519,750 Bottle of Wine? You Say You Broke It?," there was another tasting with very different results. In 1989, to celebrate the arrival of the 1986 Bordeaux vintage in the United States, a black tie gala dinner was scheduled at the Four Seasons restaurant.

William Sokolin, the New York wine merchant who wrote the book *Liquid Assets*, which gives advice on wine as an investment, had on hand one of the bottles of 1787 Château Margaux which allegedly was once connected to Jefferson. Sokolin had obtained the bottle on consignment from Whitwhams, a broker in Manchester, England. It was priced at $212,000 and Sokolin said he had insured it for that amount. Whitwhams had bought it from Mr. Rodenstock, who had been keeping it in a vault in Monte Carlo. Whitwhams had first listed the wine in its February 1988 catalogue for "only" $75,000, but by September 1988 its price had risen to $212,000.[16]

On the evening of the Four Seasons dinner, in front of 194 guests, including the owners of Château Margaux and other wine luminaries, Mr. Sokolin decided to show the bottle off to Rusty Staub, the prominent wine-loving restaurateur, and his friend and fellow retired baseball star Keith Hernandez. Since receiving the bottle and a bill for $212,000, Sokolin had raised the advertised price three times, first to $250,000, then to $394,000, then to an amazing $519,750. He had, he said, received two serious offers for the bottle.

As he was walking toward Mr. Staub, Mr. Sokolin accidentally bumped the bottle against a metal-topped table, bashing a large, oblong hole in it as shown in a photo with the *Times* story. Red wine began pouring onto the carpet as Sokolin ran for the kitchen. The unfortunate black-tie diners never got to taste the 1787 Margaux, but a manager at the restaurant who allegedly stuck his finger in it said it was clearly "maderized" and "over the hill" anyway. Sokolin kept what was left of the bottle in a plastic container in his refrigerator. The bottle itself, complete with its hole, was recently for sale at a hefty price.

Nor is this chapter of the great Jefferson wine controversy closed. As is probably fitting, a book is now being written that is devoted entirely to the subject of the mysterious bottles, and is to be published by Crown Books in 2007. Entitled *The Billionaire's Vinegar*, it is by Benjamin Wallace. Random House has the international rights.

According to the experts at Monticello, the available documentation on Jefferson's orders and receipts of Bordeaux reveal *no* evidence of the bottles' existence. In the most thorough and thoughtful study to date, Lucia Cinder Stanton of the Thomas Jefferson Memorial Foundation at Monticello totally doubts the authenticity of the bottles as Jeffersonian, while agreeing they might well be eighteenth century.

Jefferson's correspondence and papers, like his libraries, are so vast that we will likely never find every piece. They are simply too voluminous and scattered for anyone ever to be sure that we have them all. But that should be an incentive, not a deterrent. Filling in blanks was a Jeffersonian preoccupation. Why should it be different with us as we study his wines?

Intriguing also are numerous letters *referred to* by Jefferson and his wine correspondents of which we have no copies. His Summary Journal of Letters (SJL) has notes corroborating references to them, but no one has ever found the letters themselves. A number are summarized in the old State Department index called the *Bureau of the Rolls*. One-sentence summaries of them are given, tantalizingly, and it was those references which first led me to many unpublished microfilm copies of wine letters at the Library of Congress. Seldom have I searched one out that did not have some new and occasionally startling fact about Jefferson's wines that I did not know before—but none mentions these bottles.

The absence of written evidence that Jefferson ordered 1787 Château Lafite does not of course conclusively prove that he did not. In 1982, when many believed he had no Lafite because his voluminous wine records did not reflect it, an apparently authentic capsule from a bottle of "Lafitte" was found at Monticello in the excavation of a dry well there. And Jefferson did have his abbreviated signature "Th.J." engraved on his silver, although differently from the way it was engraved on the mysterious bottles from Paris.

After his 1787 trip to Bordeaux, during which he met proprietors and personally visited Château Haut-Brion, his Bordeaux correspondence greatly increased. Yet when he went back to America in 1789, for what he thought was just a visit, he took not a single bottle of red Bordeaux with him, but left them all behind in Paris, planning to return. There is also this factor to consider: Jefferson's orders for Bordeaux were often changed by his suppliers, and the fact that he left no records ordering these vintages from these châteaux is not absolutely conclusive. He did have some of his *cases*, but never his *bottles*, marked with diamonds or initials. Some unknown persons could conceivably have had the bottles prepared for Jefferson and Washington as gifts, with the delivery being interrupted by the violence of the Revolution, when they could have been hidden away, their owners killed, and the bottles forgotten.

It is always hard to prove a negative, i.e., to show that Jefferson did *not* order or possess the mystery bottles. It is even harder to prove that he *did*, however, when no documents specifically support it, especially in an area where so many documents still exist. Why, of all the thousands of wines he recorded having, many of them cheap and minor, did he fail to mention the only bottles ever alleged to have had his initials on them? And why, of all years, did 1787, which appears from several of his letters not to have been a very good one across France, turn out to be the main ones to appear? So far none of these questions have been definitively answered.[7]

To speculate credibly, Jefferson's purchases and his comments on them must be considered from beginning to end. The references in this book are just a beginning. Inevitably, as everyone who has studied Jefferson seriously has learned, sooner or later some new letter or memo may turn up somewhere, somehow.

Taking a Stand?

Faced with such a conflict, one appreciates the principled straddle taken by my old friend, the respected trial judge, law professor, and wine lover Noah Sweat, who told the Mississippi legislature in 1952, when asked if he was for or against the repealing of Prohibition:

MY FRIENDS,

I do not shun controversy. I will take a stand on any issue at any time. Here is how I feel. If when you say whiskey you mean the devil's brew that dethrones reason and creates misery and poverty, then certainly I am against it.

But if, when you say whiskey, you mean the oil of conversation, the philosophic wine that enables man, if only for a little while, to forget life's heartaches and sorrows, then certainly I am for it.

That is my stand. I will not retreat from it. I will not compromise.

(Excerpted from speech of Noah S. Sweat, Jr., April 4, 1952)

With no scientific evidence yet publicly available, and since I have studied only the Jefferson records and have not been able either to see or taste the wine or interview Mr. Rodenstock or Mr. Broadbent on the subject, it would be premature to express here any final conclusion about the authenticity of the bottles. Personally, however, I stand firmly with the experts at Monticello. Even as this book goes to the printer, rumors are circulating that a lawsuit challenging certain bottles is about to be filed in federal court in New York. Interested readers are encouraged to delve further into the extensive Jefferson records cited here and to judge for themselves, preferably with the aid of a future book devoted entirely to the subject. As with his women, it may yet take the equivalent of a vinous DNA test of the wines, the corks, and the bottles themselves to settle this latest Jefferson controversy.[18]

NOTES

1. Basic biographical data are from the late Dr. Dumas Malone's six-volume biography, *Jefferson and His Time*, unless otherwise specified. Citations to standard sources, such as the major sets of papers, are by volume number, principal editor, and page number. The magnificent edition of *The Papers of Thomas Jefferson* begun by the late Dr. Julian Boyd is still incomplete. Those papers which remain unedited have been split into two parts. Papers on the retirement years (1809 to 1826) are being edited by Dr. Jefferson Looney, formerly of Princeton and now director of the Retirement Papers Project for the Thomas Jefferson Memorial Foundation at Monticello. The papers from Jefferson's eight years as president are being edited at Princeton by the latest able successor to Dr. Boyd, Dr. Barbara Oberg.

Documents available from microfilm or originals from the Library of Congress (DLC), Princeton, the Thomas Jefferson Memorial Foundation at Monticello (TJMF), the University of Virginia (UVa), or the Massachusetts Historical Society (MHi) or Missouri Historical Society (MoHi) are similarly cited and abbreviated. The *Papers* at the Library of Congress may be found online at http://memory.loc.gov/ammem/mtjhtml/mtjhome.html. Jefferson's voluminous account records, known variously in the past as the account books, memorandum books, and pocket memorandum books, have been magnificently edited and copiously footnoted by James Bear, Jr., and Lucia Cinder Stanton in two volumes comprising 1,624 interesting pages, and are cited herein as *MB* with volume and page numbers.

There being such a bewildering proliferation of currencies and wine containers, from guilders to millreas and from butts to pipes, no overall list of such is attempted. Each item is explained in context and may also be located through the index. The same goes for capacities of wineglasses, tumblers, cups, decanters, etc. The remaining wineglasses at Monticello hold from three to five ounces each.

Introduction

1. Dumas Malone, *Jefferson and His Time* (Little, Brown 1948–1981), vol. 2, 369.
2. James A. Bear, Jr., ed., *Jefferson at Monticello* (UVa Press 1967). This volume includes the reminiscences of Isaac Jefferson, "Memoirs of a Monticello Slave," and of Jefferson's overseer Edmund Bacon, "The Private Life of Thomas Jefferson."
3. Joseph J. Ellis, *American Sphinx* (Knopf 1997); Andrew Burstein, *The Inner Jefferson: Portrait of a Grieving Optimist* (UVa 1995); Joseph Wheelan, *Jefferson's Vendetta* (Carroll and Graf 2005); Roger G. Kennedy, *Mr. Jefferson's Lost Cause* (Oxford 2003).
4. Ellis, supra, 317.
5. An excellent concise history of Jefferson's evolving image may be found in R. B. Bernstein's *Thomas Jefferson* (Oxford 2003), 191–98. See also Jack McLaughlin, *Jefferson and Monticello: The Biography of a Builder* (Holt 1988), which fairly rehumanizes Jefferson in context. To restore one's faith in Jefferson, see Eric Petersen, *Light and Liberty: Reflections on the Pursuit of Happiness* (Modern Library 2004), a 150-page compilation of his wise sayings organized under thirty-four Jefferson-like categories from "Enthusiasm" and "Fitness" to "Living in the Present" and "Life Acceptance."
6. Randall 344.
7. *Papers*, vol. 17, 493.
8. DLC, discussed in more detail in chapter 6.
9. Lyman H. Butterfield, ed., *Diary and Autobiography of John Adams* (Harvard U. Press), vol. 3, 306.
10. John C. Fitzpatrick, ed., *The Writings of Washington from the Original Manuscript Sources, 1745–1799* (GPO 1944), vol. 2, 321.
11. Ibid., 322.
12. Ibid., 481.
13. Ibid., vol. 2, 395, 436; vol. 3, 143; vol. 26, 448.

14. Harold C. Syrett, ed., *Writings of Hamilton* (Columbia U. Press 1979), vol. 8, 304–5.
15. Fitzpatrick, ed., *Writings*, vol. 2, 92.
16. William Younger, *Gods, Men and Wine* (Wine and Food Society 1966), 373.
17. Bergh, vol. 15, 186–87.
18. To Dr. J. F. O. Fernandez, December 16, 1815, DLC.
19. Letter of May 26, 1819, DLC.
20. To Don Josef Yznardi, May 10, 1803, DLC.
21. Bear, *Jefferson at Monticello*, 13.
22. Bergh, vol. 15, 178. To De Neuville, December 13, 1818.
23. Readers interested in that controversy should consult the article in *Nature* magazine on DNA tests comparing samples from Jefferson's paternal uncle Field Jefferson with samples from a direct descendant of Sally Hemings's son Eston and the well-reasoned analysis of the Hemings family story by NYU law professor Annette Gordon-Reed, then compare these conclusions with the anti-Hemings position set forth by Cynthia H. Burton in *Jefferson Vindicated* (Keswick VA 2005), critiquing the DNA study and its uses.
24. *Gourmet*, February 1991, 42.
25. See "Mazzei Brothers," *Wine Spectator*, December 15, 2005.

Chapter 1. Early Wines

1. Unless otherwise specified, all biographical information is taken from Malone, *Jefferson*, vol. 1.
2. Edwin Betts, ed., *Thomas Jefferson's Garden Book* (Am. Philo. Soc. 1944), 39 (hereafter referred to as *GB*).
3. Original documents furnished by the Colonial Williamsburg Society.
4. Jane Carson, *Colonial Virginians at Play* (UVa 1965), 39–40.
5. Ibid., 266–70.
6. George Rainbird, *Sherry and Wines of Spain* (McGraw-Hill 1966), 135.
7. Henderson, supra, 309.
8. *Oxford English Dictionary*, 1970 printing, 93.
9. John Hull Brown, *Early American Beverages* (Bonanza 1966), 115.
10. T. J. Randolph, ed., *Memoirs of Thomas Jefferson* (London 1829), 79.
11. Malone, *Jefferson*, vol. 1, 129.
12. The best short history of Madeira is in Hugh Johnson's masterful book *Vintage: The Story of Wine* (Simon & Schuster 1989), 243–51. There are

fuller histories of Madeira; the most entertaining, written in an old-fashioned style by a cousin of playwright Noel Coward's, is Noel Cossart's *Madeira: The Island Vineyard* (Christie's 1984). Zarco is referred to in some places not as "blue-eyed" but as "one-eyed," a piratical image. Perhaps it was a nickname pinned on him by his Moorish enemies, since the Arabic word "ashqar" can have both meanings.

13. Bear, *Jefferson at Monticello*, 9.
14. Betts, ed., *GB*, 618.
15. Ibid., 239.
16. Samuel Eliot Morison, *Oxford History of the American People* (Oxford Univ. 1965), 207–8.
17. Ibid.
18. Mazzei's account of his amazing career may be read in his own words, translated: *Memoirs of the Life and Peregrinations of the Florentine Philip Mazzei 1730–1816.* There is also a thorough analysis of his extensive dealings with Jefferson in Richard Garlick, *Philip Mazzei, Friend of Jefferson* (Baltimore 1933), 39–43.
19. Cyrus Redding, *A History and Description of Modern Wines* (London 1833, 1876), 281.
20. Malone, *Jefferson*, vol. 1, 197.
21. Bear, *Jefferson at Monticello*, 9.
22. Sarah N. Randolph, *The Domestic Life of Thomas Jefferson* (Charlottesville 1871), 35–36.
23. Marquis de Chastellux, *Travels in North America in the Years 1780, 1781 and 1782*, trans. Howard C. Rice, Jr. (UNC 1963), vol. 2, 369.
24. Fitzpatrick, *Writings*, 394–95.
25. Chastellux, *Travels*, vol. 1, 132–33.
26. Ibid.
27. Ibid.
28. Ibid., vol. 2, 387–88.
29. Ibid., vol. 2, 392.
30. Ibid., vol. 2, 391.
31. Ibid., 390.
32. *Papers*, vol. 6, 270; *MB* for October 31, 1780.
33. Claude Bowers, *The Young Jefferson* (Boston 1945), 24.
34. *Papers*, vol. 7, 203, 262.
35. Ibid., vol. 1, 576.
36. Ibid., vol. 7, 175.
37. Ibid., 148, 229, 363.

38. Ibid., 30.
39. Ibid., 175.
40. Ibid., 263.

Chapter 2. Thomas Jefferson Goes to Paris (1784–1787)

1. *MB*; Malone, *Jefferson*, vol. 2, 4–5. As in other chapters, all biographical details are taken from Dr. Malone unless otherwise specified.
2. *Papers*, vol. 8, 437; Ford, vol. 4, 5.
3. Marie Kimball, *Jefferson: The Scene of Europe* (New York 1950), 9.
4. Ford, vol. 4, 404.
5. Randolph, *Domestic Life*, 78.
6. Albert H. Smyth, *The Writings of Benjamin Franklin* (New York 1907), vol. 1, p. 216.
7. Ford, vol. 10, 105.
8. *Papers*, vol. 8, 558.
9. Ibid., vol. 7, 601; ibid., vol. 8, 93–95.
10. Randolph, *Domestic Life*, 103.
11. Ibid.
12. *Papers*, vol. 7, 252.
13. Ibid., 545.
14. *Papers*, vol. 8, 43.
15. Ibid., vol. 9, 465.
16. Ford, vol. 5, 293.
17. *Papers*, vol. 11, 262.
18. The material on Franklin here cited all comes from George H. McKee, "Was Revolutionary America Dry?" *Commonweal*, 609 et seq. (Oct. 26, 1932). See also Younger, *Gods*, 45, and Malone, *Jefferson*, vol. 2, 16.
19. *Papers*, vol. 8, 166.
20. Ibid., 172.
21. Ibid., 183.
22. Ibid.
23. Ibid., 183.
24. Ibid., 354.
25. DLC.
26. *MB*, November 23, 1785.
27. Ibid., November 17, December 29, 1785.

28. *Papers*, vol. 8, 568–69.

29. Ibid., vol. 9, 210.

30. Ibid., 211.

31. Ibid., vol. 10, 66; ibid., vol. 9, 298.

32. Ibid., vol. 10, 196.

33. Mazzei, *Memoirs*, 291–93.

34. *Papers*, vol. 7, 386–89.

35. Ibid., vol. 9, 252.

36. Ibid., 623.

37. Edward Dumbauld, *Thomas Jefferson, American Tourist* (UOkla 1946), 70.

38. Kimball, *Jefferson*, 129.

39. Saul K. Padover, *The Complete Jefferson* (Mentor 1952), 895, letter of January 1, 1789.

40. *Papers*, vol. 9, 350.

41. Randolph, *Domestic Life*, 53.

42. Adrienne Koch and William Peden, eds., *The Life and Selected Writings of Thomas Jefferson (Random House* 1944), 39.

43. *MB*, June 16, 1786.

44. *Papers*, vol. 7, 134–37.

45. Ibid., vol. 10, 129.

46. See reproduction of Paris cellar of May 1787, located at end of *Papers* volume for 1790.

47. *Papers*, vol. 10, 199.

48. Ibid., 356.

49. Ibid., vol. 12, 529.

50. Malone, *Jefferson*, vol. 2, 45.

51. *Papers*, vol. 10, 250.

52. Ford, vol. 7, 330.

53. *Papers*, vol. 10, 478.

54. Ibid., 460, 467, 524, 543, 594.

55. Ibid., vol. 6, 112; Kaplan, *Jefferson*, 17.

56. *Papers*, vol. 11, 203.

57. Ibid., 214.

58. Ibid., 211–13.

59. Ibid., 472.

Jefferson to Parent: à Paris ce 14me. Juin 1787. "Si vous croyez, Monsieur, que le vin de Voulenayé et le vin de Meursault de la qualité nommée Goutte d'or peuvent etre transportes à Paris pendant les chaleurs actuelles, je vous prierai de m'envoyer une feuillette de chacune de ces deux especes, en bouteilles, des meilleures crues, et de la recolte qui est la meilleure pour etre bu le moment actuel. Vous aurez la bonté de m'indiquer la personne auquel je pourrai faire toucher le montant, ce que je ferai le moment que vous me la ferez connoitre. Il faudra m'avertir un peu en avance de l'arrivée des vins, afin que je peux faire prendre les arrangemens necessaires au bureau de la douane de Paris. Je vous prierai de faire cette expedition sans perte de tems, les vins etant destinés pour le moment actuel. Il n'y a que trois jours que je suis de retour de ma voyage. J'ai l'honneur d'etre avec des sentimens d'estime tres distingués, Monsieur, votre trés humble et trés obeissant serviteur,

TH: JEFFERSON

P.S. Mettez sur toutes les lettres de voiture & c. que ce sont des Vins ordinaires, et si le voiturier consentiroit d'entrer Paris par la grille des champs elysées, ce me donneroit moins d'embarras, parce que ma maison touche à cette grille–la. C'est la partie de Paris la plus eloignée de vous, ainsi vous aurez la bonté d'arranger avec le voiturier combien il faundra lui payer d'extraordinaire pour ca."

60. *Papers*, vol. 11, 484–85.
61. Ibid., 608.
62. Ibid., 246–48.
63. Ibid., 297.
64. Ibid., 270–73.
65. Ibid., 283–85.
66. Ibid., vol. 8, 635.
67. Ibid., vol. 11, 334.
68. Ibid., vol. 13, 435.
69. Ibid., vol. 11, 270.
70. Ibid., 464.
71. Quoted in Alexander Henderson, *The History of Ancient and Modern Wines* (London 1824), 338.
72. Younger, *Gods*, 385–86.
73. Dumbauld, *Thomas Jefferson*, 105.
74. Ibid., 106.
75. *Papers*, vol. 13, 268.

76. Ibid., 415–60, excerpted.
77. Ibid., 464.
78. Ibid., 273.
79. Ibid.
80. Ibid.
81. Ibid.
82. Ibid.
83. Ibid., 271.
84. Ibid., 273–74.
85. Ibid.
86. Randolph, *Domestic Life*, 91.

CHAPTER 3. JEFFERSON STOCKS HIS PARIS WINE CELLAR (1787–1788)

1. *Papers*, vol. 12, 14.
2. Ibid., 32.
3. Randolph, *Domestic Life*, 122.
4. Ibid., 124.
5. Ibid.
6. Ford, vol. 2, 116.
7. Malone, *Jefferson*, vol. 2, 137.
8. *Papers*, vol. 11, 627.
9. An excellent full-length description of which may be found in Susan Mary Alsop, *Yankees at the Court: The First Americans in Paris* (Doubleday 1982).
10. *Papers*, vol. 12, 217; *Papers*, vol. 14, 290.
11. Ibid., vol. 11, 575.
12. A modern psychoanalytical study of it may be found in the chapter by the same name in Fawn Brodie, *Thomas Jefferson: An Intimate History* (Norton 1974), 199–227. The entire letter is reproduced in Brodie at 483–92.
13. *Papers*, vol. 12, 127.
14. Ibid., vol. 11, 644–47.
15. Alexis Lichine, *Encyclopedia of Wines and Spirits* (Knopf 1982), 223.
16. Account book for December 21, 1785. See also Gazaigner letters to Adams of April 7, 21, 1785 (MHi).

17. Louis Jacquelin and Rene Poulain, *The Wines and Vinyards of France* (Hamlyn 1962), 253–56; Hugh Johnson, *World Atlas of Wine*, 3d ed. (Simon & Schuster), 1985, 135.

18. *Papers*, vol. 13, 664.

19. Younger, *Gods*, 363. See also H. Warner Allen, *The Wines of Portugal* (McGraw-Hill 1963), 170.

20. Re Commaraine, see Hubrecht Duijker, *The Great Wines of Burgundy* (Crescent 1983), 104–9; and H. W. Yoxall, *Burgundy* (Stein and Day 1968), 81–82.

21. *Papers*, vol. 11, 431.

22. Ibid., 455.

23. Ibid., 465.

24. Ibid., vol. 12, 516.

25. From Parent, February 3, 1788.

26. Ibid.

27. *Papers*, vol. 12, 612.

28. Ibid., vol. 13, 634–36.

29. Ibid., 636.

30. Ibid., vol. 14, 656.

31. Ibid., vol. 13, 480–81.

32. Ibid., vol. 14, 570.

33. Ibid., 639.

34. Ibid., 679.

35. Ibid., vol. 15, 102.

36. Ibid., 155.

37. Ibid., vol. 8, 93.

38. Ibid., vol. 10, 66, 136, 196.

39. Ibid., vol. 11, 378.

40. Ibid., 396.

41. That letter is quoted in note 56, infra.

42. *Papers*, vol. 11, 672.

43. Ibid., 23.

44. Ibid., vol. 12, 132.

45. Ibid., 434.

46. Ibid., 435.

47. Ibid., 500.

48. Ibid., 514.

49. Ibid., 541.

50. Ibid., 560.

51. Ibid., vol. 14, 45.

52. Ibid., 45.

53. Ibid., vol. 12, 561.

54. Ibid., 593.

55. Ibid., vol. 14, 280; ibid., vol. 12, 133.

56. Ibid., vol. 12, 616.

57. Ibid., 594.

58. Ibid., 617.

59. Ibid., 648.

60. Ibid., vol. 13, 96.

61. Ibid.

62. Ibid., 171.

63. Ibid., 297.

64. Ibid., 204.

65. Ibid., 541.

66. Ibid., vol. 14, 335.

67. Ibid., 45.

68. Ibid., 353.

69. Ibid., 280.

70. See particularly Cocks and Feret, *Bordeaux and Its Wines* (Wine Appreciation Guild 1986), and Robert M. Parker, Jr., *Bordeaux* (Simon & Schuster 1991), 924–25. See also discussions in Edmund Penning-Rowsell, *The Wines of Bordeaux*, 5th ed. (Wine Appreciation Guild 1985), 192, 425–50; Michel Dovaz, *Encyclopedia of the Great Wines of Bordeaux* (1981); and David Peppercorn, *Bordeaux* (Faber & Faber 1982).

71. Penning-Rowsell, *Wines*, 309, 396.

72. Peppercorn, *Bordeaux*, 57–69.

73. *Papers*, vol. 11, 621.

74. Ibid., 622.

75. Ibid., 464.

76. Ibid., 552.

77. Ibid., vol. 12, 226.

78. Ibid., 353.

79. Ibid., 291.

80. Malone, *Jefferson*, vol. 2, 197–98.

81. See treatment in detail in chapter 6.

82. *Papers*, vol. 19, 267.

83. Ibid., vol. 12, 133.

84. Ibid., vol. 14, 280.

85. Ibid., vol. 12, 133.

Chapter 4. Jefferson Tours and Tastes in the Vineyards of the Rhine, the Mosel, and Champagne (1788–1789)

1. *Papers*, vol. 8, 10.

2. Ibid., 63.

3. Dumbauld, *Thomas Jefferson*, 110–11; Autobiography, 123–26.

4. Autobiography, 123–26; Malone, *Jefferson*, vol. 2, 146.

5. Malone, *Jefferson*, vol. 2, 191; Kimball, *Jefferson*, 212–13.

6. Dumbauld, *Thomas Jefferson*, 116.

7. Kimball, *Jefferson*, 218–23.

8. *Papers*, vol. 12, 680.

9. Ibid., 691.

10. Ibid., vol. 13, 48.

11. Ibid.

12. Ibid., vol. 12, 614–15.

13. Lichine, *Encyclopedia*, 328.

14. Begins at *Papers*, vol. 13, 12 et seq.

15. Ibid., 260.

16. Ibid., 48.

17. Ibid., 279–280.

18. Leon Adams, *The Wines of America*, 3rd ed. (McGraw-Hill 1985), 91. For an excellent discussion of Champagnes in Jefferson's time, see Redding, *History*, 96–116.

19. Malone, *Jefferson*, vol. 2, 192.

20. Ibid., 172.

21. *Papers*, vol. 13, 210–13.

22. *Thomas Jefferson—Writings* (Library of America 1984), 919–20.

23. Ford, vol. 2, 444.

24. *Papers*, vol. 13, 356.

25. Ibid., 374.

26. Ibid., 444–48.

27. Lawrence, *Jefferson and Wine*, 90.

28. *Papers*, vol. 13, 527.

29. Ibid., 642.

30. Ibid.

31. Malone, *Jefferson*, vol. 2, 205–6.

32. *Papers*, vol. 14, 343.

33. Ibid., vol. 13, 654.

34. Ibid., vol. 15, 66.

35. Ibid., 67.

36. Gouverneur Morris, *A Diary of the French Revolution*, 2 vols., ed. B. C. Davenport (Houghton Mifflin 1939).

37. Fitzpatrick, ed., *Writings*, 453.

38. Morris, *Diary*, vol. 1, xi.

39. Ibid., 106.

40. Ibid., 247.

41. Ibid., 106–7.

42. Ibid., 142.

43. *Papers*, vol. 14, 295.

44. Morris, *Diary*, vol. 1, xxxii.

45. Ibid., 17.

46. Ibid., 164.

47. Ibid., 184.

48. Ibid., 187.

49. Ibid., vol. 2, 223.

50. Ibid., vol. 1, 222.

51. Ibid., 36.

52. Ibid., 37.

53. Ibid., 83.

54. Ibid., 80.

55. Ibid., 156.

56. Ibid., 426–27.

57. Ibid., 559.

58. Ibid., 215.

59. Ibid., xvii.

60. Ibid., xxix.

61. Morris, *Diary*, vol. 2, 297, 307.

62. Ibid., vol. 1, 61.

63. Ibid., vol. 2, 303.

64. Ibid., vol. 1, 159.

65. Malone, *Jefferson*, vol. 2, 234.

66. *Papers*, vol. 14, 426.

67. Brodie, *Thomas Jefferson*, 290.
68. Malone, *Jefferson*, vol. 2, 235.
69. Morris, *Diary*, vol. 1, 167.
70. Ibid., 166.
71. *Papers*, vol. 15, 48–49.
72. Ibid., 436.
73. Ibid., 375–76.
74. Ibid., 477–78.
75. Ibid., 491–99.
76. Malone, *Jefferson*, vol. 2, 241.
77. *Papers*, vol. 8, 635–37.
78. Ford, vol. 1, 148.

Chapter 5. The Return to America
(1789–1800)

1. Bergh, vol. 10, 286. Brodie, *Thomas Jefferson*, 246.
2. *Papers*, vol. 15, 519.
3. Ibid., vol. 16, 38.
4. Ibid., 80–81.
5. Ibid., vol. 15, 563.
6. Ibid., vol. 16, 228–29.
7. Ibid., 494.
8. McKee, "Was Revolutionary America Dry?"
9. *Papers*, vol. 16, 292.
10. Ibid., 323.
11. Ibid., 493.
12. Ibid., vol. 17, 476.
13. Ibid., 573–80.
14. Ibid., 321–22.
15. Ibid., 342.
16. Malone, *Jefferson*, vol. 2, 319. Dumbauld, *Thomas Jefferson*, 159.
17. *Papers*, vol. 17, 421.
18. Ibid., 496. See also account book for August 12, 1790, noting in TJ's handwriting the memo enclosed in this letter listing the wines intended for George Washington.
19. *Papers*, vol. 17, 493.
20. Ibid., 494.

21. Ibid.
22. Ibid.
23. Ibid., 322.
24. Ibid., 653.
25. Ibid., vol. 18, 3.
26. Ibid., vol. 17, 315–18.
27. Ibid., vol. 18, 600.
28. Ibid., 355.
29. Ibid., 494.
30. Ibid.
31. Malone, *Jefferson*, vol. 2, 258. See also *The Journal of William Maclay* (1927), 265.
32. Morison, *Oxford History*, 329.
33. Malone, *Jefferson*, vol. 2, 474.
34. *Papers*, vol. 20, 623.
35. Ibid., 622.
36. Ibid., 333.
37. Ibid., 372.
38. Ibid., 418.
39. Ibid., 685.
40. Ibid., 404.
41. Ibid., 419.
42. Malone, *Jefferson*, vol. 2, 360.
43. *Papers*, vol. 20, 471.
44. Ibid., vol. 18, 513.
45. Ibid., vol. 19, 119.
46. Ibid., 334.
47. Ibid., 266.
48. Ibid., 630.
49. Ibid., vol. 20, 249.
50. Ibid., vol. 17, 342.
51. Ibid., vol. 20, 569.
52. DLC.
53. *Papers*, vol. 20, 573. The "Fox" referred to was probably the English Whig Charles James Fox (1749–1806).
54. Ibid., 590.
55. Ibid., 345.
56. Ibid., 382, 670.

57. Ibid., 646.

58. Ibid., 647.

59. Ibid., 691.

60. Ibid., vol. 18, 34.

61. Ibid., vol. 17, 297. So remarkable is that letter for its phonetic spelling and phraseology that it is reproduced here in its "original" form insofar as it relates to wine: FROM PETIT, paris Ce 3 Aaout 1790, "Monsieur je prans laliberte de vous Ecrire pour vous dire que mes parans Sesont oposé pour que jail vous rejoindre. Outre Cela Cest que les gages que vous me proposé Sont trop mediocre pour alle Siloiens. Je fais, tout henballe, tour pour le mieux. Je crois que vous de vé recevoir le tout Bien condisionné. Vous dite Si il iaduvin dele faire maittre henboutele. Voila omoiens troiy ans quil ne vous est poiens venu duvin henpieces. Il sitrouve 600 Boutele devin tont que Konyacque que grave et pagnerais et frontignon et autre vin des pagne. Il ia dons toutes les Caisses des Carte de tout les noms des vin."

62. *Papers*, vol. 20, 35.

63. Ibid., 713.

64. Kaplan, *Jefferson*, 38, 42.

65. *Papers*, vol. 20, 647.

66. Ibid., vol. 27, 842–44. Original document in the Collection of Herbert R. Strauss, first published by the Newberry Library in 1965 with an introduction by Lawrence W. Towner.

67. Bergh, vol. 8, 335.

68. Malone, *Jefferson*, vol. 3, 59.

69. Fenwick sent him fourteen cases of precisely such wine, the best *vin ordinaire* of 1788, in their strongest bottles, on May 16, 1793. Jefferson received Fenwick's letter on August 16, 1793. *Papers*, vol. 26, 45–46, 387–88, 661, 718–19, 739.

70. Bergh, vol. 8, 434. He paid the freight on a pipe of Lisbon he had ordered anyway as shown in account book of January 8, 1793, and purchased three more pipes of Termo from Lisbon on April 21, 1793, at a cost of $225. *Papers*, vol. 26, 92, 170–71, 188.

71. *Papers*, vol. 26, 746–47. Micro at Montico.

72. Dumbauld, *Thomas Jefferson*, 239. A personal note here: I once argued a case before Judge Dumbauld, who was sitting with the Fifth Circuit Court of Appeals. Neither of us realized the other was writing a book on Thomas Jefferson.

73. Randolph, *Domestic Life*, 185.

74. Malone, *Jefferson*, vol. 3, 137. Rush knew of such open-air dinners, having enjoyed one with Jefferson that year. *Papers*, vol. 26, 638.

75. *Papers*, vol. 26, 758; *Papers*, vol. 27, 60, 661.

76. Randolph, *Domestic Life*, 192.

77. Malone, *Jefferson*, vol. 3, 168.

78. Ibid., 217.

79. Randolph, *Domestic Life*, 193.

80. Ibid., 242, letter of March 3, 1802.

81. Randall, vol. 3, 333.

82. See, e.g., Karen Hess, ed., *Martha Washington's Booke of Cookery* (Columbia 1981), 168, and "claret" entries in account book of Nov. 16, 1792, Jan. 7, 1793, June 14, 1793, and August 18, 1793.

83. Malone, *Jefferson*, vol. 3, 188–89.

84. Harold C. Syrett, ed., *Papers of Alexander Hamilton* (Columbia 1979), vol. 6, 168–83, vol. 11, 143, 146–47.

85. *Papers*, vol. 28, 448–49.

86. Malone, *Jefferson*, vol. 3, 201–7.

87. Ibid., 217.

88. Le Duc de la Rochefoucauld-Liancourt, *Travels Through the United States of America*, 1795–1797, 2d ed. (London, 1800), vol. 3, quoted in Koch and Peden, eds., *Life*, 41.

89. Isaac Weld, Jr., *Travels Through the United States of North America*, 1795–97, 4th ed. (London, 1800); Malone, *Jefferson*, vol. 3, 237.

90. Ford, vol. 7, 93.

91. Ibid., 120.

92. Ibid., 113.

93. Randolph, *Domestic Life*, 343.

94. Jefferson's accounts with Francis reflect mostly just "wine," porter, etc. *Papers*, vol. 29, 469; *Papers*, vol. 30, 436; *Papers*, vol. 31, 69, 582.

95. Malone, *Jefferson*, vol. 3, 299.

96. Ibid., 267.

97. Quoted in *The Planter's Advocate*, no. 38, May 17, 1854 (document on file at Monticello).

98. Brodie, *Thomas Jefferson*, 309.

99. Foley, ed., *Jeffersonian Cyclopedia*, #4628, 494.

100. Micro at Montico.

101. Malone, *Jefferson*, vol. 3, 332.

102. Ibid., 335.

103. Micro at Montico dated March 12, 23, 1801.

Chapter 6. Wine in the President's House (1801–1809)

1. William Plumer, Jr., ed., *The Life of William Plumer* (Boston 1857).
2. M. B. Tincom, ed., "Caviar Along the Pontomac: Sir Augustus Foster's 'Notes on the United States, 1804–1812,'" *William and Mary Quarterly* (January 1951).
3. Leon Adams, *The Wines of America*, 3d ed. (McGraw-Hill 1985), 568.
4. Henderson, *History*, supra, 318–19.
5. James S. Young, *The Washington Community*, 1800–1828 (New York 1966), 167.
6. Malone, *Jefferson*, vol. 4, 159.
7. Brodie, *Thomas Jefferson*, 336.
8. Malone, *Jefferson*, vol. 4, 47.
9. Ibid.
10. Brodie, *Thomas Jefferson*, 369.
11. *MB*, end 1803.
12. Ibid.
13. Lawrence S. Kaplan, *Jefferson and France* (Yale 1967), 93.
14. Fitzpatrick, ed., *Writings*, vol. 2, 384, 398, 436, 481; vol. 3, 143.
15. Unless otherwise specified, all Jefferson wine letters in this chapter came from the microfilm at the Library of Congress, and wherever possible were cross-checked against copies at Princeton and Monticello. In such cases, no specific footnote will be added to identify them.
16. The same practice will be followed in citing the *Memorandum Books*.
17. Malone, *Jefferson*, vol. 4, 97.
18. Ibid., vol. 5, 78, 235.
19. Ibid., vol. 4, 58.
20. Some names of Champagne proprietors are only partially legible, and, eighteenth-century spelling being somewhat arbitrary, it is difficult to decipher them precisely.
21. Viz. Skipwith replies of August 7, 1803, and October 25, 1803.
22. A *milrea* was a Portuguese gold coin worth a thousand *reis*, which was worth about ten British shillings at that time.
23. Malone, *Jefferson*, vol. 4, 68–70, 80.
24. *National Intelligencer*, December 3, 1804.
25. Bryan, *National Capital*, vol. 1, 224, 337, 410.
26. Viz. George Robertson, *Port* (Faber & Faber 1982), 31–21; John Delaforce, *The Factory House at Oporto* (Christie's 1979).
27. *Family Letters*, 352–53.
28. DLC.

29. *Family Letters*, 371.

30. Henderson, *History*, 192; Penzer, *Book*, 123; Younger, *Gods*, 364

31. Penzer, *Book*, 128.

32. Fiske Kimball, *Thomas Jefferson, Architect*, 2d ed. (DeCapo Press), plate 175; Saul Padover, ed., *Thomas Jefferson and the National Capital* (USGPO 1946).

33. Bear, *Jefferson at Monticello*, 104.

34. Ibid., 13.

35. Ibid., 106–7.

36. John C Van Horne and Lee W. Formwalt, eds. *The Correspondence and Miscellaneous Papers of Benjamin Henry Latrobe* (Yale U. Press 1984), vol. 1, 232.

37. Saul K. Padover, ed., *The Complete Jefferson* (Duell, Sloan), 309.

38. Malone, *Jefferson*, vol. 4, 377–79, 382–92; see also Jefferson to William Short, January 23, 1804, LCmicro.

39. Foster's notes, supra. These are not that reliable, however, not having been written until 1833. Malone, *Jefferson*, vol. 5, 681.

40. Malone, *Jefferson*, vol. 4, 374. Later historians dispute that Plumer himself ever said this, believing his son added it when he edited his papers, supra. Plumer was actually rather pro-Jefferson for a Federalist.

41. W. P. Cutler and J. P. Cutler, eds., *The Life, Journals and Correspondence of Rev. Manasseh Cutler, L.L.D.* (Cincinnati 1888), vol. 1, 71–72.

42. Margaret Bayard Smith, *The First Forty Years of Washington Society* (Scribner's 1906), 388–89.

43. Ibid., 392–93.

44. Malone, Jefferson, vol. 5, 184.

45. Smith, *First Forty Years*, 402–3.

46. "Dr. Mitchill's Letters From Washington: 1801–1813," *Harper's*, vol. 58, 743–44; Malone, *Jefferson*, vol. 4, 374.

47. Charles Francis Adams, ed., *Memoirs of John Quincy Adams, Comprising Portions of His Diary from 1795 to 1848* (Philadelphia 1874), 60–61, 272, 316–17, 330–31, 378, 381, 457–53, 480–81.

48. Ibid.

49. Malone, *Jefferson*, vol. 4, 373–75.

50. Ibid., 106–8.

51. Ibid., 338–39.

52. Brodie, *Thomas Jefferson*, 412.

53. Randolph, *Domestic Life*, 255.

54. Malone, *Jefferson*, vol. 4, 407, 413–15.

55. "Fining" is a sort of filtering, done in the traditional way by dropping fresh egg whites in the casks to aid precipitation of extraneous matter. Jefferson,

by his comments, had become rather knowledgeable in wines, and was the classic conservative connoisseur in not fining his wines but letting their sediments drop naturally, then racking them off from the bottom of the cask.

56. See Cyril Ray, *The Wines of Italy* (Octopus 1966), 153–44, and Dorozynski and Bell, *The Wine Book* (Golden 1969), 165.

57. Maurice Healy, *Stay Me with Flagons* (London 1940), 121.

58. Source: College of William and Mary Library, James Barron Papers, Box 2, Folder 5.

59. T. J. Randolph, ed., *Memoirs of Thomas Jefferson* (London 1829), vol. 4, 79; Bergh, vol. 1, 217.

60. Bear, *Jefferson at Monticello*, 105.

61. Malone, *Jefferson*, vol. 5, 528.

Chapter 7. Retirement at Monticello (1809–1826)

1. Biographical details in this chapter are from volume 6 of Malone, *Jefferson* (*The Sage of Monticello*) and will not be separately cited except in special circumstances.

2. Ford, vol. 9, 329.

3. Randolph, *Domestic Life*, 326.

4. Statement of Benjamin Parker in 1824, on file at Monticello.

5. Brodie, *Thomas Jefferson*, 424.

6. For Scuppernong today, see Clarence Gohdes, *Scuppernong* (Duke U. Press 1982).

7. Smith, *First Forty Years*, 67–68.

8. On file at Monticello.

9. DLC.

10. DLC.

11. Koch and Peden, eds., *Life*, 602.

12. Betts, ed., *GB*, to John Dortie, 462; to William Dorsey January 15, 1812; from Bernard McMahon in Philadelphia on February 28, 1812; from James Ronaldson November 2, 1812; from William Dorsey on November 7, 1812.

13. To James Ronaldson, January 12, 1813.

14. Randolph, *Domestic Life*, 300.

15. Koch and Peden, eds., *Life*, 615.

16. DLC.

17. Padover, ed., *The Complete Jefferson*, 76–85.

18. Ibid.

19. Randall, vol. 3, 343.

20. Bear, *Jefferson at Monticello*, 12.

21. Ibid., 100.

22. *Family Letters*, 137–38.

23. Betts, ed., *GB*, 533. Two years later he wrote a nearly identical letter to Gov. James Barbour; *GB*, 566.

24. Ibid., 574.

25. Ibid., 618.

26. Ibid., 95, 100.

27. Brown, *Early American Beverages*, 39–46.

28. It appears that at one point Jefferson tried to grow his own hops as well—"manure & make up hop-hills." Betts, ed., *GB*, 473 (February 1, 1812).

29. *Farm Book*, January 16, 1816; March 11, 1817.

30. Randolph, *Domestic Life*, 109.

31. See letter of Mazzei's daughter dated May 8, 1825. Winterthur Portfolio, 126.

32. See Burton Anderson in *Food & Wine*, December 1983, Winterthur Portfolio, 126.

33. Mazzei, *Memoirs*, 123–24.

34. For a detailed history of the region, see Lamberto Paronetto, *Chianti: The Story of Florence and Its Wines* (Wine & Spirit Publications 1970), and Raymond Flower, *Chianti: The Land, the People and the Wine* (Universe, N.Y., 1979).

35. Anderson, *Wines of Italy*, 64.

36. Unfortunately the "printed paper" on Paillerols has not been found.

37. Vin Santo is a classic Italian wine, rich and sweet, made from dried grapes, often excellent.

38. Jacquelin and Poulain, eds., *Wines*, supra, 254; Morton Shand, *A Book of French Wines* (Jonathan Cape 1960), 321.

39. Jacquelin and Poulain, eds., *Wines*, 176. A wine that sounds much more like Jefferson's Ledanon is the nearby St.-Gilles-du-Gard, described in *Wines* as velvety, robust, and "sprightly," and which is often used in imitation of Port and Madeira, 175.

40. Redding, *History*, 141–42.

41. Hugh Johnson, *Vintage: The Story of Wine* (Simon & Schuster 1989), 202–5.

42. Jacquelin and Poulain, eds., *Wines*, 186–87; Redding, *History*, 149–52.

43. Bergh, vol. 19, 243–45.

44. Redding, *History*, 149–56; Henderson, *History*, 174–75. See letter of September 18, 1817. DLC.

45. Bergh, vol. 16, 139–40.

46. Malone, *Jefferson*, vol. 6, 431–32.

47. Bergh, vol. 15, 178.

48. Ibid., 186–87; Koch and Peden, eds., *Life*, 690–91.

49. Letter to Martha of July 28, 1819.

50. Redding, *History*, 423.

51. Ibid., 78.

52. Malone, *Jefferson*, vol. 6, 375.

53. Randolph, *Domestic Life*, 328.

54. Ibid., 313.

55. Ibid., 328.

56. Wendell D. Garrett, *Thomas Jefferson Redivivus* (Barre Publishing 1971), 176.

57. Randolph, *Domestic Life*, 326.

58. Malone, *Jefferson*, vol. 6, 403.

59. Redding, *History*, 147; Johnson, *Vintage*, 206. Heron Wines of San Francisco is now also making a promising Pinot Noir on the limestone soils of Limoux.

60. Malone, *Jefferson*, vol. 6, 403.

61. Marian Klamkin, *The Return of Lafayette* (Scribner's 1975), 157.

62. Malone, *Jefferson*, vol. 6, 405.

63. Klamkin, *Return*, supra, 158.

64. Malone, *Jefferson*, vol. 6, 408.

65. Padover, supra, 89–90.

66. Ibid.

67. Dr. J. Jefferson Looney, editor of the Retirement Series of the Jefferson Papers at Monticello, discovered in 2004 this last wine letter. For generations it was believed that Jefferson's last letter was written on June 24 to the mayor of Washington, D.C., declining an invitation to attend the fiftieth anniversary of the signing of the Declaration. Some Jeffersonians might be disappointed that Jefferson's last letter was not the noble discussion of human rights formerly believed. But given what we now know of Jefferson the private man, it is perhaps equally fitting that, as he clung to life, he wanted to make sure he still had plenty of good wine on hand. See "Thomas Jefferson's Last Letter," Dr. J. Jefferson Looney, *Virginia Magazine of History and Biography*, vol. 112, no. 2 (2004), 179–84.

Chapter 8: Vineyards at Monticello (1770–1826)

1. Betts, ed., *GB*, 557. Letter to Levin Gale of May 7, 1816.

2. Bergh, vol. 13, 79 (Jefferson to C. W. Peale, August 20, 1811).

3. Ibid.

4. Ford, vol. 7, 477.

5. Betts, ed., *GB*, 20.

6. Ibid., 22.

7. Ibid., 40.

8. Ibid., 52–53.

9. Ibid., 55.

10. Mazzei, *Memoirs*, 207.

11. Garlick, *Mazzei*, 43.

12. Betts, ed., *GB*, 62.

13. Mazzei, *Memoirs*, 206.

14. Betts, ed., *GB*, 43.

15. *Papers*, vol. 1, 156–59.

16. Jared Sparks, *The Correspondence of the American Revolution* (Books for Libraries 1970), vol. 7, 249.

17. Malone, *Jefferson*, vol. 1, 294–95.

18. Letter to Gallatin, January 25, 1793.

19. Louise Tharp, *The Baroness and the General* (Boston 1962), 312.

20. Bear, *Jefferson at Monticello*, 12, 23.

21. Bowers, *The Young Jefferson*, 223.

22. Betts, ed., *GB*, 67.

23. Ibid., 101.

24. Ibid., 95.

25. Bergh, vol., 19, 19.

26. *Papers*, vol. 9, 624.

27. Betts, ed., *GB*, 119. Beginning that summer and continuing through 1788 one Frenchman named Maupin bombarded Jefferson, as he had Franklin, to help him establish vineyards in America. Jefferson never did, but much later in life helped other Frenchmen do just that (DLC).

28. Betts, ed., *GB*, 126–27.

29. Foley, *Cyclopedia*, 119.

30. Betts, ed., *GB*, 135.

31. Ibid., 144.

32. DLC.

33. Betts, ed., *GB*, 116.

34. Ibid., 122.

35. Ibid., 140–41, 143–44.

36. *Papers*, vol. 15, 376.

37. Betts, ed., *GB*, 313, 430–31.

38. Ibid., 453, 480.
39. Ibid., 491.
40. Ibid., 505. His frustration related primarily to the South Carolinians' dilatoriness with the olive tree, but also the cork oak.
41. Ibid., 619–21.
42. Letter of July 21, 1792, DLC.
43. Betts, ed., *GB*, 180.
44. Ibid., 203.
45. Ibid., 248–49. The "brick dust" grape was probably the Chasselas Doré, also known as the Italian "Toccai of Friuli," according to horticulturist and Monticello vineyardist Peter Hatch.
46. DLC.
47. DLC.
48. Betts, ed., *GB*, 274, 278–79.
49. DLC, with a letter to the Pennsylvania legislature re vineyards (March 25, 1801).
50. Betts, ed., *GB*, 277. The "Cape" grape was apparently native, but part of these cuttings were claimed to have been brought all the way from the real Cape of Good Hope in South Africa.
51. DLC.
52. Re Henry Main, see Betts, ed., *GB*, 299, 308–9, 431.
53. DLC.
54. Betts, ed., *GB*, 304.
55. Ibid., 336, 340–41.
56. Ibid., 333.
57. Ibid., 348.
58. Ibid., 352.
59. Ibid., 375.
60. DLC.
61. Betts, ed., *GB*, 415.
62. DLC.
63. Betts, ed., *GB*, 423, 436, 456–57, 462–63, 475, 481, 548, 554, 557; DLC (John Adlum, March 13, 1810, April 10, 1810), (Letter to John David dated December 25, 1818, which states in part, "I have formerly been eager to introduce the culture of the vine and sunk a good deal of money in the endeavor. Altho' unsuccessful, I would still persevere were I younger, but I would do it on a small scale"), (letter from John David at Richmond dated January 1, 1816).
64. DLC.

65. Betts, ed., *GB*, 555.

66. DLC; Betts, ed., *GB*, 557.

67. Betts, ed., *GB*, 637.

68. Ibid., 565.

69. MS in UVa library.

70. Betts, ed., *GB*, 572.

71. DLC.

72. Ibid.

73. Betts, ed., *GB*, 602. Jefferson would certainly be proud to know that today a red grape native to Virginia and known generally as the Norton, a *vitis aestivalis*, is winning medals at international competitions against European varieties. Consistently the best Norton is that of the old Stone Hill Winery of Hermann, Missouri, as well as the version produced by Dennis Horton of Virginia.

74. Ibid., 602–3.

75. Ibid., 604.

76. *Family Letters*, 447. Col. Burton is Col. G. Hutchins Burton of Halifax, N.C. See *MB* for May 1, 1817.

77. Leon Adams, *Wines of America*, 3d ed. (McGraw-Hill 1985), 72–73, 90–91; Philip Wagner, *A Winegrower's Guide* (Knopf 1945), 31. Also in DLC.

78. Reproduced in John Adlum, *Cultivation of the Vine* (facsimile edition by Booknoll Reprints, Hopewell, New Jersey, 1971).

79. Bergh, vol. 18, 318.

80. Peter J. Hatch, *The Fruits and Fruit Trees of Monticello* (UVa Press 1998), 131.

81. Ibid.

Epilogue: The Latest Jefferson Controversy: A Mysterious Case of Bordeaux

1. *Wine Spectator*, November 16–30, 1985, 7.

2. The Talk of the Town, *The New Yorker*, January 20, 1986, 20.

3. *Wine Spectator*, January 1–31, 1986, 5.

4. James Suckling, "Did Cork Fall Into Forbes' Lafite Bottle?" *Wine Spectator*, November 15, 1986, 5.

5. "It Is the Oldest Bordeaux, But Was It Jefferson's?" *New York Times*, October 30, 1985, Living, 15, 17.

6. Ibid.

7. "In Defense of the Jefferson Bottle," *Wine Spectator*, March 1–15, 1986, 6.

8. "Unanswered Questions," *Wine Spectator*, March 16–31, 1986, 42.

9. "No More Doubts," *Decanter*, September 1986, 20–21, 43–44.

10. Ibid. The Robinson article, too long to reproduce here, is amusingly written and highly recommended.

11. "Historic Mouton 'Delicious to Drink,'" *Wine Spectator*, November 15, 1986, 5.

12. Francis X. Clines, "1784 Wine Fetches $56,000," *New York Times*, December 4, 1986.

13. James Suckling, "Rare 1784 Yquem Brings $56,000" and "Historical Doubts," *Wine Spectator*, January 31, 1987, 5.

14. James Suckling, "Publisher Buys 1784 Margaux," *Wine Spectator*, August 31, 1987, 10.

15. Jancis Robinson, "Survival of the Fittest at Chateau d'Yquem," *Quarterly Review of Wines*, summer 1988, 18–21. Re other tastings and sales of Yquems attributed to Jefferson, see "Jefferson's Yquem, Too," *Wine Spectator*, October 31, 1986, 5.

16. Howard G. Goldberg, "A $519,750 Bottle of Wine? And You Say You Broke It?" *New York Times*, April 26, 1989, 21.

17. *Papers*, vol. 8, 93.

18. Since those words were written in early 2006, much has transpired. In August 2006, billionaire collector William Koch sued in federal court claiming his "Jefferson" bottles are fakes. See: *KOCH vs. RODENSTOCK, aka Meinhard Goerke*, SDNY #06CV6586. Then last year came a thoroughly amusing best-seller on the subject: *The Billionaire's Vinegar* by Benjamin Wallace (Crown 2008) follows the scandal from the attic of Meinhard Goerke (Rodenstock's true name) to cellars in Palm Beach, St. Petersburg, Caracas, and Hong Kong. Throughout the controversy, the scholars at Monticello courageously ignored all insults thrown their way by "Rodenstock" and his enabler Broadbent, and refused to accept the bottles as authentic. Then one day Koch's lead investigator found the smoking gun: proof that the engraving on the bottles was produced by a modern, high-speed electric device similar to a dentist's drill. The Rodenstock response, as translated from the German was: "What's the big deal about wine fraud? Jesus did it."

   But a counterfeiter should not have the last word. That must go to Jefferson, who said in 1825 about the lap-desk on which he wrote the Declaration: "Its imaginary value will increase with years—[you] may see it carried in the procession of our nation's birthday, as the relics of the saints are in those of the church." Always the lawyer, Jefferson hand-wrote an affidavit swearing to the authenticity and provenance of his desk. He was truly a visionary and a remarkably modern man.

Select Bibliography

On Wines and Vineyards Then and Now

Adlum, John. *Cultivation of the Vine* (Booknoll reprint facsimile ed., Hopewell, N.J. 1971).

Allen, H. Warner. *Wines of Portugal* (New York 1963).

Anderson, Burton. *Vino* (Boston 1980).

Arnoux. *Dissertation sur la Situation de Bourgogne sur les Vins qu'elle produit* (London 1728).

Barry, Sir Edward. *Observations on the Wines of the Ancients* (London 1775).

Berry, Liz, M. W. *The Wines of Languedoc-Roussillon* (London 1992).

Briggs, Asa. *Haut-Brion* (London 1994).

Broadbent, Michael. *The Great Vintage Wine Book* (New York 1980).

Brown, John Hal. *Early American Beverages* (New York 1966).

Cocks and Feret, eds. *Bordeaux and Its Wines* (San Francisco 1986).

Cossart, Noel. *Madeira: The Island Vineyard* (London 1984).

Dion, R. *Histoire de la Vigne et du Vin en France* (Paris 1959).

Domine, Andre. *Wine* (Cologne 2001).

Duijker, Hubrecht. *The Great Wines of Burgundy* (London 1983).

Ensrud, Barbara. *American Vineyards* (New York 1988).

Faith, Nicholas. *The Winemasters* (London 1978).

Forbes, Patrick. *Champagne* (London 1967).

Fowler, Damon Lee, ed. *Dining at Monticello* (Chapel Hill 2005).

Frater, Elisabeth. *Breaking Away to Virginia and Maryland Wineries* (Capital Books 2002).

Gabler, James M. *Passions: The Wines and Travels of Thomas Jefferson* (Baltimore 1995).

Galtier, Gaston. "La Viticulture de l'Europe occidentale à la veille de la Révolution française, d'après les Notes de voyages de Thomas Jefferson" (Paris 1968).

Garlick, Richard Cecil, Jr. *Philip Mazzei, Friend of Jefferson: His Life and Letters* (Baltimore 1933).

Gohdes, Clarence. *Scuppernong* (Durham 1982).

Hatch, Peter J. *The Fruits and Fruit Trees of Monticello* (Charlottesville 1998).

Healy, Maurice. *Stay Me with Flagons* (London 1940).

Henderson, Alexander. *The History of Ancient and Modern Wines* (London 1824).

Hyams, Edward. *Dionysus: A Social History of the Wine Vine* (London 1965).

Jacquelin, Louis, and Rene Poulain, eds. *The Wines and Vineyards of France* (London 1962).

Jeffs, Julian. *Sherry* (London 1982).

Johnson, Hugh. *Vintage: The Story of Wine* (New York 1989).

———. *World Atlas of Wine* (New York 1985).

Joseph, Robert, ed. *The Wine Lists* (Enfield 1985).

Jullien, A. *Topographie de tous les Vignobles connus* (Paris 1816).

Lawrence, Robert de Treville. *Jefferson and Wine* (The Plains, Va. 1989).

Lee, H. G., and A. E. Lee. *Virginia Wine Country III* (Hil Designs 2004).

Lichine, Alexis. *Encyclopedia of Wines and Spirits* (New York 1982).

Lukacs, Paul. *American Vintage: The Rise of American Wine* (Boston 2000).

McBride, Duncan. *General Instructions for the Choice of Wines and Spiritous Liquors* (London 1793).

McCoy, Elin. *The Emperor of Wine: The Rise of Robert M. Parker, Jr. and the Reign of American Taste* (New York 2005).

McKee, George H. "Was Revolutionary America Dry?," *Commonweal* (Oct. 26, 1932).

Molyneux-Berry, David. *The Sotheby's Guide to Classic Wines and Their Labels* (Ballantine 1990).

Olney, Richard. *Yquem* (Godine 1986).

Osborne, Lawrence. *The Accidental Connoisseur* (North Point 2004).

Parker, Robert M., Jr. *Bordeaux* (New York 1998).

———. *Burgundy* (New York 1990).

———. *Wines of the Rhone Valley and Provence* (New York 1997).

Paronetto, Lamberto. *Chianti: The History of Florence and Its Wines* (London 1970).

Pellucci, Emanuele. *Vino Nobile di Montepulciano* (Fiesole, Italy 1998).

Penning-Rowsell, Edmund. *Wines of Bordeaux* (San Francisco 1985).

Penzer, N.M. *The Book of the Wine Label* (London 1947).

Peynaud, Emile. *Knowing and Making Wine* (New York 1984).

——. *The Taste of Wine* (San Francisco 1987).

Pinney, Thomas. *A History of Wine in America* (Berkeley 1989).

Rainbird, George. *Sherry and the Wines of Spain* (McGraw-Hill 1966).

Ray, Cyril. Updated by Serena Sutcliff. *Bollinger: Tradition of a Champagne Family* (London 1994).

Ray, Cyril. *Lafite* (New York 1969).

Redding, Cyrus. *A History and Description of Modern Wines* (London 1833, 1876).

Robinson, Jancis. *The Great Wine Book* (Morrow 1982).

——. *The Oxford Companion to Wine* (Oxford 1994).

——. *Vines, Grapes and Wines* (Knopf 1986).

Rosengarten, David, and Joshua Wesson. *Red Wine with Fish* (New York 1989).

Rowe, Walker Elliott. *Wandering Through Virginia's Vineyards* (Baltimore 2005).

Shand, P. Morton. *A Book of French Wines* (London 1960).

Sichel, Peter M. F. *The Wines of Germany* (Boston 1986).

Simon, Andre. *Bottlescrew Days* (London 1927).

——. *History of the Wine Trade in England* (London 1909).

——. *Wine in Shakespeare's Days and Shakespeare's Plays*, in the *Sette of Odd Volumes* (London 1931).

Suckling, James. *Vintage Port* (San Francisco 1990).

Wasserman, Sheldon, and Pauline Wasserman. *Italy's Noble Red Wines* (New York 1991).

Young, Arthur. *Travels during the Years 1787–1789 in France.* 2 vols. (London 1792, Cambridge 1950).

Younger, William. *Gods, Men and Wine* (Wine & Food Society 1966).

On Thomas Jefferson and His Times

Adams, Charles Francis. *Memoirs of John Quincy Adams* (Philadelphia 1874).

Adams, William Howard. *Jefferson's Monticello* (Charlottesville 1983).

——. *The Paris Years of Thomas Jefferson* (New York 1997).

Alsop, Susan Mary. *Yankees at the Court: The First Americans in Paris* (Garden City, N.Y. 1982).

Appleby, Joyce. *Thomas Jefferson* (New York 2003).

Baridon, Michel, and Bernard Chevignard. *Voyage et Tourisme en Bourgogne a l'époque de Jefferson* (Dijon 1988).

Bazin, Jean-Francois, and Pierre Duprey. *Le Bicentennaire du Voyage de Jefferson en Bourgogne* (Dijon 1986).

Bear, James A., Jr. *Jefferson at Monticello* (Charlottesville 1967).

Bear, James A., Jr., and Lucia Cinder Stanton, eds. *Jefferson's Memorandum Books*. 2 vols. (Princeton 1997).

Betts, E. M., and James A. Bear, Jr. *The Family Letters of Thomas Jefferson* (Columbia, Mo. 1966).

Bernstein, R. B. *Thomas Jefferson* (Oxford 2003).

Boorstin, Daniel J. *The Lost World of Thomas Jefferson* (Chicago 1948, 1993).

Bowers, Claude. *The Young Jefferson* (Boston 1945).

Brady, Frank, and Frederick A. Pottle, eds. *Boswell on the Grand Tour of Italy, Corsica and France, 1765-1766* (New York 1955).

Brodie, Fawn. *Thomas Jefferson, An Intimate History* (New York 1974).

Brown, Marvin L., Jr., ed. *Baroness von Riedesel and the American Revolution* (Chapel Hill 1965).

Bulletin of the Bureau of Rolls and Library of the Department of State: Calendar of the Correspondence of Thomas Jefferson (Washington, D.C. 1894).

Bullock, Helen D. *My Head and My Heart* (Putnam 1945).

Burstein, Andrew. *Jefferson's Secrets* (Cambridge 2005).

Cappon, Lester J., ed. *The Adams-Jefferson Letters* (Chapel Hill 1988).

Carson, Jane. *Colonial Virginians at Play* (Charlottesville 1965).

"Caviar Along the Potomac: Sir Augustus John Foster's Notes on the U.S., 1804-1812," *William and Mary Quarterly* (January 1951).

Cerami, Charles A. *Young Patriots: The Remarkable Story of Two Men, Their Impossible Plan, and the Revolution that Created the Constitution* (Naperville, Ill. 2005).

Chastellux, Marquis de. *Travels in North America in the Years 1780, 1781 and 1782*. Translated by Howard C. Rice, Jr. (Chapel Hill 1963).

Craveri, Benedetta. *The Age of Conversation* (New York 2005).

Cunningham, Noble E., Jr. *Jefferson and Monroe: Constant Friendship and Respect* (Chapel Hill 2003).

Cutler, W. P., and J. P. Cutler, eds. *The Life, Journals and Correspondence of Rev. Manasseh Cutler, L.L.D.* (Cincinnati 1888).

Dabney, Virginius. *The Jefferson Scandals: A Rebuttal* (Chapel Hill 1981).

Dewey, Frank L. *Thomas Jefferson, Lawyer* (Charlottesville 1986).

"Dr. Mitchill's Letters from Washington: 1801–1813." *Harper's*, vol. 58.

Duetens, Louis M. *Journal of Travels Made Through Principal Cities of Europe*. Translated by John Highmore (1782).

Dumbauld, Edward. *Thomas Jefferson, American Tourist* (Norman, Okla 1946).

Fisher, S. I. *Observations on the Character and Culture of the European Vine* (Philadelphia 1834).

Fitzpatrick, John C., ed. *The Writings of Washington from the Original Manuscript Sources, 1745–1799*. 37 vols. (Washington, D.C. 1944).

Foley, John P. *Jeffersonian Cyclopedia* (New York 1900).

Foster, Eugene A., et al. "Jefferson Fathered Slave's Last Child." *Nature*, vol. 396 (Nov. 1998).

Garlick, Richard. *Philip Mazzei, Friend of Jefferson* (Baltimore 1933).

Garrett, Wendell D. *Thomas Jefferson Redivivus* (Barre, Mass. 1971).

Gilreath, James, and Douglas L. Wilson, eds. *Thomas Jefferson's Library: A Catalog* (Washington, D.C. 1989).

Gordon-Reed, Annette. *Thomas Jefferson and Sally Hemings: An American Controversy* (Charlottesville 1997).

Hess, Karen, ed. *Martha Washington's Booke of Cookery* (New York 1981).

Hitchens, Christopher. *Thomas Jefferson: Author of America* (New York 2005).

Kaplan, Lawrence S. *Jefferson and France* (New Haven 1967).

Kelso, William. *Archaeology at Monticello* (TJMF 1997).

Kennedy, Roger G. *Mr. Jefferson's Lost Cause* (Oxford 2003).

Kimball, Marie. *Jefferson: The Scene of Europe.* (New York 1950).

———. *Thomas Jefferson's Cookbook* (Charlottesville 1976).

Klamkin, Marian. *The Return of Lafayette* (New York 1975).

Lander, Eric S., and Joseph Ellis. "Founding Father" [as in DNA analysis], *Nature*, vol. 396 (November 1998).

Lanier, Shannon, and Jane Feldman. *Jefferson's Children: The Story of One American Family* (New York 2002).

La Rochefoucauld-Liancourt, Duc de. *Travels Through the United States of America, 1795–1797*. 2 vols. (London 1800).

Lewis, Jan Ellen, and Peter S. Onuf, eds. *Sally Hemings and Thomas Jefferson: History, Memory and Civic Culture* (Charlottesville 1999).

Looney, J. Jefferson. "Thomas Jefferson's Last Letter." *Virginia Magazine of History and Biography*, vol. 112, no. 2 (2004).

Malone, Dumas. *Jefferson and His Time.* 6 vols. (New York 1948–1981).

Marraro, Howard R., ed. and trans. *Memory of the Life and Peregrinations of the Florentine Philip Mazzei, 1730–1816* (New York 1942).

McCusker, John J. *How Much Is That in Real Money?* (Worcester 1992).

———. *Money and Exchange in Europe and America 1600–1775: A Handbook* (UNC 1978).

McLaughlin, Jack. *Jefferson and Monticello: The Biography of a Builder* (Holt 1988).

Morison, Samuel Eliot. *Oxford History of the American People* (Oxford 1965).

Morris, Gouverneur. *A Diary of the French Revolution.* Edited by Beatrix Cary Davenport. 2 vols. (New York 1939).

Padover, Saul K., ed. *Jefferson* (Mentor 1952).

———, ed. *The Writings of Thomas Jefferson* (Norwalk, Conn. 1967).

Parton, James. *The Life of Thomas Jefferson* (Boston 1784).

Petersen, Eric S., ed. *Light and Liberty: Reflections on the Pursuit of Happiness* (New York 2004).

Peterson, Merrill D. *The Jefferson Image in the American Mind* (London 1960).

———, ed. *Visitors to Monticello* (Charlottesville 1989).

Pick, Franz, and Rene Sedillot. *All the Monies of the World* (New York 1971).

Plumer, William, Jr. *The Life of William Plumer* (Boston 1857).

Randall, Henry S. *The Life of Thomas Jefferson*. 3 vols. (1858; reprint New York 1972).

Randall, Willard Sterne. *Thomas Jefferson: A Life* (New York 1993).

Randolph, Mary. *The Virginia House-wife*. Facsimile edited by Karen Hess. (Columbia, S. C. 1984).

Randolph, Sarah N. *The Domestic Life of Thomas Jefferson* (Charlottesville 1871).

Randolph, T. J., ed. *Memoirs of Thomas Jefferson* (London 1829).

Rice, Howard C., Jr. *Thomas Jefferson's Paris* (Princeton 1976).

Roquette-Buisson, Odile de. *The Canal du Midi* (London 1983).

Schiff, Stacy. *A Great Improvisation: Franklin, France, and the Birth of America* (New York 2006).

Seale, William. *The President's House: A History*. 2 vols. (New York 1986).

———, ed. "Thomas Jefferson's White House," *Journal of the White House Historical Association* #17 (Washington, D.C. 2006).

Shackelford, George Green. *Thomas Jefferson's Travels in Europe* (Johns Hopkins 1995).

Smith, James Morton, ed. *The Republic of Letters: The Correspondence between Jefferson and Madison, 1776–1826*. 3 vols. (New York 1995).

Smith, Margaret Bayard. *The First Forty Years of Washington Society* (New York 1906).

Smyth, Albert H. *The Writings of Benjamin Franklin*. 10 vols. (New York 1907).

Sowerby, E. Millicent, ed. *Catalogue of the Library of Thomas Jefferson*. 5 vols. (Washington, D.C. 1959).

Sparks, Jared. *The Correspondence of the American Revolution* (Books for Libraries, 1970).

Stanton, Lucia C. *Free Some Day: The African-American Families of Monticello* (Charlottesville 2000).

Stein, Susan. *The Worlds of Thomas Jefferson* (Abrams 1993).

Tharp, Louise. *The Baroness and the General* (Boston 1962).

The Tour to the Northern Lakes of James Madison and Thomas Jefferson (May–June 1791). Facsimile edited by J. Robert Maguire (Fort Ticonderoga 1995).

Weld, Isaac, Jr. *Travels Through the United States of North America, 1795–1797* (London 1800).

Wheelan, Joseph. *Jefferson's Vendetta: The Pursuit of Aaron Burr and the Judiciary* (New York 2005).

Wilson, Douglas, and Lucia Stanton, eds. *Jefferson Abroad* (New York 1999).

Wood, Gordon S. *Revolutionary Characters: What Made the Founders Different* (New York 2006).

Young, James S. *The Washington Community, 1800–1828* (New York 1966).

INDEX